→16.1 April 4/94.   **Date Due**

APR 0 7 1994

THE
DREAM
OF
NATION

A Social and Intellectual History of Quebec

Susan Mann Trofimenkoff

162669094

Macmillan of Canada
A Division of Gage Publishing Limited
Toronto, Canada

Canadian Cataloguing in Publication Data

Trofimenkoff, Susan Mann
   The dream of nation

Bibliography: p.
Includes index.
ISBN 0-7715-9730-4

1. Quebec (Province) - History.   2. Nationalism -
Quebec (Province).   I. Title.

FC2911.T76   971.4   C82-094721-0
F1052.95.T76

Unless otherwise specified, chapter opening photographs
were supplied courtesy of Public Archives of Canada.

Macmillan of Canada

A Division of Gage Publishing Limited

Printed in Canada

TABLE OF CONTENTS

Preface

This is how I see Quebec. It may contradict others' visions; it may complement them. It is intended to provide English-speaking Canadians with an interpretive synthesis of the history of Quebec in which the focus is upon French-speaking Quebecois since they have always been the source of greatest puzzlement to English Canada. English Quebec is only beginning to produce its history partly because it rarely saw itself as a distinct entity in Canada. Such has never been the case for French Quebec. There a dream of nation has hovered over historical circumstance with changes in one always affecting the other since the earliest days of French settlement. The kaleidoscopic results have been contradictory, startling, sometimes amusing, and sometimes frightening to French and English alike. They have seldom left anyone indifferent. Nor have they ever solved the dilemma of being French in North America.

Had it not been for a circumstance and dream of my own this book would have been written in quite another way and at quite another time. At the meetings of the Canadian Historical Association in Saskatoon in 1979, Virgil Duff, then with the Macmillan Company of Canada, armed himself with a petition signed by a number of historians (mutual friends, I suspect) to convince me to undertake a history of Quebec for both the college and trade market. I, with seventy-nine other projects in mind, resisted, only to find myself awakened one night with the book and chapter titles dictated by a dream. That and the nonchalant observation of my parents (Marjorie and Walter Mann who have always considered me their contribution to bilingualism) that such a book was the obvious outcome of "all that studying" set me to work.

The book draws upon my reading, teaching, and research in Quebec history over the past fifteen years. The general bibliography and the specific ones after each chapter indicate my indebtedness and offer suggestions for readers to pursue. At a time when historical studies in Canada have expanded into social, labour, urban, and women's history, I have been fortunate in having the help of not only specialists in Quebec history but also of so many of the new practitioners in my own department at the University of Ottawa. In particular I wish to thank Cornelius Jaenen, Fernand

Ouellet, Jacques Monet, Andrée Lévesque, Don Davis, and Michael Piva who were generous with their time and knowledge. Graduate student assistants Mark Entwistle and André Cellard dug up verifications on demand. Lynne Trépanier of the Geography Department drafted the maps. Thanks to the financial assistance of the Social Sciences and Humanities Research Council of Canada and the University of Ottawa, I was able to spend full time on the book during sabbatical leave in 1980–1981. And in the final stages, editor Alicia Myers put her pencil through every obscurity of language, fact, or meaning; those that remain are my doing. Through it all I have counted on the unspoken but obvious moral support of my husband Nicholas and daughter Britt-Mari who tolerated my physical and mental absences.

I hope everyone concerned likes the result.

Susan Mann Trofimenkoff
Ottawa, May 1982.

"In the beginning was the river."
Cap Tourment by John J. Bigsby.

1 The Dream of Empire

In the beginning was the river, frozen six months of the year. Both link and barrier, the river drew Indian nations to trade among themselves at choice locations—Tadoussac, Quebec, Montreal— long before Europeans slipped along its shores in the sixteenth century. It marked the frontiers of various Indian nations. Those to the north, Montagnais, Huron, and Algonkin, attempted to keep it as the limit of European contact. The Europeans themselves, awed by the river, were nonetheless dismayed: the route to Asia was once again blocked. Yet perhaps something could be made of the obstacle. The immense gulf that opened and shut the river once a year teemed with fish, food for the asking for an equally immense European market where religious conviction turned half the year into meatless days. The narrower shoreline upriver sheltered, if only temporarily, friendly Indians eager to offer surplus furs for surplus trinkets, both decorative and deadly. The profit margin was large and again the European market insatiable, animated this time by the dictates of social convention: what the

Indians wore on their bodies, the Europeans would wear on their heads. Some of the rockier shores glittered like gold to the inexperienced eye of a Jacques Cartier; at a time when Spain was shipping treasures back to Europe from its South American conquests, France could easily be lured by a tiny sparkle in the gloomy land that fate had assigned it in North America. The lower coastline, hugging the hills to the north, opening out flat and distant to the south, hinted, at least to the more experienced eye of a Samuel de Champlain, able to see beyond the forest, of agricultural possibilities sufficient for a settled population if not for export. Moreover the very currents and eddies of the river suggested, as did Indian tales, distant lands and seas. Perhaps a way could yet be found, through the barrier if not around it, to reach the known wealth of Asia. Only the river could tell. In the summer it dazzled the imagination of Europeans; in the winter it damned them, body and soul.

Europeans in the seventeenth century were prepared for both. The adventure might lead to material wealth; the hardships might ensure eternal salvation. Such was the impulse that led the French to America, late on the European imperial bandwagon but eager to catch up to their Spanish, Portuguese, and European rivals in wealth and prestige. Of course French fishermen had long since known the route to the Canadian cod; the few among them who actually landed to dry their catch before returning to Europe filled any extra space in their ships with furs bartered from coastal Indians. Jacques Cartier's first encounters with Indians in 1534 had surprised neither the French nor the natives although the giant crosses he insisted on planting along his path no doubt aroused some curiosity. The few attempts at wintering in Canada had dismayed the Europeans and added to the Indians' sense of superiority. It was not until the early seventeenth century, however, when France resolved internal religious and political problems, that the country began to feel the full weight of the European impulse to empire. To the stretching of mind and muscle occasioned by geographical and intellectual discoveries, to the social ferment thrown up by the clamour of a new commercial class, and to the technological advances in shipping and navigation, France added a centralized state and a religious fervour. By the early seventeenth century both were nurturing dreams of North American empire.

The state's dream was the feeblest. For almost three-quarters of a century, the French government experimented with companies and colonies before determining, in the 1660s, to put its own military and organizational skills fully behind the Canadian colony. In the interval it had sanctioned settlements in Acadia and in Canada, had pondered using them as dumping grounds for unwanted Protestants, and finally settled on Catholic exclusivity. It participated in a rather desultory fashion in the rivalry with England over Acadia, watching the territory change hands continually through the century depending on which European power, or mere band of raiders, could make the claim of prior discovery or prior settlement stick. Even Quebec changed hands momentarily in this fashion in the late 1620s, indicating the very tentative foothold that Champlain had gained there since 1608 under the interested eye but not very long arm of the French state. The French government had in fact waited impatiently for news of the route to Asia as Champlain slowly charted the eastern Canadian river systems as far as Lake Huron; it politely shelved his detailed plans of 1618 for a thriving commercial and agricultural colony on the banks of the St. Lawrence.

Lacking the funds for any direct involvement in the overseas enterprise, the French state contracted the mapping, the trade, and the settlement first to rich individuals and subsequently to large commercial firms. In return for a monopoly on all the trade in and out of New France, the Company of One Hundred Associates was to raise the population from barely one hundred in 1627 to over four thousand within fifteen years. The trade flourished but the settlers did not. Indeed, the two were in many ways incompatible. Settlers drained the Company's profits, since in the early years they had to be provided with everything. They were also more interested in trade themselves than in agricultural or artisanal production. And yet any continuing tie with the Indians necessitated settlement. The Company could not simply appear each spring and expect the Indians to be awaiting cheerfully, their arms loaded with *castor gras*, the greasy beaver that was the favoured fur. The Europeans had to adapt to the Indian trading system, not vice versa, and the adaptation required a permanent French presence in order to maintain the Indian alliances so carefully constructed by Champlain early in the century. All the gifts, exchanges, speeches, and ceremonies, of both a peaceful and war-like nature—necessary to keep the Indians coming to the river with their furs—demanded French settlement.

In spite of the demands of the trade and the requirements of the French government, the Company of One Hundred Associates never could or would fulfil its obligation to settle the colony. The French villages of Quebec, Trois-Rivières, and Montreal were fragile entities, clinging to the life line of the river and exposed, after mid-century, to the vengeance of the Iroquois for the alliance the French had nurtured with the enemy Huron. Even a second Company, the *Communauté des Habitants*, composed of settlers in the 1640s, was unable to ensure profits for itself and development for the colony. On numerous occasions the dream even appeared to be more of a nightmare: many a night the twenty-five hundred settlers of 1660, shivering in their beds from cold and fright, hoped they would awaken in France. Only in 1663 did the French government decide to fashion the dream directly, in its own guise.

The religious dream was far more powerful than that of the state in the early seventeenth century. Indeed without it there might have been no New France at all. Out of France's religious turmoil of the sixteenth century and its struggles for religious conformity in the seventeenth came the most extraordinary group of hard-nosed religious zealots: mystics who knew how to run a business; wealthy nobles and bourgeois with an intense longing to change the world for God and, in the process, if He were particularly gracious, to transform themselves into martyrs. They saw New France in their dreams and speculated about a new Christian race composed of French and Indians. They also had the money, the connections, the zeal, and the determination to realize their dreams. Many of them were women.

To New France such people came, cutting their personal ties but rarely their powerful connections in France. They came as missionaries, teachers, nurses, and social workers, sometimes as individuals, sometimes in groups. They founded schools for Indian children, colleges for French boys, convents for the daughters of the colonial elite, hospitals for the sick, asylums for the needy, and day schools for girls in the countryside. In 1642 they established Montreal or Ville Marie in order, as they described it, "to bring about the glory of God and the salvation of the Indians." Their letters home were advertisements and pleas for the colony and rarely did they go unheard. Money, settlers, and supplies followed in the wake of the religious, whether they were Jesuit missionaries wandering with the Indians far from the settlement, or Ursuline nuns cloistered in Quebec City but privy to all the politics of the colony and directing some of the most prosperous seigneuries, or Sisters of the Congregation tramping the unprecedented path of non-cloistered nuns, carrying schooling to youngsters in the countryside. Long before New France had a secure economic or political footing on the St. Lawrence, these mystics established a network of clerically administered social institutions that would not only outlive New France but be an enduring feature of Quebec society until well into the twentieth century.

Not that all their dreams were realized. New France never did become a "New Kingdom" and the goal of turning Indians into French, sedentary Christians encountered cultural resistance as strong as the mystics' own zeal. Moreover, some of the missionaries were unwitting transmitters of disease; they probably killed more Indians than they converted. Smallpox, measles, and simple respiratory ailments passed through Indian communities with the speed and devastation of a fire. With equal ravage other aspects of European culture—clothing, tools, guns, and brandy—took their toll. Usually the missionaries disapproved, and once the Canadian church acquired strong leadership and organization under Monseigneur François de Laval, appointed vicar apostolic in 1659, its major battle was against the liquor traffic. And yet the battle was a lost cause since the lines of friendship, trust, and knowledge that bound the missionaries and the Indians together had also opened many routes of the fur trade and thus had helped create the very problem the church was fighting.

If the French could hold their liquor better than the Indians, they were no more immune to other by-products of the fur trade. Warfare was the major one. Sometimes the French were caught in inter-tribal crossfire, as in the 1640s when Iroquois and Huron battled for control of the supply lines to the French along the river and to the Dutch to the south. Sometimes they bore the brunt of Iroquois cultural and economic hostility as in the 1650s when their tiny settlements were under constant Indian attack. In either case the mystics found their desire for martyrdom and the settlers their dread of torture amply fulfilled. It took another forty years, the direct involvement of the French state, and a massive influx of soldiers and settlers before the French could say with any ease that they were here to stay. The infant colony hobbled for generations.

The precariousness of the settlement clinging to the shores of the St. Lawrence between Quebec and Montreal finally dawned upon civil servants in France, and even upon King Louis XIV. At the same time came a recognition of the value of colonies, both in terms of prestige and, if possible, in terms of wealth. Much of this awareness was fostered and then translated into action by Jean-Baptiste Colbert, successively and cumulatively through the 1660s intendant of French finances, then controller general, and finally Minister of the Marine and hence responsible for colonies. In 1663 New France took on the trappings of a French province, with a governor and an intendant to look after military and civilian affairs respectively and a sovereign council to perform judicial and administrative functions. Depending on the talents and inclinations of the various individuals who held these posts over the next one hundred years, the government of New France oscillated between scrupulous control, inspired planning, military ventures with a distinct odour of *castor gras*, brilliant administration, and the lining of individuals' pockets. Like all administrators, they quarrelled among themselves. Unlike most, their work was complicated by distance and climate: eighteen months or more could easily pass between a request for assistance or advice and a response from France. The colony moved at its own pace — that of the seasons and of the river.

On occasion, an administrator tried to hurry the pace. Jean Talon, intendant in the 1660s and present in the colony for a mere five years, had grand plans. He envisioned a larger population, a larger territory, and the development of commerce, the fur trade, agriculture, fishing, mines, and forests. Ships built at Quebec to strengthen the French navy! But the dream soon encountered some of the persistent traits of New France. Settlers would not live in circular villages inland, surrounded by agricultural lands. Neither the dictates of defence nor the promise of prosperity could convince them to abandon the rectangular river-front lots that offered them transportation, sustenance, and distance from the seigneur. Nor was capital easily available. Investment from France followed the tides of European warfare rather than those of the lower St. Lawrence.

When it did come, it expected a quick return and only the fur trade could guarantee that. Of the massive private investment in the trade, at least three-quarters of the profits returned to France, the remainder settling into the hands of a few Canadian families little inclined to diversifying their interests. In fact, actual coinage, let alone capital, was a scarce commodity in New France. But then too, so were people, both skilled labour and consumers. Neither imported nor home-grown labour ever sufficed. Indentured immigrant workers returned to France as soon as their contract expired and finances permitted. Children of imported wives—the famous *filles du roy* sent out from the orphanages of Paris between 1665 and 1673 with education in their heads and money in their pockets to marry settlers and army officers— showed little inclination for the cribbed existence of a steady worker. Those who did, and acquired a trade by means of the apprenticeship system, merely filled and sometimes even overstocked the colony's immediate needs for bakers, bootmakers, or butchers. There never was a surplus of money for innovation nor a market for consumption. Moreover, any dream of economic development crumbled against the purpose of colonies: they existed to serve the mother country, not to compete with it.

And yet France took seriously her obligation to defend the colony. The sending out of French regular troops in the 1660s was in fact of much more significance in setting the tone for Canadian society than economic planning that came to naught. The Carignan-Salières regiment contained the Iroquois menace in the St. Lawrence valley although there was no end to the threat until the formal peace of Montreal in 1701; along with other companies of soldiers subsequently sent from France, they stamped a military pattern upon the colony. Moreover, the soldiers brought money with them for their own sustenance and their expenditures. So great did the military needs of colony and empire eventually become that during the eighteenth century, approximately three-quarters of French government expenditures in New France were on the military. Many of the soldiers were also settlers: the common soldier stayed in the colony as a labourer or farmer; the officers often married into wealthy Canadian families once the demographic imbalance in favour of men righted itself early in the eighteenth century. Their children continued the pattern as the military provided some of the more interesting and prestigious occupations in the colony: the boys soon Canadianized the officer ranks of the Marine companies, the girls wove the intricacies of social stability through marriage, family connections, and social power.

The local militia appears to have traced a similar pattern. As of 1669, all male settlers aged between sixteen and sixty were automatically members of the militia, organized into geographical units based upon the parish. Their function was to defend the immediate area, or, when necessary, to accompany the far fewer regular French troops on major expeditions into Indian or English territory. Until the Canadians assimilated the French soldiers, there was much mutual astonishment and disdain between them. The Canadians fought in the Indian manner—by stealth, speed, surprise, and ambush; they had no respect for the formal lines and calculated volleys of European battles. They also survived better in the forest, without requiring the massive supply trains of European armies. But they did not escape the lure of office. Rank in the militia was often a stepping stone to higher things: many a Canadian seigneur requesting ennoblement from the French king during the seventeenth century emphasized his service as a militia officer; many a status-seeking bourgeois imitated the process in the next century. The need for, and the presence of the military in New France helped maintain an *ancien régime* society of hierarchy, order, place, propriety, and honour.

Yet, not everyone behaved as expected. The river and the forest were much too close and much too fascinating, the moral guardians too distant, and the people themselves both too many for the handful of priests and administrators to control and too few to feel bound by the social norms of any community. Clerics in particular found this difficult, but since most of the people were in the countryside and most of the clerics in the towns with their bishops as often as not in France, there was little they could do but fret. That the clerics did well. They fretted over fashions and gambling, over swearing, drinking, and dancing; they looked dimly upon the theatre and even more so upon horseracing in the churchyard during sermons; they bemoaned the successful reduction of the tithe from one-thirteenth of all production to one twenty-sixth of wheat production and the successful evasion of that amount; they wailed that they could not persuade people to repair a church roof. Even adding their voice to that of the state did not seem to help. In spite of the church's moral strictures and the royal government's economic incentives, Canadians persisted in marrying well into their twenties and having families, on average, only about half the size of the clerically or state sanctioned dozen. The *habitants* quite stubbornly and quite deliberately refused to bend their ways to the demands of a tiny elite.

Just as the settlers often behaved in unexpected ways, so some of the colonial social structures evolved differently from the original intention. The seigneurial pattern of land holding was less a system than an idea based upon a European reality which had little to do with social, political, or even economic conditions along the St. Lawrence. In France, a noble held a fief for the king; in return for a livelihood from the land, he and his vassals owed military service to the monarch. Both rank and way of life sharply distinguished noble from peasant. In New France, seigneurs acquired land on the condition that they concede sections of it to settlers. In many ways the obligations weighed more heavily upon the seigneur than upon the settler. In return for a certain prestige and minimal annual payments in cash and in kind, the seigneur had to provide and maintain a mill and a manor house, support the parish church, assist in community road building, and keep a census of the land, the people, and their production. No wonder few of them fulfilled their obligation to settle the land. Until they had thirty or forty families with cleared land, they could not expect a financial return; unless they or their sons engaged part time in the fur trade to acquire some capital and part time on the land, clearing it and growing crops, they made no profit. Moreover, the division of the seigneury among all the heirs at death meant that any accumulation of capital was decidedly difficult. Many seigneurs did not even bother with their land, where their position was often indistinguishable from that of their *habitants*. Instead they lived in town and considered their holdings merely part of their social status. Some attempted to acquire more seigneuries for that very purpose. But others may have been just as pleased to have the state revoke their title for failure to colonize the terrain, as happened in one or two instances. As a plan for settling the country, most of the seigneuries held by individuals were a failure.

Those held by the church or by religious orders were much more successful. Partly because the seigneury stayed intact across time, neither church nor order having personal heirs among whom the property had to be divided, and partly because the religious had to make a living from the lands to finance, in part, their social and educational undertakings, these seigneuries were carefully tended. They began with capital investment from the religious orders and their patrons in France, and developed under the continually interested eye and entrepreneurial talent of a Marie de l'Incarnation, mystic and founder of the Ursulines, or even a Bishop Laval. They also tended to be the best land in the best locations: one-third of the conceded river frontage in 1663 was in the hands of the church; the entire island of Montreal was the seigneury of the Sulpicians as of 1657. One hundred years later, the church and its religious affiliates controlled one-quarter of all conceded lands in New France, most of it in the area surrounding Quebec City and Montreal. More than a third of the population lived on those lands.

The agriculture undertaken on the seigneurial lands only slowly acquired a commercial form. During the seventeenth century, barely enough was produced for the farm families themselves. On occasion, in fact, climate or wars actually brought famine. Even the line between subsistence and provision of the towns was often precarious. A scarcity of labour affected agricultural undertakings as it did all others; there were few enough people to tend to the land let alone expand the growing area, every inch of farmland having to be wrenched from the forest. Only in the early eighteenth century did agriculture even become a major occupation, let alone acquire a commercial colouring, as the fur trade began to suffer from overproduction and an increasing population had to seek employment elsewhere. *Habitants* then began growing wheat for export, mostly to the newly constructed and hungry fort of Louisbourg on Ile Royale (present-day Cape Breton). The countryside itself changed as a consequence with tiny villages emerging to service a more commercial farming. So too did the social structure change as *habitants* sorted themselves out into affluent, self-sufficient, and poor. Moreover, commercial agriculture in New France leaves much behind for the historian to ponder: the 1730s appear to have been lean years with crop failures, export cutbacks, a shortage of jobs, and general misery.

In fact, agriculture never was a major commodity in the economy of New France. Furs and soldiers were the real money-makers in an economy based on trade and warfare. Most male settlers appear to have taken part in one or the other, or both, at some point during the one hundred and thirty years of settled existence in New France. By 1760, four thousand people of a total population of approximately sixty-five thousand in the St. Lawrence valley were officially employed in the trade and no one knows how many took an unofficial part. Certainly, before 1660, when the Indians still came to Montreal for the annual fairs, everyone had at least a small hand in the trade. Thereafter it became more specialized. By the end of the century seasoned *voyageurs* in the employ of merchant traders had taken over from the individual, haphazard, and somewhat libertine *coureurs de bois* in the colonial trade. In the spring, the *voyageurs* headed out from the colony, north and west in canoes big enough for seven men, carrying immense loads of trade goods. They returned sometimes in the autumn, sometimes the following summer, bearing furs, mostly beaver in the seventeenth century, a greater variety in the eighteenth. For all the romantic aura that surrounded the *voyageurs*—songs and strength and adventure—they were the mere transporters of the trade. They neither stalked animals nor pocketed profits. And theirs was the most dangerous activity. They slipped between enemy Indian tribes, over contested territory; they ran the risk of river and portage; they raced ice and ambush back to Montreal. And they often died. All this they did merely to turn their furs over to the ever-decreasing number of commercial agents. For as the length of the trips into the interior increased, along with Indian demands for more and better goods, the trade became concentrated in the hands of a small number of wealthy, interrelated families able to sustain lines of credit often three and four years long. These families, either agents of large metropolitan companies or independent business associates, kept all their profits within the rather closed circuit of the trade. Most of the profits returned to France, the rest went into supplying and servicing the trade. Occasionally a seigneury was purchased for status rather than profit; more often extravagant entertainment with imported wines and finery from France maintained the friendly ties of officials, officers, merchants, and traders. Rarely did any of the money from the fur trade branch out into other commercial or industrial undertakings.

In fact, the furs themselves merely changed hands as they passed through the colony. Providing work only for transshippers in Montreal and Quebec, the furs followed the dictates of the French, not the Canadian economy. There they suffered competition from continental suppliers and ran the risk of changing hat fashions. Depending on the European market, the Canadian trade ebbed and flowed, now overstocking the French storehouses as at the beginning of the eighteenth century, now diminishing and diversifying its output as in the mid-eighteenth century. Always raw furs remained the colony's major export.

Many of the furs were actually exported illegally. The route via Albany was hazardous since it went into alien Indian and English territory, but it was also shorter and promised quicker and better returns. It avoided the twenty-five percent export duty imposed on the value of furs leaving New France and it provided English trade goods which the Indians, and even some Montrealers, preferred. Fine English woollens appeared in the French trader's pack in the western territories, while English silver and china graced the tables of fur merchants in Montreal. One of the links was certainly the Desaulniers sisters operating out of Caughnawaga, on the south shore of the St. Lawrence west of Montreal. The two women were related to enough of Montreal's fur trading families to avoid official inspection; they did business with Indian couriers who mastered the shadowy route to Albany. Indeed, for all the official disfavour of this contraband activity, it was perhaps the life line of the Canadian trade, permitting a continuing movement of furs when the French market was glutted and providing access to better trade goods, thus enabling the Canadians to maintain their economic and political alliances with the insatiable Indians.

These alliances gradually drew the Canadians, with French military backing, further and further into the North American interior. Just as the original trade had required a permanent, albeit small, presence in the St. Lawrence Valley, so now the expanding trade and the continuing peace with the Indians after 1701 required a French presence in the interior. Only if the French brought trade goods, and good ones, close enough would the Indians refrain from establishing direct trade links themselves with the English colonies. Only if the French military was somewhere in the vicinity would the Indians be sufficiently impressed or persuaded to stay on the French side in any skirmish with the English. And only if the French claimed, by physical presence, the right to the territory beyond the St. Lawrence and beyond the English colonies along the Atlantic coast, could France maintain its prestige in Europe. Hence the extraordinary expansion of New France from a colony clustered along a major river to a far-flung web of empire, north, west, and south across a continent. By the beginning of the eighteenth century New France had sent explorers and traders well beyond the original lands of Acadia, Newfoundland, and Canada into the territory of the Hudson Bay, the Great Lakes, the Iroquois lands south of the lakes, and down the Mississippi River to the Gulf of Mexico. As in the early seventeenth century, the lines of exploration became lines of mission, of trade, and then of defence. By the late 1730s the French had posts at all strategic locations in what would later be the Canadian and American mid-west.

The soldiers and the trade marched hand in hand. Defence of the empire offered the extra rewards of the fur trade. Sometimes even the high administrators were in on the profits. Governor Frontenac in the late seventeenth century may well have allowed the attraction of fur to decide the location of military posts financed by the French government. And once installed in defensive positions around the Great Lakes, a French garrison was bound to pass its time bartering with the Indians. Meanwhile, *voyageurs* in the employ of the troops packed as many trade goods as military materials into their canoes. Soon too many people were making too much money for the French government ever to be able to extricate itself with any delicacy from what soon became an overextended position.

But then France may not have wanted to withdraw. Although the French government recognized that, except for the fisheries, New France had become an economic liability in the eighteenth century, it remained keen to checkmate its European rivals, notably England. For that purpose, New France represented an enormous political and military asset. It could contain the English settlers along the Atlantic seaboard as well as the traders of the Hudson's Bay Company fringed around the northern sea; it could secure Louisiana's hinterland; and, in case of a major European conflict, it could keep many a British soldier entangled in the North American backwoods instead of on the battlefields of Europe. Such a conflict would also occupy the British fleet, bound to defend that country's prize colonies. And always there seemed to be an occasion for European conflict. The succession to thrones could easily spark international duels as it did when France and Britain warred over Spain's new monarch in the early 1700s and again over the Austrian royalty in the 1740s. Each time the war extended to the colonies, leeching onto age-old Indian rivalries, modern fur trade competition, and antagonistic colonists. Each time the Canadians won in the forests of North America and lost at the peace tables of Europe. Perhaps for that reason they were eager to strengthen the economic and military hold on the west after 1713. If in that year the Treaty of Utrecht, signalling the end of the war of the Spanish succession, gave England, at least on paper, so much of what New France considered hers—the watershed of Hudson Bay, Newfoundland, Acadia, the Iroquois territory south of the Great Lakes—neither France nor the Canadians intended to let Britain profit from the victories. In 1717, France began the extensive fortification of Louisbourg to watch the British in Acadia and to guard, as much as it could, the cod fishery and the entrance to the St. Lawrence. The Canadian officers and soldiers in the French Marine companies in New France manned the posts in the western interior and maintained the Indian alliances. Britain might have suzerainty on paper, but the French and the Canadians had the physical presence and hence the power. No one in 1713 saw a European treaty as the beginning of the end for France in America.

Indeed, both France and New France went on to enjoy some of their best years in the generation of peace between 1713 and 1744. French international trade increased, while the growing French navy successfully challenged Britain's assumed control of the seas. Neither country could afford another war and France profited most from the respite. In New France too, the colony seriously began to take hold. France's distraction during the European wars of the early eighteenth century encouraged the colonists to make more of their own goods: agriculture, fishing, commerce, and even some industries began to flourish. After the war, wheat and biscuits constituted the base of a busy trade with Louisbourg; ships from Quebec could be spotted off Martinique. The French navy's growing strength provided a second wind for Canada's shipbuilding industry: royal subsidies financed colonial construction for imperial use; once the subsidies were withdrawn, the well-equipped shipyards began producing smaller craft for the highly lucrative coastal trade. Shipbuilding in France itself called upon Canadian timber, although never in a systematic fashion. Iron mines near Trois-Rivières went into production with royal subsidies for the Forges du St. Maurice. Textile makers, tanners, and brewers produced for a local market as did cabinetmakers and silversmiths, the latter a sure sign of prosperity in the colony, making articles modelled on French medallions for the fur trade and vessels modelled on household utensils for the churches.

Quite visible in all this commercial activity were a great number of women. In the upper echelons of the fur trade, marriages were as much business partnerships as love matches: the absent partner in the interior, usually the male, left the other in charge of stores and accounts in the colony. The garrison officer along the Great Lakes often had his wife and daughters with him at the post; they tended the trade while the soldiers were off trafficking or battling. Lower down the fur trade hierarchy, widows of merchants often branched into profitable businesses: Marie-Anne Barbel, the widow Fornel, diversified her inherited place as merchant, supplier, and shipper to the northern trade into real estate and a pottery factory. Lower still, the wives of *voyageurs* in the towns often opened taverns to profit from the many thirsty soldiers that France sent and the colony produced after 1663. Wives in the countryside tended the farms, often for years at a stretch, and, given their generally superior education, likely kept the farm accounts. Industrial establishments also profited from having women at the helm. Agathe de Saint Père began making textiles early in the eighteenth century, ransoming English weavers from Indians who held them prisoner. Her successor, a Madame Benoist, employed women to make shirts and petticoats for the fur trade. Louise de Ramezay had extensive lumbering operations on the Richelieu. Nothing in New France society hindered, and much in fact fostered, commercial undertakings by women.

Less visibly, women also helped to mould and maintain a social structure that slowly developed through the eighteenth century. In a society where the family was the basic social unit, and often the only political one, where the household was a centre of economic production, where laws protected women's property rights before, during, and after marriage (the chances of being a widow, if not for long, were high), where women were at first scarce and subsequently often alone, and where people themselves were even more scarce, women had ample scope for valued activity. They made their voices heard at the bottom end of the social scale convening an assembly to elect a midwife in 1713 or rioting against rations of horsemeat during the dire winter of 1757–58. And they made their presence felt at the top end of the social scale. Louise Elisabeth Joybert de Soulanges, the Canadian wife of Philippe de Rigaud de Vaudreuil, governor of New France from 1703 to 1725, spent years at Versailles paving the way for her sons' entry into places of prestige and command, protecting her husband's interests, and advising France's Minister of the Marine on colonial matters. Between the two social extremes, women cemented business alliances and perpetuated the military society by having their marriageable daughters introduced to officers and their other daughters serve as nurses to the soldiers in a hospital of a religious order. The women, of course, produced the children who gradually Canadianized all ranks of society, from *habitants* up through tradespeople, merchants, traders, the clergy and the religious, the military and the administrators. They may even have smoothed (or perhaps added to) the social rivalry that remained at the very top: social engagements, lavish entertainment, and polite *salon* accomplishments possibly kept the number one French administrator or trader talking to the number two Canadian.

What the women were never able to do, nor the men for that matter, was to overcome some of the basic flaws in the social and economic structure of New France. There never were enough people. In particular, the lack of skilled labour was chronic. Immigration was always minimal, a mere ten thousand between 1608 and 1759, the entire period of New France, and most of them appear to have been ordinary, poor labourers. The colony in fact had little to offer prospective immigrants and whenever the state indicated a bit of industrial incentive, it encountered the lack, and hence the expense, of skilled labour. There was never enough money in the colony and, by always importing more than it exported, New France perpetually sent more money out of the colony than it attracted. Only the military presence, the ten percent duty on imports, the royal subsidies for the administration of the colony, the church, and the few industries ensured that some cash returned to New France. Even then wars and weather could easily disrupt the flow. On occasion the lack of money in the colony led to experiments with card money and bills of exchange—the cards redeemable for cash when the next shipment arrived from France, and the bills for goods on the French market, thus avoiding the hazard of sending money by ship. Neither experiment worked and everyone in the colony was a loser as the French government halved the face value of the cards and French suppliers undercut the value of the bills of exchange. With no surplus money in the colony and the economy tied to the exporting of an untransformed natural resource, there was neither willingness nor ability to develop local money-making ventures.

Only in wartime did Canadians enjoy the steady flow of coins through their purses, and even then this only happened when the French government took the colonial aspects of its European wars seriously. Such was the case after 1743 when Britain and France warred again, this time seriously competing for trade and colonial supremacy. French money poured into the colony and enabled it not only to look more prosperous but to attend to immediate military concerns. Border raids on the English colonies indicated once again Canadian military skill, in spite of the numerical odds. On the Atlantic coast, however, Louisbourg fell easily to the English in 1745. Both events disrupted the flow of trade goods—illegal ones from England via Albany and legal ones from France via Louisbourg and resulted in restiveness among the Indian allies in the western interior. Once they no longer received from the French trade goods of the accustomed quantity, quality, and price, the western Indians were quite prepared to discard the alliance, forcibly remove the French, and engage in commercial transactions with English traders now anxious to move west across the Alleghenies into the Ohio territory. Only the brief duration of the war and the restoration of Louisbourg to France in 1748 permitted the fragile alliance to continue. It would not be for long. In the 1750s the French attempted to garrison their flimsy hold on the west by building a series of forts in the Ohio valley. Meanwhile in the east, the British began taking seriously their control of Acadia, an English paper conquest since 1713, by founding Halifax as a naval base and fortress in 1749 and plotting the expulsion of the French-speaking inhabitants of the territory. The carefully planned but so terribly fragile eighteenth century empire of France in North America began to crumble.

Perhaps the end was visible all along. The colony lacked so much — money, people, talent, enterprise, peace, leadership, luck—that it was surprising it lasted as long as it did. It had the zeal to found a new people, and the military prowess to stamp its name across a continent. But few people came to stay and fewer dreams were realized. Always the base was a thin line along a treacherous river, inviting people inland or sealing their fate with the arrival of the first ships from Europe. Nothing in Quebec's future would assuage the insecurity bequeathed by New France.

SELECT BIBLIOGRAPHY

Bosher, John F. "The Family in New France." In *In Search of the Visible Past: History Lectures at Wilfrid Laurier University 1973–1974.* Edited by Barry M. Gough. Waterloo, Ontario: Wilfrid Laurier University Press, 1975. Pp. 1–13.

Dechêne, Louise. "La croissance de Montréal au XVIIIe siècle." *Revue d'histoire de l'Amérique française* 27(1973):163–79.

Dechêne, Louise. *Habitants et marchands de Montréal au XVIIe siècle.* Paris: Plon, 1974.

Dictionary of Canadian Biography. Toronto: University of Toronto Press, 1966—.

Eccles, William J. *Canadian Society During the French Regime.* Montreal: Harvest House, 1968.

Eccles, William J. *The Canadian Frontier, 1534–1760.* Montreal: Holt, Rinehart and Winston, 1969.

Eccles, William J. "The Social, Economic and Political Significance of the Military Establishment in New France." *Canadian Historical Review* 52(1971):1–22.

Frégault, Guy. *Le XVIIIe siècle canadien: Etudes.* Montreal: Editions HMH, 1968.

Groulx, Lionel Adolphe. *Histoire du Canada français depuis la découverte.* Volume 1: *Le régime français.* Montreal: Fides, 1960.

Hamelin, Jean. *Economie et société en Nouvelle-France.* Quebec: Les presses de l'Université Laval, 1960.

Harris, Richard C. *The Seigneurial System in Early Canada: A Geographical Study.* Madison, Wisconsin: University of Wisconsin Press, 1966.

Jaenen, Cornelius, J. *The Role of the Church in New France.* Toronto: McGraw-Hill Ryerson, 1976.

Moogk, Peter N. "Apprenticeship Indentures: A Key to Artisan Life in New France." *Historical Papers/Communications historiques.* Canadian Historical Association, 1971. Pp. 65–83.

Noel, Jan. "New France: les femmes favorisées." *Atlantis* 6(1981):80–98.

Ouellet, Fernand. "Propriété seigneuriale et groupes sociaux dans la vallée du Saint-Laurent (1663–1840)." In *Mélanges d'histoire du Canada français offerts au professeur Marcel Trudel.* Edited by Pierre Savard. Ottawa: Editions de l'Université d'Ottawa, 1978. Pp. 183–213.

Trudel, Marcel. *Initiation à la Nouvelle-France: Histoire et institutions.* Montreal: Holt, Rinehart and Winston, 1968.

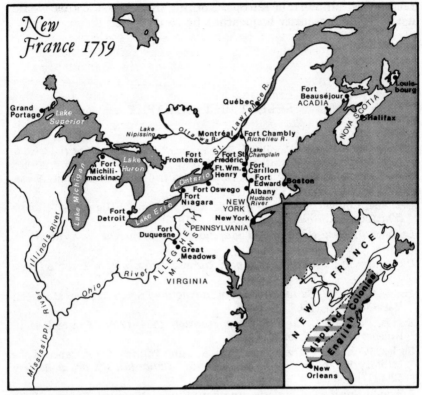

New France in 1759
Inset derived from the Fourth Edition of the National Atlas of Canada
© 1974 Her Majesty the Queen in Right of Canada with permission of
Energy, Mines and Resources Canada.

2 Conquest

By the 1760s conquest was added to the legacy of New France and
the question of being French in North America took on another
dimension. Just what that dimension was has been the subject of
much historical debate. Some of that debate has illuminated aspects of the society of New France; more of it has revealed the
contemporary political stances of the historians themselves. By
turning New France's military loss at the hands of the British
into a psychological trauma, historians have in fact played roles in
the drama almost as significant as those of the eighteenth century
protagonists. Certainly they have been less polite than the generals of two centuries ago who gravely sent each other enquiries as
to health and the latest news from Europe before engaging in a set

battle. The European soldiers of the eighteenth century were imperial employees; their work was one of duty and honour, rarely of passion. The historians, particularly those of the mid-twentieth century, were ideologues and, in their passionate devotion to *la patrie*, nationalists—a species rare and incomprehensible in the eighteenth century. Their weapons— speeches, lectures, scholarly articles, learned treatises, and tracts—were physically less harmful than the muskets, cannon, and hatchets of two centuries ago but perhaps ultimately more devastating. For behind the political debates that continue to rage today both within Quebec and between Quebec and the rest of Canada lies the spectre of the Conquest, a spectre fed and fostered by historians.

As an historical problem the Conquest raises three major questions. The least controversial appears to be what actually happened in Canada during the Seven Years' War (1756–63 for a European; 1754–60 for a Canadian) or during the crucial year between the fall of Quebec on September 13, 1759, and the capitulation of Montreal on September 9, 1760. Military historians, strategists, armchair generals, and war games enthusiasts ponder the movement of troops and supplies but rarely engage in heady debate. Only the very latest of them, W.J. Eccles, combining military and social history, now argues with his predecessors and contests the generally held view that the military collapse of New France was inevitable. Much more controversial, however, has been the question of just what that military collapse meant for the economic, political, and social structures of the time. Historians such as Jean Hamelin and Fernand Ouellet have argued that the change was minimal; others such as Guy Frégault, Michel Brunet, or Maurice Séguin have contended that the change was catastrophic. The debate raged in the late 1950s and early 1960s and turned on the questioned existence and the lamented behaviour of an indigenous French Canadian bourgeoisie in the eighteenth century. Of even broader scope has been the question of the meaning of the Conquest for subsequent generations of French Canadians. Coming to terms with that event appears to have been one of the major preoccupations of French Canadian intellectuals ever since.

The actual battle between the French led by Montcalm and the British led by Wolfe on the Plains of Abraham on September 13, 1759, took only fifteen minutes, but the preparations had been lengthy. New France was a military society and warfare had always been just around the corner. The years of the Seven Years' War, 1756–1763, harsh though they were, constituted no more than what Canadians were accustomed to: insecurity, disease, the possibility of famine, military threats, and economic instability. True, this was the first time since the Kirkes unceremoniously took Quebec in 1629 and held it for three years that the English had succeeded in a military expedition against Canada. But they had always been skulking about, posturing from the south, the north, or the sea. Perhaps too the thirty years peace between England

and France in the early eighteenth century had lulled a few souls
into temporary security. But anyone having anything to do with
the fur trade—and almost everyone did—was aware of the continuing rivalry in the west and north, over the contraband coun-
ters in Albany, or even in the commercial bustle of the supply
centres at Louisbourg. Given the politics of the fur trade, the extraordinary growth of the American colonies, and the recurring
rivalry of the European states, an outright confrontation was probably inevitable.

The outcome however was by no means inevitable. Mere numbers might make the Canadian cause appear hopeless as some sixty-
five thousand faced more than a million Anglo-Americans in the
British colonies to the south. But the Canadians were more than a
fighting match for the English colonists. Indeed had they been left
alone to fight on their grounds and in their own manner, the results might have been quite different. Instead, France inflicted upon
the Canadians its own death wish for the colony in the person of
Louis-Joseph, the Marquis de Montcalm. Nor was the question of
supply, whether locally or from France, as crucial to the outcome
as some historians have contended. The intendant François Bigot
may well have been lining his pockets and gambling away some of
the profits made from lucrative army contracts, but supply the
army he did. The food shortages noticeable among the civilian
population as early as 1756 and becoming increasingly severe by
the winter of 1758–59 were familiar to the local *habitants*: a largely
self-sufficient agriculture had always been prone to the vagaries
of season and climate. Moreover the French supply ships succeeded
in slipping past the British watch in the Gulf of St. Lawrence until
1759. And even after the fall of Quebec, the French victory at Ste.
Foy in April 1760 raised the possibility of recovering the city. Sheer
chance, and perhaps the negligence of the French navy which appears to have given up on Canada as early as the autumn of 1759,
brought British ships up the river first as the ice cleared in the
spring of 1760. Only then was defeat a certainty.

There never has been agreement about the significance of this
defeat; the Conquest has meant different things to different generations and indeed to different social groups. Perhaps not surprisingly clerics of the late eighteenth century saw the hand of
providence in the English victories of 1759 and 1760, sparing the
French settlement in North America from the ravages of the French
Revolution and, coincidentally, catapulting the clergy into positions
of power and prestige it had never known during the French Regime. Clearly providence had backed the right side. By the early
nineteenth century other views prevailed. The historian Francois-
Xavier Garneau was not at all enamoured of the clergy and in
spite of expurgations from subsequent versions of his *Histoire du
Canada* his view of the Conquest as a tragedy entailing the decap-
itation of the social elites (and hence making room for clerical ones)
became the major interpretative strain until well into the twenti-

eth century. Later in the nineteenth century French Canadian politicians and journalists, fascinated by the positions of power and prestige that the parliamentary system had provided them, began to see the Conquest as the happy introduction of liberty into a backward land. British political ideas and practices, they surmised, provided infinitely more scope for individual endeavour than did the ties of family and deference that patterned the *ancien régime*. Moreover, as the very few but much more radical pointed out, those same liberal institutions permitted French Canada to survive in spite of clerical tyranny.

By the early twentieth century, as French Canadians reeled under successive blows of English Canadian intolerance, industrialization, and imperial wars, the Conquest emerged as a challenge to French Canada's survival instincts. Misreading the society of New France as agricultural and clerical, the historian Lionel Groulx saw the persistence of such traits in the Quebec of the 1910s as a sure sign that struggle and survival were the valued, perhaps even providential, legacy of a nonetheless tragic Conquest. The more secular historians of the mid-twentieth century saw fewer clerics and fewer farmers in New France; rather Frégault, Brunet, and Séguin spotted a normal society in infancy, arrested in its growth by the Conquest. This view of Conquest-as-thalidomide, hotly contested by Hamelin and Ouellet, raised the question of the nature of society in New France, one of the more fruitful although by no means yet resolved historical enquiries engendered by the Conquest debate. Most historians in Quebec today have turned resolutely away from the debate: the older among them concentrating on the early adaptability, or lack thereof, of French Canadians to economic and social changes of the early nineteenth century; the younger asking similar questions about the late nineteenth and early twentieth centuries.

Behind the varying interpretations of the Conquest are two very different approaches to the place of French Canada in North America. Each recognizes the minority position of French Canadians, but one makes of it a problem, the other a challenge. For some French Canadians being a minority has entailed subordinate economic, political, and social status. They have been able to point to foreign observers such as Lord Durham in the nineteenth century who said it would be so or to federal enquiries such as the Royal Commission on Bilingualism and Biculturalism in the twentieth century that recorded the fact. And they have sought the cause in the Conquest, and the cure, albeit with some reluctance, in independence. For other French Canadians, however, being a minority has entailed a complex challenge, rather than an obstacle. For some meeting this challenge has meant arguing and displaying a certain superiority to English Canadians. For others it has meant denying the ethnic dimension altogether and claiming that the interests of class and politics are paramount. This approach thus emphasizes either healthy competition or interested co-operation between French and English Canadians and implies, for its adherents, adaptation and coping rather than blaming and whining. To its opponents it spells compensation or, worse still, collaboration. The two approaches have fuelled the debates of historians, intellectuals, and politicians throughout the history of French Canada. René Lévesque and Pierre Trudeau are merely the latest manifestations of the two points of view. Without the Conquest neither would have existed.

Perhaps because dipping into the debate over the Conquest gives one the distinct feeling of being the uninvited guest at a family squabble, English-speaking historians have contributed relatively little to it. Nineteenth century writers such as William Smith or William Kingsford shared current liberal notions of progress and development and tied them closely to British political and economic institutions. Like many of their Protestant compatriots they had little use for Catholicism and tended therefore to see the French colony in North America as lost in the misty wafts of clerical obscurantism. The Conquest could only be a deliverance. Such views died hard in English Canada bolstered as they have been by such prominent twentieth century historians as Donald Creighton. For him the Conquest brought the true builders of the northern commercial empire to power, although British officals themselves did not always recognize it, and much of Creighton's post-Conquest history is the tale of obstinate resistance by foolhardy French Canadian politicians and peasants to the progress and development planned by English Canadian merchants. On occasion a more sympathetic voice was heard. An Arthur Lower, a George Stanley, or a Ramsay Cook has valiantly attempted to paint a picture of what conquest really means, of what being a minority actually feels like. But English Canada has never known conquest nor enforced minority status. Therefore a great leap of imagination is required, as great as that of French-speaking historians who would dearly love to wish the Conquest away or to have had their predecessors react differently to it. Perhaps only an analogy can assist the leap of imagination. Conquest is like rape. The major blow takes only a few minutes, the results no matter how well camouflaged, can be at best unpredictable and at worst devastating.

Long before the devastation of Quebec in 1759, there was trouble in the western interior. In the rich lands west of the Allegheny Mountains, imperial dreams were bound to collide. The French dream involved the maintenance of Indian alliances for both strategic and economic reasons. A chain of forts constructed in the 1750s to encircle the American colonies from the eastern Great Lakes to Louisiana would knit the French empire in North America together and also guarantee a steady supply of furs to the French market; the Indian alliance would ensure the safety of the forts and the production of the furs. Together, French and Indians would be able to keep the Anglo-American settlers from moving west. Moreover, if the flimsy European peace of 1748 settling the War of the Austrian Succession degenerated into open warfare between Britain and France again, the French and American proximity in the North American mid-west, coupled with an Indian threat to the American settlers, would necessitate the presence of many more British troops in America. The more troops and ships on the west side of the Atlantic, the fewer there would be for war in Europe.

The policy made sense, at least to the French. To the British, the Anglo-Americans, the Canadians, and the Indians things appeared in quite another light. The British were hardly keen to have the French second guess their attempt to contain French naval and commercial expansion. The Anglo-Americans, particularly land agents from Pennsylvania and Virginia, were not about to permit the French to block their westward expansion. They had their eye on Indian lands and on the profits to be derived from sales to their compatriots. Some of the northern colonies, however, notably New York which engaged in surreptitious and profitable trade with Canada, were less keen on confrontation with their French-speaking neighbours. As for the Canadians, they saw a threat to their own commercial stability in French imperial designs on the interior. French military strength in the west depended on the Indian alliance which could only be kept intact through trading practices profitable to the Indians. Therefore the price of trade goods had to be kept low and the ordinary officer or soldier was not to engage in trade. But there was not much profit for Canadian commercial agents in such a system. Not surprisingly then Canadians moved reluctantly into the Ohio valley in the 1750s as the French slowly constructed a road southeast of Lake Erie to the headwaters of the Ohio River and a series of forts further south after 1753. Nor were the Indians particularly content for French imperial plans were of scant interest to them. Anxious to keep white colonists from settling permanently on their lands, to maintain their own intermediary position with fur supplying tribes further west, and to obtain trade goods as cheaply as possible, the Indians sided with whoever offered the better deal.

Usually, but not always, it was the French. So anxious were the French to maintain their Indian alliances that they often took a loss in order to supply the British trade goods so admired by the Indians. The Indians in turn easily recognized that the French were merely blocking direct access to British traders; and yet any direct trading might lead to Anglo-American expansion and white settlement in the west. The French clearly had no such intention and claimed even to protect the Indians from it. The play was subtle and shrewd as the Indians eyed the ebb and flow of strength between their present and potential allies. They could not know in 1754 that they would be the ultimate losers in skirmishes that saw the French dislodge Virginians, construct Fort Duquesne on the Ohio, and send out a party to order approaching Anglo-Americans off, only to have the group ambushed by George Washington and some members of the militia. Two years before the European outbreak of the Seven Years' War, North Americans were already feuding over unsettled terrain far in the western interior. The wavering Indians, once the French had forcefully defeated Washington at Great Meadows, sided, for the time being, with their erstwhile allies.

Within a year the feuding, continuing in the west, had engulfed the Atlantic coast and the St. Lawrence region as well. On the east coast, the British, unsuccessful in blocking the passage of French military ships bound for Louisbourg and Quebec, captured Fort Beauséjour on the Nova Scotian isthmus and undertook the most dramatic of all early Canadian events: the expulsion of the Acadians. Of the seven thousand French-speaking settlers forcibly evicted from homes, farms, and villages throughout present-day Nova Scotia and New Brunswick during the summer of 1755, some two thousand made their way to Quebec where they added to the fright of the inhabitants as well as to the housing and supply problems of the city. In the western interior, the Anglo-Americans abandoned a planned attack on Niagara while a small group of Canadians with their Indian allies defeated a major force of twenty-two hundred under the British General Braddock near Fort Duquesne on the Ohio in July. Among Braddock's abandoned baggage were plans for attacks on the other Canadian nerve centres. While the information sped east, the French and Indians engaged in systematic raids on the frontiers of present-day Pennsylvania and Virginia. And in the St. Lawrence lowlands, both British and French fortified their bases along the Richelieu—the former invasion route of the Iroquois was now being used by the British. The French built Fort Carillon at the southernmost tip of Lake Champlain while the British constructed Forts William Henry and Edward on Lake George and the Hudson River, respectively. The British won an engagement by Lake George in September but were unable to capture Fort St. Frédéric which would have furnished stores, shelter, and munitions for the marauding forces. All along the hazy border from the Atlantic to the Ohio, fear haunted the settlers.

In 1756, with war officially declared in Europe, France sent out Montcalm to command the *troupes de terre*. And then the trouble began. Officially Montcalm was subordinate to the governor of New France, Pierre de Rigaud, Marquis de Vaudreuil, who commanded all the forces available to the Canadians: *troupes de terre*, *troupes de la marine*, the militia, the naval detachments, and the Indian allies. Vaudreuil was a Canadian, indeed the first Canadian governor, with powerful connections that had been carefully cultivated by his mother at the French Court. He and Montcalm did not take to each other. Their personalities clashed and their positions were much too close for comfort. Moreover their military strategy differed dramatically. Vaudreuil, raised on the French dream of empire, saw military advantage in the extended lines of potential offense throughout the North American interior. He was convinced that a combination of Canadian and Indian warfare could eventually harass the enemy into submission. Montcalm, trained in European set battles, could see only the St. Lawrence as in any way defensible; a sortie into distant territory might on occasion be envisioned, but always the French should draw back to the surely impregnable line of the St. Lawrence. Yet even of that the French commander was not always sure. Montcalm conveyed his uneasiness, even his disinterest, to his own officers who then clashed with the much more determined Canadian officers and soldiers.

Not that Montcalm was inactive. In the summer of 1756 he captured and destroyed the Anglo-American fort of Oswego on the south side of Lake Ontario. Earlier Canadian raids on the supply routes to the fort had facilitated the capture, but the victory was his. It ensured French control of the entire Great Lakes and Ohio area, cutting off both any reprisal for periodic Canadian attacks on the American borders and any possibility of an Anglo-American invasion of the St. Lawrence region via the Great Lakes. The same French strategy worked a year later on the second possible invasion route, the Richelieu-Lake Champlain entrance to the St. Lawrence. But here Montcalm's hesitancy came into play, and perhaps too his lack of understanding of the Indian allies he was obliged to tolerate among his troops. Fort William Henry fell easily to Montcalm's onslaught, but he refused to pursue his advantage. He could neither rein in his Indian troops who proceeded to massacre the garrison and the inhabitants of the fort nor could he stomach their tactics sufficiently to use them to frighten the American colonists into submission all the way to Albany. Instead he drew back.

Montcalm's hesitancy reflected that of France. More interested in the European developments of the war, France lost its dream of empire. A mere toe hold on the North American continent would suffice as a bargaining tool at the post-war peace talks. France therefore sanctioned Montcalm's notion that only the inner St. Lawrence was defensible. As if to emphasize the point, Montcalm managed to fend off an attack on Fort Carillon early in July 1758, but he refused to turn defence into offence. France also sent far fewer reinforcements to New France than Britain did to its American colonies—a mere seven thousand compared to twenty-three thousand—thereby indicating its lack of interest as well as its success in tying down more British than French troops in North America. The problem with the strategy was obvious: more British troops meant more British victories. And for the rest of 1758 that is precisely what happened. On the Atlantic coast, Louisbourg fell to the British later in July. Although the gain was minimal since the French navy was not in port and the sixty-day siege occupied the British too long to dare an autumnal race against the ice up the St. Lawrence for an attack on Quebec, the strategic acquisition was enormous. In the western interior, a surprise Anglo-American attack in August destroyed the boats and provisions at Fort Frontenac in the northeastern corner of Lake Ontario thereby crippling French supply and communication links to Niagara and the Ohio country. For once the Indians did not tip the French off about the attack. Having thanked the French two years earlier for removing Anglo-Americans from Oswego, just across the lake, the Indians now seemed prepared to thank the other side for removing the French. This switch of Indian favour persuaded the French to abandon Fort Duquesne on the Ohio in November; in response to an Indian peace treaty with the Pennsylvanians who renounced all claims on the Indian territory west of the Allegheny Mountains, the French destroyed their own presence in the American midwest. By then the French government had added insult to injury. It elevated Montcalm above the Canadian governor, giving him command of all French, Canadian, and Indian forces in North America. Vaudreuil fumed. He was convinced that Montcalm's disinterest, now honoured by France, would eventually seal the fate of his homeland.

Thus during 1759 the British had easy access along the three possible invasion routes into the heart of the St. Lawrence colony. From the west came Anglo-American troops planning to descend upon Montreal from Lake Ontario. In spite of the capture of Fort Niagara in mid-summer, thereby cutting off the final French link to the Ohio country, this line of attack did not succeed until the late summer of 1760. From the south came other English forces along Lake Champlain toward the Richelieu River. In the face of that advance, the French retreated, destroying Forts Carillon and St. Frédéric as they went. But there too the advance halted, at least until the following year, as Major-General Jeffrey Amherst, betraying a sense of unease hardly befitting an invader, decided to repair the forts and construct a new one at Crown Point rather than continue north. Was he expecting to confront Canadian troops advancing south along the Richelieu? Or was he so sure of the failure of Major-General James Wolfe's invasion along the St. Lawrence from the east that he dared not place himself too far inside enemy territory?

Certainly Wolfe was in an awkward position by late summer 1759. His eight thousand soldiers were perched precariously on three separate landing points: on the western tip of the Ile d'Orléans, on Point Lévis, and on the east bank of the Montmorency River. They ought to have been easy targets for the sixteen thousand troops available to Montcalm and had Canadian tactics prevailed, the French might easily have picked off the British soldiers from the rear, slowly but surely antagonizing them into retreat. But Montcalm stayed put within the walls of Quebec City and would not be drawn out by Wolfe's summer-long bombardment. Neither British attacks along the Beauport coast east of Quebec nor American destruction of some fourteen hundred homes and farms on the Ile d'Orléans and along the two coasts succeeded in baiting Montcalm into a pitched battle. Perhaps he was awaiting winter as anxiously as Wolfe was dreading it. Hesitating over a final attempt to take Quebec from the Beauport side or an immediate withdrawal to the Gulf before the river froze, Wolfe finally decided on a wild gamble. With dark and stealth and luck, the British might be able to climb the almost perpendicular cliff west of Quebec, cut off the French line of supply and reinforcement, and draw up in proper European battle formation on the flat land outside the walls of the city, high above the river. It might just work. Certainly if it did not, the British would have to retreat with no dark, no stealth, and no luck: they would all tumble over the cliff in an ignominious clatter. But it did work. On the morning of September 13, much to the surprise of the generals on both sides, the British confronted a hastily gathered lot of French soldiers, only half of those available to Montcalm. Within fifteen minutes the battle on the Plains of Abraham was over and the two generals dead, a peculiar commentary on the state of readiness of both sides. Wolfe and Montcalm were at least spared the Canadian winter.

For the Canadians, the outcome was less decisive. The city itself, in ruins and housing more people than it could feed, surrendered conditionally to Wolfe's brigadier James Murray on September 18. The French forces withdrew west of the city, still sufficiently numerous to harass Canadian farmers who might be tempted to supply the city with food or firewood, but not yet strong enough to ponder an attack on the British. How far Murray's authority extended beyond the city was unknown; how long his presence would last was equally unknown. How the city would survive the winter, whether there would be food or fuel for the morrow let alone seed grain for next year's sowing, whether the French suspension of payment on Canadian bills of exchange would be merely a postponement or an actual repudiation—the worries were endless. Only the nursing sisters maintained their usual serenity, healing Canadians, French, and British indiscriminantly. Murray never forgot them in his subsequent plans for the new British colony.

Those plans, however, were at least a year away. In the interval, the French and Canadian soldiers from the Montreal region regrouped under François, the Duc de Lévis and designed a spring attack upon Quebec to coincide with the arrival of the first supply ships of the year from France. By April 1760, with French forces just west of Quebec at Ste. Foy, Murray learned of the intended attack but not of the size of Lévis' troops, equal to his own at about thirty-eight hundred. Deciding on an immediate battle rather than a prolonged siege which the city might well not withstand after the harsh winter, Murray brought his forces out of Quebec for a confrontation with the French and Canadian soldiers on April 28. In an engagement of more military merit than that on the plains the previous autumn, the British were defeated. Lévis then prepared to retake Quebec, awaiting only the first ships up river. May 15 brought the ships, but they were not French. Chance, the weather, and, it seems, total French disinterest as of the late autumn of 1759 determined that British warships would be the first up the St. Lawrence after the break-up of the winter ice. Lévis had to withdraw. From then the end was but a matter of time. By September 1760, invading forces finally mastered the three traditional, but seldom successful, routes towards the control of Montreal: Murray came up river from Quebec, William de Haviland reached the St. Lawrence from the Richelieu, and Amherst came down river from Lake Ontario. With no fortifications, no provisions, no ammunition, and a force of two thousand against the seventeen thousand of the British, Montreal was an indefensible town. The Indians had already made peace with Amherst, the militia had returned home, and on September 9, Montreal, as well as all of Canada, Acadia, and the western interior, surrendered.

Even then the conquest might have been temporary. One never knew how the European powers would settle their differences once the war was over. Who could say that France would prefer a couple of sugar islands in the Caribbean (Guadeloupe and Martinique) to its vast North American territories? That would not be known until the Treaty of Paris in February 1763. In the meantime a military regime governed Quebec until the establishment of civil government in August 1764, almost a year after Britain's plans for the colony were expressed in a Royal Proclamation in October 1763. Just how that military regime would function was another unknown in 1760. The British themselves were not too sure, their most recent experience in coping with foreign captives having been the expulsion of the Acadians. Although many Canadians feared the same fate, that solution seemed impracticable if only because of numbers and the ever-freezing St. Lawrence. Instead, the articles of capitulation in September 1760 reflected more the gentlemanly conduct of eighteenth century warfare. French regular soldiers could return to France on the condition that they not take up arms again in the war. Half of them, some sixteen hundred, did so. French government officials could also return to France and Canadians wishing to accompany them there or to any other French colony were welcome to depart. A few seigneurs and some of the Canadian officers of the *troupes de la marine* trained in the French imperial dream left the defeated colony. Except for a handful of merchants hoping to cut their losses by an immediate presence in Paris or the port cities of France, everyone else stayed, assured of humane treatment if sick or wounded, assured of protection for themselves, their property, their religion. This was not conquest with a vengeance; it behooved the military leaders of the eighteenth century to display their honour, having stripped the other side of theirs by their very defeat. And they demonstrated that honour throughout the period of military occupation. British officers fitted their rule into the existing framework of French laws and practices. And they paid their way, in cash. After the devalued and eventually repudiated paper money of the final years of the French regime, the British could not have found a better means of ensuring an appreciative population.

The French may indeed have had the last laugh. To leave Britain stuck with the endless military expense that was North America was a fitting turn of events even if the strategy of tying down vast British forces in America had failed by 1760. The British victory in New France released troops for service elsewhere in the war that continued for another three years. But the victory and the eventual peace settlement of 1763 left Britain holding all of North America. That, the French foresaw, would aggravate the already restive Anglo-Americans to the south. The latter would soon revolt and thereby bring an end to the envied British commercial empire. England would be left holding those disdained few acres of snow north of the rich American states. French foresight extended no farther, but one can easily imagine the largest guffaw in response to de Gaulle's *"Vive le Québec libre"* cry of July 1967 coming from somewhere in the vicinity of the tombstone of Louis XV.

Still, at the time few people were laughing. The surrender, for all its urbanity and perhaps even profit, did mean insecurity. Some things would change, some things would remain. No one quite knew what or when or how. People from two European states, at odds with each other for centuries were now to live together in a far-flung colony the value of which no one was quite certain. The two differed in language, religion, laws, political and juridical practices. And yet they also shared monarchical, religious, and familial values of hierarchy, loyalty, honour, order, and grace. They bore a grudging admiration for each other: educated Englishmen spoke fluent French while educated Frenchmen discoursed on the merits of British parliamentary institutions. Flung together by the fortunes of war, their capacity for coping would now be put to the test.

Some of the Canadian elites displayed the least ability to cope. The nobility, the officers, and many seigneurs (often the same people) had played their roles in New France as close to the French administrators as possible. Their own livelihood and status had depended upon it. Careers in the military and the civil service, with easy access, one always hoped, to the fur trade, had necessitated social and preferably familial ties to French officials both in the colony and at Versailles. Those ties now made them suspect to the British while their military experience made them potentially dangerous. The days of the Canadian aristocracy were thus already numbered as British officers and British administrators moved into positions of command vacated by the French. Even the few positions that might be available to some trustworthy individuals as interpreters of customs and usages could never employ all the Canadians accustomed to such patronage appointments. Those seriously interested in the agricultural development of their seigneuries might foresee some benefit in the new and large imperial market for wheat. But such people were few. Like their British aristocratic counterparts, most Canadian seigneurs regarded their land holdings as a mark of social prestige rather than as an economic investment. Moreover, no one knew what the future held in store for seigneurial tenure, a system quite foreign to the British. Those who thought they saw the writing on the wall departed for France, often leaving parts of their families in Canada just to be on the safe side. Some forty seigneuries, about one quarter of all the seigneurial land, changed hands with other members of the Canadian nobility and newly arrived British military officers acquiring it. The departed counted on royal pensions, official protection, access to public office, and perhaps even on business contracts, thanks to their connections in France. Those who stayed, and they were the majority, trusted in the traditional patterns of marriage and warfare to re-establish their social pre-eminence.

Merchants had always been more adept at coping than the traditional elites. They lived by their wits and their pockets although in the tiny society of New France their connections had often been close with the aristocracy. Now the merchants were valuable to the British for they knew the intricacies of the fur trade: distances, equipment, *voyageurs*, and trade goods. But they also needed credit, long lines of it stretching from metropolitan centres, be they Paris or London, to the outer reaches of known North American terrain and across three or four years. Here the Canadian merchants were at a disadvantage, while the French ones simply departed. The incoming British and Americans had ready cash and ready credit, and they were prepared to make this new hinterland their own. Moreover they were young and dynamic; the one glimpse we have of Montreal merchants in the late 1750s suggests that most of them may have been beyond the age of adaptability to a new commercial framework. Yet for some, the novelty was not that great. Canadian merchant families like the Baby family and others easily had their Paris credit ratings transferred to London. Less easily, however, could they assuage the fears of the British military that Canadian traders in the interior might foment trouble with the Indians.

Indian trouble was in fact the least of the worries of the Canadian or British merchants. The fur trade itself had been in trouble since the beginning of the war and neither Canadians nor British had a ready answer. The war had cut off shipments of trade goods and had raised prices. With the British military victory, the trade changed from the highly regulated monopoly system of the French regime to one of individual and free competition. Montreal merchants hardly had time to catch their breath after the capitulation before there were American and British traders swarming through the town on their way west, armed with English trade goods. By 1765 there were fifty new British or American merchants established in Montreal and the competition was fierce both among themselves and with the traditional rivals out of Albany and

Hudson Bay. The Canadians appear to have more than held their own in terms of numbers, investment, and technical know-how until the overexpansion of the trade in the late 1770s necessitated capital and technological change. Only in the patronage traditionally associated with the interior did the Canadians lose out; unless they were bonded associates of British merchants, they were rarely given the lucrative contracts to supply the British military posts in the mid-west. Those contracts alone could keep many a merchant prospering for years. And of course the right word supplied by the right person in the right place could make all the difference with a supplier, a shipper, or a credit agent. Often those words were spoken in English.

Soft words in the right places are usually associated with the clergy. This group too used its particular talents to cope with the new Protestant rulers in a Catholic land. And it used them well. For of all the varying social groups in New France at the time of the Conquest, the clergy had perhaps the most to lose; yet it was the ultimate winner. Clerical numbers were few and they became fewer still in proportion to the population until well into the nineteenth century: in the immediate years after the Conquest, the barely two hundred priests of 1759 dwindled to a scant one hundred and forty by 1764. With no bishop to consecrate new priests (the last one, Henri-Marie Dubreil de Pontbriand, having died in 1760), there was real fear that the clergy would simply wither away. Moreover, the few that were left were in dire financial and legal straits. Buildings, churches, seminaries, and presbyteries had all suffered heavy damage during the war; some had been requisitioned by British troops and were not returned. Seigneurial land held by the church also had been ravaged with the result that agricultural produce and seigneurial dues dwindled. Even clerical title to the land was now open to legal questioning, as the British eyed the seigneurial system with perplexity. The royal subsidies which had helped finance the schools and social services provided by religious men and women now came to an end. Accustomed to earning their status by their services in a close but subordinate alliance with the state during the French regime, the clergy was now unsure of its position in an Anglican state that sanctioned the same intimate connection with religion but not with Catholicism. Nonetheless clerics were used to preaching obedience to the sovereign. As for the women religious who numbered about two hundred, none of them left the colony. They were all Canadians and since most of them had brought dowries to their communities they were in a better financial position than the male religious orders. Moreover, unlike the men, they enjoyed official recognition from the new rulers for their nursing services during the war. For many reasons therefore—practical, personal, political, financial, social, traditional, and even religious—the clergy was tempted to put in good words for the British authorities. To do otherwise would have been foolhardy, risking the loss of spiritual comfort and direction for a practising, if not very pious, population. At the same time, the clergy knew well enough that the British also required a form of consolation. Of all the links to the people, the British were likely to trust the clergy more than the former militia captains or the seigneurs. And they needed those links to the people if the transition from French to English, from surrender to acceptance, was to be made calmly. The clergy moved softly and spoke smoothly. Of all the elite groups, it survived the best.

Among the people, the echo of conquest was least distinctly heard. In many ways their lives had always been ones of coping. Political change may in fact have been less trying than plague, famine, the death of a husband in the west, or a wife in childbirth. The women had protested the substitution of horsemeat in the civilian rations in 1757; now they heard the sound of hard cash for the first time in many a year. Townsfolk in particular could see the change as prices dropped and coinage circulated. All the lower ranks of merchants below the importers, wholesalers, outfitters, and traders—the artisans, shopkeepers, innkeepers, and money lenders—may even have smiled. Those in Montreal had at least been spared the destruction of the city wrought upon Quebec. The *habitants*, most of whom lived in the areas surrounding the two major towns, likely all knew of damage or loss to the farm or crop of a relative or neighbour, if not themselves. Visions such as that, transmitted orally over the generations and through the long winter nights, are burned into the collective memory. And yet the British presence brought peace and cash for agricultural products. If ever the *habitants* were required to provide communal labour or, more rarely, commandeered wheat, they performed these duties with the same grumbling that had accompanied similar functions demanded of them during the French regime. They quickly surmised the delicate position of the seigneur and the clergy and became even stingier with their payments of dues and tithes. The Conquest may well have demanded the least of the *habitants* and for that they may have been glad.

In the twilight years of New France, between the British military victories of 1759 and 1760 and the Treaty of Paris in 1763 by which France ceded its North American empire, no one behaved quite the way historians two centuries later would have liked. The nightmare which later writers have made of the Conquest was probably less frightening in real life when it demanded the rational powers of judgment, discretion, and action. Coping is a long way from collaboration. In 1760 the colony's economy based on an exportable raw material—furs—and a subsistence agriculture remained intact, as did the structure of the colonial government with a governor and hand-picked favourites reporting to a distant capital. The military retained its pride of place in a continuing colonial society where both old and new social groups jockeyed for position. Two legal systems, two religions, two languages—most visible and audible in Quebec and Montreal—merely added to the cosmopolitan nature of the two towns, used to strange sights and sounds since their founding.

And yet it was conquest. And conquest is like rape.

SELECT BIBLIOGRAPHY

Brunet, Michel. *Canadians et Canadiens: etudes sur l'histoire et la pensée des deux Canadas*. Montreal: Fides, 1954.

Brunet, Michel. *Les Canadiens et les débuts de la domination britannique, 1760–1791*. Ottawa: Société historique du Canada, 1962.

Cook, Ramsay. "Some French-Canadian Interpretations of the British Conquest: 'Une quatrième dominante de la pensée canadienne-française'." *Annual Report*. Canadian Historical Association, 1966. Pp. 70–83.

Eccles, William J. *The Canadian Frontier, 1534–1760*. Montreal: Holt, Rinehart and Winston, 1969.

Eccles, William J. *France in America*. New York: Harper and Row, 1972.

Frégault, Guy. *La guerre de la conquête*. Montreal: Fides, 1955.

Frégault, Guy. *Le XVIIIe siècle canadien: Etudes*. Montreal: Editions HMH, 1968.

Igartua, José. "A Change in Climate: The Conquest and the *Marchands* of Montreal." *Historical Papers/Communications historiques*. Canadian Historical Association, 1974. Pp. 115–34.

Igartua, José. "The Merchants of Montreal at the Conquest: Socio-economic Profile." *Histoire sociale/Social History* 8(1975):275–93.

Miquelon, Dale, ed. *Society and Conquest: The Debate on the Bourgeoisie and Social Change in French Canada, 1700–1850*. Vancouver: Copp Clark, 1977.

Nish, Cameron, ed. *The French Canadians, 1759–1766: Conquered? Half-conquered? Liberated?* Vancouver: Copp Clark, 1966.

Ouellet, Fernand. *Histoire économique et sociale du Québec, 1760–1850: structures et conjoncture*. Montreal: Fides, 1966.

Ouellet, Fernand. "Dualité économique et changement technique au Québec (1760–1790)." *Histoire sociale/Social History* 9(1976):256–96.

Ouellet, Fernand. "Propriété seigneuriale et groupes sociaux dans la vallée du Saint-Laurent (1663–1840)." In *Mélanges d'histoire du Canada français offerts au professeur Marcel Trudel*. Edited by Pierre Savard. Ottawa: Editions de l'Université d'Ottawa, 1978. Pp. 183–213.

Séguin, Maurice. *L'idée d'indépendance au Québec: Genèse et historique*. Trois-Rivières: Boréal Express, 1968.

Stanley, George F.G. *New France: The Last Phase, 1744–1760*. Toronto: McClelland and Stewart, 1968.

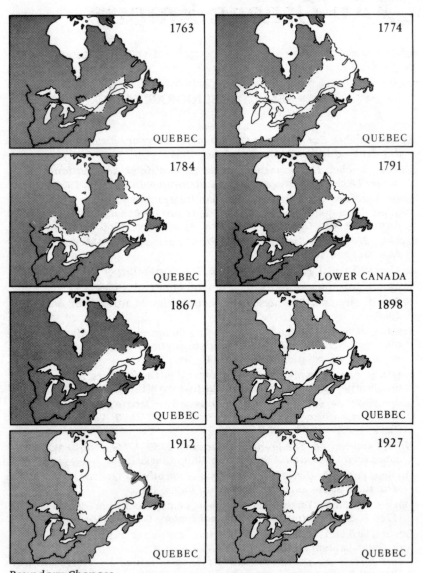

Boundary Changes
Derived from the Fourth Edition of the National Atlas of Canada © 1974
Her Majesty the Queen in Right of Canada with permission of Energy,
Mines and Resources Canada.

3 An Other's Empire

For thirty years after the Conquest Britain attempted to make Quebec an English colony. It never quite worked. The English dream of empire vacillated more than the French one—three different policies in as many decades—but the result was no different: the colony never did conform to imperial expectations. Governors and merchants in Quebec, colonial secretaries and parliaments in London all tried to fit the new colony not only into their own image, but also into an imperial puzzle of incredible dimensions. That confusion was often the result is hardly surprising. For this was a period of tremendous upheaval in the western world. What historians have termed the Atlantic Revolution spared few in the last decades of the eighteenth and opening years of the nineteenth centuries. If England was able to take the pace of change in stride at home, putting off even its political ramifications until the 1830s, the same was not true abroad. Canada, the United States, and France all underwent revolutionary military, political, and social change, Canada's punctuated by conquest in the 1760s and rebellion in the 1830s. As an imperial power England bore the brunt of these changes, acquiring a new empire in North America only to have the old one break away.

With the Treaty of Paris, Britain acquired all former French territory in North America, except for a fishing shelf off Newfoundland's north shore and the two gulf islands of St. Pierre and Miquelon. Britain added to its thirteen colonies along the Atlantic coast a vast northern and western empire of unknown dimensions. The tiny settlement along the St. Lawrence was the least of its worries. True some seventy thousand French-speaking Catholics had to be integrated into an English-speaking and largely Protestant empire. But that was assumed to be easy: the same format used in the other American colonies should suffice. The real problem lay in the west, a vast Indian territory surrounding the Great Lakes and bordering the American colonies all the way to the Gulf of Mexico. Control and administration there would not be so simple.

As if to accentuate the point, the western Indians took up arms in the spring and summer of 1763 before the ink was even dry on the Treaty of Paris. Indeed, the news of the peace between England and France had not reached the western interior. There, numerous groups of Indians were unhappy over the interruptions in the fur trade occasioned by the lengthy European rivalry in the North American forests. The war had not only cut the flow of trade, it had raised prices of trade goods. The Indians resented having to pay for fewer goods with more furs. Moreover the British did not display quite the same generosity towards the Indians as had the French. Whether it was ceremonial hospitality in the form of greetings and speeches or concrete hospitality in the form of guns and rum, the British appeared parsimonious. There were sporadic attacks throughout the summer of 1763 as Indians, sometimes acting alone and sometimes led by Pontiac, took out their hostility upon British posts all the way from Michilimackinac on the northwest end of Lake Huron to those in the area south and west of Lakes Erie and Ontario. By autumn the Indian hunting season had begun: eating, clothing, and trading were more important than attacking British forts. And the French withdrawal from the area, once the terms of the European peace were known, emphasized the isolation of the Indians. They could count on no help from their erstwhile allies and the uprising petered out.

It left its mark, however, in subsequent British policy for the new North American acquisitions. Imperial strategists in London foresaw Indian unrest as the greatest danger; they therefore designed the Royal Proclamation in the fall of 1763 primarily to contain it. By making the western territories a vast Indian protectorate under the Crown, Britain hoped to ensure the defence of the area, keep white settlement out, and break the historic link between French and Indian. The attempt would require a British presence, just as had the old French policy of containing the Anglo-Americans and appeasing the Indians. And it would mean trade with the Indians on advantageous terms to them. Thus, no sooner did the British acquire the central North American continent than they were obliged to behave just like the French before them, manning a string of military posts throughout the area and permitting their military officers to be closely involved in the fur trade. The American continent and commerce had a logic of their own which defied the divisions of European states.

Another way of breaking the link between French and Indian was to limit severely the frontiers of the St. Lawrence settlement. As of October 1763, the territory of Quebec was reduced to a mockery of the former French empire. Its natural link by river and canoe to the west, to the north, and even to the east was broken by the boundaries Britain imposed. Divested of the fur trade and of the fisheries, Quebec was to be a roughly rectangular sandwich, the St. Lawrence a circumscribed filling from the western tip of Anticosti to Lake Nipissing. Beyond those boundaries settlement was discouraged, just as outward expansion was discouraged in the thirteen colonies to the south. Quebec was to be the fourteenth, a colony just like the others.

Like the others it would enjoy British laws and British institutions. That meant a governor and his council as well as an elected assembly to enact laws and raise the necessary taxes to pay for them. It probably also meant a freehold system of land tenure and an influx of new agricultural settlers, both from the overcrowded colonies to the south and perhaps even from the British Isles. Eventually it might well mean the English language and Protestant religion. Certainly it meant that Quebec was to become an integral part of the British commercial empire: Britain's Navigation Acts imposed trading patterns and restrictions on Quebec which the other colonies were soon to reject rather unceremoniously.

The only realistic aspect of the Royal Proclamation as it concerned Quebec was the acknowledgment that circumstances might not permit its immediate implementation. How indeed could one have an elected assembly where the majority of potential electors were Roman Catholics, barred by British law from holding office? And supposing new settlers did not materialize in numbers great enough to warrant drastic changes of laws, habits, and beliefs? Or even for the few newcomers who did appear, how were they to enjoy English laws as promised by the Proclamation when there were no English laws in Quebec? What then?

These were questions British officials in Quebec would ponder for the rest of the century. Neither changes of personality, position, or politics could alter the fact that Quebec did not quite fit. Governors from James Murray to Guy Carleton to Frederick Haldimand and back to Carleton again, as Lord Dorchester, wrestled with the problem only to let their personal penchants and often their wishful thinking get the better of them. They all discovered that even the best of British proclamations could not quite encompass legality and justice, trade and fair play, institutions and customs. Also, they each tended to be charmed by the Canadian seigneurial and clerical elites, dismayed by American and British merchants, and probably deceived by the few Canadian *habitants* they encountered. In a late eighteenth century setting of commercial pushiness and democratic pretensions, there was something soothing about the aristocratic, military values harboured in certain sectors of Canadian society. The governors were, after all, soldiers. Thus, when time or the occasion permitted, they often let their orders from London slide under the council table.

Around that council table, once civilian government was established in the late summer of 1764 with James Murray as governor, sat a group of hand-picked men. In a time of dubious loyalty, only one was French, a newly arrived Huguenot at that. The others were British: officers, officials, and an increasingly noisy group of merchants, present because of their financial weight in Quebec City or Montreal. There was no sign of clerical presence; that would have been both impolitic and illegal. Indeed only in 1766 was a bishop, Jean-Olivier Briand, surreptitiously consecrated in France and permitted to return to Quebec. Neither his title nor his church was secure until after the turn of the century. Long before then, a rival Anglican bishop was at the governor's right hand. Although not on his council, he was actively engaged in anglicizing a nascent school system and dreaming of the end of Catholicism in a British colony. Council members too wondered how long all the trappings of a British colony could be avoided. Especially when rumblings from the King's "old subjects"—English, Scots, or Irish arriving from the Atlantic colonies or from the British Isles—began to be heard in the land.

Even though it became clear as early as 1766 that a separate policy for Quebec was required, eight long years of delays and ditherings lay between that recognition and actual legislation in the Quebec Act. Lawyers and officials on both sides of the Atlantic fussed over the complications of separate but equal, all the while keeping a wary eye on growing indications from the thirteen original colonies that they desired not only equality but separation too. The new colony of Quebec housed many a former Anglo-American; they could hardly be denied the political institutions and legal framework to which they were accustomed. But how could one grant such institutions in a Catholic, conquered colony? Even supposing some way could be found around the vexing question of Catholic toleration (Britain did not find the answer for itself until the late 1820s) should one really be tolerating them if assimilation was the ultimate goal? As historian Hilda Neatby described the dilemma: "an English colony without an assembly seemed unthinkable, an assembly including Roman Catholics unreliable, and an assembly excluding Roman Catholics unjustifiable."

The dithering continued into the early 1770s. By then it was clear that trouble was brewing in the more southerly colonies and that immigration was not going to flow into Quebec. The Canadians themselves showed no signs of assimilation. Indeed proliferation was more the pattern. Some of their elites were using Carleton's obvious sympathy to get a good word through to London. Meanwhile the economy showed few signs of turning the territory quickly into a commercial gem in the imperial crown. With the fur trade so closely tied to the military presence in the west, Britain found itself bogged down in the very quagmire that France had been so pleased to abandon in the late 1750s. And those military forces tied up in the western posts might soon be required closer to the western fringes of the restive American colonies. They might even need a secure base of operations from the north.

Out of that imperial, North American, and Canadian context came the Quebec Act, an attempt by Britain to keep Quebec British without making it English. The effort lasted only slightly longer than that of the Royal Proclamation, for a French regime Quebec could no more survive in late eighteenth century Anglo-America than could a pseudo-English colony made up of French-speaking Catholics. Moreover the Anglo-Americans were not content. They interpreted the Quebec Act of 1774 as another intolerable act, justifying revolt against Britain. The territorial clauses of the Act gave Americans every cause for fear. Britain reattached to Quebec the entire western, northern, and eastern territory cut off by the Royal Proclamation. What appeared only proper to Canadians and a godsend to British and indeed American merchants in the colony seemed more like a military threat to people in the American colonies.

Hadn't they lived for a century or more under the constant danger of surprise attack from the north and from the west? Now Britain was not only re-establishing the traditional military threat, it was sanctioning the peculiar society to the north as well. All the French institutions, language, civil laws, and religion were to be officially tolerated. The seigneurial system, tithes, everything that to the Americans had made New France appear so archaic was now to have the force of British law. Worse still there was to be no elected assembly, an unheard of negation of every English citizen's birthright. Instead a few Canadians would find their way by appointment, and thus no doubt by favouritism, into the council of the governor. There, thanks to a rewording of the oath required of all office holders, Catholics could have their say in the direction of Canadian public affairs. The imposition of British criminal law was minor compared to the enormous concessions made to the Canadians.

If the Quebec Act annoyed the Americans, it also irritated certain groups in Quebec itself. Seigneurs and clerics were of course delighted, seeing places of power and prestige open up in the new but familiar administration. They even pretended to greater social ascendancy than they had, assuring Governor Carleton that his military wishes would be their command through to a docile population. But merchants of British and American origin in Quebec were not so pleased. They might have welcomed the extended boundaries, but they disliked the social and political aspects of the new law. They had been insisting since the early 1760s that a British colony without an assembly was a contradiction in terms. What they really meant was that an administration they did not control was intolerable. There would be nobles and seigneurs on the governor's seventeen to twenty-three member council and they were bound to maintain "feudal" practices and laws, among them French civil law. That would mean no freehold tenure and therefore no registry office to record landholdings, debts, mortgages, or encumbrances; it would mean no banks or established credit agencies since the latter fell under the religio-legal frown of usury; it would mean the power of the law behind seigneurial dues and religious tithes. No accumulation of capital there. The merchants were angry. Their anger was even shared by a growing number of Canadian merchants convinced of the need for elective institutions if they ever expected to dislodge the traditional elites. Had any of the merchants known of the instructions that accompanied the Quebec Act, they might have tempered their annoyance. Contrary to the dictates of the Act, Governor Carleton was to have his council introduce *habeas corpus* into the colony and consider the introduction, by ordinance, of English laws concerning debts, promises, contracts, and agreements. He was to undermine the Catholic religion by gradually imposing restrictions on the bishop, the seminaries, the male religious orders, and the missionaries. Carleton kept these instructions well hidden for fear of displeasing seigneurs and clergy and indisposing an amenable council. He was not at all interested in debates and discussions; such practices were too American for Carleton's aristocratic and increasingly despotic nature.

Unfortunately for Carleton, those American practices were in the air. Some Americans even thought they should bring them to the very doorstep of this British resurrected New France. One of the earliest undertakings of the American Revolution was an invasion of Quebec in 1775. Whether the Americans expected to liberate Quebec or merely to show their annoyance with the Quebec Act is a debatable point. Certainly they coveted the northeastern fisheries and the western fur trade. The very month the Quebec Act took effect, in May 1775, the Americans appeared along one of the traditional invasion routes, the Lake Champlain-Richelieu waterway, to attack British Forts Ticonderoga and Crown Point. By the autumn they had the official backing of the Continental Congress and the able leadership of Richard Montgomery. That force took Chambly and St. Jean on the Richelieu in November and proceeded overland to Montreal for a winter sojourn among the startled and not always displeased inhabitants. Carleton meanwhile evacuated the British troops from Montreal, pulling them back east of Sorel, in order to avoid American division of the British forces had the invaders decided to continue north along the Richelieu to its mouth at Sorel on the St. Lawrence.

The Americans also appeared in Quebec by a more unusual route. That same autumn of 1775 troops under Benedict Arnold struggled over an old Indian route from Maine towards the Chaudière in the Beauce country. From there they advanced straight north to the St. Lawrence for an attack on Quebec City. The local *habitants* greeted the invaders with open arms and open stores, not from any ideological sympathy with the Americans, but to show their surprise and admiration that anyone, let alone equipped soldiers, could succeed across such inhospitable terrain. The refreshed troops proceeded gallantly on their way towards Quebec where they joined with some of Montgomery's forces from Montreal. There they dug in for a rather uncomfortable siege of Quebec through the winter of 1775–76. Neither they nor the British had sufficient troops to engage in a set battle and a New Year's Eve attempt by the invading forces to capture Quebec's lower town and thereby take the city did not succeed. The two sides simply sat out the winter, the British uneasy about leaving the town in any case, so unreliable was the local population. The river once again came to the rescue of the British, bringing ten thousand reinforcements with the first free navigation in the spring. The besieging American force melted away too, back down the Richelieu with, surprisingly, no British in hot pursuit.

Perhaps Carleton was by then too fearful of Canadian activity in the rear if his forces advanced through the countryside. Certainly there was no great rallying to the cause of the King to repulse the invader. For all Carleton's catering to the seigneurs and the clergy, neither group was able to call up any popular enthusiasm, let alone any military activity. The seigneurs, seeing the American military threat as a means of re-establishing their own social status, were most chagrined by the lack of interest on the part of the *habitants*. Military service to the state was their traditional calling; if they provided such service to the new state, they would be assured of position, place, and power. The clergy also had good reason for urging the *habitants* to unite in support of Britain during the American Revolution. Experiencing financial, recruiting, construction, and even parish difficulties, the Catholic church in Quebec, led by Monseigneur Briand, was eager to have the arm of the state within close reach. The bishop and many of the local *curés*, therefore, publicly stated that loyalty to the Crown was proper payment for British political and religious generosity in the colony. Less openly Bishop Briand also let it be known that a few troops might serve as a useful prod to *habitant* loyalty. Clearly, the church's message was not meeting with complete acceptance. In fact, the one recorded note of dissonance probably hid many others: in mid-sermon, an annoyed parishioner shouted back at the priest, "That's enough preaching for the English." In spite of the efforts of the clergy and the seigneurs, then, *habitant* loyalty was far from being an absolute certainty.

The *habitants* in fact were playing a waiting game. Accustomed to bearing the brunt of military adventures, either as members of the militia or suppliers to troops, they intended this time just to wait and see. Their indifference to the seigneurial call was blatant; their hesitancy in the face of clerical persuasion was just as obvious. None of them behaved the way government, seigneurial, or clerical elites wanted them to. Perhaps it was just a matter of distance: there were few resident seigneurs and fewer resident priests in most of the parishes of Quebec. Most likely the people were afraid, knowing full well that they would pay the costs of the victory or the defeat of either side. Stolid neutrality was therefore the best course, with a dose of self-interest thrown in when conditions warranted. So the *habitants* sold food to the American invaders for ready cash, but the minute paper money appeared, the food vanished. They would not, however, join the militia and they would not take up arms, the military obligations of the French regime having been broken, it seems, at least in the popular mind, by the Conquest.

Curiously enough, some of the merchants so despised by Carleton were his best allies during the American invasion and the years of the Revolution (1775–1783). Some of them, indeed, were better able than clergy or seigneur to raise some patriotic interest on the part of the *habitant*. In spite of their vehement opposition to the political and legal aspects of the Quebec Act, those merchants with any interest in the fur trade saw that their own future lay in the maintenance of the tie to Britain, especially now that the west had been reattached to Quebec. The Revolution was in fact useful to them since it cut off American fur trading competition out of Albany. The Montreal merchants reaped the advantage. They also profited from the very state of war: the military had always been a major prop of the Canadian economy.

Little wonder then that Carleton had military difficulties during the remainder of his stint as governor. With his former enemies now his best supporters and his cossetted allies feeble hangers-on, he could hardly be expected to defend the colony mightily or even attack the rebels to the south. Though a second invasion never materialized, there was sufficient fear on all fronts until well into 1782 to keep old and new subjects in Quebec nervous. Moreover in 1778 France openly declared the European war games it had been playing in North America since 1775 by siding officially with the American rebels against Britain. For a time, the naval and then military assistance that France offered began to look like backing for another attempted invasion of Quebec. But France was neither interested in recapturing Quebec for itself nor in assisting the American rebels to acquire it. Two powers in North America would suit France just fine: one British and the other American. With British troops and vessels in the colony, they could not at the same time be threatening France in Europe. Carleton, however, did not stay around to see the French finessing of the American Revolution. He resigned the governorship and returned to Britain in 1778, slighted by the choice of another to command a British advance south in 1777. Haldimand governed Quebec for the next five years through the rest of the ultimately victorious revolution.

The victory in 1783 brought more economic and social repercussions to Quebec than had the invasion or even the entire war. Much to the dismay of the merchants in Montreal and Quebec, the boundaries of the colony changed once again. The lucrative fur trade area south of the Great Lakes vanished forever as the new international boundary followed the mid-line of the St. Lawrence west of Montreal through the middle of Lakes Ontario, Erie, Huron, and Superior. With a gesture at a European peace table, Britain turned over its land and Indian allies in the Illinois, Ohio, and Mississippi areas to the United States. It then attempted to protect not the hapless Indian, but the white settler in the area from possible Indian reprisals by maintaining British control of the military and fur trade posts at Niagara, Detroit, Michilimackinac, and Grand Portage. The ten year lease on the American mid-west which had begun in 1774 with the Quebec Act was now brought to an abrupt end. The British and Canadian merchants' dream of a commercial empire based on favoured access to the best fur lands vanished.

With the boundary changes of the American peace settlement in 1783, the disadvantage which Canadians in the fur trade had only begun to experience in the late 1770s became chronic. Not only could Americans and Canadians now ply the Great Lakes equally, but also, by this time, the only way to compete on the Great Lakes was with the larger, more expensive *bateaux*. If one still favoured canoes, one had to reach even farther west, beyond Lake Superior, west and north into the Saskatchewan country. Either way the expenses mounted. Technological change or distance coupled with rising prices for trade goods, increasing demand for quality products on the part of the Indians, and higher wages for boat and canoemen all spelled ruin for individual or even partnered traders. The only way to survive was to remove competition by forming associations, groupings that could amass more capital and call on greater credit. Here the Canadians balked. Either for personal or financial reasons they were unwilling to make the leap from a familial enterprise or an individual partnership to a fullfledged company. For example, the North West Company was an association of Scots that dominated the fur trade out of Montreal from the 1790s until the 1820s when it succumbed to overpowering competition from the Hudson's Bay Company further north. Initially, the Nor'westers had come as individuals and formed partnerships with Canadians—the Scots providing capital, credit, and occasionally knowledge of the French language; the Canadians offering technical knowledge and oftentimes marriageable daughters—but when the company was formed in the late 1780s few Canadians were among its partners or backers. The Canadians continued to man the boats and canoes of the trade, while the Scots vicariously lived the life of the *voyageur* in the great mansions and clubs of Montreal. Nonetheless, it was eventually a Scot, following the dictates of the fur trade ever further west, who found the western sea, the original *raison d'être* of France in North America in the sixteenth and seventeenth centuries. On the Pacific coast Alexander Mackenzie left his mark, "from Canada by land 22nd July 1793."

There was of course another possible response to the American proximity in the Great Lakes region. Instead of fleeing it as the Nor'westers tended to do in their search for a Canadian fur trade route beyond Lake Superior, one could confront it squarely. The St. Lawrence might become the major access route into the American mid-west, drawing out furs for the time-being and whatever other product the area might produce once settlers had flowed in, to say nothing of all the imported goods those very settlers would need. But such a dream would require immense political and economic backing: a river closed six months of the year had to have a superlative competitive edge over alternative routes to America's year-round port in New York. That political and economic backing could only come from a state with favourable laws, sound currency, efficient administration, and massive public spending. The quickest way to ensure such backing was by means of an elected assembly. Thus, without quite intending to, the American Revolution gave the impetus to a merchants' dream as well as to a political and economic program that certain Montrealers would doggedly pursue for the next hundred years.

The American break with Britain also brought a more immediate reality. It dumped thousands of Loyalists into the British colonies to the north. Most of these American opponents of the Revolution went to Nova Scotia, in such numbers in fact that a separate colony was created for them in 1784 by breaking off the northwestern portion to form New Brunswick. Seven years later the same would happen to Quebec, the portion this time being to the southwest, present-day eastern and southern Ontario. Instigating that eventual separation were the approximately seven thousand Loyalists whom Governor Haldimand placed west of the last line of seigneurial settlement along the St. Lawrence above Montreal. Even though the Loyalists gave a boost to the continuing dream of turning Quebec into an English colony, they were nonetheless living at a considerable distance from French Canadians. Even so, no sooner were they engaged in breaking the land along the river and the Lake Ontario frontage than commercial interests in Montreal began adding them to their own dream. Transportation, supplies, financing, and credit would all be required to support the agricultural production and the basic needs of the Loyalists. With a bit of luck and a lot of sound organization Montreal merchants could capture the business. Less alluring because far less numerous was the trickle of Loyalists into what came later to be known as the Eastern Townships, the unsettled land behind the innermost line of seigneuries south of the St. Lawrence below Sorel and east of the Richelieu. Barely noticed even farther east in Quebec, Loyalists sprinkled themselves among the few escaped Acadians on the south shore of the Gaspé peninsula.

In spite of its distance and lack of settlement, the Gaspé would, by the end of the eighteenth century, predict in microcosm much of the rest of Quebec's economic development in the early nineteenth century. The fur trade had long since vanished, as it was slowly to do after the turn of the century in Quebec and the west. Three occupations of growing importance for the rest of Quebec had already emerged in the Gaspé, though none in a very developed stage: fishing, farming, and logging. The peculiarity for the Gaspé and later for the rest of Quebec was the combination of the three. Families undertook all three concurrently, a sexual and seasonal division of labour had women tending the sown crops and cleaning the beached fish while men combed the sea and the forest. Occasionally an ethnic specialization altered the picture as Acadians and Loyalists farmed while British and French settlers fished; but neither occupation alone could keep entire families alive. In the Gaspé too, the one exportable product—fish—was in the hands of external agents. The Robin family, French-speaking from the English Channel Islands, had, within a few short years of its establishment in the region in the 1760s, distinguished itself from compatriots along the entire eastern tip of the Gaspé. Indeed it held most of those compatriots as well as the other settlers in an intricate web of indebtedness while reaping the profits of major fish exports to Europe, the West Indies, and Brazil.

But the Gaspé, then as now, was not where the action was. In both economic and political terms, the original St. Lawrence settlement was the centre. There the fur trade still captured imaginations and young men from the farms and the towns. Fishing was a minimal commercial investment, the few seal and oil dealers from Quebec rivalling those from Newfoundland off the Labrador coast. Logging only became a profitable export activity at the very end of the century when the costs of war could justify the high costs of shipping; in the meantime wood was whittled down to the more easily transportable barrel staves to furnish the insatiable international market for barrels, the major containers for shipped goods. Locally, wood served for fuel and construction. But the growing economic undertaking was agriculture, occupying increasing numbers of people throughout the eighteenth century. The gradual commercialization and even export possibilities of agriculture—including selling to towns, fisheries, the army, the West Indies, and eventually breaking into the British market for wheat— began making it an attractive occupation. As agriculture prospered at the end of the century, specialized occupations developed in its wake: blacksmiths, bakers, general storekeepers, notaries, and even the occasional doctor. They all congregated in villages whose very existence testified to the growing agricultural prosperity. The result was that fewer young men were available to hire on for a season in the west and if they did go they could command higher wages. Not that agricultural development was a steady and sure thing. It followed the vagaries of demand and climate. The American Revolution, for example, increased both illegal exports along the Richelieu and the demands of the British troops in Quebec. The end of the war cut off both outlets. A crop disease one year could mean famine the next as was the case in 1788 and 1789. Farming new land rather than using new techniques on old land —a common approach to agriculture throughout North America at the time—appears to account for the colony's rather uneven agricultural development as a growing population filled out the seigneurial holdings. Wheat was the favoured crop since any surplus could be relatively easily marketed for the prized imports of tea, sugar, molasses, rum, and fine cloth. Storage and transport were constant problems, especially as new farms opened the hinterland.

In the towns, particularly Quebec and Montreal, another occupation was increasingly important to certain French Canadians and was beginning to take the limelight. This was politics. Initially an activity of English-speaking merchants in the colony, accustomed from their British or American backgrounds to using political institutions for their economic benefit, politics now began to intrigue the Canadian commercial and trading class as well. Both the homegrown and the imported merchants found that they had every reason to co-operate. Their economic and social interests coincided since they both spotted their own prosperity in the commercial development of the colony and each group was uneasy with a government dominated by a military and landholding class. Even where their interests diverged, strategy dictated co-operative tactics. The Canadians realized they would never have a larger voice in government until they dislodged the few Canadian councillors, seigneurs all, from their much too subservient positions next to the governor. An elected assembly was the only means to gain power and in order to ensure its implementation, the Canadians needed vociferous, forceful allies. Vociferous the British merchants had certainly been, ever since it became obvious in the mid-1760s that an assembly was not in the offing; forceful they were not simply because of numbers. They too needed allies, numerous ones and, they gradually realized, Canadian and Catholic ones. The path to power, it seemed, was to be shared even if each group fully expected to dominate the other once their mutually agreed upon aims were realized.

No sooner was the American Revolution over than British and Canadian merchants discarded their self-imposed support for the governor and his military activities and began to agitate. For five years they acted in concert. Working in committees in Quebec and Montreal, they drafted petitions, drummed up signatures, and shipped their demands to London. They wrote for and read the new papers: the Montreal *Gazette*, English when it began in 1778 and bilingual by 1785, and the English language Quebec *Herald* from 1788. The international articles reproduced in both papers convinced them that theirs was a cause common to the western world. To London and to the governor they made their requests known in November 1784 and January 1785. They wanted an elected assembly of both old and new subjects chosen by town and country dwellers alike. They wanted English commercial law, as enacted by an assembly, added to the continuation of English criminal law and the maintenance of French property laws. They wanted more legislative councillors but with fewer powers since only the assembly was to have the right to impose taxes or initiate money bills. And they backed their demands with some twenty-three hundred signatures, two-thirds of them Canadian.

By the late 1780s, the two groups of commercial interests appear to have gone their separate ways. Not that they changed their demands. They seem merely to have chosen distinct paths to the King's ear in London. Reports and petitions of 1788 now bore the signatures of one group or the other. The Canadians even added a number of particular requests. Perhaps Monseigneur Briand got to them. Perhaps they sought clerical support themselves. In any case the new demands were both religious and political. They wanted the qualification "subject to the King's supremacy" removed from the Quebec Act's tolerance of Catholicism and they wanted religious communities to have guaranteed property rights. At the same time they wanted Canadians and British to have access to public office in proportion to their numbers and they wanted the elected assembly to appoint and pay government officials. French Canadians were beginning to bare their political teeth. While doing so, they also foreshadowed the lines of a political alliance with the clergy that would not be fully confirmed until the 1840s.

Apart from the merchants, the French Canadians were by no means united. In December 1784 the seigneurs organized a counter petition to the merchants'. Presuming to speak in the name of the nation, the first but by no means the last of such pronouncements in Quebec history, the seigneurs argued against an elected assembly. They maintained that such an institution would undermine religion, property, and personal security; the best future for Quebec was in strict adherence to the Quebec Act. The seigneurs, mostly members of the governor's legislative council and mostly from the region between Longueuil and Sorel on the south shore of the St. Lawrence below Montreal, managed to acquire twenty-four hundred signatures. Among them were a large number of crosses in lieu of names; were they the marks of intimidated *habitants*? Certainly one of the fears the seigneurs raised was that of land taxes, a fear bound to evoke a responsive chord among *habitant* farmers. What the seigneurs really feared was the loss of their own privileged political and social position. An elected assembly would raise the social status of two inferior groups. Vulgar traders would dominate the assembly and make laws in their favour by imposing, for example, a land tax in place of the existing import tax on trade goods. And even more vulgar *habitants* would elect the traders on an equal basis with their seigneurs. It was unthinkable even to the very people who had been facing the unthinkable since the Conquest. Only the Quebec Act stood between them and oblivion. Small wonder they spoke so loudly or evoked the nation to protect their property rights.

All the noise emanating from Quebec was the last thing British officials in London needed in the late 1780s. Having barely settled the American war and still smarting from the international loss of face that rupture had evoked, the British were now confronted with the possibility of another war in Europe. For an even greater clamour was bursting out of France and no one knew where it might lead after the popular outbreak in the summer of 1789. And now this pesky inheritance from France in America was insisting on still more constitutional changes. Was there no end to it? Moreover was there any way of seeing clearly through the myriad problems involved? The colony had to be maintained as a colony; Britain was not about to let the rest of its empire in North America simply slip away. At the same time the colony, housing British subjects, had to have representative institutions. Yet those institutions had to be checked: too much popular say had obviously sparked the American Revolution. But now too little appeared to be sparking the French Revolution. Somehow the various groups in the colony had to be reconciled to each other and to the Crown. Seigneurs and clergy, officers and officials, merchants, townspeople, and rural *habitants*, British, Americans, and Canadians, to say nothing of the Loyalists, all had to be moulded into a viable polity which might even pay its own way and which certainly should be open to immigration from the mother country. That in turn raised the land question, both as legal tenure and as the measure of social distinction. The dilemmas appeared insoluble.

Nevertheless, Britain took one more stab at trying to make Quebec into an English colony. In 1791 the Constitutional Act imposed upon Quebec the British constitutional pattern, considered to be the only stable one in the Atlantic world, but refurbished to fit the times. The Act strengthened the monarchical element by means of crown reserves—land specially marked to provide an independent income to the governor and his retinue. The Act also stabilized the aristocratic element by maintaining the appointed legislative council and the legal and property guarantees of the Quebec Act. Seigneuries could remain, but beyond their present boundaries freehold tenure was to prevail. The latter might even foster the growth of a new landed aristocracy if the proper people gained access to the territory. Finally, the Act introduced the democratic element by according an elected assembly: a voice for, but not necessarily power to, the people. In essence a little Britain. The only cutting of Quebec required to fit the pattern was the lopping off of the west once again. In response to Loyalist demands and perhaps in recognition of the fact that Quebec showed every sign of remaining French no matter how British it became, Britain separated the Loyalist land west of the seigneuries from the rest of Quebec. Upper Canada (present-day Ontario) and Lower Canada (present-day Quebec) would now pursue a similar constitutional path but on a separate legal and, in all estimations, ethnic course.

Although the balanced constitution of 1791 was designed to keep everyone content, it actually provided the framework for increasing difficulties over the following decades. As Quebec emulated and contributed to the Atlantic trend toward more democratic institutions, how long would its elected assembly agree to the aristocratic elements embedded in the constitution of 1791? An economically independent governor, reporting to London, hand-picking the members of his legislative council and those of the newly added executive council in 1792, and able to veto the assembly's wishes was bound to clash eventually with a democratically elected body. And as the composition of the assembly altered over the years, it became increasingly restless with its own limited functions. It resented seeing political opponents cosying up to the governor and finding powerful places in his councils. Gradually it designed the means to attach popular favour to that resentment.

The ramifications of the Constitutional Act would, however, take forty years to work themselves out and few of the difficulties were visible in the 1790s. Economic prosperity and external military threats from both France and the United States easily papered the social and political cracks visible before and after the decade. The

French-speaking English colony began taking its place in an imperial market for wheat and wood. From the former metropolis in France came fear, intellectual excitement, a few *émigré* priests, and a commodity that would sound the death knell of all anglicizing efforts. A French revolutionary song gave birth to *les enfants de la patrie* and for Quebec the fun had just begun.

SELECT BIBLIOGRAPHY

Brunet, Michel. *French Canada and the Early Decades of British Rule, 1760–1791.* Ottawa: Canadian Historical Association, 1963.

Burt, A.L. *Guy Carleton, Lord Dorchester, 1724–1808.* Ottawa: Canadian Historical Association, 1955.

Creighton, Donald. *The Empire of the St. Lawrence.* Toronto: Macmillan, 1956.

Eccles, William J. *France in America.* New York: Harper and Row, 1972.

Hare, John E. "Le comportement de la paysannerie rurale et urbaine de la région de Québec pendant l'occupation américaine, 1775–1776." In *Mélanges d'histoire du Canada français offerts au professeur Marcel Trudel.* Edited by Pierre Savard. Ottawa: Editions de l'Université d'Ottawa, 1978. Pp. 145–50.

Neatby, Hilda. *Québec: The Revolutionary Age, 1760–1791.* Toronto: McClelland and Stewart, 1966.

Ouellet, Fernand. *Lower Canada, 1791–1840: Social Change and Nationalism.* Toronto: McClelland and Stewart, 1976.

Ouellet, Fernand. *Economic and Social History of Quebec, 1760–1850.* Toronto: Macmillan, 1980.

Tousignant, Pierre. "Les Canadiens et la réforme constitutionnelle 1783–1791." Unpublished paper presented to the annual meeting of the Canadian Historical Association, June 1972.

Tousignant, Pierre. "Problématique pour une nouvelle approche de la constitution de 1791." *Revue d'histoire de l'Amérique française* 27(1973): 181–234.

Tousignant, Pierre. "The Integration of the Province of Quebec into the British Empire, 1763–91. Part I: From the Royal Proclamation to the Quebec Act." In *Dictionary of Canadian Biography.* vol. IV. Toronto: University of Toronto Press, 1979. Pp. xxxii–xlix.

"Montreal ... a town of twenty-five thousand inhabitants in the mid-1820s."
Montreal by S. Davenport, 1825.

4 The Birth of Nationalism

Early in the nineteenth century French Canadians gave birth to a Quebec version of one of the most powerful ideas of the western world. In doing so they began a dream of their own, different from that of the French regime or that of the early years of British presence in Quebec. No longer an imported dream of imperial dimensions, this nationalist dream was grounded in the social, economic, and political realities of Lower Canada. And yet it had its connections abroad. "We the people" had just created a new nation to the south; across the Atlantic, liberty, equality, and fraternity had just transformed an old nation. When France attempted to export its revolution by force it encountered not just the resistance of mercenaries but a new ideological and popular force emanating from its European neighbours. Spokesmen for the new idea used a common language: with equal fervour they all condemned the social and political restrictions of the *ancien régime*. So much so that they were often mistaken for liberals, advocating individual rights, group freedoms, unrestricted commerce, and a popular say in government. But the same spokesmen used another common language: with equal reverence they all cherished the popular elements of their own culture. So much so that they were often mistaken for conservatives, clinging to language, religion, territory, familial and legal customs. In fact they were both and they were neither.

Nor were they everybody. And yet, one of the more successful of the fantasies of nationalists was that they did in fact speak for everyone. They convinced themselves and they convinced their opponents. They persuaded British governors at the time and through one governor in particular—Lord Durham in the late 1830s—they persuaded subsequent generations of historians. They aroused suspicion among the British and American newcomers to the colony just as they continued to do among English Canadians over the next century. They always had the ear of the press; they never missed a headline, favourable or disparaging, then or since. They were in fact skilful communicators, using whatever means were at hand to develop and extend a particular message. But still they were not everybody. Rather they emerged as part of a particular social class, thrown up by the turmoil of the Atlantic Revolution and the peculiarities of the Lower Canadian situation. They had their own aims, different from those of other social groups. They had their own means—the ideology of nationalism—to justify their existence and their pretensions to social and political power. And given the time and the place they had a magnificent opportunity to spread their dream to other classes of society. The economic difficulties of the period provided fertile soil for recruiting the masses to their cause. And the political institutions, so obligingly put in place by Britain in 1791, provided the medium of communication.

None of this happened overnight and historians dispute much of the mechanism. That the process was already underway before the end of the eighteenth century is an argument dear to historians Jean-Pierre Wallot, Gilles Paquet, and Pierre Tousignant. Certainly one can find nationalist-oriented arguments used to veil the social ambitions of groups left out of the cosy alliance of seigneurs, clerics, and British officials that constituted the upper echelon of Quebec society before 1791. One can even spot the word nation sprinkled in the occasional petition. And there is no doubt that the agricultural prosperity of the end of the eighteenth century was beginning to produce educated sons for new occupations, different from the customary farmers, artisans, merchants, or traders. If these new people eventually became nationalists, just when and how they did so is another matter of debate. Fernand Ouellet attaches their evolution to agricultural difficulties which, he contends, began in the first decade of the nineteenth century. Others say the turning point was later still. The dispute is fuelled by the new methods and approaches of economic history and has been going on since the 1960s, creating much fine historical analysis but never an entirely persuasive picture of *habitant* behaviour. That there were serious agricultural difficulties after 1815 and even worse after 1830 no one now disputes. Yet whether or not this directly caused the birth of nationalism in Quebec or whether its origins go back even further is a question that continues to be a subject of much debate today. In any case, in the Lower Canadian political arena there were no self-styled *patriotes* in the 1790s; by the 1830s they cannot be mistaken. Somewhere between the two dates they, as nationalists, and nationalism along with them were born.

Between those dates much of the social structure of Quebec also changed. The close weaving of mutual interest and fear that brought British army officers and administrators, Canadian seign-eurs and clergy together after the Conquest into what historian Alfred Dubuc has called the aristocratic compact disintegrated in the late eighteenth and early nineteenth century. It disintegrated partly because one of its component groups, the Canadian seign-eurs, disappeared as a social class. But partly too it disintegrated because of the birth of nationalism. Where once the bonds of birth, class, and station and the values of aristocracy, hierarchy, and deference had held various groups at the top of the social struc-ture together, now the ties of ethnicity began to exercise their pull. Not surprisingly, therefore, the largely English-speaking merchant traders, the group just beneath the aristocratic compact in the late eighteenth century, began moving up. By the 1830s they had totally displaced the seigneurs and were happily sitting in the councils of the governor and supping with his army officers. The one group of Canadians that managed to stay on top, the clergy, did so with great difficulty, threatened as it was by the suspicion of British officials, the scepticism engendered by the Atlantic Revolution, dif-ficulties in its own ranks, and its own ties of friendship, family, and sympathy with the very group beginning to make nationalist noises. That group, emerging from the mass of people, educated largely by the clergy for new middle-class professional occupations, was beginning to eye the top positions itself. Just as for the mer-chant traders, economic or social pretensions may well be suffi-cient to explain their behaviour. Then, at the bottom of the social structure remained the great mass of the people, little altered by any lure of social mobility. The only mobility they knew was either geographic or economic (and that mostly downward), both of which made them susceptible to a nationalist message to explain their woes. Thus a social structure, born of the *ancien régime*, took on modern trappings with a nationalist twist.

The Canadian seigneurs were the first to disappear under the onslaught of the Atlantic Revolution. Their uselessness to the aris-tocratic compact was apparent at the time of the American Revolu-tion when they were unable to summon the *habitants* to military duty. Nonetheless they clung to their prestige and the few offices that the Quebec Act afforded them in the council, as administra-tors, judges, or even occasionally as military officers. Accustomed from the days of the French regime to associating status with prox-imity to government, they rarely attended to their seigneuries and thus lost the one opportunity of establishing themselves concretely as prosperous, even adventurous agricultural entrepreneurs in a time of rising prices and expanding markets. Indeed, the one exploitable product most of them saw on their seigneurial domains, until the wood trade became promising well after the turn of the century, was the *habitant*. As agricultural prices rose, so too did seigneurial dues. Newly conceded lands also promised some income as the seigneur demanded increased payments both in cash and in kind. Needless to say, in such circumstances, the *habitant* lost little love upon the seigneur.

And yet the seigneurial system of landholding itself lasted another half century. Partly this was because some individual seigneurs survived, if not as a class, at least as powerful personages. They were present in the assembly for at least the first four years after 1792 as well as being members of the legislative council. Some of them even managed to redeem themselves militarily during the War of 1812. Partly too, the system survived as long as it did because so many newcomers, not members of the traditional seigneurial class at all, stepped in as seigneurial landowners. Merchant traders, many of them English-speaking, purchased seigneuries as social investments in the eighteenth century and then discovered their commercial value first in agriculture in the 1790s and then in wood in the nineteenth century. Some of the English and Americans in Quebec grumbled about this vestige of the *ancien régime*, but those who actually owned seigneurial property, and they tended to be rich, were seldom to be found advocating abolition. Another factor contributing to the prolongation of the life of the seigneurial régime was the attraction it exerted on a new class of people entirely: the middle class professionals. The very people whose existence, education, and beliefs gave the lie to a landholding system based on caste, inheritance, and allegiance nonetheless hankered after the social status that the land continued to convey. Where they could scrape together the capital, they often bought a distant and presumably cheap seigneury. Such was the case of the surveyor Joseph Papineau who later sold *Petite Nation* on the Ottawa River between Montreal and Hull to his son Louis-Joseph who turned out to be one of the more heartless of the nineteenth century seigneurs. But the final reason for the longevity of the seigneurial system was the nationalist dream, spawned by the very people who were perhaps personally unable to purchase their way to social status by means of a seigneury. Papineau might have one, but few of his colleagues in the legislative assembly, in the newspapers, or on the hustings possessed one. Still, they could dream about it. And in any dream intended to differentiate French Canadians from others, the seigneurial system of land tenure was an obvious element.

So too was the Catholic clergy. Its position is, however, much more difficult to define. The clergy certainly played a key role in the aristocratic compact. It facilitated the entrenchment of the British regime by acting as a channel of communication. It may even have constituted the one brake on open popular favour for

the American invaders in 1775–76. And yet the clergy hardly constituted a social class, stemming as it did from all levels of society
and, at least among the men, importing many of its leaders from
France. But even with those internal differences and perhaps because of them, the clergy did offer a path of social mobility.
Through its ranks one could acquire an education, status, and even
power. But the clergy never constituted a political party definable
like the others beginning to take loose shape in the early nineteenth
century. Its political views remained as varied as its social origins. And yet it always managed to stay close to the source of
political power, ever sniffing out the changes in direction and moving that way. Guarding its home base near the governor, it nonetheless reached out tentatively to the increasingly popular party
in the assembly in the 1820s.

For all its proximity to power, the Canadian Catholic church in
the early nineteenth century was neither omnipotent nor omnipresent. Its spiritual and social roles were both severely restricted by
numbers, finances, and the general scepticism to which all of the
institutions of the *ancien régime* were being subjected throughout the Atlantic world. There never were enough priests to serve
all the parishes of Lower Canada, let alone provide teachers for
schools and colleges. One priest for seven hundred and fifty
people in 1780 declined to one for just under fourteen hundred in
1810 and to one for just over eighteen hundred by 1830. Without
the women religious, none of the social obligations of the church—
schooling of the young and the girls, care of the sick and the
elderly, sustenance for the poor—would have been fulfilled. Nor
were the indigenous priests particularly well trained since they
lacked any rigourous theological education. They had to accept
the barely disguised hostility of immigrant French priests and
the open denigration of Anglican ones. The priests bore the religious indifference of their parishioners with difficulty while trying to control their troublesome behaviour in church and change
their scandalous behaviour outside. Even the assembly had to be
called in to enact a law in 1808 to preserve a semblance of order
during religious services. And, as always, the clergy had to
wheedle its financial support from the local population in the
form of tithes or church repairs.

The "Superintendent of the Roman Churches" was just as insecure as his priests. Under attack from Anglican pretenders with
both money and friends to make their case for Church of England
supremacy, Bishop Joseph-Octave Plessis had neither legal recognition nor political place to make his views known. He could not
name priests without the governor's approval. He could not con-
stitute parishes, now a civil matter. He could never be sure that
church property was safe from the governor's acquisitive gaze.
Already by 1800 the government had taken over the lands of the
Jesuits and the Recollets, purportedly to support education. But
would it be Catholic education? Plessis' survival and that of his

church was largely left to chance, the chance arising more from external circumstances. Britain's wars with France in the early nineteenth century left officials in London anxious to avoid religious strife in Quebec; the subsequent war with the United States in 1812 gave the Canadian clergy the opportunity to show its loyalty once again. By 1818, Plessis was the officially and legally recognized bishop of Quebec, pocketing an annual salary from the governor since 1813 and sitting on the legislative council since 1817.

The delicate political position of the church was not lost upon the new political groupings in the assembly. Indeed, had the church been stronger in the early nineteenth century, those political groupings and their nationalist message might not have taken form at all. Harbouring democratic ideas and political pretensions of their own, those members of the new professional classes who had a voice in the assembly regarded the clergy somewhat suspiciously. Their suspicion was grounded partly in the anti-clericalism typical of their time and class and partly in their annoyance over the church's too close collaboration with the governor, a person with whom the assembly members were constantly quarelling. But there was also a certain jealousy. For the clergy and the new professionals were competing for the same thing—the ideological dominance of Quebec society. Their weapons and tactics were similar too: the prestige of education, the skill of communication, the play of ideas. The only difference was in the nature of those ideas. Even then the distinctions were not always clear. The clergy might order the faithful to support the governor in his dispute with the assembly in 1810 and at the same time continue to subscribe to the assembly members' favourite newspaper, *Le Canadien*, which was the source of the dispute. And from the other side professional men might look askance at clerical political behaviour but continue to send their sons to be educated by those same clerics. Not surprisingly then the two groups began approaching each other in the 1820s, each anxious for the other's political support. Coincidentally the nationalist message began making more room for religious values now considered characteristically French Canadian and therefore deserving protection. At the same time the new bishop of the new diocese of Montreal, Monseigneur Jean-Jacques Lartigue, began, in a most unusual fashion, to combine nationalist values in his religious messages. If the differences between the clergy and the new professional classes never completely disappeared, an alliance was taking shape.

With another changing group there was little possibility of alliance. The merchant traders of the very early nineteenth century had had little in common with the groups that had formed the aristocratic compact in the late 1700s; they had even less in common with the rising middle class in the professional occupations in the early 1800s. The merchants' activities were commercial, their networks continental and imperial. They chafed at political and geographic restrictions on their trade; the division of Quebec into

Upper and Lower Canada in 1791 infuriated them. They attempted to dominate the early assemblies but as they dropped from fifty percent of the members to thirty percent by 1810, they slowly lost out to the new middle class. Even during that process they changed internally. Major traders took on the trappings of an aristocratic way of life; minor ones proliferated in the wake of a commercialized agriculture and a developing timber trade. The first gave a new lease on life to the aristocratic compact, all the while displacing the seigneurs; the second began demanding state assistance and intervention to realize their commercial dreams for the St. Lawrence. With no electoral success via the assembly, they used their financial power, even altering their political tune, to acquire positions in the councils close to the governor. From being the governor's major opponents during most of the years after the Conquest, the merchants, albeit in a modified and more varied form, became the governor's staunchest allies by the 1820s.

Ensconced as they were, close to the governor and mostly speaking his language, the large commercial elements of Quebec society became the target for the new middle class. The merchant class had both economic and political power which the professionals coveted. For the most part the middle class disdained commerce and used their sense of intellectual importance derived from the studious professions to claim their position in society. When no one listened, they added the nationalist note: those in power were English; those without power were French. They believed that favouritism towards one group and discrimination towards another accounted for the relative positions of the two different classes. The remedy was then simple. Replace the English favourites with the French, putting them in key political positions, close to and perhaps even in control of, the administration; the economic tables would then be turned and all of society would benefit.

Who then was this professional or middle class, so ready to cloak its political ambitions in nationalist garb? It could be counted on the fingers of one hand in the 1780s and 1790s—a notary here, a lawyer there, a doctor in the next village. By the 1820s there were in fact too many of them, more than an agricultural society in economic decline could support. They emerged at a time of agricultural prosperity from the upper levels of *habitant* families able to spare a son for schooling. They plied their various trades— notaries, surveyors, lawyers, doctors, small merchants, journalists —among the rural population and maintained those ties even when they lived in villages, then in towns, and even in the larger urban settings of Quebec City and Montreal. When agricultural difficulties began, they expressed the *habitant* fears. In short they gradually replaced the seigneur, the militia captain, the priest, even the local prosperous farmer as social leaders of the rural population, supplying knowledge, advice, sometimes money, and, by the 1820s, political organization. They mastered the political institutions of 1791 easily since their education and their interests prepared them for debate, political intricacies, and procedural finesse. In 1810 they were already more than one-third of the assembly members; by the 1830s they dominated the assembly entirely as members of the *parti canadien.*

The peculiarity of the new middle class lay precisely in its social and political interests. Unlike the seigneurs, the traders, and even the *habitants* of the French regime, the developing middle class had no economic base. Most of them did not even have the military function that made both seigneurs and *habitants* valuable to the state. And yet they may well have modelled their behaviour on that of the seigneurs, attempting to assure social leadership by acquiring proximity to power. What they did not discern was that the decline of the seigneurs and the attendant rise of the commercial trading class had its basis in economics. The seigneurs neglected to develop an economic base for their political pretensions; the commercial class rose precisely because it had that base. The only economic function attached to the new middle class was that of a service industry. But it was a service industry ahead of its time, affordable during agricultural prosperity and again much later in the nineteenth century as an accompaniment to industrialization. But with neither condition prevailing early in the nineteenth century, the new middle class was economically superfluous. Probably it knew it. Hence its rather frenetic political activity to provide for itself a place in society. The larger the political space it occupied, the greater would be its control of the patronage that went with political power. Patronage meant jobs: did not the new professions provide just the right training for government appointments?

Without the economic base to bolster its social and political ambitions, the middle class turned to something for which its education had prepared it—an ideology. The principle of nationalities, imported from Europe and sounding like liberalism, could make a people look like an individual: distinguishing characteristics developing in accordance with natural laws and therefore justifiably seeking their full expression. How simple then to distinguish French Canadians by their language, their religion, their social institutions. And how pleasant to name oneself their spokesman.

Having the mass of people believe it was another matter. With neither the time, the patience, nor the training for philosophical discussion, the *habitants* could only be reached through the land. The land in fact housed about three-quarters of all the inhabitants of Lower Canada. As the population grew, the farmland spread, tentatively feeling its way along the south shore of the St. Lawrence, filling in the areas of the southern Richelieu which had been devastated after both the American invasion of the eighteenth century and the brief American visit during the War of 1812. It crept slowly into the lower Laurentians along the north shore of the Ottawa River, filling out and expanding the seigneuries. In the 1820s it nudged the Eastern Townships, supposedly reserved for

English settlers, and in the 1830s approached the Saguenay River. But when farmland became scarce and unproductive by the late 1820s, people turned elsewhere and a trickle of emigration began to the United States. The mobility of the *habitants* was indeed geographic, not social or intellectual. They may have adapted to the growing demand for wheat and then wood in the late eighteenth and early nineteenth century just as later they may have registered the decline of an export market for wheat and began to grow peas, beans, and potatoes. Many may have lost incomes and adventures as the western fur trade dwindled. Yet whatever their behaviour, all indications point to their increasing impoverishment over the first half of the nineteenth century. Nonethelss the vast majority of them did have votes and it was here that the middle class took an interest and played upon *habitant* fears—of taxes, of land takeovers, of English immigration—in order to gather those votes. By the mid-1820s one can trace *habitant* economic difficulties in direct proportion to the degree of electoral support for the *parti canadien.*

One final group of people was largely forgotten by everyone. Both Montreal and Quebec City, centres of about twenty-five thousand inhabitants each in the mid 1820s, harboured an urban labour force, growing, differentiating itself, and more than one-quarter female. The women of Montreal worked in 1825 primarily as domestics, day labourers, prostitutes, nuns, and teachers, although occasionally a position as a governess, washerwoman, mid-wife, dressmaker, blacksmith, innkeeper, or seller of yard goods could be found. Many of the women may not have declared an occupation to Jacques Viger, a most inquisitive census taker, or he may have caught them in a period of seasonal unemployment, cruelly common to workers in Montreal and Quebec throughout the nineteenth century. Their male counterparts were also domestics, day labourers, and carters serving Montreal's busy, but seasonally limited import and export trade. Artisans working in their own shops with the odd apprentice continued to make and sell shoes, clothing, and household utensils directly to the public. But unskilled workers were also present in larger scale shoe and food production. Molson's brewery was a large employer. In Quebec City the same trades and occupations prevailed, augmented by a large number of ship labourers, sailors, loggers, and undoubtedly prostitutes serving the vast, but again seasonal, export timber trade. The only interest such people aroused among the middle class was for their political usefulness. Few except the highly skilled among them had the property qualification or paid the requisite rent in order to vote, but many of them could and did serve as head bashers. At a time of open voting, with electors stepping forward in public to declare their choice, a gang of strongmen often proved useful.

With the exception of most of this group of urban labourers, the new middle class managed to have its nationalist message heard throughout Lower Canada in the early decades of the nineteenth century. That it was able to do so was largely a result of the buffeting Quebec underwent in the same period. In fewer than thirty years, the entire structure of the Quebec economy changed. The fur trade disappeared, agriculture went into a long, steady decline and only the new wood trade offered some regional respite. The ideological consequences, in the form of nationalism, are still with us. Even a middle class without a solid economic base, both a product and a manipulator of the economic transformations of the time, continued to exist in Quebec for another hundred years.

As the fur trade declined so too did Quebec's attachments to the continental west. After 1800 ever smaller numbers of French Canadians headed west from Montreal in the employ of the North West Company. That company itself faced declining demand in England and increasing competition in the west. No sooner had it absorbed one rival in the XY Company in 1804 than it encountered others on the far west coast. Always the Hudson's Bay Company with its easier access to the northwestern interior was present. By giving financial assistance to the Selkirk settlement on the Red River from 1812 on the Hudson's Bay Company hoped it would block the western routes of the traders from Montreal. But by then fur trade exports from Quebec had already fallen to a fraction of their former volume and importance. In the 1790s they made up half the value of all exports; by 1810 they managed a bare ten percent. Even that was to disappear in the face of relentless competition from the Bay. By 1821, the Montreal traders of the North West Company gave up, combined forces with their northern rivals, and, now as members of the Hudson's Bay Company, continued the Canadian trade out of the northern ports. The activity that had linked Quebec to empire, both continental and imperial, disappeared. The trade that had shaped the geography and the economy of Quebec for two hundred years vanished.

Occupying far more people than the fur trade ever had, Quebec agriculture appeared momentarily on the imperial stage and then it too declined into barely self-sufficient obscurity. Just when this occurred is a matter of debate. Certainly in the 1790s, grains, flour, and biscuit from Quebec could be found on the imperial markets in London and the West Indies; by 1810 they were no longer there. During the war of 1812 Quebec agriculture did respond to increased demand from the British troops and Canadian militia fighting the Americans. But no sooner was the war over than serious signs of difficulty emerged. As of 1815 no one disagrees: Lower Canadian agriculture was in a state of crisis, little relieved until after 1850.

If the crisis itself is clear, the causes are still in dispute. Historians have in turn attributed the pitiable state of agriculture to lower British demand, fluctuating imperial prices, higher shipping rates, cheaper American produce, and the declining quality and quantity of production in Lower Canada itself. In particular, questions concerning methods and amount of production have raised

strong arguments. Were inefficient *habitants* refusing to modernize their agricultural techniques? Did they then turn to raising
only those crops that would sustain their families: oats, barley,
potatoes, hay, and livestock? Or were shrewd and commercially
sensitive *habitants* developing the new products in response, not
to an export market, but to the closer and more lucrative outlet in
the towns and the new timber trade? Or did the *habitants* hire on
in the logging camps themselves and thus diminish their own agricultural production?

Certainly the land was no longer kind. Soil exhaustion in the old
seigneuries was evident by the 1820s and, except for the Eastern
Townships where few French Canadians had ventured, any new
land was better fit for growing trees than wheat. And yet new
land was needed, as the population bulged beyond the existing
seigneuries. There was a limit to the possible division of land among
inheritors: once a farm was the width of a wagon road it was not
likely to produce much. Nor could it support young people. Some
of the daughters may have found jobs as domestics in the towns
as they were to do later in the century; most of the sons could
only become landless labourers, roaming the seigneuries in search
of work, deprived even of a paternal inheritance with which to
purchase increasingly unavailable land. Their presence simply aggravated the agricultural crisis since they added to the numbers
of non-farm people who had to be fed. By the late 1820s Quebec
was importing foodstuffs from Upper Canada.

The ramifications of the agricultural crisis touched all social
groups. As the *habitants* became increasingly impoverished, their
few ties to the outside world were cut by the lack of wheat for
export and cash for imports. Subsistence agriculture and revived
domestic production of household goods undermined the rural e-
conomy of small-scale merchants and independent artisans.
Habitant poverty meant fewer demands for the services of the
professional middle class and yet the numbers of that class were
growing daily. *Habitant* difficulties enraged the commercial class
whose import and export business suffered; attempting to recoup
their losses they began looking to transporting the products of
Upper Canadian and even American mid-western agriculture. But
to capture that trade they needed credit institutions—the first
banks in Lower Canada date in fact from 1816—and they needed
improvements in communications, notably roads and canals. Ties
to empire were bound to clash with those of an increasingly isolated Lower Canada where the St. Lawrence was becoming a lake,
no longer a river. Finally, even the seigneurs and clergy felt the
pinch of agricultural hardship. They may even have added to it as
the seigneurial and religious dues increased the burdens of the
habitant and the occasional seigneur refused to concede new land
to poor farmers. Where the *habitant* simply could not pay, seigneur
and clergy both lost income.

Only one light glimmered on Quebec's gloomy economic horizon.

The timber trade, in response to Britain's massive demands during the Napoleonic wars, provided jobs and income. With the supply from the Baltic cut off by the French blockade of continental ports after 1806, Britain was prepared to absorb the higher costs of timber shipped from North America. The wood trade initially offered individual *habitants* an alternative cash income as they cut into their own woodlot. As the trade expanded it opened a local market for agricultural products, food for the logging crews in the winter camps. Jobs were to be had in those very camps, to say nothing of the booming shipping out of Quebec. Since timber ships were loaded by hand, they required massive numbers of labourers, if only for a short season. In 1810 some six thousand dock workers and sailors crowded the port of Quebec. They too had to be fed, their demands calling not only on local agricultural produce but also on imports from the United States. Their activity made timber the major export commodity, accounting for three-quarters of the value of all shipments out of Quebec in 1810. The subsequent decline of the timber trade was purely relative since British preferential duties kept the trade, and with it much of the Quebec economy, alive until the 1840s.

Besides the economic results, the timber trade had two social repercussions in Lower Canada. Where the trade prospered, nationalism did not. As if timber kept the tie to empire, those areas touched by it maintained their distance from ideological and political attempts to break the tie. The Quebec City region in particular but also the Ottawa Valley were largely immune to nationalist arguments. But at the same time the timber trade brought in its wake a problem that would exacerbate the agricultural crisis and add an unhealthy ethnic note to the nationalist message. Poverty-stricken immigrants crowded the holds of the returning timber ships, providing ballast in exchange for cheap fares across the Atlantic. They poured into Quebec City and Montreal looking for jobs and into the countryside looking for land. More than one hundred thousand of them streamed through Quebec between 1815 and 1830 and if most of them continued through to Upper Canada and the American west, they left their mark indelibly on the popular conscience. Surely they had come to take our land and take our jobs. Granted they were poor like us, but they were also English-speaking. And sometimes they were diseased. Perhaps it was all deliberate.

The new middle class professionals did little to dispel such fears. Anxious about their own livelihood and tending to see the British commercial presence as a hindrance to their social and political mobility, they were not likely to offer a different explanation to their rural relatives, clients, and voters. They might even play upon those ethnic fears. Certainly the economic changes of the period, the disappearance of the western fur trade, and the dire straits of agriculture created a potential popular base for the nationalist message. Both the *habitants* and the new middle class felt threatened. Nationalism allowed them both to spot the source of the threat in the outsider, the other. Ironically, the other had provided the instrument for the public expression of such ideas. The parliamentary institutions that Britain had introduced into the colony in 1791 offered a public, and often noisy, forum for the precise formulation of the growing sense of French Canadian uneasiness. Over the first decades of the nineteenth century, French Canadian politicians, almost all members of the new professional class, mastered the techniques of parliamentary procedure and gradually moulded themselves and their electorate into a highly disciplined political party, the *parti canadien*.

Troubles began very early in the century. Rival groups clashed in the assembly and the press over economic policy in 1805. Merchants attempted to have aspects of the seigneurial regime modified only to meet the hostility of, and defeat by, the increasingly numerous representatives of the new middle class. The same groups argued over the appropriate source of funding for the building of new jails in Montreal and Quebec. Much to the chagrin of the merchants, it was decided that duties on imported goods rather than a tax on land furnish the necessary revenue. The merchants recorded their annoyance in the Quebec *Mercury* and the Montreal *Gazette* and the assembly retaliated by having the editors arrested for libel. A number of assembly members then backed one of their colleagues, Pierre Bédard, in founding the first solely French language newspaper, *Le Canadien*, in 1806. The democratic leanings of the paper pleased neither the governor nor the clergy. Bédard's very early expression of the idea of ministerial responsibility as a logical deduction from British constitutional principles and practices was seen as an affront to the British tie and to proper notions of subordination. When Sir James Craig, who served as governor from 1807 to 1811, sided with the merchants in another assembly row over the presence of judges and Jews in the colony and then dissolved the assembly and called elections in 1809 and again in 1810, he attacked *Le Canadien* directly. With clerical support he had the presses seized and Bédard arrested. The issue only served to increase popular support for the emerging *parti canadien* in the assembly. One of the Craig-inspired elections, that of 1809, in fact produced the one person who later would successfully tie all the political, economic, and social issues together—Louis-Joseph Papineau.

Momentarily interrupting the play of Lower Canada politics was the reminder that Quebec was still very much part of the British empire. The War of 1812 barely passed over Quebec but it gave a brief respite to the traditional elites and also revealed some of the new elite's true colours. The British-American feud, once again over the western interior, found little sympathy among the northern American states bordering on Lower Canada. Exchange along the Richelieu tied the two areas together and made St. Denis into a busy port. Movements of population also linked the areas as many French Canadians migrated south to work in the forest trade of

Lake Champlain. In spite of these links, the area served once again as an invasion route during the war and permitted one of the old seigneurial families to relive a few moments of military glory as lieutenant-colonel Charles-Michel de Salaberry rebuffed American troops at Lacolle in 1812 and again at Châteauguay in 1813. De Salaberry's aristocratic relatives were keen to defend old values which they now saw embodied in the British connection; they feared the social more than the military repercussions of an American victory. Clerical voices echoed the same sentiment and bolstered it with the religious obligation to defend the existing government. Only one cleric, the future Bishop Lartigue of Montreal, added the novel concept of national obligation. As for the English merchants in Quebec their ties to empire had always been solidly economic and they were not about to break them now, especially when the military victories in Upper Canada and the west regained for Britain all the original fur trade lands south of the Great Lakes and west to the Mississippi. The merchants' old continental dream revived even as the war increased local commerce in the St. Lawrence valley. But they were bound for disappointment once again when, at the end of the war, Britain blithely handed back to the United States all the western gains. The war merely confirmed the separate existence of two entities in North America. And even though the new French Canadian middle class would later flirt with American democratic and republican ideas, it too was interested in a separate, and for the moment, British existence in North America. Middle class voices were numerous in expressing a nationalist sentiment in the face of the military threat.

Finances served to further link the war and Lower Canadian political reality. Additional British troops brought income into the colony, income on which the governor as chief military and political officer could draw; once the war was over in 1814, their withdrawal accentuated his financial difficulties. The assembly was not slow to spot the weakness and as of 1817 it squabbled interminably with the governor over control of the purse. As determined by the imperial government, the governor held those purse strings attached to military funds, the Jesuit Estates, crown revenues from certain lands, and import duties. The assembly held the other strings leading to the taxes raised by provincial statute. The governor's monies rarely expanded and yet his expenditures kept growing for he had to pay the salaries of public servants and the costs of the judicial system. The only limit on the assembly's access to funds was popular resistance to taxation.

Co-operation between the governor and the assembly was very limited. In return for paying some of the governor's bills, the assembly insisted on a close look at the charges. If the governor balked, the assembly simply refused to vote monies for some of the pet schemes of its political opponents, increasingly close to the governor in the legislative and executive councils; they could just wait for their precious roads, canals, banks, and registry offices. If the governor gave in a bit, as was sometimes dictated by his financial needs or by revelations that public servants were speculating with public funds, and allowed some scrutiny of his expenses, the assembly tended to pursue its quarry further. By voting each item of the governor's budgetary demands separately it slowed down the entire system of government. Always the assembly balked at the governor's insistence that it vote the civil list—the salaries of certain officials—on a permanent rather than an annual basis. The tussle was an even draw: the assembly's political power matched the governor's imperial power. Occasionally a congenial governor such as Sir John Sherbrooke in 1818 or a sympathetic British committee of enquiry like the Canada Committee in 1828 almost managed a solution. Invariably, however, a new governor, a haughty colonial secretary, or a twist of political fate in the assembly brought further intransigence. By the late 1820s Governor Sir George Ramsay, Earl of Dalhousie, was refusing to sanction any money bills coming from the assembly for local projects if the assembly did not vote the sums required to pay the governor's expenses. When even that brought no breakthrough he dissolved the assembly twice in a row while assembly members took a mammoth petition of complaint to London.

Behind the squabble and the constitutional principles used to justify it lay a struggle for power. By the 1820s that struggle was clearly channelled into two opposing political groups. On one side was a loose alliance under the name of the English party. On the other, a slightly more coherent group rallied behind the *parti canadien* banner. In fact neither was as ethnically pure as its name implied; the English party, mostly composed of merchants, harboured French-speaking seigneurs and members of the governors' councils, the *parti canadien*, while predominantly French and middle class, attracted some English-speaking journalists, doctors, and the occasional merchant. The two groups in fact distinguished themselves more by their interests and their political behavior than by their ethnic origin.

Members of what would become the English party gradually lost the little electoral strength they had in the very early assemblies of the 1790s. As compensation, they sought the political favour of the governor. With places in his councils they hoped to ensure their voice in government. Their interests in fact dictated that behaviour and necessitated the voice. Tied economically to Britain and in competition with American merchants for western commerce, they needed government backing for the reforms they sought: banks to provide credit, canals to facilitate communications, registry offices to record land transactions and monetary ventures. When particularly pressed, the developing English party would also have liked to abolish the seigneurial system and all French civil laws. Because it could not make its views prevail in the assembly, it tended to denigrate that body, referring to it as conservative and backward. In fact its own clinging to privileged positions near the governor made it increasingly conservative. Even when it succeeded, in the mid-1820s, in having the Lachine Canal completed with public funds, it complained that the lengthy delay occasioned by obstreperous assembly members had permitted the Americans to gain the edge with the Erie Canal.

So uneasy indeed was the English party that it engaged in some underhand activities. Its proposal to unite Upper and Lower Canada in 1822 was a well-kept secret only leaked from London long after it had been on the desks of the colonial office. A single government for the two colonies, with the electoral qualifications raised and French abolished as an official language would favour commercial and English expansion. It would free Montreal from the dead weight of seigneurialism and unprogressive French Canadian politicians. Moreover, and here the scheme was attractive to Upper Canada, it would solve the vexing question of the division of customs duties between the two colonies. That question had been a sore point between the two since the 1790s: Lower Canada collected the dues on imported goods and then paid to Upper Canada a proportion that was always the subject of dispute. But all the English party achieved from its vast scheme of union was a temporary solution to the customs issue in the Canada Trade Act of 1822. The rest of the proposal took Britain too much by surprise and aroused too much opposition among French Canadians to be enacted. Licking their wounds, the members of the English party started muttering about annexing Montreal alone to Upper Canada. Like the Loyalists before them, English commercial interests in Montreal constituted Canada's first separatists.

The opposition to union gave new coherence to the *parti canadien*, brought its leader Louis-Joseph Papineau to the fore, and broadened its following. The group was in fact discernible in opposition to Governor Craig in 1809 and 1810, already displaying remarkable organizational abilities in the electoral ridings of the countryside. It tossed up and argued over any number of leaders from Pierre Bédard to Joseph Stuart, Louis-Joseph Papineau, Andrew Stuart, Augustin Cuvillier, and Joseph-Remi Vallières de Saint-Réal, all members of Lower Canada's new professional class. Members from the Quebec region vied with those from Montreal for prestige and position. As the party's hold over the assembly grew, passing eighty percent of the seats in 1824 and more than ninety percent in 1827, its aims became equally clear. It intended to control the positions of power by removing the English place holders and appointing Canadians in their stead. Hence the acrimony of the dispute over finances: if the assembly could control the spending of public funds, it could name the spenders. Hence also the early interest in responsible government: if the governor had to choose his advisers from among people enjoying the support of the assembly, he would have to choose Canadians. And one of the reasons the party began flirting in the 1830s with American notions of electing all public officials was that it was sure it could guarantee the election of Canadians.

In the 1820s that steady electoral support was solidified by popular anger over the proposed union, by increasing agricultural difficulties, and by Papineau's charismatic personality. A new note of outright distrust of the English crept into the party's messages. The petitions Papineau and John Neilson took to London in 1823 to oppose the union all stressed the cultural, institutional, and economic differences between Lower and Upper Canada. The defeat of the union was perhaps the first nationalist victory. It certainly gave the assembly the strength to be magnanimous for it subsequently recognized the Eastern Townships' right to representation in the assembly. It also voted funds for the construction of the Lachine Canal on the St. Lawrence and the Chambly Canal on the Richelieu as well as for banks, roads, and education. Spending on education in 1824 may even have been the pay-off to the Catholic church which had long been demanding public assistance but had only recently displayed its political colouring in opposing the union. The possibility of the governor naming priests (as the designers of the union had wished) was enough to make the church speak out publicly, but it was insufficient for any real alliance with the *parti canadien*. Moreover in 1829 the assembly revealed its increasingly democratic and secularizing tendencies in another school bill: locally elected school trustees were to oversee parish schools. The clergy was not amused. But by then the party had flexed its muscles and rather liked the feel. It began calling itself the *parti patriote*, clearly advertising its nationalist pretensions. In that guise it entered one of the more turbulent decades of Quebec's history.

SELECT BIBLIOGRAPHY

Bernard, Jean-Paul, Paul-André Linteau, and Jean-Claude Robert. "La structure professionelle de Montréal en 1825." *Revue d'histoire de l'Amérique française* 30 (1976):383–415.

Creighton, Donald. *The Empire of the St. Lawrence.* Toronto: Macmillan, 1956.

Dubuc, Alfred. "Problems in the Study of the Stratification of the Canadian Society from 1760 to 1840." *Annual Report.* Canadian Historical Association, 1965. Pp. 13–29.

Le Goff, T.J.A. "The Agricultural Crisis in Lower Canada, 1802–12: A Review of a Controversy." *Canadian Historical Review* 55 (1974):1–13.

Manning, Helen Taft. *The Revolt of French Canada, 1800–1835: A Chapter in the History of the British Commonwealth.* Toronto: Macmillan, 1962.

Ouellet, Fernand. *Histoire économique et sociale du Québec, 1760–1850: structures et conjoncture.* Montreal: Fides, 1966.

Ouellet, Fernand. *Lower Canada, 1791–1840: Social Change and Nationalism.* Toronto: McClelland and Stewart, 1976.

Ouellet, Fernand. "Le mythe de 'l'habitant sensible au marché': Commentaires sur le controverse Le Goff-Wallot et Paquet." *Recherches sociographiques* 17(1976):115–32.

Paquet, Gilles, and Jean-Pierre Wallot. "Crise agricole et tensions socio-ethniques dans le Bas-Canada, 1802–1812: Eléments pour une ré-interprétation." *Revue d'histoire de l'Amérique française* 26 (1972):185–237.

Wallot, Jean-Pierre. "Religion and French-Canadian Mores in the Early Nineteenth Century." *Canadian Historical Review* 52 (1971):51–91.

". . . poorly armed and undisciplined comrades . . ."
The Insurgents at Beauharnois by Jane Ellice.

5 For Whom the Bell Tolls

Within the span of a single decade Quebec experienced the liberalism and the imperialism of its tie to Britain and the political hopelessness of a nationalist cause. From the Canada Committee's supporting of many of the colonists' grievances in 1828 to the Durham Report of 1839 advocating the union of Upper and Lower Canada, the political groupings in Quebec played out the penultimate act of a lengthy drama, starring a popularly elected assembly and a group of privileged office holders. The liberalism of the times and the similarity of the Lower Canadian play to that being staged in Upper Canada, the Atlantic colonies of Nova Scotia and New Brunswick, and even in Britain and parts of continental Europe allowed the final act, resulting in responsible government, to be presented relatively peacefully in the 1840s. But like all plays, this one masked another reality. The social and economic dislocations, evident since earlier in the century, continued to take their toll. Indeed they were aggravated by local and international economic conditions peculiar to the decade. Together they gave the play an unexpected twist as during the decade members of the liberal professions donned military garb and staged a brief rebellion to emphasize their plea for social leadership. The incongruence defeated them as much as the presence of imperial troops.

By the late 1820s, the British government recognized the fact that the governor and assembly in Lower Canada were thoroughly fed up with one another. Monetary and political obstinacy on both sides had brought the administration of the colony virtually to a standstill. With similar problems emerging from Upper Canada and changes in Britain's own electoral system in the offing, the British parliamentary Canada Committee was charged with hearing colonial grievances. From Lower Canada the grievances, taken to London in petitions and by personal envoys from the assembly, were explicit: Lord Dalhousie who had served as governor since 1819 was impossible; the legislative council as presently constituted was an insult; the thwarting of the assembly's will concerning finances was intolerable.

In its report in 1828 the Canada Committe endorsed many of the complaints. Although the only concrete result was the recall of Dalhousie that year, the Committee made other recommendations which served to remind moderates that a constitutional path to reform was still possible. For example, the committee regretted the presence of so many place holders in the legislative council and suggested that somehow that body should be rendered more independent, more representative of the interests of the colony. The committee also recommended that the assembly, soon to be enlarged from the original fifty seats of 1792 to eighty-four, was the most appropriate body for controlling public revenue; it should supervise the raising and spending of all monies. At the same time the committee urged that the colony retain the divergent customs of both French and English. French Canadians should continue to enjoy their religion and their laws; they might even extend the seigneurial system, if they so wished, into new territories, although not those of the Eastern Townships. The English, however, had as much right to their freehold system of land tenure. Indeed, the transfer of seigneurial holding to freehold tenure should be facilitated. True to its liberalism, the Canada Committee was convinced that good will, tolerance, and impartiality could make a fundamentally sound constitution work.

Unfortunately those qualities were in increasingly short supply in Lower Canada in the early 1830s. By naming a few more French Canadians to the legislative council, governors did succeed in having most of the bills of 1830 and 1831 become law. But the assembly was increasingly suspicious and eyed with hostility any of its own members who accepted places in the council. It turned down a conciliatory offer from London to control most of the colony's finances and even the Jesuit Estate funds in order to continue voting the civil list annually rather than for the life of the sovereign as the offer suggested. The speaker of the assembly, Louis-Joseph Papineau, was much too wary to fall into the trap proposed by Lord Aylmer, governor from 1831 to 1835, that he be named to the executive council. Aylmer, Papineau had already concluded, was another of the robbers of the country. In turn the governor began thinking that only a union of Upper and Lower Canada could contain Papineau and his ultra-liberal followers in the *parti patriote*.

Aylmer was not the only one worried about ultra-liberalism. The clergy and indeed many moderates looked askance at a radical bill which the assembly passed in 1832. The *loi des fabriques* proposed secular control over the educational and monetary activities of parish vestries by means of popularly elected church wardens with legally defined powers. Given the *parti patriote's* political skill, it could count on electing its own—the local notary, doctor, surveyor, or general store merchant—and thereby successfully challenge the *curé* for power and prestige in the parish. The clergy spotted the threat and used its influence with the leglislative council to have the bill rejected. In fact, some assembly members disliked the bill as well. A minority group of more moderate members, among them Papineau's long-time colleague from Quebec City, John Neilson, objected to the radical stand of the majority whom they considered too democratic and too anticlerical. Neilson, first elected to the assembly in 1818, had taken colonial petitions to London in 1823 and 1828 and, as a member of the *parti canadien*, had always supported Papineau. After 1832 the two went their separate ways.

So too, in large measure, did French and English after the election that same year. In one of the Montreal ridings, the election became so contested by rival gangs bent on breaking each others' heads that the troops were summoned to maintain order. In the melee, three French Canadians were killed. As the church bells tolled the defeat of reform, a government enquiry exonerated the soldiers and an assembly enquiry registered its scepticism. Armed hostility was now a distinct possibility.

Orchestrating that possibility, although always afraid to look it in the face, was Louis-Joseph Papineau. A second generation representative of the new middle class, Papineau was forty-six years old in 1832 and had already spent half his life in the assembly. His early education in the classics of liberalism led him away from a paternally designed career in the clergy. He never practised law for which he had the rudimentary, quasi-apprenticeship training typical of the time; rather his literary talents, oratorical skills, and a penchant for taking the opposite point of view led him into politics. Among his first electors in 1809 was his mother, exercising the female suffrage that was tolerated in the colony until 1834. He became speaker of the assembly in 1815, a position then entailing the power and the prestige of the leader of the majority. Fighting off all subsequent competitors for the speakership, Papineau gladly accepted the annual salary of £1000 that was attached to it in 1817. He left the management of his seigneury *Petite Nation* to his younger brother and ignored the increasing indebtedness of his *habitants*. Instead he waxed nostalgic about life on the land, pocketed his seigneurial dues, picked up profits from the timber trade on the Ottawa, lived in the grand manner in Montreal, and complained of poverty.

Papineau may have been looking for a new career in the early 1830s. At some point he began imagining himself as the president of a French Canadian republic. He had the skill, the following, and the experience; his career was a combination of ambition and altruism. He delighted in the adulation of his supporters in the assembly and even more so in that of the crowds on the hustings. Like other nineteenth century liberals, he genuinely believed in popular control of the mechanisms of government, but the people to exercise that control were men like himself, members of the new and responsible middle class. To ensure control, however, required the addition of some particularly French Canadian elements to the liberal creed. Toward this end Papineau glorified the seigneurial system and even tempered his own scepticism to give national due to the clergy. He claimed to be an unwilling patriot, drawn into political and later military skirmishes against his will. But he knew of the financial dealings of his friend the Montreal bookseller Edouard Fabre who collected and administered funds for patriotic purposes; as of 1834 there appear to have been distinct plans for organizing and financing a resort to arms. But when the armed rebellion materialized in late 1837, Papineau proved to be a poor rebel. His political ambitions disintegrated as he took flight into exile just after the first outbreak of violence.

That rebellion might well not have occurred had Papineau's magic not marked an entire generation. He was the first of Quebec's nationalist leaders with all the charisma such leaders have subsequently displayed. He had immense personal charm and spoke with great passion. He made *la nationalité* and *les canadiens français*, innovations of the 1820s, into tangible entities under attack from greedy merchants, superior officials, and biassed governors. Much of his popular appeal was a result of his thumbing his nose at the English and tweaking the ears of the clergy. But at the same time he was able to blend *habitant* mockery of people in high places with *habitant* fear of change into a defence of French Canadian language, religion, and laws. Just what that defence might entail Papineau rarely specified, but the crowds that he touched were willing to follow him anywhere. In a time of economic distress, institutional transformation, and political tug of war, Papineau's magic was a heady mix of democratic logic, popular uneasiness, liberal rhetoric, *habitant* indocility, and nationalist dream.

In contrast, the *parti patriote* was much more prosaic. It was never as united as Papineau wished in spite of the fact that most of its members came from the same overcrowded middle class. Assembly members quarrelled among themselves for positions of prestige in the party; they represented different regional, economic, and ideological interests. Often their only point of agreement was hostility to the governor and his councils. Accentuating the disunity were the great number of newspapers claiming to carry the *patriote* message. *La Minerve* was the most consistent, *The Vindicator* added a virulent Irish tone, *Le Canadien* provided a more moderating voice from Quebec City, *Le Libéral* was more doctrinally liberal while *L'Echo du pays* introduced a rural Catholic note. The program of the party always appeared hazy, if not deliberately negative, to people at the time and historians ever since. It opposed public expenditures from both a liberal and nationalist perspective: the government ought not to be favouring a certain class especially since the institutions desired by that class might mean eventual assimilation. And yet on occasion *parti patriote* members could be found dreaming of canals on the Richelieu to favour north-south trade, local manufactures to diminish dependency on British imports, free trade with the United States rather than preferential treatment from Great Britain, even the accumulation of local capital through a *Banque du peuple.* But there never was much precision in defining, let alone agreement over what the party stood for.

It was much easier to unite the party with a few sure slogans. Assembly control of finances worked well in the 1820s but gradually broke down as neither assembly nor governor ever conceded enough to satisfy the other. English hostility to the French was vastly more malleable. It could be combined with a reform demand by pointing out that a predominantly English legislative council consistently blocked the wishes of a predominantly French assembly. One sure way of changing things was to render the council elective and by 1832 this had become the rallying cry of the party, convinced that its electoral success in town and country would carry over from assembly to council. Or it might even abolish the council altogether as the *parti patriote* ally in the British House of Commons, John Roebuck, suggested in 1835. But by then another simple slogan was attracting certain members of the party: independence.

If the slogans rallied, they also repelled. Some adherents of the *parti patriote* began to hesitate early in the 1830s in the face of the secularizing tendencies of the proposed *loi des fabriques*. Others doubted the wisdom of radical constitutional change such as having complete elective institutions. Still others, particularly those from the Quebec City region where British preferential tariffs kept the wood trade closely tied to empire, would have nothing to do with independence. Some too simply did not share Papineau's conviction, expressed to his wife in 1835, that England's aim was to denationalize French Canadians by attacking their religion, laws, customs, and language. The slogans could be as disruptive as they were unifying.

In terms of actual behaviour, the much despised English party was not very different. Indeed, *patriote* hostility lent more cohesion to that loose group than did any internal mechanism. Admittedly its economic program had been clear and consistent since the late eighteenth century: it wanted the assistance of government in designing a commercial empire linking the continental interior to imperial markets via the St. Lawrence. And some of its members avowedly considered French Canadian institutions a hindrance to that plan. But others actually enjoyed and profited from those institutions. The few who had favoured positions of political power clung to them with as much tenacity as the *patriotes* coveted them. They too used constitutional and nationalistic arguments to bolster their case: to tamper with the legislative council was to flirt with dreaded American republicanism. Still others were quite prepared to do just that: if Britain gave in to *patriote* demands, the English in the colony would threaten independence themselves. Some even sanctioned violence as young men formed rifle corps and flaunted their military prowess in the streets of Montreal. From Quebec City, however, came voices of moderation: adherents of the English party there simply did not believe the Montreal *Herald* when it argued that the foreign—meaning French—character of Lower Canada sullied the national honour of England.

In spite of the differences of opinion within the two political groups in Lower Canada, it was actually the economic despair of

great masses of ordinary people that caused the two parties'
competing dreams of nation to come to blows. As long as many
habitants could remember they had known agricultural hardship:
crop failures in 1805, 1812, 1816, 1818, 1828, 1833, and 1836 competed with depression between 1819 and 1821, 1825 and 1828, 1833
and 1834, and again in 1837 to make their lives miserable. There
was no escape because there was insufficient arable land for an
increasing population. The attendant poverty of too many people
on too little land increased as both seigneur and priest demanded
higher payments for the economic and religious services they provided. The habitants grumbled but reserved their anger for the
English immigrants pouring through the countryside in search of
land and jobs. That the British government was saving immense
tracts of land in the Eastern Townships for these newcomers by
means of the British American Land Company, formed in 1832, only
aggravated the situation. While desperate French Canadian farmers began squatting on Township lands, the assembly petitioned
the King in opposition to the Company and the legislative council
prepared resolutions in its favour. By 1837 bad harvests throughout the Atlantic world diminished crops and raised prices to such
an extent that farm families in Lower Canada could not even feed
themselves let alone procure seed grain for the following year.
When British and American banks faced imminent collapse in 1837
and suspended payments, the credit shocks were felt throughout
the Lower Canadian economy. It was easy enough to combine radical politics and economic disaster and seek the cause elsewhere,
among the English.

Patriote leaders knew full well that agricultural problems had
little to do with the English. As assembly members, they had often
deplored the state of agriculture and had created committees of
enquiry. Those committees tended to attribute the agricultural difficulties to bad farming techniques, an accusation that has been
repeated in history books ever since. Precisely what the Lower
Canadian farmers should have been doing was rarely specified.
Certainly notions of crop rotation, summer fallow, effective fertili-
zation, and drainage were known if not always practised techniques, but they all presuppose decent land to begin with, commercialized agriculture, and an easily accessible market. None of
those conditions prevailed in Lower Canada in the 1830s. Like others throughout eastern North America, French Canadian farmers
tended to reap what the soil would offer for as long and as easily
as they could. Then they would break new land, either cutting into
their own woodlot or emigrating to new territory. When both of
these "techniques" became impossible, as was increasingly the case
by the late 1820s, they switched products from wheat to vegetable
and roots crops better able to ensure the family's subsistence. Little
ethnic variation alleviated the scene. The productivity of English
farmers in Lower Canada was scarcely greater than that of the
habitants. Upper Canada produced better wheat because the land

was newer. Agriculture in Quebec was only to come into its own much later in the nineteenth century when a growing urban demand permitted farmers to use mediocre land for its only paying purpose—as pasturage for dairy cattle.

As the economic situation worsened in the 1830s, however, so too did the political scene. In 1834 a committee of radical *parti patriote* members of the assembly drafted ninety-two resolutions as the basis of their electoral program. They accused the governor, Lord Aylmer, of acting contrary to the interests of both Britain and the colony. They damned the legislative council for its servile lackeying to the governor, for its blocking of assembly bills, and for its undemocratic nature. They condemned the administration of justice in the colony that tolerated confusing cases carried on in two languages, sometimes more than two legal traditions, and at great expense. They drew on French and American precedents, as well as their own previous demands, for both the tone and the content of the resolutions and they repeated their already public preference for elective institutions throughout the entire system of government.

If the Ninety-two Resolutions were designed to distinguish the radical from the more moderate members of the *parti patriote*, uneasy with each other since 1832, they succeeded. Some of the moderates may even have agreed with the governor's dismissal of the resolutions as "sham grievances." In any case, twenty-four of them voted against the resolutions when they were debated in the assembly. Seventeen of the twenty-four then decided not to risk the following election campaign and simply disappeared from politics. For them, the charge of republicanism and disloyalty—so easily made by the English party—sat heavily. For the radicals, however, the tremendous popular support they were able to arouse in the countryside for sending the resolutions to London was sufficient sanction for their stand. One of the few priests to take the radical course, *abbé* Etienne Chartier, claimed that the revolutionary intent of the resolutions was quite clear: either England would have to concede or the colony would have to take up arms. Was this in the back of people's minds as they voted in the last election before the Rebellion? Papineau's re-election in Montreal in the late autumn of 1834 was one long street fight. Elsewhere in the province the radical *patriotes* swept out the moderates. Even the respected John Neilson was defeated in Quebec City. The increasingly uneasy governor reported to London on the "character of nationality" displayed in the elections; he had not seen such a display before.

Aylmer's description undoubtedly coloured the approach of his successor. The British government dispatched Lord Gosford to govern the colonies as gently as possible and to enquire into the seemingly perpetual state of political unrest. While attempting to understand the grievances behind the Ninety-two Resolutions and to formulate an appropriate British response, Gosford tried to solve what he saw as a basically ethnic problem with good will. He even behaved so generously towards Papineau and his radical colleagues that many of the English in Lower Canada began to complain. They need not have worried. Gosford had secret instructions in his baggage: affable he could well be, but adamant too, in the maintenance of certain constitutional principles. There was to be no question of an elective legislative council, let alone assembly control of crown lands; nor was there to be any further concession in the financial tug of war between governor and assembly. Somehow Gosford's secret instructions became known in Upper Canada and a fellow radical there, William Lyon Mackenzie, busy copying much of the spirit and even some of the letter of the Ninety-two Resolutions into his own Seventh Report on Grievances of 1835, informed Papineau.

While Gosford blithely prepared his report for the British government, the Lower Canadian assembly balked. After seeing half of its bills disappear into the legislative council, never to be seen or recognized subsequently, while the same council spent months on paltry bills of its own, one of which was intended to suppress charivaris, the assembly decided that further co-operation was impossible. Once again finances provided the lever. As of 1836, the assembly decided to vote government funds for six months only. Gambling that the governor and his councils would not dare dip into provincial funds without the proper constitutional sanction, the assembly expected to gain for itself complete control of all monies raised in the colony. When the governor and council still had not given up after the first six months, the assembly effectively went on strike by adjourning itself. In that instance it gambled that voters would not object too violently to there being no funds for public works or even for schools.

Meanwhile Gosford penned his report. As expected, he could not agree to an elective legislative council although he did think some of the French *patriote* leaders should be appointed to it. Nor would he tolerate any notion of local control over the governor: the tie to Britain had to be maintained with the governor continuing to be responsible solely to London. The Crown too had to maintain some financial independence even if this meant having the civil list voted for a mere seven years rather than for the life of the sovereign; in exchange the assembly could control all other provincial revenues. It could even make laws concerning the crown lands although it could not interfere with the executive's prerogative to manage those lands. The whole, containing nothing that *patriotes* had not seen and rejected years before, was respectfully submitted to His Majesty's government at the beginning of March 1837.

By then the British government had had enough. Within four days of the receipt of Gosford's recommendations, Lord John Russell, government leader in the British House of Commons, had drafted ten short resolutions. Another three days and parliament had given its approval to them. In answer to *patriote* demands and to Gosford's attempt at conciliation, Russell's resolutions said

"NO". There would be no responsible executive council, a demand the *patriotes* had only lately borrowed from Upper Canadian radicals. There would be no elective legislative council. There had to be a civil list voted for a reasonable length of time by the assembly. The British American Land Company was there to stay. If the governor could not obtain his required funds by a vote of the assembly, he now had London's authority simply to take them. What was more, if matters did not right themselves in the colonies, the British government would impose a union of Upper and Lower Canada upon them.

Ten years earlier the Russell resolutions might have seemed relatively mild. In 1837 they were inflammatory. French Canadians in the assembly no longer had any confidence in the governor and simply rejected Gosford's last minute dickering in the summer of 1837 as he offered a suspension of the resolutions in return for a vote of funds. Gosford's response was to dissolve what would be the last Lower Canadian assembly. While the members headed for their ridings to suggest that the die was cast, the English population counted the number of British soldiers in the colony and smiled upon the young men of the Doric Club, a paramilitary organization in Montreal. Among the people in general, the agricultural crisis, immigration, cholera, and political propaganda had all made their mark. Well might Sir Robert Peel, Tory leader of the opposition in the British House of Commons, suggest that an army accompany the Russell resolutions to Canada.

Trouble was certainly brewing throughout the summer and fall of 1837. The *patriotes*' Permanent Central Committee, a centre for political discussion in Montreal since 1834, very easily orchestrated a series of mass meetings in most of the populated districts of Lower Canada. There the passions of both *patriotes* and the people were aroused. Papineau preferred to believe that the meetings were merely exercises in popular pressure, preliminaries to a vast constitutional convention planned for December. But the language used suggested otherwise. At St. Ours, on the Richelieu north of St. Denis, *patriotes* informed unhappy farmers that Britain was an aggressor to be checked by economic boycotts and illegal trade with the United States. At St. Marc, south and across the river, farmers were warned to prepare for a fight. In Montreal, Papineau reminded the crowds that the English had used violence in the past to secure their rights. Some of the young men took him seriously enough to form a military group rivalling the English Doric Club. This group, the *Fils de la liberté*, paraded around Papineau's house indicating to all who cared to see that they had revolution in mind with Papineau at the head of it. North of the city, crowds of up to four thousand gathered to hear Papineau justify the American revolt against England; reading their own fears into the *patriote* speeches, many of the listeners dispersed to harass their English neighbours. Back in the Richelieu region, at St. Charles, Papineau phrased resolutions in the stirring language of the French and American Revolutions; French liberty caps were prominently on display and the *habitants* cheered the suggestion that they melt their spoons to make bullets.

The convention planned for December was to be the last attempt at peaceful change. If it did not succeed, Lower Canada might well have to follow the American example and gain independence by armed rebellion. But perhaps it was not intended to succeed. By December the river would be frozen, facilitating all sorts of movements more expeditious than the penning of resolutions or the framing of constitutions. Moreover since the radical *patriotes* were now quarrelling among themselves, perhaps an armed uprising rather than a convention would prove more useful in uniting them. On the one side were people like Etienne Parent in Quebec City, now using the *Le Canadien* to denounce the foolishness of revolution. On the other side were much more radical spirits hoping that revolution would rid them of seigneurs and clergy. In the middle was Papineau, dithering. And watching them all was Lord Gosford, as governor charged with keeping the peace.

Whether or not the convention would have united the *patriotes* or led to any peaceful resolution of the developing conflict was a question left far behind with the outbreak of violence in early November 1837. On November 6, the *Fils de la liberté* and the Doric Club took to the streets of Montreal battling at the offices of the *Vindicator* and at Papineau's residence. Gosford summoned British troops from the other colonies. He also prepared arrest warrants for Papineau and the other *patriote* leaders but did not issue them until they, hearing of the warrants, departed precipitously from Montreal. Assuming that Papineau, last spotted heading east toward St. Hyacinthe, was on his way to rouse the rebellion, Gosford ordered him arrested.

Whether prepared for an armed uprising or not, the *patriotes* were now obliged to show their strength on the spur of the moment. Under Wolfred Nelson's direction, the *habitants* and townsfolk of St. Denis actually defeated a force of British soldiers on November 23. In their glee they may even have believed that Papineau's presence had been required elsewhere, that his leaving St. Denis was not in fact flight. Unfortunately their newly dubbed general, Thomas Storrow Brown, followed Papineau's example in the midst of a battle two days later at St. Charles, further south on the Richelieu. The defeat there took the spirit out of the rebels gathering at St. Mathias and the British troops emphasized the point by attacking and destroying St. Denis on December 1. Those rebels who had fled across the American border rallied momentarily on December 6 only to be pushed back again by English volunteers. A week later British soldiers put a quick halt to the rebellion by destroying the village of St. Eustache, north of Montreal. There some five thousand *patriotes* had been gathering since mid-November, but the actual armed fighting force was a mere five or six hundred. Once again the *patriote* leaders vanished after the initial skirmish, leaving their poorly armed and undisciplined comrades to confront two thousand government troops. By December 14, the three week Rebellion of 1837 was at an end.

Among the rebels who made a hasty escape to the United States was a radical group plotting not only revenge but social revolution. Shunting Papineau aside they planned to make use of a secret society, the *Frères chasseurs*, with members purportedly throughout Lower Canada, to rekindle the Rebellion by staging uprisings all along the Richelieu and simultaneous attacks upon Montreal, Sorel, and Quebec City. Once victorious, the radical rebels would create an independent and democratic republic complete with universal suffrage, the separation of church and state, and the abolition of the seigneurial regime and of French civil law. But after the crushing defeat of late 1837 there was little popular enthusiasm for rebellion, let alone revolution; indeed only by calling upon Papineau's name could the radicals raise the least spark of interest. Neither in February nor in November 1838 did the tiny forces of invasion make the slightest dent on Lower Canadian defences. As an uprising, the Lower Canadian rebellion, like its counterpart in Upper Canada, had been a fiasco.

Numbers had much to do with the failure. In a population of close to 450 000 French Canadians in Lower Canada, the Rebellion engaged only some five or six thousand in 1837 and perhaps a few more the following year. Even allowing for family members—there appear to have been a number of women directly involved in the uprisings—one still has only a fraction of the population implicated in the Rebellion. So small indeed were the numbers that historians can count them. Fernand Ouellet has located on hundred and eighty-six professionals (seventy-six notaries, sixty-seven physicians, and forty-three lawyers), three hundred and eighty-eight small merchants, seven or eight hundred tradesmen and labourers in Montreal, and a few thousand farmers, tradesmen and labourers from the districts north and south of Montreal. For a socio-economic analysis of rebels the numbers are fascinating and Ouellet is able to confirm his view of the conservative nature of the Rebellion by investigating the interests of the professional group in particular. But the numbers are also minuscule. They included neither all groups in society nor all members of any particular group. And they were heavily concentrated in the Montreal region. Timber workers in the Ottawa Valley, for example, carried on their Irish-French disputes sublimely unaware of the troubles in either Lower or Upper Canada. Geography, economics, and ideology restrained the size of the Rebellion.

Leadership had also been a problem. As a group the clergy frowned upon the increasingly rebellious temper of the late 1830s. Monseigneur Lartigue, the bishop of Montreal, made his position clear in 1837 and 1838: good citizens do not rebel against constituted authority and those who do are quite properly denied the sacraments. A number of local parish priests, however, were caught between their doctrinally correct bishop and their economically bewildered and politically aroused parishioners. Two of them actually took up arms with the *patriotes*. More serious was the obvious lack of military skill or even bravery on the part of the middle class fomenters of rebellion. Only Dr. Wolfred Nelson appears to have had any notion of military strategy. The others relied upon words and grand gestures—the stuff of politics—to transform themselves into revolutionary leaders. When that failed, they fled. The *habitants* therefore had two choices: they could stand and watch the skirmishes, waiting to see which way the dice would fall, or they could fight and take the required leadership into their own hands. Most of them did the former, but those who took an active part produced too many leaders for the number of followers. In the face of clerical disapproval, middle class incompetence, and *habitant* hesitation on the one hand and impatience on the other, the Rebellion disintegrated.

No matter how small, localized, badly organized, and badly led, the Rebellion nonetheless left in its wake a number of broken dreams. Those most personally affected were the twelve hanged culprits, the fifty-eight exiles deported to Australia, and the unknown number of rebels who chose flight to the United States. Of a more public nature, the dream of the middle class came to an abrupt halt. Once that class stepped outside the purely political realm, it was out of its depth. If it really did envisage independence, and that appears to have been only a last-minute addition to an incoherent program, it would have to plan for it politically, not militarily. The much more inarticulate *habitant* dream also disintegrated. Land for themselves and for their children was no more abundant or fertile after the Rebellion than before. The English, the immigrants, the seigneur, and the clergy were still there, unmoved and possibly more powerful because of the defeat of the Rebellion. Barely discernible but also definitely shattered by the Rebellion was the hazy notion of the Richelieu River as a major grain and trade route between Lower Canada and the United States. Emigration paths out of the area in the 1840s clearly marked the despair. Perhaps there had been too many dreams for one small rebellion. The land that tossed up the troubles simply could not accommodate them.

Although the British had suppressed the rebellions in both Lower and Upper Canada by military force, they nonetheless sought a political solution to the troubles in the colonies. The British government therefore dispatched a liberal aristocrat, Lord Durham, to investigate the Canadian situation. Engaged in trade and radical politics, Durham was a modern businessman with racist views. Even before he set foot in Quebec, Lord Durham had a solution to Canadian ills: a federation of all the British North American colonies. He came as supreme governor, overriding both the martial law that had been imposed in December 1837 and the special council that was to govern in the absence of a constitution. He arrived in late May 1838 and departed a scant five months later, spending just enough time to make a few enquiries, confirm a few prejudices, and draft a report.

Durham's sympathies, experiences, and whirlwind tour of the Canadas led him to pen a most curious prescription, both liberal and imperialist, for Canadian problems. In Upper Canada his political predilections led him to associate with the reformers. Their idea of an executive responsible to the assembly took his fancy; it was, he thought, precisely the pattern already traced by British reformers in the 1830s. Reconciling such a plan with the maintenance of the governor's responsibility to London was not easy, as Durham was to discover upon the publication of his report. But he was convinced that responsible government would rectify the common problem of all the colonies. This problem, in Durham's own words, was "some defect in the form of government ... the combining of apparently popular institutions with an utter absence of all efficient control of the people over their rulers."

There was, however, something peculiar about Lower Canada. Here Durham's commercial interests led him to associate with the merchant class of Quebec and Montreal. He therefore found it hard to believe that they could be the villains in a similar play, pitting liberal and democratic French Canadians in the assembly against conservative and reactionary English place holders in the councils. That political skirmish surely masked the true problem of "two nations warring in the bosom of a single state." Astute enough to recognize that "it is not anywhere a virtue of the English race to look with complacency on any manners, customs or laws which appear strange to them," Durham nonetheless marked the French Canadians with the more grievous faults. They were uneducated, unprogressive, lacking in history or literature, clinging to ancient prejudices, ancient customs, and ancient laws. They were doomed to hopeless inferiority, to becoming "labourers in the employ of English capitalists." They could not possibly survive as a distinct national entity in the face of English immigration and English progress. Britain had in fact erred ever since the Conquest in encouraging the illusion of a French future in North America.

According to Durham, the kindest solution that the imperial government could now offer French Canadians was assimilation. Not brutal or dramatic—Durham was after all a liberal, he had already expressed sympathy for European peoples struggling to maintain their nationality—but assimilation nonetheless. Union of Upper and Lower Canada was to be the means with the united province having an executive responsible to the popularly elected assembly. A stroke of genius, Durham thought, to solve the political and national problems of the colonies with a simple administrative reorganization. With that, the business oriented aristocrat, the liberal imperialist from the coalfields of Durham County in northern England began spinning his own dream: once French Canadians were attached by political and economic ties to Upper Canada, they would see the superiority and the advantages of the English way of doing things. Prompted too by immigration which would soon make them a minority, French Canadians would choose their own assimilation.

Alas, poor Durham. His dream of assimilation was as unrealizable as the *patriote* dream of independence.

SELECT BIBLIOGRAPHY

Creighton, Donald. "The Economic Background of the Rebellions of Eighteen thirty-seven." *Canadian Journal of Economics and Political Science* 3(1937):322–34.

Creighton, Donald. *The Empire of the St. Lawrence.* Toronto: Macmillan, 1956.

Durham, John George Lambton. *Lord Durham's Report.* Edited by Gerald M. Craig. Toronto: McClelland and Stewart, 1963.

Jones, Robert Leslie. "Agriculture in Lower Canada, 1792–1815." *Canadian Historical Review* 27(1946):33–51.

Lewis, Frank, and Marvin McInnis. "The Efficiency of the French-Canadian Farmer in the Nineteenth Century." *Journal of Economic History* 40 (1980):497–514.

Manning, Helen Taft. *The Revolt of French Canada, 1800–1835: A Chapter in the History of the British Commonwealth.* Toronto: Macmillan, 1962.

Ouellet, Fernand. *Histoire économique et sociale du Québec, 1760–1850: structures et conjoncture.* Montreal: Fides, 1966.

Ouellet, Fernand. "Les insurrections de 1837–1838: Un phénomène social." *Histoire sociale/Social History* 2(1968):54–82.

Ouellet, Fernand. *Lower Canada, 1791–1840: Social Change and Nationalism.* Toronto: McClelland and Stewart, 1976.

Ouellet, Fernand, ed. "Lettres de L.-J. Papineau a sa femme." In *Rapport de l'Archiviste de la Province de Québec.* vols. 34–5. (1953–1954). Pp. 187–442.

Ouellet, Fernand, ed. *Papineau: Textes choisis et présentés par Fernand Ouellet.* Quebec: Les presses de l'Université Laval, 1958.

Ouellet, Fernand, and Jean Hamelin. "La crise agricole dans le Bas-Canada, 1802–1837." *Annual Report.* Canadian Historical Association, 1962. Pp. 17–33.

Public Archives of Canada. *British Colonial Office Papers, Copies of Correspondence from Canada, 1830–1835.* Series "Q", vols. 195–222.

"... the international demand for ... timber"
Ships loading lumber in Quebec, mid-century.

6 Alliance for Survival

With the Durham Report hanging the threat of assimilation over
their heads, French Canadians in 1840 had every reason to be gloomy.
Nor was there anything in their immediate surroundings to give
them cause for cheer. The defeat of the Rebellion left in its wake
exile for political leaders (Papineau among them), destruction of
farmlands and property in the Richelieu region where most of the
battles had been fought, disappointment and despair among *patriote*
supporters, and apathy among the more sceptical. A special Crown-
appointed council carried out the governor's orders and approved
the Act of Union in November 1840 which imposed union on Lower
and Upper Canada, now to be known as Canada East and Canada
West. Although the Act reinstated representative institutions in the
colony in the form of a new united legislative assembly, it also
provided equal representation for the two provinces even though
the population of Lower Canada surpassed that of Upper Canada
by close to 200 000. Furthermore, not only did it impose a fixed
civil list on the provinces and an executive and legislative council
quite free from popular control, the Act also proscribed the French
language and, in establishing one revenue fund to cover the expenses of both provinces, it saddled Lower Canada with the much

higher public debt of Upper Canada. Certainly in 1840 the political situation looked bleak for Lower Canada.

Nor did anything in the spiritual or material world offer any solace. The new bishop of Montreal, Ignaçe Bourget, was just beginning to document the religious indifference and outright disobedience among many of the presumed faithful. The colleges that were supposed to turn out priests in fact produced far too many aspirants to the liberal professions—notaries, doctors, lawyers— for the society to support. Elementary schools barely touched a fraction of the largely illiterate population. Since the assembly had not been in session since before the Rebellion, the last school law dated from 1836; thereafter there were no more funds to pay teachers. The few schools that did remain open depended upon the local teacher's goodwill, frequently superior to her knowledge. The economic situation was equally depressing. Three years of bad harvests were an unnecessary reminder that the land in general and the seigneurial system in particular could no longer support the eighty percent of the population who were rural dwellers. Urban activities—trade, commerce, imports—all slowed to a snail's pace; as Durham had noticed, French Canadians' only economic advantage was to be slightly ahead of the despised and feared immigrants. Decidedly 1840 was a dismal year.

Everything in the next fourteen years, however, was to give the lie to the dismal picture of 1840. Defeated in rebellion and condemned as an inferior race meriting only assimilation, French Canadians suddenly burst forth with extraordinary energy, enthusiasm, tenacity, and vigour. They revived and remodelled their political institutions and thereby undermined the assimilationist purpose of the union. For example, they succeeded in bringing the executive under the control of the assembly, thus solving the most vexing pre-rebellion political problem. They even achieved an elective legislative council, if only for a short period, 1855 to 1867. They shook out their religious lethargy and gave form and substance to the faith and the church. They organized a school system and municipal institutions. They scrutinized their civil law, queried its basis in the *Coutume de Paris* and amended it according to the *Code Napoléon*. They produced a generation of historians, novelists, even would-be philosophers; they formed national, cultural, educational, and political interest groups. They investigated agricultural practices, organized the settlement of areas of the Eastern Townships, and opened registry offices. They gave the green light to canal development along the St. Lawrence and the red light to the seigneurial system, abolishing it in 1854. And they did it all, or most of it, in French, in spite of Durham.

Or perhaps all this activity came about because of him. To account for the effervescence of the 1840s is a complex task. Durham may indeed have been both villain and catalyst. François-Xavier Garneau certainly undertook his *Histoire du Canada* as a direct response to Durham's deriding of French Canadians as a people without a history. The Rebellion itself may have served as both a dividing point and a lesson. The vogue of liberalism sweeping the Atlantic world no doubt had some effect as a new middle class with intellectual and political pretensions came into its own. In Quebec a new generation of this same class, some barely touched by the Rebellion, would find places of prestige in a reorganized political arena. Some would even stage, in the decades to follow, a Quebec version of the contemporary European debate between liberty and authority. The context of political peace and economic prosperity, interrupted only at the end of the 1840s, may also account for the zeal.

As an illustration of that zeal and perhaps even as partial explanation of it was French Canada's coming to terms with the British presence. After eighty years and no doubt a good deal of wishful thinking on both sides, it was obvious the British were here to stay. The acknowledgment of that reality is evident in the re-aligning of groups. From 1840 to 1854, French Canadians experimented with every conceivable form of alliance among themselves or between some of them and similarly inclined English Canadians in the now united province of Canada. They toyed too with various forms of constitutional alliance before finally settling on responsible government. Along the way they tested out religious alliances, cultural alliances, economic alliances. They even witnessed old English tories and young French radicals joining together momentarily to reject any further connection with Britain. Decidedly, much of the tumult of the times was the constant shifting of characters.

Accompanying that shifting was a major debate, sometimes overt, sometimes implicit, over the place of nationalism in public life. One strain of nationalism, stressing territorial and cultural distinctiveness, yearning for the independence that political theorists attached to nationality in the nineteenth century, and tending to blame the other for problems big and small, had ground to a halt with the defeat of the Rebellion. In the 1840s one occasionally heard a faint echo of this strain, especially after Papineau's return from exile in 1845 and his re-entry onto the political scene in 1847. But more often a great variety of nationalist voices intermingled with and commented upon the various alliances taking shape. Sometimes they provided a justification for those alliances, sometimes a questioning of them. Most often they insisted that problems big and small were of French Canadians' own making, solvable therefore by a common effort. Nationalism, in short, moved out of the political spotlight and took on all the moving shades of a cultural force.

Of the various political alliances French Canadians entered into, the most obvious, because success and history and even a statue on Parliament Hill have sanctioned it, came to be that between Lower and Upper Canadian reformers to mould the new union to their will. In 1840, however, no one knew that either Lower

Canada's Louis-Hippolyte LaFontaine or Upper Canada's Robert Baldwin could even form an alliance let alone discipline their scattered and indecisive followers into a vaguely recognizable political party. LaFontaine himself did not have much of a political program in 1840. His opposition to the Union was only the normal reaction of someone who had been a member of the *parti patriote* in the assembly since 1830. But he had also been out of the country during the troubled times of 1837 and 1838 and that tempered his opposition. So too did the persuasiveness of Francis Hincks, an Upper Canadian businessman and ally of the Baldwin reformers, whom LaFontaine had known since 1835. Although not yet set on a course of action that would lead to such a precise constitutional formulation as responsible government, LaFontaine nonetheless did see as early as 1840 the necessity of working within the Union.

In preparation for the first elections in 1841, therefore, LaFontaine carefully indicated both his opposition to the Union and his hopes for it. As he told his electors, the Union was unjust. It had been imposed without popular approval and its sanctioning of English as the only official language of the assembly, burdening Lower Canada with Upper Canada's debt, and providing equal representation for provinces of unequal population was quite simply unfair. To condemn these aspects of the Union was in fact politically necessary and by doing so LaFontaine, a Montrealer, hoped to encompass all opposition to the Union and thereby head off a resurgence of the old regional rivalries within the *parti patriote*. In Quebec City, John Neilson of the *Gazette de Québec*, erstwhile *patriote* but never radical or rebel, was hoping to revive his own political career, sullied by his membership on the hated special council which was set up after the Rebellion to impose the governor's orders. He organized massive petitions in the Quebec region against the Union, rallying priests and *patriotes* in a common expression of fear for the survival of French Canadian institutions. Spotting the popularity of the petitions, LaFontaine did the same in the Montreal district. Unlike Neilson, however, he did not send his petitions to London. Instead he pointed out to his electors that there was no alternative to working within the new constitution. Nothing else was likely to come from Britain and, even if it did, French Canadians had to have a voice in government in the meantime. Moreover, the Union might even permit a larger voice; by joining forces with political reformers from Upper Canada, French Canadians might gain greater strength to force concessions from the governor and his councillors who, by the terms of the Union and in spite of Durham's recommendations, were to behave no differently from before the Rebellion.

Some of these appointed officials, in fact, were to behave with even less circumspection than others had before the Rebellion. Lord Sydenham, the first of the Union governors, schooled by Durham and the Colonial Office in London, casually manipulated the electoral ridings in the first election with the result that LaFontaine was defeated. At that point the beginning ties of one of the alliances of the period came into play. Robert Baldwin, the Upper Canadian reform leader named by Sydenham to the executive council in the interest of "harmony"—the conciliation of opposing groups by having members of each present in the council—resigned his position to protest the lack of French Canadians at the governor's right hand. Having been elected from three different ridings in Canada West, Baldwin offered one of them to LaFontaine. The by-election was simple and LaFontaine entered the assembly of the United Canada in 1842 as a member for Toronto and made his first speech in French. Although official recognition of the language did not come until 1849 when Lord Elgin as governor used French in his opening speech to the assembly, LaFontaine had in effect already killed one of the assimilationist purposes of the Union.

Sir Charles Bagot, the second Union governor, more affable and diplomatic than Sydenham, recognized the impossibility of ostracizing French Canadians from the councils of government. He also envisaged the executive council as an expression of the majority members in the assembly rather than a place to harmonize divergent interests. He therefore offered LaFontaine the position of Attorney General for Canada East and with it an automatic place on the executive council; before accepting LaFontaine bargained successfully for spots for his Montreal and Quebec City colleagues, Augustin-Norbert Morin and Etienne Parent (the latter as clerk of the council), and for his Upper Canadian ally, Robert Baldwin. He confirmed the alliance and returned Baldwin's earlier favour by finding him the safe riding of Rimouski after Baldwin had lost the by-election which he needed to win in order to hold public office. Decidedly political friendships could pay off. Parent began philosophizing about the link between British institutions and French Canadian survival while LaFontaine assured his followers that *la nationalité* had triumphed over the Union. To the sceptical and perhaps jealous eye of John Neilson in Quebec City, now joined by Denis-Benjamin Viger, it looked more as if LaFontaine had gained office by political compromise with an English-speaking radical from Canada West. Governor Bagot, however, listened politely, often favourably, to the comments of his councillors. He was of course under no obligation to consider their comments as advice, let alone act upon them, and neither LaFontaine nor Baldwin demanded that of him.

However, it was on precisely that issue—of whether or not the governor should act on his councillors' advice—combined with the more shady one of patronage that the council and the next governor, Sir Charles Metcalfe, came to an impasse. In 1843, LaFontaine and Baldwin, respectively Attorneys General for Canada East and Canada West (their positions alone revealing the federal path that the Union, in spite of its name, would gradually trace) insisted that Governor Metcalfe assign only their nominee to a particular civil service post. The governor did not agree. He was not about to have "rebels" and "republicans" take over his task of naming the government's servants. Metcalfe in fact had instructions from London not to go any further than Bagot had in naming and listening to councillors who pretended to represent majority interests in the assembly. He also had a personal distaste for the party politics that were emerging in the united Canada. They threatened to sully the governor's own image as a non-partisan conciliator of interests. Worse still, they threatened to undermine his authority. How indeed could a governor exercise any authority if he had to obey instructions from London and impertinences from colonials? That the latter might have some legitimate grievances, Metcalfe was quite prepared to admit. He even attempted to alleviate some of them. He hinted to London that many a French Canadian ruffled feather might be soothed if there were an amnesty for the exiled and deported *patriotes*, if the policy of assimilation were dropped, if the assembly could have a peek at the civil list, and if the capital were moved from Kingston to Montreal. But London would not budge. So when Metcalfe named a minor official without consulting his executive council, he had no peace offering for that offended body. He refused to rescind his nomination and the council refused to sanction it. LaFontaine and Baldwin resigned.

They claimed they were acting on principle, but LaFontaine and Baldwin were also interested in the power of patronage. Both principle and patronage were linked to the emerging notion of responsible government. The principle required that the governor choose his councillors from the majority in the elected assembly and that he act upon their advice. The power to make him do so depended upon the councillors' ability to command a majority in the assembly. That in turn required the careful crafting of political parties and patronage was one of the tools. By distributing varied jobs in different locations, a political leader could design a network of loyalty that would reveal itself most clearly on election day. The governors knew that full well and LaFontaine was fast learning. If he controlled the distribution of government jobs, he might be able to give substance to his dream of a political party uniting all French Canadians with a congenial group from Canada West. The result would be continuous electoral victories and thus a solid base from which to exercise control over the governor. Moreover, the jobs might also solve the major problem of Quebec's middle class. All those trained professionals might find a niche in the civil service. If they could not all aspire to be legislative councillors, judges, or justices of the peace, they might well become clerks in the courts or the newly opened registry offices, land commissioners, surveyors, inspectors at ports, or even custodians of Her Majesty's mail at the inns that served as post offices. The openings were varied and almost limitless. So was the gratitude. If LaFontaine could control such economic largesse, he could both cement developing political alliances among French Canadians and show, once again, that the Union was beneficial to *la nation*.

Not everyone agreed with LaFontaine's strategy or ideas. The governor had some strong French Canadian allies in his struggle against the unseemly rush for offices and the even more unseemly suggestion that anyone other than he control that rush. Viger, Neilson, and their followers in Quebec City thought LaFontaine was insulting the Crown by his insistence on naming public servants: by assuming the governor's authority, he was actually undermining it. They also suspected that LaFontaine was merely solidifying his own political position by demanding control of patronage. If LaFontaine should win his point, the entire system of government would degenerate into a mad scramble for jobs; it would be worse than the American "spoils" system, whereby patronage was used for party purposes, since it would be sanctioned by a lofty (and they thought quite mad) political principle of responsible government. Besides it was all so unnecessary. All French Canadians had to do was to stay close to the governor's good graces and the nation's needs would eventually be recognized. Was not Metcalfe about to arrange an amnesty, perhaps even the return of the exiles, and even produce the arrears in Papineau's salary as speaker of the pre-Rebellion assembly?

The two differing political viewpoints tested their strength in the following years. Metcalfe's clash with his council, which had caused LaFontaine and Baldwin to resign, led to a futile attempt to find more congenial councillors and then to an election in 1844. The results in Canada East placed almost all French Canadian assembly members behind LaFontaine, but they also reduced his reform allies to a minority in Canada West. Baldwin was therefore ignored as the governor constructed his executive council; in protest, LaFontaine refused a position for himself. The alliance was all important. Even so, it left a number of French Canadians dubious. There they were, with a majority of the Lower Canadian seats in the assembly and yet deprived of places on the executive council because of LaFontaine's curious flirtation with reformers from Canada West. LaFontaine's own followers began to wonder. Indeed they tried his political patience and skill with their protests as they watched electorally unrepresentative figures like Denis-Benjamin Viger and Denis-Benjamin Papineau take their places in an executive council beside moderate conservatives from Canada West. LaFontaine held out for a constitutional principle backed by an alliance of people holding similar political views. His uneasy followers and his opponents in Quebec began considering an alternative form of alliance. A "double majority" would ensure that whatever political colour the two sections of the united Canada produced, each would have its place in the councils of the governor. Proximity to the governor would thus be ensured; French Canadians would always be on the side of authority. But since they could not control that authority let alone exercise it themselves because the governor was not obliged to act upon the advice of his councillors, LaFontaine would have nothing to do with the notion. Being in opposition with twenty-nine of the forty-two seats assigned to Canada East in the assembly was nonetheless a tricky situation. LaFontaine dealt with it by looking for alliances elsewhere. If he could not counteract Viger's "double majority" and nationalist argument directly, he could undermine it by drawing to his side a force of growing national importance in French Canada.

That force was the church. And its major proponent in the 1840s was Monseigneur Ignace Bourget, bishop of Montreal. If the first governor of the Union considered him of little talent and objected to his becoming bishop, the last governor of the decade had only praise for him as a staunch ally of the British connection. Both governors and bishop came a long way in those few short years. Bourget of course knew his history; the church had survived since the Conquest by staying close to the British authorities and being useful to them. Now that that authority was being whittled away by the political developments of the period, Bourget, as political an animal as LaFontaine, steered his church close to the new powers in the land.

Before any of that could happen, however, Bourget had to revitalize his church. Catholicism in 1840 was insipid, he noted dismally while collecting statistics on religious indifference: there were far too many non-practising Catholics, too many apostates, drunks, and people living in concubinage. Such a motley collection would never resist the assimilation intended by the Union let alone counteract the intense Protestant propaganda that was flooding the countryside. What they required was inspiration, organization, direction. Bourget had it all and what he did not have he imported from Europe. The imports were of a particular kind: preachers and teachers imbued with popular Catholicism and conservative philosophy. The most spectacular was a former French bishop, Monseigneur de Forbin-Janson, complete with aristocratic title to match his royalist philosophy and extraordinary preaching talents. For more than a year he paraded about the parishes of Quebec instilling and reviving religious enthusiasm in the huge crowds that greeted him. He and Bourget organized immensely popular religious retreats. And then Bishop Bourget consolidated the fervour. From France again he brought new religious orders— Oblates, Jesuits, *Clercs de Saint-Viateur, Dames du Sacré-Coeur, Soeurs du Bon-Pasteur, Pères, Frères, Soeurs de Sainte-Croix*— men and women to fill the thin ranks of Montreal's diocesan clergy. He presided over the founding of two Canadian religious communities for men and of the secular social work agency, the Saint Vincent-de-Paul Society. And he looked on benevolently as Canadian women displayed even more organizational enthusiam, creating four new religious orders within the decade: *Soeurs de Charité de la Providence, Soeurs des Saints Noms de Jésus et Marie, Soeurs de la*

Miséricorde, Soeurs de Sainte Anne. They also expanded another order established in the eighteenth century, the *Soeurs grises,* into four independent communities in different parts of the province.

Religious enthusiasm was only one of the reasons for the extraordinary burst of organized clerical activity. In fact the communities had work to do. Where an individual priest, and there were still so few of them, had to be a jack of all trades for the many religious and secular needs of his parishioners, the communities specialized their labour. Some of them indeed took on tasks that had become too much of a burden for a *curé.* There were only so many women left widowed by cholera epidemics, homeless victims of fires, and poor people that the priest could care for personally. And his moral charges were just as heavy. He had to provide religious instruction, offer alternative reading to the "immoral pamphlets" in circulation, and persuade people that a temperance society was of more value than a theatre. He may well have been pleased therefore to have some of his charitable functions undertaken by others. Most of the male orders engaged in teaching; most of the female orders in social work. The poor, the deprived, the disgraced, the old, and the sick all received care and attention from the members of one or another of the new religious orders. The religious communities also provided jobs from the 1840s and increasingly throughout the rest of the nineteenth century. Vast ranges of occupations opened to young men and women. For the men the religious orders relieved some of the pressure on the liberal professions; for the women they offered a varied alternative to the one occupation by which most women earned their living, that of childbearing.

Bourget's particular interest was education and that interest slowly brought him into contact with the politicians. All of the religious communities he brought from France were teaching orders. Although some, particularly those formed by women, found their way into small, local schools, most came to strengthen the teaching in the classical colleges, the private, church-administered secondary and post-secondary schools for boys which, in an eight year program, stressed the classical literature and philosophy of Greece, Rome, and France. Bourget hoped they would instill more religious enthusiasm among the students and thereby produce more priests. During and after his long tenure as bishop of Montreal (from 1840 to 1876), they in fact did both. Many of the graduates who did not become priests found their way into politics; in doing so they maintained their old school ties. The link of course was hardly an innovation in the 1840s. Many of LaFontaine's political allies were already close friends not only of Bourget's religious personnel but also of the religious in Quebec City. The ties became closer still when Bourget gave his backing to a newspaper as a further means of promoting religion in public life. *Les Mélanges religieux* never did confine itself to religious matters and it added the bishop's unofficial voice to the public debate in the local press.

Into that debate it also tossed two volatile notions that French Canada was to live with for many a year. The first was the link between religion and language as the mainstay of French Canadian nationality. And the other, a direct import from Europe by means of reproduced articles from the Catholic, conservative, and even royalist press, was the link between Catholic theology, conservative philosophy, and political action.

The issue that brought Bourget, his ideas, and his newspaper into the LaFontaine camp was, not surprisingly, education. Since the 1820s the assembly had been taking a sporadic interest in elementary schooling, alternately wishing to counteract the growth of schools under the auspices of the Royal Institution, a Protestant body dating from 1801, and to curb the power of the *curés* in the local schools. But the interest was always subordinate to the tug of war between assembly and council. After 1836 there was no school bill voted at all so that funds and any semblance of coordination vanished. In the 1840s things changed. With the businesslike and joint administrative activity that characterized the early years of the Union, Canada speedily provided itself with two superintendents of education. The one for Canada East, Jean-Baptiste Meilleur, like his counterpart from Canada West, Egerton Ryerson, worked against considerable odds to establish elementary schooling for the great mass of children. The problems of organization, financing, control, and administration were immense. Teachers had to be found and trained, programs designed, and schools built all in the face of popular hostility to any form of taxation. Meilleur laboured under the additional burden of the Durham Report's desire to see the schools serve as agents of assimilation. The combination of difficulties led to increasing government and clerical control.

Arguing in support of the intimate link between education and religion, the *Mélanges religieux* attacked a proposed education bill in 1845. The bill, put forth by executive councillor D.-B. Papineau of the Viger-Neilson group, political opponents of LaFontaine, did not give sufficient place to the clergy in the control of local schools. Instead it left them, as a previous school act in 1841 had specified, under the guidance of locally elected school commissioners. The only acknowledgment of increased clerical interest and presence was to permit the clergy to be "visitors" to the schools: without any legal status, they could cast an eye over the religious instruction in the schools. This was insufficient for a clergy exercising its muscle against local lay elites and at the same time invigorating popular religion. They found allies in LaFontaine and Morin, anxious for an issue to rally their followers in the assembly in opposition to the minority group in office. Together they forced amendments to the bill, giving centralized control to the superintendent but in effect local control to the clergy by permitting them to be elected school commissioners. A year later the local priest acquired veto power in the hiring of teachers. Bourget did not forget LaFontaine's assistance.

Even when that assistance did not always produce the desired results, the developing alliance held. In 1846 Bourget claimed that the church should become the rightful inheritor of the Jesuit Estates. Confiscated by the British authorities at the time of the Conquest but only turned over totally to the Crown on the death of the last remaining Jesuit in Canada in 1800, the lands had subsequently been placed under the control of the Lower Canadian assembly in 1832. Since their revenues were to be used for education and since, argued Bourget, the church was the proper educator, the church should have the lands. The Viger group in office, to whom the request was made, refused. Again Bourget turned to LaFontaine and again he found support. This time the budding alliance did not produce sufficient assembly votes for victory but the debate over the question in the press had all the pro-LaFontaine papers, *La Minerve, Le Journal de Québec, La Revue canadienne*, siding with Bourget's *Mélanges religieux* and posing as defenders of the faith. From then on *Les Mélanges* and *La Minerve* tended to be sympathetic to each other, particularly at election time.

By the mid-1840s, however, there were other voices and other groups stirring in the province: some added a cultural justification to the developing political alliances; others criticized those very alliances and the educational issue which cemented them, and others still reflected the shifting ideological priorities of the period. They all added to the effervescence of the time.

One of the new voices introduced an historical element and a contemporary message into the slowly brewing nationalist ideology. François-Xavier Garneau published his three volume *Histoire du Canada* between 1845 and 1848. Long before the motto *Je me souviens* adorned the emblem of Quebec, Garneau told his readers that they constituted a particular people whose past was one of perpetual struggle. And given the daily insults to which French Canadians were subjected in the present, Garneau implied that their future was not likely to be any different. For him, the French regime provided the best illustration of a people surviving all odds, engaging boldly in the adventures of settlement, exploration, military expeditions, and actual warfare against Indians, Americans, and the English. The early settlers did so with a spirit proper to the new world, a spirit of liberty and enterprise unencumbered by the theological and monarchical weight of the middle ages that hung over Europe. Garneau was a liberal, an anticlerical, enamoured of the *philosophes* of the eighteenth century enlightenment and fascinated by the French Revolution. He was quite prepared to sanction popular revolt, at least as an idea, as the appropriate response to inappropriate political behaviour by governing groups. In Canada that inappropriate behaviour had been coloured by a racial struggle imposed upon the country since the Conquest. Garneau's warning was clear: if Britain tempered its assimilationist policies, particularly those of the Union, with wisdom and liberality and if Canadians resisted as a people, then all might be well. If not, anything might happen.

Garneau's somewhat chaotic combination of every idea to hit the western world in the previous one hundred and fifty years was typical of the new middle class in French Canada. So too was his job. As a clerk in the parliament of the united Canadas, he was dependent on government patronage. And as a writer he was dependent on critical acclaim. Like other Canadian artists in the nineteenth and even others well into the twentieth century, he had to hope for a friendly reception abroad before being assured of a wide audience at home. Much of his *Histoire* therefore assumed a European frame of reference and with it a not always flattering portrait of the clerical figures of the past. At a time of religious revival in Canada, clerical figures were not overly sympathetic to Garneau. Sensitive to the criticism, Garneau added a different note to the third volume of his *Histoire* which appeared just as LaFontaine's political, ethnic, and religious alliances bore fruit in the achievement of responsible government. To survive, Garneau now boldly declared, French Canadian nationality required the triple support of religion, laws, and language. What was more, a Great Britain enlightened by the struggles of French Canadians might even assist that survival. Perhaps indeed the two went hand in hand: Britain's own survival in North America might just depend upon the survival of French Canada. By weaving together the ideological and political alliances of the 1840s, Garneau not only justified them but also provided a cultural contribution to nationalism that has affected nationalists and historians ever since.

For the journalist, politician, and would-be philosopher, Etienne Parent, social and economic undertakings of the middle class were the missing ingredient in the recipe for French Canadian survival. He was much more critical of his contemporaries than was Garneau and yet he too provided intellectual justification for the alliances in the making in the 1840s. To the political and clerical leadership that French Canadians had been developing since the Conquest but were now moulding and intertwining in happy conjunction with the liberal institutions of Great Britain, they must add the economic and social enlightenment of the middle class. But that enlightenment required a change of attitude and here Parent clearly indicated that French Canadians were the makers of their own misfortunes. If they did not have such an intellectual aversion to manual labour, they would not overcrowd the professional occupations and then, because there were so few jobs, spend their time seeking government employment. If they did not teach their children to despise industry, those children would not become the inferior employees of English Canadians. If they would only overcome their distaste, they could easily co-operate and even compete with the industrialists, businessmen, and exploiters of Quebec's natural resources. Only if they became as practical and accommodating as the politicians and the clerics of the time would French Canadian survival be ensured.

As of 1844, Parent's ideas found an eager audience in the *Institut canadien* and he was always a welcome speaker. Formed in 1844 by some two hundred young Montrealers as an educational organization outside the existing framework of elementary schools and classical colleges, the *Institut* shared Parent's concern for and critique of contemporary education. But the *Institut* did not share Parent's admiration for the coziness between Bourget's priests and LaFontaine's politicians. In fact, in the future the *Institut* was to provide the groundwork for a number of experimental alliances involving markedly different groups such as the returned Papineau in 1847, the Montreal tories in 1849, and the Clear Grits of Canada West in the early 1850s.

In the meantime the *Institut* may well have fancied itself the popular and social element in Parent's intellectual recipe for preserving French Canadian nationality. It was, in effect, an adult education centre with a library, a reading room, and an organized program of debates and lectures on the intellectual, economic, and political questions of the day, both European and North American. The young men it attracted were part of a new generation of the middle class: too young for the tumultuous times of the late 1830s, they nonetheless were tracing the same path towards the professions and some kind of public occupation. That they were uneasy with their choice is obvious from the repeated questioning of their formal education. All we received was Latin and Greek, Philosophy, History, and Literature, they moaned; all we hear on the streets is politics, trade, taxes, and laws, even sports, fashion, and theatre. What do we know of such things? What they taught themselves about fashion or the theatre is unknown but of politics and economics they were zealous students. They taught themselves so much indeed that they began querying many of the ideas and institutions of their own society. In the *Institut's* lecture halls and in the pages of *L'Avenir*, an increasingly radical paper edited by some of its members and read by them all, appeared arguments for secular, state-controlled schools. The American model was there for the copying, as it had been for some of the radical *patriotes* in the 1830s, with its promise of industry and prosperity. Montreal needed commercial schools; its workers needed practical instruction beyond the rudiments of reading, writing, and arithmetic. The Eastern Townships needed settlement but not by means of the seigneurial system. Perhaps indeed the seigneurial system could be scrapped entirely. And maybe tithes were not such a good thing either. The more the *Institut* members debated topics such as education, progress, science, industry, or the separation of church and state, the more some of them became intrigued by American republican patterns and European revolutionary ideas.

Into that scene stepped someone quite familiar with both. Thanks to the amnesty finally arranged by Governor Metcalfe, Louis-Joseph Papineau returned from exile in Paris in 1845. Just what his political intentions were no one knew. LaFontaine was afraid of him, wary of the place he held in the popular imagination. D.-B. Viger and D.-B. Papineau, respectively Papineau's cousin and brother, looked forward to his joining and thereby strengthening their ranks. Papineau after all owed his return to the governor; surely he would be grateful. Moreover his presence would be useful to Viger in the next elections; for all his intellectual defence of his position in the executive council, Viger felt the lack of assembly support. But Papineau gave the nod to neither faction. Only in 1847 did he decide to return to active politics, the ally of no one. With a great splash, he rejoined the assembly after the mid-winter elections of 1847–48 demanding repeal of the Union and annexation to the United States. His program surprised everyone but particularly delighted the young radicals of L'Avenir and the Institut canadien. Louis-Antoine Dessaulles, Joseph Doutre, Antoine-Aimé and Eric Dorion, Gustave Papineau, young men in their twenties, saluted the ageing radical in their midst. Was he not speaking the language of European liberal nationalism: a separate nationality requires a separate state. Was he not also heralding contemporary civilization: American trade, commerce, industry, and prosperity were the sure marks of progress. Was he not also uneasy about the growing power of the priests? Papineau may well have named the church a necessary national institution in the 1830s, but that did not entail direct political activity by priests in the 1840s. Again the young radicals cheered.

The church, obviously, did not agree. The more noise Papineau and L'Avenir made, the closer the clergy moved towards LaFontaine. In the public debate with L'Avenir, the Mélanges religieux found welcome support from the pro-LaFontaine papers. Indeed the editor of the Mélanges in 1847 was Hector Langevin, a law student in the office of LaFontaine's close Montreal ally, A.-N. Morin. Needless to say they all supported each other in the elections of 1847–48 and many of the clergy made their political views known in their sermons. If anything, the Papineau alliance with the young rouges or radicals strengthened that between Bourget and LaFontaine.

The result was a clear victory for the LaFontaine group. Coupled as it was with an equally strong victory for the reformers in Canada West, the stage was now set for the final insistence on responsible government. All the governor had to do was take LaFontaine and Baldwin and some of their allies into the executive council, as representing the majority group in the assembly, and agree to take their advice and act upon it. The new governor, Lord Elgin, did the first and the new "ministers" in the council prepared the second, a bill to indemnify those people who had suffered property loss or damage during the suppression of the "troubles" in 1837 and 1838.

As Elgin pondered his reply to what could be seen as a very cheeky proposal, he was closely watched by another group used to being near the centre of political power and now being shoved aside. The English commercial group was not at all happy with the political or economic events of the 1840s. In some ways the adjustment required of it during the period was greater than that of French Canadians under the threat of assimilation. French Canadians, after all, had had fifty years of parliamentary practice; they knew how to use political tools for their own benefit. But the political power of the commercial group had always been connected to its economic power and in the 1840s, as Britain moved toward free trade which would eliminate the merchants' preferred place in British markets, the imperial underpinnings of that economic power were crumbling. Indeed one might well argue that responsible government was less a result of political efforts than a consequence of British economic indifference. Certainly the philosophic stand on which the British government had rejected Durham's recommendation of responsible government in 1839—the indivisibility of sovereignty—quickly evaporated in the light of free trade ten years later.

Dispelled also by the times and by British economic developments was the dream of empire that Canadian commercial agents had harboured for generations. True they now had their canals and a unified political route to the centre of the continent; the Union had assured that and Britain had provided loans as well as poor Irish workers for the completion of the St. Lawrence canal system. And new immigrants settling massively in Canada West provided a tempting economic source and market. But success depended on speed, geography, American co-operation, and British preference. In the 1840s, every one of these let the Canadian commercial class down. By the time the St. Lawrence canal system was in full operation towards the end of the decade, American railways, along with the older Erie canal whose route they followed, were already drawing produce not only from the American mid-west but also from Canada West towards the year-round port of New York. The American government also facilitated that path in 1845 and 1846 with Drawback Laws that permitted Canadian imports and then exports to pass through the United States, in bond, without paying duties, on their way from or to transatlantic markets.

The British government even favoured the American route by its gradual move toward free trade inaugurated in 1842 but only completed in 1849. The first hints of free trade dismayed merchants in Canada. Their livelihood, they argued, depended on their having easier access to British markets than did other suppliers of food-stuffs and timber. Surely the British empire depended upon that too. By the 1840s Britain was no longer so sure. Its industrial demand for raw products and markets far surpassed the colonies' supplies and needs and the only way to break into non-imperial markets was to accept non-imperial raw materials in exchange, freely, without any import duties. A slight concession was tossed Canada's way in 1843 by means of the Canada Corn Act which permitted American grain to be milled into flour in Canada and enter the British market as Canadian flour hence paying a lower entrance duty than the similar American product. Montreal grain speculators, millers, and shippers rejoiced until the American Drawback Laws cut into their supplies. And then in 1846 the British government simply repealed all its Corn Laws, eliminating all import duties on all grains from any source. At the same time, it undermined the preferred position of Canadian timber in the British market by reducing the import duties of wood coming from other sources. The double blow left merchants in Montreal and Quebec reeling. The final dismantling of the imperial economic system occurred in 1849 although its importance for Canada was more symbolic than real. The Navigation Acts by which imperial commerce had to be conducted in imperial ships came to an end. For many Canadian merchants, the empire came to an end too. They might as well have responsible government. And when the newly responsible governor announced, in French, that he would sanction the payment of public funds to former rebels, they might as well burn the parliament buildings. Which they did.

In spite of the merchants' complaints, the period was by no means one of economic disaster. The grain trade responded to rising prices on the international markets until 1847 and again after 1850. Commerce along the St. Lawrence shifted west and bene-fited Montreal greatly. The timber trade expanded its territory into the Saguenay and further up the Ottawa. The American market for sawn lumber began to look promising in the 1840s and developed phenomenally in the 1850s. Local agriculture, still with imports from Canada West, fed those involved with the timber trade as well as the vast number of canal workers. Slowly it climbed out of the disasters of the early nineteenth century; by the 1850s there were even exportable products, with the north-south route an in-creasing attraction. Already a new form of transportation to facil-itate that route was inching its way across the land: Quebec's first railway dates in fact from 1836 and joined the St. Lawrence south of Montreal to the Richelieu at St. Jean. By the 1850s railway fever had taken hold of Montreal business interests and they once again began dreaming of harnessing the American mid-west to their commercial empire. One of the reasons for the recurring dream was the developing ethnic differentiation in commercial activities: former Americans dominated the north-south trade; French Cana-dians directed local commerce in the St. Lawrence valley, and the English controlled the western ties to empire. They all, along with everyone else, had to cope with the depression that struck in the late 1840s: bad harvests, declining international prices, lagging commerce, business failures, diseased immigrants, and poverty-stricken emigrants characterized the years 1847, 1848, and 1849.

But that was temporary and the new decade opened a period of unrivalled activity and prosperity in the Canadian economy. What then were some Canadian merchants doing rioting in the streets of Montreal in the spring of 1849? What were they doing a few months later in a momentary alliance with the young radicals of *L'Avenir* advocating annexation to the United States? Lord Elgin spotted the incongruity, referring to the allies as old tories and *jeune France*, the former bemoaning an economic loss and the latter heralding a new society. In fact the merchants were soothing more their self-esteem than their pocketbooks. Their unhappiness, and the alliance, lasted only the time of the depression. So too did the annexation sentiment, Louis-Antoine Dessaulles of the *Institut canadien* being the only one to continue carrying a torch for the American utopia. What really troubled the merchants was the political meaning of the economic and legislative activities of the 1840s. Having carefully spent the last half century currying favour with the governor and gradually acquiring key places in his councils for a public display of their political and economic power, they were now being unceremoniously shoved aside. Under Sydenham's direction, the legislative council lost its pre-eminence and took second place to the executive council. Its members even had to bear the final insult in 1855 when the council was made elective. In the meantime, as the executive council took on greater importance the governors of the 1840s tended to fill it with assembly members and French ones at that. Since the commercial class had rarely been successful in electing many of its members to the assembly, it was increasingly cut off from the offices of political power. No wonder they burned the parliament buildings in 1849. By then British institutions meant less to them than to many French Canadians.

Some of them in fact were closely connected to a peculiarly French Canadian institution. There were many English owners of seigneuries by the late 1840s; they and their French Canadian and clerical counterparts came under increasing attack from their erstwhile radical allies. Ironically, the *rouges* of *L'Avenir* and the *Institut canadien* were taking up one of the very early cries, long since abandoned, of the English merchants in Quebec; they even used some of their same arguments to denounce the seigneurial system. It was a hindrance to progress, they claimed, sapping initiative and enterprise, paralyzing both agriculture and industry. They also added their own ideological perspective. The seigneurial system was undemocratic in that it placed seigneur and *habitant* in a hierarchical relationship one to the other, with the seigneur taking on the airs of a lesser god and exploiting his dependent *habitants*. Instances of the exploitation were legion: seigneurial dues rose constantly as the seigneurs took advantage of a change of tenant to raise the payments; certain requirements, such as the milling of *habitant* grain in seigneurial mills, were increased to the benefit of the seigneur; at the same time, the seigneurs let their mills and other obligatory facilities fall into disrepair. The *Institut canadien* headed the organized campaign for the abolition of the regime from 1848 until 1854. It called meetings and organized petitions, it used the pages of *L'Avenir*, and it invited seigneurial tenants to meet in its lecture rooms. In doing so it lost the support of Louis-Joseph Papineau who was engaging in all the ills which the *Institut* decried on his own seigneury of *Petite Nation*. But it gained the support of the assembly and by 1850 there were resolutions to end the system. By 1854 the *Institut* had succeeded in its campaign to abolish the seigneurial system, although the proposed process was not to its liking. Seigneurs were to be indemnified for their loss of property and prestige; tenants, with some assistance from the state, would gradually buy their holdings from the seigneur and transfer them to freehold tenure. Well into the twentieth century, numerous people were still paying off their seigneurial obligations.

Like the seigneurial system, certain individuals of the 1840s disappeared in the next decade while certain patterns of political behaviour continued on. LaFontaine, Baldwin, Viger, and Papineau all faded from public view in the early 1850s. Only Bourget and the *Institut canadien* went on to conclude a tremendous battle in the 1870s. But the lines of political demarcation remained, as did the nationalist justification and critique. So too did the major question posed by the period: just how was Quebec to come to terms with the rest of British North America? Thanks largely to LaFontaine's politics and his skilful insistence on full and responsible British political institutions, assimilation was no longer one of the answers. Rather, as one historian, Jacques Monet, has suggested, three possible responses to that question arose in the 1840s and continued to colour politics in Quebec: federalism stemming from the LaFontaine alliances, provincial autonomy from the Viger group, and separatism from Papineau. Certainly recognizable political parties were a direct result of the shifting political alliances of the time. On the one side were LaFontaine's reform connections in both Canada East and Canada West who gradually transformed themselves into Conservatives, the Quebec wing acquiring the nickname *les bleus*; on the other side by the early 1850s were the more radical political graduates of the *Institut canadien* and *L'Avenir*, in turn dubbed *les rouges*, in a somewhat more uneasy alliance with the Clear Grits of Canada West. Even the merchants and businessmen gradually crept back into the political fold in the 1850s as allies of the larger, more conservative group. Where French Canadian politicians and English business interests had quarreled over canals in the 1820s, they joined forces over railways in the 1850s. By no coincidence did George-Etienne Cartier, long-time protégé of LaFontaine, member of the assembly from 1848, become a lawyer for the Grand Trunk Railway. The same combination was also to create Confederation.

SELECT BIBLIOGRAPHY

Bernard, Jean-Paul. *Les Rouges: libéralisme, nationalisme et anticléri-calisme au milieu du XIXe siècle.* Montreal: Les presses de l'Université du Québec, 1971.

Careless, J.M.S. *The Union of the Canadas: The Growth of Canadian Institutions, 1841–1857.* Toronto: McClelland and Stewart, 1967.

Hardy, René. "L'activité sociale du curé de Notre-Dame de Québec: aperçu de l'influence du clergé au milieu du XIXe siècle." *Histoire sociale/Social History* 6 (1970):5–32.

Monet, Jacques. "French-Canadian Nationalism and the Challenge of Ultramontanism." *Annual Report.* Canadian Historical Association, 1966. Pp. 41–55.

Monet, Jacques. *The Last Cannon Shot: A Study of French-Canadian Nationalism, 1837–1850.* Toronto: University of Toronto Press, 1969.

Nish, Elizabeth, ed. *Racism or Responsible Government: The French Canadian Dilemma of the 1840s.* Toronto: Copp Clark, 1967.

Ormsby, William G. *The Emergence of the Federal Concept in Canada, 1839–1845.* Toronto: University of Toronto Press, 1969.

Pouliot, Léon. *Monseigneur Bourget et son temps.* Montreal: Editions Beauchemin, 1955.

Robertson, Susan Mann (Trofimenkoff). "The Institut Canadien, an Essay in Cultural History." Unpublished M.A. thesis, University of Western Ontario, 1965.

Tucker, Gilbert Norman. *The Canadian Commercial Revolution, 1845–1851.* New Haven: Yale University Press, 1936.

Tulchinsky, Gerald. *The River Barons, Montreal Businessmen and the Growth of Industry and Transportation 1837–53.* Toronto: University of Toronto Press, 1977.

Wallot, Jean-Pierre. "Le régime seigneurial et son abolition au Canada." *Canadian Historical Review* 50 (1969):367–93.

". . . and spilled over into the Eastern Townships."
New clearing, Brompton, 1865.

7 The Confederation Risk

Confederation was the sixth and, to the present, most durable attempt at having French and English live together in the same territory. It was the only one in which French Canadians had much of a say. None of the previous attempts—the Conquest with its military regime in 1760, the Royal Proclamation of 1763, the Quebec Act in 1774, the Constitution of 1791, or the Union of 1841—had requested even a by-your-leave of French Canadians. Each moreover had offered assimilation or separation: French and English must live together or live apart. Neither formula had worked. Now in the 1860s French Canadians were to have their say in the risky endeavour of combining the two formulae: French and English would live both together and apart at the same time and in the same territory. The risk seemed foolhardy to many, then and since. Indeed most of the flaws that later generations have indicated in the agreement are mere echoes of the fears expressed at the time. And yet the risk was taken, abetted by the political, economic, and ideological climate of the 1850s and 1860s. The same forces have made the experiment both viable and fearful ever since.

Canadians were not the only ones taking national risks in the mid-nineteenth century. Just to the south in the early 1860s, Americans were tearing themselves apart in civil war in order to reconstruct themselves on a pattern designed by certain groups in the north. Across the Atlantic, France experimented with yet another revolution in 1848, another republic, then an empire once again in 1852 only to return to a republic in 1870. In the 1860s both Germany and Italy were undergoing unification with particular groups imposing their will and their plans for the future state upon others. The politicians, the military, and the press each took a hand in organizing and justifying the new national arrangements. The Canadian press followed it all, picking up the latest European developments by the new telegraph from Halifax, quoting large extracts (only a week old thanks to the new steamships) from the European press, and sometimes even taking sides. Organizing states was in the air and Canadians were not immune. The only peculiarity they added to the international scene was the absence of force. Politicians and their allies in business, not the military, created Confederation in the mid-1860s. Only afterwards did the people voice their opinion, electing old politicians to new positions.

The absence of force did not mean the absence of soldiers in Canada. All sorts of them were lurking about. Some were real and present in the colony, others more in the imaginations of fearful Canadians. Among the real ones were members of the British garrisons in various Canadian towns. But they were anxious to be gone, as was the British government to withdraw them. Indeed, Britain had been hinting ever since the 1840s when its own economic retrenchment coincided with colonial political swagger that Canada take on more of its own defence. More troublesome were the American soldiers, using the confused military and political situation of the American Civil War to dart in and out of Canada. A handful of southern Confederate soldiers staged a raid on St. Alban's, Vermont, from a base in Quebec and stirred up an international dispute involving Britain, Canada, and the northern American states. Then there were the American members of the Irish Fenian Brotherhood who, by a series of surprise attacks on Canada, hoped to annoy the British government into rendering justice to their native Ireland. No one knew what the reaction might be among the many Irish in Canada. Even more disturbing, however, were the imaginary soldiers Canadians conjured up. Supposing a victorious army from the American north decided to turn its battle laurels into conquest? What could anyone, let alone the few British soldiers in Canada, do in the face of that? One suggestion was that the British North American colonies join together; they could thus strengthen each other's defences and relieve Britain of the bother. The risk was evident and so was the folly, as some

French Canadian opponents of Confederation pointed out: the border was far too long and the expense would be monumental. The last thing Canada needed was more expenses. Already the combined Canada East and Canada West had managed to triple its public debt in the single decade 1850 to 1860. Most of the expense had been incurred for canal and railway construction. And most, wailed a number of unhappy voices, profited Canada West. Certainly the major railway construction was there although improvements in the St. Lawrence channel below Montreal were made to facilitate the movement of ocean-going vessels. Above Montreal, the Grand Trunk Railway crept along north of the river and the two lower lakes towards Sarnia, built to high British construction standards and low Canadian traffic. It was the latest and most expensive version of the old commercial dream of Montreal's English business interests: the new railroad would draw the produce of the American mid-west out along the St. Lawrence route, all to the benefit of Canadian shippers and forwarders. Like the earlier dreams, this one also was too grand and too late. Even the gauge of the Grand Trunk was wider than that of American lines, rendering the transfer of goods at the western border difficult and therefore expensive. Before the line was completed, the New York Central had already captured much of the American mid-west market and linked it to New York. The Grand Trunk attempted to counter the competition by acquiring its own line to the American port of Portland, but it always hauled a greater burden of debt than of freight, and over a longer distance, than did the American railways. Nevertheless the expansion continued. The Grand Trunk added a Lévis to Richmond line to give itself a roundabout route through the Eastern Townships to Quebec City; it also constructed a new line from Lévis to Rivière-du-Loup.

Expensive railways may have made some sense in the boom years of the 1850s. With the international demand for grain and timber soaring because of British involvement in the Crimean War and American industrial development, Canada could never move its products fast enough. Indeed, far more rail lines inched their way south from Canadian sources to American markets than headed east or west. In 1854 reciprocity sanctioned the mutual north-south interest by permitting free trade in natural products between the United States and Canada and free use of each other's transportation routes for the export of natural products beyond North America. Together, the boom, the railways, and the trade agreements emphasized the double direction of Canada's external trade: south to the United States and across the Atlantic to Britain. From Britain in particular, the prosperity attracted immigrants and investments by the hundreds of thousands.

Those same transatlantic and North American ties also rendered the Canadian colonies vulnerable. When financial difficulties beset both Britain and the United States after 1857, the repercussions were felt in Canada. Investors held back their largesse and demanded payment on earlier loans. The Grand Trunk could neither complete its lines nor repay its debts and as its problems increased, so did those of the Canadian government. Not only had the government backed the Grand Trunk financially, it had done so politically. Numerous government members with direct interests in the railway had carefully guided its business through the shoals of an elected assembly. Among those members were two key people from Canada East, both of whom would later appear as "fathers" of Confederation: Alexander Tilloch Galt from the Eastern Townships and George-Etienne Cartier from Montreal. By the late 1850s they were toying with a risky solution to the Grand Trunk's virtual bankruptcy and the Canadian government's consequent problems. The answer lay not in retrenchment, much less in a declaration of insolvency, but rather in expansion. If the British North American colonies joined together they could add markets, people, and territory to Canada's underused transportation system. By increasing trade and expanding traffic, the financial burdens of both railway and government could be lessened. More people could absorb a smaller amount of the larger debt. Of course still more railways would have to be built, to the east and perhaps to the west. . .

The idea began to appear even more interesting in the troubled years of the early 1860s when Canada's two major international trade connections pulled in opposite directions. From Britain the sources of credit, tarnished by the financial crises of the years 1857 to 1862, dried up, leaving the Grand Trunk stranded and causing numerous bank failures in Canada. Declining commerce meant declining government revenue, the duty on imports having always provided the major source of funds. Fewer funds meant an increased public debt. The holders of much of that debt, powerful British backers of the Grand Trunk such as the Baring Brothers, began to add their voice to the wild Canadian scheme to consolidate all the British North American colonies and thereby stabilize the financial situation. At the same time contradictory pulls from the south affected the Canadian economy much more favourably although they too ultimately pointed toward a union of the British North American colonies. Between 1861 and 1865 the American Civil War created such enormous demands for agricultural products that even Quebec's sluggish agricultural economy responded. The war also kept American manufacturers so busy supplying the domestic market that they exported little to Canada. Into the vacuum stepped Canadian industries, many of them in Quebec. Quebec textiles, leather, shoes, and clothing found a ready local market in Canada East and Canada West. But what would happen once the war was over? The Americans were already threatening an end to reciprocity. And their manufacturers would surely try to regain their Canadian markets. Could Canadian agriculture and industry withstand the post-war changes? Perhaps they too should seek wider markets and maybe even protection in a union of the British North American colonies.

With the promise of economic development, the Confederation dream acquired substance. New industries might provide employment for the increasing number of French Canadians having to search for work beyond Quebec, particularly in the United States. They would certainly increase the urban market for agricultural products, construction timber, and firewood. Maybe they would even attract capital although it was painfully evident that Quebec lacked the natural sources of power that were turning the industrial wheels of England and America: coal, steam, and iron. Hydro-electricity came at the very end of the century and all Quebec had to offer in the meantime was the tamer water power of streams and rivers for the turning of mill wheels. Yet Quebec did have people, lots of them. Not surprisingly then, light industries blossomed in Quebec using water power as well as cheap, and more often than not, female, labour. As far as its promoters were concerned, Confederation would create new markets and impose import duties on competitive textiles, shoes, and clothing, thereby protecting these industries in Quebec.

In the meantime, the abundant labour supply spilled off Quebec's farms throughout the 1850s and 1860s. Sometimes departing from modernized farms where proximity to markets made machinery possible and children redundant, but more often abandoning traditional farms that could not feed all the offspring, young people by the thousands headed for the towns. The young men often took a circuitous route via the lumber camps. They followed Quebec's expanding wood trade ever farther up the Ottawa Valley or beyond the Saguenay into the Lac St. Jean region. They appeared in new towns like Chicoutimi, and they acquired skills in the sawmills and in the sash and door, shingle, and furniture factories that were the early industrial offshoots of the wood trade. Then they bartered their skills for industrial jobs in the larger urban centres of Quebec or New England. There they caught up with their female counterparts who had taken a more direct route to town. With little prospect of job or marriage in a rural setting, young women set out to find both in the cities. By the 1860s they already formed the majority of young people in Montreal and Quebec City, willing workers for the new industries and tractable servants for middle and upper class families. Their presence heralded the urbanization that characterized the rest of the nineteenth century.

Other people persisted in trying their luck on new farms. Sometimes as individuals and sometimes in organized groups spurred on by colonizing dreams of the clergy or local politicians, new settlers from older rural areas tested out the territory north of Trois-Rivières, broke new land on the south side of Lac St. Jean, filled out that of Beauce county, following the Chaudière River south, and spilled over into the Eastern Townships. The movement into the townships actually changed the ethnic character of that area, as the northern townships became almost totally French Canadian and the southern ones increased their French-speaking population to one quarter. But the economic picture did not alter. Without a nearby lumber camp or better still a road or a railway, there was no ready market for agricultural products. Politicians would soon promise colonization roads and railroads as bounty from Confederation's new provincial governments, but in the meantime French Canadians arrived poor, stayed poor, and, for some of them, moved on poor.

In some ways the politicians spinning dreams of political innovation by means of Confederation were as isolated as the settlers eking out a living in the lower reaches of the Canadian Shield. The politicians were a mere handful of the population separated from their constituents by barriers of class and education and from each other by sectional and sectarian interests. But they had organizing skills at their fingertips and means of communication at their disposal. Confederation was to be their field day, but they could easily make it appear a national undertaking. Few workers or farmers, much less domestic servants, had anything to say about the new political arrangements and only some of the opponents of the scheme thought this was even worth pointing out.

The increasing political difficulties of the Union were almost reason enough for devising a new constitution. Depending on issues and personalities, political groups and alliances crystallized or disintegrated. As far as they were discernible, the lines of political parties joined George-Etienne Cartier's *bleus* from Canada East (conservative inheritors of LaFontaine's political and religious alliances to which were added the English commercial element of Montreal) to John A. Macdonald's Conservatives from Canada West (tory and eastern Ontario remnants of Baldwin's alliances). By deft political manoeuvring this group usually managed to control a majority of the seats in the Union parliament. In opposition was a more fragile association of Antoine-Aimé Dorion's radical *rouges* from Canada East and George Brown's reforming Grits from Canada West. Not the least of the difficulties of these loose alliances was the fact that the vagaries of electoral politics kept tossing up largely *bleu* majorities in Canada East and reform majorities in Canada West. No one was interested in Viger's old idea of double majorities, incompatible as it was with party government, but still everyone grumbled. Particularly the reformers from Canada West. They muttered about "French domination" and complained of bills being forced upon one section of the united Canada by a majority from another section. When they began counting numbers, they became even more annoyed. The population of Canada West had surpassed that of Canada East as early as 1851 but the two sections were locked into a united assembly where each had an equal number of representatives. "Rep. by pop!" cried the reformers with one eye on electoral reform and another on the possible addition of western territories to Upper Canada's domain.

By the early 1860s the difficulties had become impossibilities. Governments could rarely sustain a majority for more than a few months as the four-way pulls in the assembly tugged at the political fabric. In 1863, for example, the assembly's divisions constituted an equal draw from whatever point of view: as many *bleus* and conservatives as reformers and *rouges*; as many *bleus* and *rouges* as reformers and conservatives. The politicians at the time were as dizzy as history students since. There seemed no way out of the impasse, unless of course one risked an even larger political alliance, consolidating and separating at the same time. A federal union might be the answer to Canada's political problems just as it might be to its military, financial, and economic problems. The idea itself was nothing new. Durham had wondered about it on his way across the Atlantic to investigate the rebellions in 1838; Joseph Howe, a prominent member in the assembly of Nova Scotia, had suggested it as Nova Scotia became the first of the British North American colonies to achieve responsible government in 1848. *Le Canadien* wrote about it in 1847. Joseph-Charles Taché discussed it in a pamphlet in 1858 as did Joseph-Edouard Cauchon in the *Journal de Québec.* Cartier and Galt appear to have been convinced of it about the same time; Macdonald was slower, awaiting some break in the political impasse that would make the risk worth taking. The break came from George Brown in 1864. Swallowing his pride and his intense dislike of both Cartier and Macdonald, Brown offered most of his reform group in the assembly as political support for the *bleus* and the Conservatives on the condition that they all work together to realize a federation. No one, it seems, approached Dorion and his *rouges* and they were left in opposition, joined by a few unrepentant reformers, wondering bitterly about Brown's motives. Needless to say the *rouges* subsequently constituted the major opponent of Confederation.

The coalition was no sooner in place than it had plans for the federation clearly delineated and a timetable for putting it into place. In September 1864 at Charlottetown, the Canadians convinced Maritimers debating a union among themselves to join the larger venture. By October, delegates from the five British North American colonies (the united Canada, Nova Scotia, New Brunswick, Prince Edward Island, and Newfoundland), were meeting in Quebec to frame the new constitution. After that each assembly would debate the Quebec Conference proposals for federation, presumably pass them, and London would give its final sanction. With any luck, a year would suffice. The year extended to three, mostly because two of the Atlantic colonies desisted from the scheme and a third, New Brunswick, had the temerity to hold an election on the issue, only to see its pro-Confederation government defeated. By the time another election was held, carefully arranged to ensure victory for the new plan, and a suitably decorous conference held in London, it was 1867. The British parliament then gave its quick accord, actually spending more time debating a dog tax, and the British North America Act became law with royal sanction at the end of March and implementation on July 1.

Confederation both joined and separated the constituent parts. The new Dominion of Canada was to be a federation of four provinces with a central parliament consisting of an elected House of Commons and an appointed Senate. Members of those two bodies would come from all the regions of the new country. At the same time each of the federating colonies retained a distinct existence as a province with its own provincial parliament. Between the federal and provincial governments was a fairly strict division of powers and interest: trade, commerce, defence, banking, general taxation, and criminal law concerned the federal government; property, civil rights, direct taxation, schools, hospitals, and public lands concerned the provinces. The federal government was assigned those powers of general interest as well as anything not specified as being under provincial jurisdiction.

The speed with which the proposals and later the BNA Act were passed as well as their content dismayed the *rouges*. Their opposition, expressed in pamphlets and in the press, at public meetings and in the Canadian assembly, was in fact more strident than the support orchestrated by George-Etienne Cartier and the *bleus*. Ultimately it was less successful because Cartier could orchestrate elections as well. But while the debate raged in public, the *rouge* opposition revealed much of the character and many of the risks of the proposed Confederation.

The *rouges* never did share the fear of the United States that was one of the determinants of Confederation. On the contrary, their admiration for American democratic institutions and American commercial bustle knew few bounds. Some of them even wondered whether for Quebec, the status of a sovereign state in the United States might not be preferable to the great unknown of Confederation. Certainly they argued that the new federation could not expect to emulate American progress unless it adopted American institutions. The Civil War, they claimed, was not the result of a faulty constitution but rather was the inevitable clash between the "progressive" north and the "obscurantist" south. The Confederation proposal to avoid American problems by reversing the division of powers and giving more to the central government than to the provinces was no guarantee of peace or stability or progress. Much less could it ensure defence against any potential American invasion. If a successful northern army chose to invade Canada, there was little to be done. As good nineteenth century liberals, the *rouges* saw the path to peace through trade, commerce, and international good will rather than through the expenditure of large amounts of money on defence.

Government expenditures in general troubled the *rouges*. They were familiar with the financial past of the united Canada and they did not think it augured well for the future. Canada East had picked up more than its fair share of the accumulating debt. How much of the vastly increased expenditure entailed by expansion to the Atlantic and dreams of the Pacific would it also have to bear?

And to what advantage? Cartier and his business allies could only hold out the prospect of increased intercolonial trade and international investment and thereby a return to the prosperity of the early 1850s. But supposing it did not work? The *rouges* were sceptical and fearful. To them, the notion of lessening the financial burdens of Canada by spreading them out over a larger territory and greater population made no sense. If anything, the two parts of the present Union should simply recover their own autonomy, perhaps creating a tiny federation between them for their few common problems.

The larger federation, the *rouges* suspected, was a grand design to profit railway promoters and their political backers among the *bleus* of Canada East and the Conservatives of Canada West. Railways, notably the Grand Trunk, had been so intertwined with Canadian politics over the previous decade that there was little reason to think they would play any different role in an even larger country. The *rouges* had protested the connections ever since their first appearance in the Canadian assembly in the early 1850s. Now they wondered just how many Grand Trunk agents were hanging around the periphery of the Quebec Conference. Certainly there were some at the conference table itself, two indeed were from among the six Canada East delegates—Alexander Tilloch Galt and George-Etienne Cartier. One of the resolutions of that conference stipulated the completion of an intercolonial railway at government expense from the eastern end of the Grand Trunk line at Rivière-du-Loup through New Brunswick and into Nova Scotia. Even minuscule Prince Edward Island was holding out for a railroad. Everyone was in on the act and the *rouges* wondered whether the entire show was not a benefit performance for the railway companies.

To their political cynicism about Confederation, the *rouges* added a philosophic opposition to certain aspects of it. The proposal for a senate whose members were appointed by the government for life, for example, was undemocratic. Moreover it was an anachronism, as the Union government had already recognized when it made the legislative council elective in the mid-1850s. Now there was to be an unfortunate return to the old ways. Besides the danger of the majority party in the new federal government simply filling the senate with its friends, there was the principle, debated in Europe and practised in the United States, of the sovereignty of the people. They, and not any intermediaries, should choose their government. And they should also have a say in designing the new constitution. The *rouges* therefore insisted on a plebiscite or at least an election before Confederation became law.

Neither of the democratic demands of the *rouges* had any effect upon the makers of Confederation. To them, the *rouge* notion of popular sovereignty was not only foreign but frightening. It implied rule by the mob; the new senate, the "sober, second thought" of parliamentary democracy, was designed to counter that very danger. What concerned the "fathers" of Confederation was not the nature of the senate but the number and regional distribution of its membership. They haggled over that issue for weeks at the Quebec Conference and were almost prepared to abandon the entire project for the sake of a few senate seats. They certainly had no intention of consulting the people at any stage in their deliberations. The people would have their say later. Once the details were worked out and the entire proposal given the sanction of the British parliament, then the people could elect their representatives to work within the new constitution. Following British political practice and principle, the new Canada, like the old, would be a representative democracy with built-in safeguards to offset the potential dangers of even that amount of democracy.

Almost as a last resort, the *rouges* added a nationalist argument to their arsenal of weapons against Confederation. What place would French Canadians have in the new federation that was really a legislative union in disguise? According to the *rouges*, the central government was to have all the powers, the provinces none. They did not dispute the plan for the central government's prominence in trade, commerce, finance, and defence. But there was a host of other, seemingly innocuous powers that revealed the immense weight the new federal government would carry. It was to control criminal law, marriage, divorce, and indirect taxation; it could name all judges and it could disallow provincial laws; it retained all the powers not specifically assigned to the one or the other level of government. And it offered the provinces paltry sums to conduct their paltry affairs. Not only were the provinces not to do much, they were to do it in the pay of the federal government. And in that overwhelming federal government, the Quebec representation was to be fixed at sixty-five members. Shades of Durham danced in the heads of the *rouges* as they saw his plans to eliminate French Canadians come true. In the new central government French Canadians would be totally and permanently outnumbered. Confederation was, in short, a national risk.

From that followed a whole series of bleak predictions. French Canadian politicians, a minority in the new House of Commons, would easily be tempted to trade their nationality for personal favours. They would even do so in English, for the French language would never survive its minority position in the federal parliament. Moreover, in any national or religious crisis English Canadians would forget their political differences and unite to defend their racial interests; there too the force of numbers would crush the French Canadians. The federal government could even, given its control of defences and its numerical composition, force French Canadians to take up arms against their will. In the face of those dire possibilities, what could a powerless provincial government in Quebec do, even if it did have a French Canadian majority? Precious little, warned the *rouges* whose list of national perils provided many a future nationalist, rarely of *rouge* vintage, with ready-made complaints against Confederation.

The *rouge* opposition failed to stop or even amend the plans for Confederation. It did give some people pause as a mere four votes divided French Canadian supporters from French Canadian opponents in the Canadian assembly's vote on the Quebec Conference resolutions in 1865. But the assembly as a whole adopted the resolutions by a vote of ninety-one to thirty-three, eleven English Canadian opponents joining the twenty-two *rouges*. The *rouges* themselves disagreed over what possible alternative they could propose. Some of them backed off from the battle once the six Quebec bishops, after much dithering among themselves, publicly endorsed the new arrangement: clerical sanction followed royal sanction in the early spring of 1867. And in the federal elections the following autumn, clerics and *bleus* used their considerable electoral expertise to slash *rouge* representation in the new House of Commons. It was easy enough to smear the *rouges* with anticlericalism and annexationism, two popular phobia of the 1860s carefully cultivated by the press, the priests, and the politicians. Leader Antoine-Aimé Dorion, for example, retained his riding of Hochelaga by a mere twenty-three votes. Although the popular vote was closer than the number of seats, fifty-four percent of the vote and forty-seven seats in the new federal House went to the *bleus* while forty-five percent of the vote and seventeen seats went to the *rouges*, the latter were now divided over the question of continuing their opposition or accepting the *fait accompli*.

In spite of, or perhaps because of, their nineteenth century liberal enthusiasm, the *rouges* ignored an essential ingredient that would make Confederation work. Behind the risks which everyone saw was the will and even more the ability to organize and control. The economy, politics, the nation itself—whether it be French Canada or the new nationality the Confederation promised—came under the organizing spell of the late nineteenth century. Weaving that spell was a network of communications of every imaginable sort whose tremendous expansion characterized the period. From railways to ideology, Confederation came out the winner, its message of assimilation accompanied by separation written large across the land.

In response to the economic risk, Confederation offered to organize and control a viable commercial economy on the northern half of the North American continent. Internal organization entailed the creation of commercial links between the British North American colonies where few had existed before. Confederation therefore abolished intercolonial tariffs and constructed intercolonial railroads. The promise was prosperity for all, but the means was central control as the new federal government directed interprovincial trade and enticed the provinces by taking over their debts and paying them an annual subsidy. Similarly, the central government was able to entice or warn the new country's trading partners by skilful use of the tariff. The offer not to impose tariffs at all, repeated on numerous occasions throughout the rest of the nineteenth century, might persuade the Americans to renew the reciprocity agreement. If not, severe tariffs could serve both as retaliation and as a declaration of commercial independence from the United States and Great Britain. Tariffs supplied funds which the federal government used primarily for railway construction and the payment of the subsidies to the provinces. Later they were to protect Canadian industries and entice American ones to establish branch plants in Canada. As means of communication, the tariff and the railway perhaps gave the outside world the clearest message: the new nation was healthy, stable, and reliable. The response was immediate and just what the framers of Confederation hoped it would be in the form of international investment in Canada, all of it confirmed by Canadian agents in London, by the imperial post, and soon by the new transatlantic telegraph.

Linking the economic to the political organization of Confederation was George-Etienne Cartier. A Montreal lawyer and director of the Grand Trunk Railway, Cartier had legal, business, and social connections with the English- and French-speaking elites of Canada's major commercial city. As an assembly member since 1848 and Quebec's, perhaps Canada's, most prominent politician, he had allies throughout the country. With them he shared conservative values, a respect for property, a suspicion of American political practices, a horror of universal suffrage, and a disgust for the messiness of Union politics. Confederation was a means of clarifying the politics and confirming the values. By a skilful division of powers between the central and provincial parliaments, Confederation would permit the assimilation of those economic and political interests common to all and the separation of those cultural and political interests peculiar to each. Where there was any overlapping as concerned French Canadians, Cartier was convinced that Quebec ministers in the federal government would safeguard their rights. But then he used a separatist argument to convince French Canadians that Confederation was a good thing. A parliament of their own in the old capital of Quebec City would protect the French language, the Catholic religion, and the civil law that was characteristic of Quebec but not found in any of the other provinces. Even if some seats in the new provincial parliament were reserved for the English-speaking element, they would always be a minority. Quebec could develop its own affairs in its own way. Agricultural, commercial, and railroad development was all there, waiting for Quebecois to undertake. Besides, threatened Cartier, there was no alternative. Better to do the organizing ourselves, even as a minority at Ottawa but a majority in Quebec, than to have it done by Americans. Confederation or annexation: there was no other choice.

Cartier had numerous means of conveying his message. His

political network extended the one designed by LaFontaine in the 1840s and he controlled it so thoroughly that, for example, his three French Canadian colleagues at the Quebec Conference barely whispered a word. Elections themselves, still without secret ballot and with additional property qualifications for both electors and elected, were also a means of controlling votes. Cartier and his allies had all the organizational skills to ensure victories and the new federation tossed in a bonus by permitting the same politicians to seek election to both the federal and the provincial parliaments. The politicians themselves spread government patronage into the farthest riding and carefully cultivated the *curés* and the local elites of the tiniest towns. Between political visits, newspapers confirmed the links. So did the Sunday sermon of the local priest. Cartier was not always sure of the benefits of a clerical alliance and he was sensitive to the *rouge* charge that the priests exercised undue influence in politics. Moreover, he and Bishop Bourget did not always see eye to eye on matters secular or spiritual. Still, if the priests could be kept in hand, there was no doubt they were the closest and most continuous tie to the electors.

Many of those electors were sensitive to the double national risk of Confederation. A distinctive British North America might be as difficult to achieve as a distinctive French Canada. But that was precisely the Confederation promise: a new nationality was being created and at the same time French Canada was being preserved. To realize the promise and also to mock it, all the agents of cultural communication were called into play, with some specially fashioned for the cause. Proponents of Confederation fed on anti-Americanism and some actually spun dreams of French and Catholic expansion to numerical superiority in the new country. Opponents of Confederation fed on minority status and quoted the designs of western expansionists to outnumber French Canadians. Both the *rouge* pessimism about Confederation and Cartier's optimism about the opportunities open to a French Canadian provincial government were attempts to organize the French Canadian nation, just as conservatism and rejection of the American federal model were attempts to organize the Canadian nation. Each stance had cultural allies in the churches, in the newspapers, in literary and intellectual associations such as the *Institut canadien*, in the popular festivals organized by the Saint Jean Baptiste Society, in the schools, in the mails, in poems, songs, and novels, and in the family.

One idea simplified the attempt at intellectual organization by all these cultural agents. This was the notion of separate spheres. Originating in the western world's experience of industrialization and its social ramifications, and usually associated with the family, the theory of separate spheres is discernible in the economic, political, and national organization that made Confederation viable. According to the theory, two spheres divided human undertakings into complementary but separate functions and assigned them to the two sexes. Whether as an ideological prerequisite to industrialization with its specialized tasks, or as a justification of the process or even of its results in removing economic production from the family household and placing it in standardized factories elsewhere, the notion of separate spheres provided codes of behaviour for the growing number of middle class families. Men departed from the home to undertake economic activities in a public work place; women remained in the home to accomplish emotional tasks in private. Men were rational and intellectual; women were emotional and cultural. Men designed the state; women organized the family. Men created and women sustained.

Canadians were familiar with the notion as it pertained to the sexes. Sermons of the 1850s and 1860s reiterated the theme of separate spheres, adding theological justification to a secular and historical development. And in the 1870s the topic became even more popular as the "woman question" became one of public debate. The application to other areas of experience was easily made, especially when growing numbers of French Canadians began consciously seeking the differences that bound them to and yet distinguished them from their English-speaking compatriots. The linguistic and religious differences were obvious but the search for differentiation did not stop there. Rather there were cultural characteristics peculiar to the two people. Curiously, those characteristics resembled the very ones assigned to the two sexes: French Canadians had a cultural, emotional, artistic, sustaining, and civilizing function to play in a country dominated by English Canadian commercial, economic, rational, and materialistic activities. To the makers of Confederation, the complementarity was as essential as the differences and hence they easily devised double spheres of political, economic, constitutional, and national activity where each would specialize and the whole would profit. Only much later would historian Lionel Groulx speak disdainfully of Confederation as a mixed marriage, and thereby justify dissolution; later still would politician René Lévesque use the image of the incompatible marriage bed to present his argument for separation. At the time of Confederation the task for Quebec was to consolidate and organize ideological unanimity within one of the spheres. A particular brand of the Catholic clergy set about it assiduously.

114   THE DREAM OF NATION

SELECT BIBLIOGRAPHY

Bernard, Jean-Paul. *Les rouges. Libéralisme, nationalisme et anticléri-calisme au milieu du XIXe siècle.* Montreal: Les presses de l'Université du Québec, 1971.

Bonenfant, Jean-Charles. *La naissance de la Confederation.* Montreal: Leméac, 1969.

Careless, J.M.S. *The Union of the Canadas: The Growth of Canadian Institutions, 1841-1857.* Toronto: McClelland and Stewart, 1967.

Cornell, Paul G. *The Alignment of Political Groups in Canada, 1841-1867.* Toronto: University of Toronto Press, 1962.

Cornell, Paul G. *The Great Coalition.* Ottawa: Canadian Historical Association, 1966.

Creighton, Donald. *The Road to Confederation: The Emergence of Canada, 1863-1867.* Toronto: Macmillan, 1964.

Cross, D. Suzanne. "The Neglected Majority: The Changing Role of Women in 19th Century Montreal." *Histoire sociale/Social History* 6 (1973): 202-23.

Faucher, Albert. *Québec en Amérique au XIXe siècle.* Montreal: Fides, 1973

Groulx, Lionel Adolphe. *La Confédération canadienne: ses origines.* Montreal: Le Devoir, 1918.

Hamelin, Jean, and Yves Roby. "L'évolution économique et sociale du Québec, 1851-1896." *Recherches sociographiques* 10(1969):157-69.

Hamelin, Jean, and Yves Roby. *Histoire économique du Québec, 1851-1896.* Montreal: Fides, 1971.

Harris, R. Cole, and John Warkentin. *Canada Before Confederation: A Study in Historical Geography.* Toronto: Oxford University Press, 1974.

Ullmann, Walter. "The Quebec Bishops and Confederation." *Canadian Historical Review* 44(1963):213-34.

Waite, P.B. *The Life and Times of Confederation, 1864-1867: Politics, Newspapers and the Union of British North America.* Toronto: University of Toronto Press, 1962.

Young, Brian. *George-Etienne Cartier, Montreal Bourgeois.* Montreal: McGill-Queen's University Press, 1981.

"Catholicism held out an option to women via the religious communities."
Hotel Dieu Hospital, Quebec, 1870s.

8 The Clerical Offensive

In the last third of the nineteenth century the clergy was as much
a means of national unity as the railroad. The clergy in fact had
better networks across Quebec than did the railway, for all its
frenetic promoters. Some clerics even attempted to harness the iron
horse to their cause, urging railways as colonization routes when
politicians were desperately seeking commercial traffic and votes.
The attempt required political pressure and certain members of
the clergy became very adept at using their privileged and increasingly numerous positions in society to exercise that pressure. They
also developed a vast ideological justification for their activities,

drawing on European sources of ultramontanism and Quebec sources of nationalism in order to spin a dream of French Canadian unanimity under clerical direction. They would be the ones to guide French Canadian destinies along paths different from and more worthy than those of English Canadians. The message was heard in every corner of the land thanks to a vast array of communicators, some direct, some more subtle. Given that array it is surprising that the dream of nation inspired by the ultramontanes never did become a reality. Instead, most Quebecois chose the path of the railway towards its promised destiny of North American prosperity. Along the way, however, they witnessed, sometimes with gratitude, sometimes with amusement, and sometimes with annoyance, clerical struggles for their national souls.

Like all ideologies, ultramontanism was a mix of social, cultural, and intellectual forces. Looking "beyond the mountains," that is, over the Alps to the papal presence in Rome, became a common pastime of certain conservative groups in Europe in the nineteenth century. Fearful of the revolutionary ferment on the streets and in people's minds, certain Catholic spokesmen turned to Rome for guidance and assurance in a world turned topsy-turvy by free-thinkers, liberals, socialists, and anarchists. Having found that all their cherished notions of hierarchy, order, place, *noblesse oblige*, and working class deference were under fire, such people responded by developing, with papal assistance, a strong antidote of ultra-Catholic dogmatism that denied any place in the intellectual, social, or political spectrum for notions other than theirs. The framing of an ultramontane ideology allowed its adherents to make sense of their environment, to cope with the many changes of the nineteenth century, and even to suppose that they might mould some of the changes in their own favour. Like any ideology, ultramontanism reflected and legitimized the social status and aspirations of particular groups of people.

In Quebec, looking "beyond the mountains" was one of the favourite activities of certain bishops in the latter half of the nineteenth century. Monseigneur Ignace Bourget, bishop of Montreal from 1840 to 1876, was the most adamant looker, although he was later joined by the younger and more systematic thinker, Monseigneur Louis-François Laflèche, highly placed in the diocese of Trois-Rivières since the early 1860s and bishop of Trois-Rivières from 1870 to 1898. Bourget in fact spent much time peering at Rome in person: he made eight trips to the papal see during his tenure as bishop. He imported Roman costume and Roman liturgy for his Montreal priests; the religious communities he brought from France all owed their ecclesiastical foundations to Rome. He spoke the language of papal infallibility and of the *Syllabus of Errors* long before either was formulated in Roman minds or before Laflèche produced a systematic Canadian version of ultramontanism in *Quelques considérations sur les rapports de la société civile avec la religion et la famille* in 1866. He and Laflèche sympathized with papal efforts to retain temporal power over the pontifical states; they even sanctioned the sending of the *Zouaves*, a small contingent of French Canadian soldiers, to Italy in 1868 to assist the pope in his military tribulations against Italian nationalist insurgents bent on unifying Italy and confining the pope to matters spiritual. Yet Bourget's interest in things Roman was more than a matter of aesthetics or dogma. Power was involved. By providing the Quebec clergy with the international stature and prestige of Rome, Bourget might enhance its prominence in Quebec society. Indeed the aura of a European intellectual justification of clerical intervention in civil affairs was perhaps just what the clergy needed to bolster its pretension to speak for the nation. The nation itself might profit from the aura since nothing else would distinguish it more clearly in the new Confederation. Decidedly, ultramontanism could prove most useful in a Quebec setting.

European politics bred ultramontanism; Canadian fears imported it to Quebec. Throughout the nineteenth century intellectual debates and popular uprisings reiterated the great division of the French Revolution, that between liberty and authority. Those Europeans, and Canadians too, who were scandalized by the turmoil traced it back to the Revolution's unceremonious tossing aside of the church and the moral authority of religion in 1790. And they were horrified by what they saw as the logical conclusion of such behaviour in the movement for Italian unification in the mid-nineteenth century: the pope would be deprived of his political control of much of central Italy and Rome would be a secular, not a spiritual capital. How could the pope maintain his moral authority and the independence of the church without having temporal power as well? And if the pope had no temporal power, how could civil society be anything but immoral? Those who suggested a division of the spiritual and the temporal were obviously mistaken for their views would undermine the pope's moral authority and society's moral cohesion. The pope said so, in no uncertain terms in 1864 in his *Syllabus of Errors*, intended primarily for Catholic clergy. In it the pope decried every imaginable form of wrong-thinking from liberal ideas of the separation of church and state to such heretical views as the necessary acceptance by the Roman pontiff of progress, liberalism, or modern civilization. Along the way he insisted upon the precedence of ecclesiastical over civil authority and the right of the church to defend its temporal power by force. He even disputed the right of his opponents to voice their opinions: liberals, socialists, and communists, members of secret societies, of bible societies, even of liberal clerical societies were all engaging in the malpractice of freedom of speech; it led inevitably to the corruption of minds and morals. Papal opponents were appalled, but to his advocates he spoke the word of God. Within a few years the church admitted as much by declaring the doctrine of papal infallibility. The pope could not err.

Such views were reassuring to a fearful and beleaguered French

Catholic church in Canada. For just as Monseigneur Bourget was beginning his long campaign to revive Catholicism in Quebec, he had to confront groups of organized liberals, first in intellectual associations and then in political parties, who thought the clergy should remain within the spiritual fold or even, for some very radical thinkers, disappear entirely. Later he had to counter still other politicians, conservative ones at that, who had very decided views about the subordinate place of the church as one institution among many others under the aegis of the state. Moreover that same state was beginning to take an interest in matters which Bourget considered his alone. The new provincial government in 1867 actually established a ministry of education and Bourget had to use all his increasing political influence to have it abolished eight years later. Some lay personnel, notably women of the upper classes, were also undertaking social and charitable work outside the clerically prescribed forms and outside the control of the religious communities. Bourget did not deny that there was work to be done; he was after all bishop of Canada's first industrializing city. Nor did he eschew a place for lay workers in supporting the charitable work of the church. But he was quite clear about the lines of command: they extended from the church down.

In 1866 Monseigneur Laflèche combined the European awareness and Canadian fears into a coherent statement of ultramontanism as befitting Quebec. His *Quelques considérations* . . . were part of a heritage common to many Quebecois, cleric and lay alike, and they found various forms of expression in the press and the pulpit of the time. His was the most thorough argument for the subordination of the temporal state to the spiritual power of the church. For Laflèche everything followed logically from the place of God in the universe. Laflèche's God was creator and guide and protector, omnipresent at the beginning of time and throughout history. He assigned missions and roles to families, to nations, and to states which they ignored at their peril. He assured his own institutional presence in the form of the church and spoke through the pope. He delegated his authority to the father in the family and to the civil leader in the state. Thus, Laflèche considered all three human institutions—the church, the family, and the state—as being of divine origin although their functions made some more divine than others. The church's duty to teach the law of God put it in closest touch with the source of that law. The family's duty to transmit the law of God across generations linked it to the church for knowledge but directly to God for permanence. The state's duty was the lowly one of policing, protecting against disorder. Given the divine origin of the three, Laflèche saw all of them as subordinate to the will of God. But since the church formulated that will, it was necessarily superior to the other two.

To fortify the place of the church, and thus the role of the priest in society, Laflèche added his idea of the nation. Formulated by the family through the transmission of language, tradition, and faith, the nation, according to Laflèche, had a quasi-divine status to begin with. But since faith was the most important national ingredient, the nation required the supervision of the church. That supervision entailed the control of education to ensure the continuance of the faith. Moreover the state must lend its support to the church since the state could not exist without the foundation of faith in the nation. The state thus had religious duties and would in fact be acting against the interest of the nation if it denied them. But the state in turn required the assistance of the church not only to define those duties but also to ensure that the best people were at the head of the government to carry them out. The church must therefore have a voice in the selection of governments; by means of its priests, the church must help electors choose the right candidates. With what may have been a deliberate confusion of the nation as cultural entity and the nation as political state, Laflèche was able to reinforce his argument for the dominant position of the priest.

One final, peculiarly Canadian note, capped Laflèche's ultramontane argument: thanks to God and history, the French Canadian nation had a religious mission to fulfil in North America. It must spread that mission by evangelizing the heathens of today and tomorrow just as Cartier and Champlain had done in the days of New France. And it must do so with all the courage and tenacity bequeathed by the early settlers. But to propagate the faith required its internal consolidation: French Canadians had to secure unity within before they could spread the Christian message abroad. They must therefore combat anything that threatened not only the Catholic faith, the essence of the nation, but also any menace to the nation itself. Once again, who could define the menace better than the priest? If French Canadians were to understand their divinely ordained mission and be sensitive to all the perils surrounding it, Laflèche urged that they must take their lessons from the priests.

To unite French Canadians behind such views took more than one book by a bishop. In spite of the solidity of the ultramontane argument—with God on its side and any doubters branded as national enemies—the entire campaign for ideological unity met remarkable resistance even from some of the priests themselves. Bishops and lower clergy of a more accommodating nature than their colleagues Bourget and Laflèche seriously wondered about the potential harm to Catholicism of such doctrinaire views. But they did not question the growing clerical presence in Quebec; indeed they rejoiced in it. Numerous paths, opened by sheer numbers of clergy and nuns, permitted the ultramontane assumption of clerical superiority, if not the entire logic, to find its way into most households. By means of the pulpit and the press, schools and popular processions, colonization movements, social work, the law, and politics, the clergy managed to reach almost everyone. Eventually almost everyone had to come to terms with the priests and did so with more or less good grace.

Monseigneur Bourget's investment in religious enthusiasm in the 1840s paid off handsomely later in the century. Vocations multiplied as young men found a calling, and a job, in the ministry. Although there were fewer than five hundred priests in Quebec in the 1840s, by 1900 they were more than two thousand. In contrast, the overall population of Quebec merely doubled in the same period. One priest for every two thousand Catholics in 1840 became one for every five hundred by the 1880s and the spatial distribution may even have accentuated the difference. In the 1840s many parishes rarely saw a priest, the people contenting themselves with twice-yearly visits from a missionary. Some even preferred it that way and objected strenuously to the permanent and therefore expensive establishment of a resident *curé*. By the 1880s the church was much more thoroughly organized: more dioceses mapped out the territory and more priests occupied it systematically. What was once popular protest turned into popular pride as parishes vied with each other for sumptuous churches and spacious presbyteries. Almost every family acquired a personal tie to the clergy, through a son, a nephew, a cousin, or a neighbour. In a society where training for the liberal professions was still haphazard and offered no guarantee of work for the many aspirants, training for the priesthood ensured not only an education and an occupation but also status and social mobility. Ultramontane ideology may even have enhanced the status of priests. In any case they were increasingly present and increasingly able to offer their parishioners their superior education, their spiritual and material succour, and their information networks.

Elements of those information networks were the pulpit and the press. Both provided links to worlds larger than the parish, larger than the country. In some rural parishes, the pulpit was the sole source of information with the priest carefully filtering the outside world for the benefit of the local farming community. By controlling both secular and spiritual information, a rural *curé* could easily confuse the two. He even kept an eye on local news by having the wide front steps of the church serve as a general meeting place before and after mass. There the *curé* may have read aloud from *La Gazette des campagnes*, a clerical newspaper supporting the agricultural college in Ste. Anne de la Pocatière from the early 1860s. If so, his listeners would certainly catch the analogy between progress and cholera, the one as deadly to the soul as the other was to the body. City newspapers carried the same message, if less blatantly. In Montreal, the moderate *Mélanges religieux* of the 1840s disappeared in 1852, but *Le Nouveau Monde* took up the ultramontane argument in 1867. And in Quebec City in the 1880s *La Vérité* did so with a vengeance. Even so ultramontane papers never did dominate Quebec journalism. Politics was always more profitable than religion and most papers were in the pay of *bleus* or *rouges*. The latter's *Le Pays*, for example, had spotted ultramontane sophistry in certain clerical minds in the early

1850s and continued to sound the alarm until its own demise in 1871, in part a victim of that clerical onslaught. But by the mid-1880s a new mass circulation paper, Montreal's *La Presse*, played up local, political, and even scurrilous news and easily outsold the preachings of the clerical press.

In the schools, the clergy had a more powerful instrument for claiming its place in society. The abolition of the ministry of education in 1875 was symptomatic of growing clerical power. From then until 1964 when a ministry was re-established, the state bowed to clerical authority in education. A provincial Council of Public Instruction administered the public school system through a Catholic and a Protestant committee. Since the Catholic committee was dominated by bishops, even the lay teachers, a continuing but diminishing majority in the elementary schools, had to bow to a curriculum and a discipline designed by priests. If not direct paths of ultramontanism, the schools certainly instilled a sense of the importance of religion into the minds of young French Canadians. Those few boys who continued on to a private classical college or the even fewer girls who went on to a convent for secondary education received the same message in a larger dose. There all the teachers were priests or nuns, most of them members of religious orders and all of them on the hunt for new recruits. Nine new colleges founded after 1850 stressed the growing importance of secondary education for boys and of teaching as a profession for priests. Some of the colleges innovated industrial and commercial programs; others retained the strict classical curriculum. In the latter, carefully screened supplementary reading leaned towards the conservative Catholic writers of contemporary France. By the 1890s prize-winning students in at least one of the colleges were awarded bound collections of *La Vérité*. Solid, Catholic souls emerged from such training. Even if they did not all go on to become priests, let alone ultramontanes, they all had school chums who did. The few radical spirits who resisted the clerical message, many of them products of the college at St. Hyacinthe, imbibed sufficient diplomacy to ensure acceptance. As for the girls, their convent training was both less doctrinal and less serious since it led to no further studies. Access to the clerically staffed and controlled Laval University, established in Quebec City in 1852, with a branch in Montreal after 1876, was allowed only to males who had passed through a classical college. The girls could do neither but they may have noted that teaching as a member of a female religious order had advantages of status and material comfort denied to the lay schoolmistress.

From the schoolrooms the clergy took its message into the streets and into the woods. With a calendar full of saints' days, the least occasion provided the setting for processions which the clergy deftly organized. Popular entertainment may well have been one of the motives: politicians were always able to draw huge crowds and the priests were not to be outdone. Popular protection may

have been just as compelling: the nineteenth century diseases—
cholera and then smallpox—were so sudden, so devastating, and
so recurring that public penance and public prayer were often the
only solace. More joyous and attracting equally large crowds were
the festivities surrounding the sending of the *Zouaves* to Rome in
the late 1860s. The ultramontane attempt to make the papal cause
a popular one was quite evident in the careful selection of the four
hundred volunteers to defend the pope's territories against the republican insurgents of Garibaldi. The young men came from all
the dioceses of Quebec and from all social classes. Even though
they saw no active service in Italy, their departure and return were
carefully marked by parish and diocesan celebrations and capped
by mammoth demonstrations in Montreal. The Grand Trunk Railway even offered special excursion rates for people from the countryside to swell the urban crowds. After their return, the *Zouaves*
kept alive their popularity, and that of the pope, by forming a
veterans' association to parade about on anniversaries and take
part in processions. Some *Zouaves* even took up the message of
colonization that the priests were also delivering, taking off into
the woods of the far Eastern Townships to found the settlement of
Piopolis, named for Pope Pius IX, by Lake Megantic. The clergy
were not far behind, inspiring and organizing colonization movements in the late nineteenth century. Neither leaders nor led were
ever very numerous, but the clerical presence reinforced the message of spiritual direction and involvement in very practical matters. One of the priests involved in the settlement of the Laurentians
northwest of Montreal actually went on to become a senior civil
servant: *curé* Antoine Labelle was deputy minister of colonization
in the late 1880s when Honoré Mercier was premier.

In a much less spectacular fashion and in a more private domain
the church may have succeeded best in making its presence vital
to Quebec society. Little ideology accompanied the assistance nuns
provided to women in families, but probably none was needed. The
women knew the source of the aid and the family spread the word.
The nuns in fact were in an even better position than their male
counterparts to offer help: their numbers increased ten times between 1850 and 1900. A mere six hundred at mid-century, there
were more than a six and a half thousand women in religious communities by the turn of the twentieth century. At the same time
when the clergy could offer one priest for every five hundred Catholics, the sisters were able to provide a nun for every one hundred
and fifty. The growth undoubtedly reflected a greater religious presence and intensity in Quebec society. Some of the newly designed
devotions and much of the cult of Mary were specifically intended
for women. Even the large numbers of young women drawn only
temporarily into a religious life testified and perhaps contributed
to its attraction. Twice or even three times the number of permanent nuns spent a few years in a novitiate and then took religious
training back to their families and neighbourhoods. But the growth

in the number of nuns may also have reflected increasingly limited activities available to women in the late nineteenth century. The notion of separate spheres both accompanied and justified a restriction of women's roles to very narrowly maternal functions. In such a situation, common to the western world, Catholicism held out an option to women via the religious communities. That option had always been available but it seems to have become particularly attractive only in the latter half of the nineteenth century. Certainly for the women of Quebec, becoming a nun added a choice to the limited possibilities of marriage, spinsterhood, or emigration. Only in the mid-twentieth century, when varied and valued secular activities became open to women, did the numbers of nuns begin to decline.

In the late nineteenth century, religious women undertook a vast array of social services. Education was only the most obvious one. The nuns themselves acquired an education they would not have received in secular society and they passed that training on to youngsters across the province. Their presence added to but did not in fact account for the early and increasing feminization of elementary teaching in Quebec; it also reinforced the intimate link between religion and education. As well, nuns directed elite boarding schools, training young women of the upper middle classes either to become nuns or to take their religious duties within their families very seriously indeed. Both Henriette Dessaulles and Joséphine Marchand, for example, although critical of the intellectual training they received, understood that theirs was the task to keep their future husbands and children on the straight and narrow path of religion. Both in fact absorbed with their education very clear notions of the separate spheres of men and women and they repeated the lessons in their later careers as journalists.

An increase in the number of boarding schools permitted the nuns not only to teach more girls at both the elementary and secondary levels but also to provide other services. By 1900 two hundred boarding schools attracted eleven percent of all female students; the number of both schools and girls had more than doubled since the 1860s. Besides revealing the enterprising spirit of the nuns, the new schools also indicated the increasing value placed on schooling for girls. Certainly the longer girls spent in the full-time company of nuns, the more likely they were to link the religious presence with their daily lives. But the schools also took in temporary boarders and thereby served another purpose. Critical moments of family life often produced orphans, if only for a while. A death, the remarriage of a mother or father, temporary unemployment, or even emigration often brought young girls to the boarding school. Their parents or relatives paid what they could and the nuns kept the girls for a few months or a few years. This type of assistance, as much as the education received, created a valued and lasting link between religion and the family.

Nuns were also present in areas beyond the classroom and the message they brought to families, particularly to women, was the same: the church provides aid in times of trouble. Trouble there was aplenty in the working class districts of Quebec's industrializing towns and the nuns were among the first to tend to it. Besides confronting dramatic problems such as those of prostitutes, criminals, delinquents, and infants born out of wedlock, the nuns soothed the more ordinary evils that afflicted the working poor. Childbirth, seasonal unemployment, sickness, death, alcoholism, or old age could destroy the fragile equilibrium of the family economy. In order to survive, a working class family required the financial contributions of at least two of its members, but who those contributing members were varied depending on the ages and stages of the family. They might be father and son, father and daughter, father and mother. Whatever the combination, a single hazard could disrupt it. Often the mother then had to cope alone by taking in washing or sewing, or by hiring herself out as a domestic and sending the younger children elsewhere. If there was a relative nearby and if that relative was not in dire straits too, the problems might be contained within the family. If not, the nuns were always there. They might come into the home itself to help out or they might take the children into their day care centres or orphanages. In either institution, the children stayed only temporarily until the family re-established itself, until an older daughter was of age to care for the youngsters, or until a relative was able to undertake the task. Sometimes the nuns protested the return of a child to parents known for alcoholism or irreligion; always they used the institutional surroundings to offer religion along with some elementary technical training to the children. The parents were in no position to protest. If anything, the mother was probably grateful. And in the women-talk of doorstep, kitchen, and street corner, she probably said so. Without either of them knowing it, she may well have been Monseigneur Bourget's best advocate.

Bourget, however, left little to chance and in his long struggle with the *Institut canadien* dating back from the 1850s, he eventually had recourse to lawyers to argue his case. From the mid-1840s to the mid-1870s some two thousand people had expressed sufficient interest in liberal ideas to become members of the *Institut canadien* in Montreal. Sometimes they were pulled away by age or occupation or the occasional religious scruple, but there was always a new contingent of young men to replace them, eager to debate ideas in general and politics in particular. In the 1840s they formed *rouges*, among them the subsequent leader Antoine-Aimé Dorion; in the 1860s they formed Liberals, among them the subsequent leader Wilfrid Laurier. They scoured the international press and debated the merits of British, European, and American political ideas and practices. At their banquets they raised toasts to progress and the sovereign people; in their assemblies they argued political rights for women. Priests playing with politics left them decidedly uneasy as did the growing ultramontane justification for such activity. They saw no social benefit from the association of spiritual and temporal powers in Rome or in Canada where the diversity of religious beliefs made such a pretension not only impracticable but intolerable. They were freethinkers in an era of increasing Catholic conservatism and they insisted on stocking the *Institut* library with the classics of contemporary liberalism: Voltaire, Lamennais, Bentham, Mill, Thiers, Guizot, Blanc. That most of the authors were suspect in clerical eyes and many were even on the papal Index of Forbidden Books did not disturb them in the least.

Needless to say it did disturb Monseigneur Bourget. In a series of pastoral letters in 1858, the bishop of Montreal warned of liberal tendencies abroad in the land. He particularly mentioned reading rooms of certain associations where the books lacked clerical sanction. Justifying his own position with impeccable ultramontane logic—the priest as representative of Christ must be able to exercise His influence in all realms of human endeavour and any suggested diminution of the priest's power constituted an attack on divine authority—Bourget told the *Institut* to purge its library. If it did not he would brand the association anti-Catholic and prohibit Catholics from being members. The threat was sufficient to scare away one hundred or so of the seven hundred members at the time. The rest declared their own competence in judging the morality of the books. By the mid-1860s, however, with membership dwindling, thanks in part to Bourget's more subtle tactics of having his priests influence the wives and mothers of members, the *Institut* sought some accommodation with the intransigent bishop. If he would indicate which of the books in the submitted catalogue were not to his liking, the *Institut* would undertake to remove them from the open shelves and place them under lock and key. Bourget kept silent. By 1865 some of the Catholic members of the *Institut*, among them Wilfrid Laurier, were anxious to have the matter settled. They appealed to Rome, the Rome of the *Syllabus of Errors*, to complain of the bishop's unfair treatment and to ask whether they, as Catholics, could belong to a literary society that had Protestant members and Indexed books in its library.

Eighteen signatories waited four years for a reply from Rome. Sixteen of them were prominent Montreal citizens, lawyers, and doctors; two were printers without social status. By 1869 when the reply was finally received one of the printers was working for the ultramontane newspaper *Le Nouveau Monde* and the other, Joseph Guibord, just happened to die a few months after. In that reply the pope placed the yearbook of the *Institut canadien* on the Index and condemned the association as a teacher of pernicious doctrines. While the *Institut* prepared further appeals to Rome, revealing thereby either its acceptance of spiritual direction or its increasingly uncomfortable position in Quebec society, Bourget interpreted the Roman decree as permission to deny the sacraments to any member. Joseph Guibord suddenly became a *cause célèbre*. As an unrepentant member of the *Institut*, he was denied burial in consecrated ground.

During the controversy over the library, the bishop of Montreal and the *Institut canadien* found other grounds for quarreling. One was ideological. In 1864 Gonzalve Doutre, younger brother of Joseph Doutre the prominent Montreal lawyer and *Institut canadien* member who would take the Guibord case through all the courts of the land, exposed his views on the *Principe des nationalités* before the *Institut canadien*. For Doutre, nations consisted merely of the inhabitants of the same country. There was nothing divine about them; they had merely developed as a result of discoveries, science, and civilization. Their coherence lay not in a common religion but in the tolerance they accorded to individuals of different faiths and in the harmony they fostered by means of self-government. Nothing could have been farther from ultramontane notions of nationality and Monseigneur Bourget was not amused. Nor were some *rouges* who were busy tacking on a nationalist argument to their opposition to Confederation. Bourget was caught. He could hardly rebuke Doutre's ideas without siding with the *rouges* and although he may have shared *rouge* worries about the threat Confederation posed to French Canadian nationality, he could hardly espouse their liberalism.

A more practical dispute also divided Bourget from the *Institut*. A number of Montreal lawyers, *Institut* members all, were negotiating with Victoria University, then in Cobourg, Ontario, to have the law courses which they gave under the auspices and in the lecture rooms of the *Institut canadien* recognized for credit towards a law degree from the Ontario university. By 1867 they had the agreement. Some thirty students, more than in Laval's or Victoria's programs combined, were about to undertake secular legal training and have it sanctioned by a Protestant university. Bourget was not only furious but fearful. His own battle to have a Catholic university in Montreal, independent from Laval—a battle he lost in 1876—was not going well and here was the *Institut canadien* looking for all intents and purposes as if it were forming the nucleus of a secular university in Montreal. No wonder he pounced on the coffin of poor Joseph Guibord in the fall of 1869.

That coffin kept some of Canada's brightest legal minds occupied for six years. Guibord's wife refused to accept her *curé*'s verdict that her husband be buried in the unconsecrated part of the cemetery, the section reserved for thieves, murderers, and unbaptized infants. She took the *curé* to court. Behind her was the *Institut canadien* claiming that burial was a civil right and that the papal condemnation of the *Institut*, besides being still under appeal, was not of the legal sort that would deny entry into the consecrated part of the cemetery. Behind the *curé* was Monseigneur Bourget exercising the full weight of ultramontane authority. At issue was the question of civil or ecclesiastical supremacy in society. Such a question was not decided in a day. While Guibord rested in a vault in the Montreal Protestant cemetery, the lawyers argued world history, church history, and Canadian history through all the appeal courts of the land and on to the final one, the Judicial Committee of the Privy Council in London. From there the verdict came in 1875: burial was indeed a civil right and Guibord should have his final resting place on top of his now deceased wife (the family was too poor to afford a double plot) in the consecrated part of the cemetery.

It took two tries to get him there. Alerted no doubt by legal poor sports in religious garb, a great mob greeted "Joseph Doutre and his corpse" and prevented their passage into the cemetery. How much was entertainment and how much religious conviction is hard to know. Perhaps wondering that too, Monseigneur Bourget urged calm during the subsequent attempt to bury Guibord. Let the British soldiers use their military power, their concrete, and their scrap iron to place Guibord in a legal plot; Bourget would use his ultimate ecclesiastical power and deconsecrate that section of the cemetery. Would Bourget's curse be lateral or horizontal, queried one Montreal wag. And how would he determine its boundaries so as not to affect neighbours near by or, worse still, Madame Guibord below? Certainly the case, if not the curse, put an end to the *Institut canadien*, unable to survive a purely legal victory in such inhospitable surroundings.

The same setting also affected political liberalism in Quebec. Far from being buried, however, liberalism merely transformed itself. In response perhaps to clerical analogies that heaven was *bleu* and hell *rouge*, and certainly by accommodating the clergy on some issues and confronting it on others, eventually the liberals skilfully sloughed off much of their *rouge* radicalism, attracted moderate *bleus*, and emerged as a viable Liberal party. Indeed, within fifteen years of the end of the Guibord case and much to the chagrin of the ultramontanes, Liberals dominated Quebec provincially and federally. In another six years Liberals governed all of Canada with Wilfrid Laurier, a French Canadian and one-time member of the *Institut canadien*, as prime minister. The change owed much to the ultramontanes taking their ideology too seriously and playing with the fire of politics.

Both clerical and lay adherents of ultramontanism had thought that political truth, like spiritual, ideological, and social truth, could only be found by following the directives of the church. They therefore attached themselves, from mid-century on, to the more sympathetic of the political groups in Quebec, the conservative *bleus*, in the hopes of making political issues and elections into struggles for the expression of divine will. But there they often found the going rough as their ideological instransigence prohibited the compromises necessary to political life. To George-Etienne Cartier, leader of the *bleus* until his death in 1873, they were a thorough nuisance. They stirred up trouble where none existed and they insisted upon impossibly doctrinaire solutions to complex problems.

One example was the *programme catholique* drawn up by ultramontanes in 1871 to guide the elctoral behaviour of all good Catholics. In it the ultramontanes stated their clear preference for the conservative *bleus*. But since even they might not be sufficiently pure, the electors should screen candidates carefully for their adherence to ultramontane views. Proper candidates should indicate their willingness to take the advice of bishops and priests in initiating and amending laws such as those regarding marriage, education, the creation of parishes, and the keeping of civil registers. With that criterion in mind electors could easily decide a contest pitting two Conservatives or a Conservative and a Liberal against each other. Between two Liberals, electors should choose the one who comes closest to the *programme*. But they should simply abstain from voting if they had to choose between a Liberal who accepts the *programme* and a Conservative who rejects it. The *programme* had the explicit backing of bishops Bourget and Laflèche but three others, Taschereau of Quebec, Langevin of Rimouski, and Larocque of St. Hyacinthe, pointedly informed their clergy that the episcopacy had had nothing to do with its elaboration. Many Conservatives were just as alarmed: Cartier, Hector Langevin, and Joseph Cauchon, all moderate leaders of the Quebec Conservatives, shuddered as they foresaw electoral victories compromised by such ultramontane daring. In fact, neither their fears nor ultramontane hopes were realized as most candidates refused to have anything to do with the *programme*.

The ultramontanes, however, thought they had a perfect issue in 1871 when the New Brunswick government legislated an end to provincial support for Catholic schools. With the religious and linguistic rights of French Canadians outside the province of Quebec in jeopardy, the ultramontanes counted on Cartier to use his considerable presence in the federal government to have Ottawa disallow the New Brunswick legislation. Ultramontanes claimed there must be no compromise. Legally, however, the British North America Act guaranteed only those minority school rights that had legally existed prior to Confederation and the Acadian schools in New Brunswick had never been sanctioned by law. Moreover, the federal power of disallowance could be a dangerous weapon. Supposing someone wished to turn it against Quebec? What would ultramontanes say then? And if used in this case, might it not imply that the federal government had the ultimate power over education? Could ultramontanes accept that? Cartier, Langevin, and Jean-Charles Chapais, ministers in the Macdonald government, hesitated to invoke such power. In turn, from the press and pulpit, ultramontanes branded them as traitors and the issue spilled over into the federal election of 1872. There the clergy divided again: Bishop Langevin of Rimouski, brother of the minister (Hector Langevin), and Archbishop Taschereau of Quebec forbade their priests from making any public statement. Meanwhile Bourget, Laflèche, and the ultramontanes found odd allies in one-time *rouges*, delighted to point out the accuracy of their predictions for Confederation. Disguised as liberal nationalists and even attempting to form a *parti national*, these *rouges* joined with the ultramontanes to cause some electoral surprises. They even managed to defeat Cartier in his home riding of Montreal East.

By 1875 politicians were openly accusing the clerics of undue influence in elections. Most politicians actually liked to claim clerical support whenever they faced the electorate. By doing so they unwittingly lent some weight to the political pretensions of ultramontanes. But what troubled Liberal politicians in particular was that clerical support went so handily to the Conservatives. Even a Liberal federal government from 1874 to 1878 was unable to change some priests' views of the party as infamous, dangerous, and an enemy of religion. Some went so far as to threaten their parishioners with eternal damnation if they voted Liberal. Temporarily overcoming their differences, the bishops united in the autumn of 1875, at the time of the last act of the Guibord case, to make a collective statement about the church's rightful voice in public debate and to condemn liberal Catholics. Archbishop Taschereau, fully aware that condemnation would not cause such beings to disappear and temperamentally prepared to tolerate them, unhappily signed the document. Less than a year later he issued a single statement of his own in which he treated both political parties, Conservative and Liberal, equally. Taschereau's tolerance could not prevent angry Liberals from taking the clergy to court, convinced that defeats in two ridings were caused by priests swaying the votes. One of the disputed cases, contesting Hector Langevin's victory in Charlevoix, northeast of Quebec City, offered a curious glimpse into political relationships of the time. Langevin had sported his clerical backing, even his relationship with Monseigneur Langevin, the bishop of Rimouski. Ever since the death of Cartier in 1873 Langevin had been attempting, against great odds and even greater rivals, to hold the Quebec wing of the federal Conservatives together, united behind his leadership. For that he was willing to tolerate the embrace of the ultramontanes, something neither Cartier nor Joseph-Adolphe Chapleau, a rival for the succession to Cartier, had been able to stomach. The contested case was thrown out of court by Judge Routhier, a former ultramontane politician, on the grounds that the state could not control the clergy: since voting was a moral question it required the direction of priests. On appeal to the newly created Canadian Supreme Court, Justice Taschereau, brother of the archbishop, reversed the decision of the lower court: the clergy had in fact exercised undue influence and the election was annulled. A decided odour of family chicanery hung over the whole affair.

Moreover, it was messy, both for the church and the politicians. From Rome and from the Eastern Townships came two attempts, both in 1877, to soothe matters. The pope dispatched an Irish envoy, Monseigneur George Conroy, to investigate the troubled politico-religious scene. Conroy found clerical interference in politics bad enough but the division it created among the priests even worse. How could Catholicism itself survive in a country such as Canada where so many different religions co-existed if the priests continued to engage in such unbecoming behaviour? They should desist, forthwith. At the same time, Wilfrid Laurier, federal Liberal MP for Arthabaskaville in the Eastern Townships, was arguing that there was no connection in any case between the liberal Catholicism denounced by the church and the political liberalism he and his party espoused. Canadian Liberals drew upon the British liberalism of Gladstone. They harboured not an ounce of revolutionary zeal. They were neither annexationists nor anticlericals. For his pains Laurier was treated to defeat in a by-election necessitated by his accepting a cabinet position in the government of Alexander Mackenzie; the ultramontanes had not yet abandoned the Conservative ship. Within a month, however, Laurier found a safe Liberal seat in Quebec East, in Monseigneur Taschereau's diocese; from there he was elected handily until his death in 1919.

In spite of judicial, papal, and public rebukes, ultramontanism lingered on. Strong enough to make life awkward for the Conservatives through the early 1880s and determined enough to join forces even with former *rouges* when a question of principle arose, as in the Riel crisis of 1885, it nonetheless troubled so many moderates that they began moving in Laurier's direction once he had cleared the Liberal air of the *rouge* taint. By the late 1880s Quebecois were voting Liberal, and Conservatives were scurrying for cover. Not that the ultimately victorious Liberals ever forgot the clergy; the two in fact developed a *modus vivendi* that kept both in the public limelight well into the twentieth century. The reason the church shared part of that limelight was not because of the political pretensions of ultramontanes, a tiny, albeit outspoken group within Canadian Catholicism, but because of the social services the church was able to provide. Thus, ultimately the explanation for the strong religious presence evident in Quebec society from the last third of the nineteenth century until the 1960s may well lie with the schools and the family. And in the latter women were the key, not in the presumed sense of their being more religious but rather in the fact that they had more reason to be grateful to the clergy, particularly to the nuns. The women after all, were the ones bearing the brunt of the urbanization and industrialization of the late nineteenth century.

SELECT BIBLIOGRAPHY

Bernard, Jean-Paul. *Les Rouges: libéralisme, nationalisme et anticléri-calisme au milieu du XIXe siècle.* Montreal: Les presses de l'Université du Québec, 1971.

Bradbury, Bettina. "The Family Economy and Work in an Industrializing City: Montreal in the 1870s." *Historical Papers/Communications historiques.* Canadian Historical Association, 1979. Pp. 71-96.

Bradbury, Bettina. "The Fragmented Family: The Family Life Cycle, Poverty and Death Among Mid-nineteenth Century Montreal Families." Paper presented to the annual meeting of the Canadian Historical Association, Montreal, 1980.

Danylewycz, Marta. "Taking the Veil in Montreal, 1840-1920: An Alternative to Marriage, Motherhood and Spinsterhood." Unpublished Ph.D. thesis, University of Toronto, 1981.

Dumont-Johnson, Micheline. "Les communautés religieuses et la condition féminine." *Recherche sociographiques* 19(1978):79-102.

Dumont-Johnson, Micheline. "Des garderies au XIXe siècle: les salles d'asile des Soeurs Grises à Montréal." *Revue d'histoire de l'Amérique française* 34(1980):27-55.

Eid, Nadia F. *Le clergé et le pouvoir politique au Québec: une analyse de l'idéologie ultramontaine au milieu du XIXe siècle.* Montreal: Hurtubise, 1978.

Fadette. Journal d'Henriette Dessaulles, 1874-1880. Montreal: Hurtubise, 1971.

Hamelin, Jean. *Les premières années de la Confédération.* Ottawa: Commission du centenaire, 1967.

Hamelin, Jean, John Huot, and Marcel Hamelin. "Aperçu sur la politique canadienne au XIXe siècle." *Culture* 26(1965):150-89.

Hamelin, Louis-Edmond. "Evolution numérique séculaire du clergé catholique dans le Québec." *Recherches sociographiques* 2(1961):189-241.

Hamelin, Marcel. *Les premières années du parlementarisme québécois, 1867-1878.* Quebec: Les presses de l'Université Laval, 1974.

Hardy, René. "L'ultramontanisme de Laflèche: genèse et postulats d'une idéologie." *Recherches sociographiques* 10(1969):197-206.

Hardy, René. *Les Zouaves.* Montreal: Boréal Express, 1980.

Robertson, Susan Mann (Trofimenkoff). "The Institut canadien, an Essay in Cultural History." Unpublished M.A. thesis, University of Western Ontario, 1965.

Rumilly, Robert. *Mgr Laflèche et son temps.* Montreal: Editions du Zodiaque, 1938.

". . . thousands of people living in close proximity."
Champlain Street, Quebec, 1870s.

9 Nobody Meant to Stay

One of the most telling responses to clerical definitions of place and function was for French Canadians to pack up and move elsewhere. Sometimes the moves were temporary, seasonal, or sexual adjustments to the parsimony of the land. More often they were permanent, flinging French Canadians into all the habitable areas of Quebec, into the Canadian and American west, into New England, and into the cities. Even in the new locations, the people did not stay put. They followed seasonal offers of employment in timber camp or factory; they shifted from town to town and within the towns from tenement to tenement. The wailings of clerico-nationalists followed them wherever they went, decrying the promised land which French Canadians persisted in seeing beyond the rural parish. Sometimes the bemoaners were right: the industrial reality of Montreal in the 1880s was hardly idyllic. But still the numbers of the urban working class kept growing, pulling people from presumably worse conditions in the countryside.

Like many other North Americans, French Canadians spent most of the latter half of the nineteenth century moving about. In that, they were little different from their ancestors in New France or their descendants in Quebec. The pattern of geographic mobility can be traced clearly from the indentured labourers, the *voyageurs*, even the missionaries of the seventeenth and eighteenth centuries to the domestic servants and factory lasses of the nineteenth century, the miners of Abitibi in the 1920s, and on to the construction workers of James Bay in the 1970s. Moreover, except for the missionaries, the attraction was always the same: cash. The land constantly sent its daughters and sons scurrying for income elsewhere. They moved around the province during the bad years of the mid-1870s, the good years of the early 1880s, and the mediocre ones thereafter. They left the Quebec region and headed for Montreal; they departed from the Richelieu and the Laurentians and traipsed into the Eastern Townships, the Gaspé, and other regions surrounding Lac St. Jean and the Ottawa River. They claimed most of the land of the province, but the land did not always claim them. Instead, in far greater numbers they left the province entirely. More than half a million emigrated to the United States to add to a similar number that had already trickled, and then flowed, into New England by 1870. Relatively few scattered to Manitoba or the American mid-west, distance and finances, rather than cultural factors, likely being the prohibitive force. Whether their move was outside the province or within it, they had a decided preference for those towns that offered industrial jobs. Their numbers and their willingness to work determined in fact the type of light industry that developed in New England and southwestern Quebec. Long before the economists spotted it, their very roaming about indicated the peripheral nature of the Quebec economy. There was no reason to stay because there was not enough to do.

Agriculture, whether in a good or bad state, produced most of the migrants. Where adaptation of techniques or produce was occurring, fewer farm workers were required; where stagnation marked the farmland, there were too many mouths to feed. In either case temporary migration was a first resort. A season at a lumber camp in the Ottawa Valley might provide enough cash for the farm's running expenses; six months in a New England brick factory might begin the savings needed to purchase another farm or clear the debt on the present one. More permanent migration may have been initiated by young women since the jobs they went seeking—domestic service as maid or housewife—did not lend themselves to seasonal interruptions. In either case movement off the farms was steady and continuous as agriculture changed or succumbed in the face of external pressures.

Agricultural changes were the most noteworthy. The latter third of the nineteenth century witnessed a growth in the amount of cultivated land and a better distribution of it between pasture and cropland. Productivity also increased: the same amount of land grew twice as much wheat, oats, barley, and potatoes. While new lands and new techniques enhanced some of the traditional agricultural products, the major difference in the late nineteenth century was the change to dairy farming and stock raising. The American Civil War had encouraged the latter in the 1860s; increasing urban demand favoured the former from the 1870s until well into the twentieth century. The shift also signified the beginning of regional specialization in agriculture both within Canada and within Quebec. Wheat was abandoned to the new lands opening ever further in the Canadian west; in Quebec milch cows and cheese factories clustered around the towns and railway lines of the Eastern Townships and the Montreal plain. The expanding communication network, its main component being the railways, drew people as well as products to the towns.

Milk, cheese, and butter thus provided the momentum for Quebec's agriculture and for its mobile population in the latter half of the nineteenth century. The three products required new forage crops like hay and buckwheat. Gradually, they also demanded mechanization: field machines for the crops and factory machines for the dairy products. These in turn reduced the number of farm hands; young people were free to become "hands" in urban factories. The mechanization of cheese and butter making in particular may also have meant a masculinization of these activities, as they moved out of the kitchen or shed and into small factories. In the process they undermined the farm family as an economic unit and displaced young women who then emigrated. By the end of the century cheese factories were producing eighty million pounds of cheese, a more than eighty-fold increase since 1851. The expansion and the mechanization required money; a marketable product and excess young people both went in search of it in the towns.

The trend toward specialization and mechanization did not, however, solve all the agricultural problems of Quebec. Many areas were unsuitable for the raising of dairy cattle; others were too inaccessible. Subsistence farming continued, with its attendant poverty and its seasonal movement of young men into timber camps. Even the areas of dairy development were not exempt from difficulties. Unless a railway or a good road passed nearby, marketing or the pooling of milk for factory production of cheese and butter was next to impossible. In fact, the factories were frequently misnomers, often being no more than small, family enterprises with the occasional hired hand. Neither the "factories" nor the "workers" revealed much scientific awareness and, until the 1890s when standards and regulations were set by the government, the poor quality of the products entailed great losses. The animals themselves were a poor lot, producing only half the quantity of milk of European cows. Even marketing, where transportation permitted it, created problems: without standards or regulations, a weighty cheese in a Montreal shop might reveal a large stone in its centre; oily butter might be rancid before reaching the shops of London where it could not compete with Scandinavian products.

Just as some people came to terms with agricultural changes by moving out, others attempted to organize those changes in the hope that they might thereby stem the exodus. From the late 1860s, government agents worked incessantly to educate farmers to the new commercial possibilities of dairy farming. Agronomists, of whom the most prominent was Edouard Barnard, wrote and spoke as well as edited agricultural newspapers. They organized agricultural societies with local circles to which the farmers in a region would belong. The circles and societies in turn hosted fairs, exhibits, and contests, brought in lecturers, and kept their members informed of the latest farming and marketing methods. In addition, the agronomists backed the establishment of model farms, urged the teaching of agriculture in the elementary schools, suggested new industries such as sugar from beet roots, and imported new breeding stock. They also developed the first agricultural schools in the province from the early one at Ste. Anne de la Pocatière in the late 1850s to the specialized dairy school in St. Hyacinthe in the 1890s, and the more short-lived ones at Richmond, Rougemont, and Compton, all in the Eastern Townships, and another in Oka, northwest of Montreal. In the late 1880s, the provincial government created a separate ministry of agriculture and colonization, distinguishing it from public works and placing the province's prime minister, Honoré Mercier, and a colonizing priest, *curé* Labelle, at the head of it. The department instituted government inspection of cheese and butter factories; it developed a system of government contracts stipulating that farmers bring their milk to certain factories within a given length of time. The transportation companies also responded to the development and increased organization of the dairy industry. Refrigerated trains and ships by the mid-1890s took more than half the produce to foreign markets.

But still the people departed and their exodus disturbed priest and politician alike. Religious and political battles both needed numbers and French Canadians seemed determined to take those numbers elsewhere. Perhaps they could be tempted by new lands within the province. If the government provided the roads and facilitated the acquisition of land, the clergy would provide the leadership. Colonization might solve the economic wanderlust of French Canadians.

A grand total of forty-five thousand people heeded the call of colonization in the last half of the nineteenth century. For all the increasing emphasis that the clergy put upon the rural characteristics of the French Canadian people, fewer than a thousand per year settled in the impossible terrain of the Laurentians and the upper Mauricie or even the considerably better lands of the Town-

ships or of the Lac St. Jean or Temiscamingue regions. French
Canadians were headed for the cities and no one could stop them.
For those who did brave new areas of settlement, they faced a
three year struggle of backache and heartache, clearing the land,
constructing a house, pulling in a first crop. They depended on
the wood merchants for temporary employment and on the priest
for moral support. The government with its promised road was
usually far in the distance.

Actually, the government was much more interested in railroads
than in colonization routes. If the former could serve as the latter,
so much the better. But a railway that carried only settlers and
their effects did not pay. Even those that were intended to do far
more frequently failed. In the early 1880s the provincial government gladly disposed of the north-shore railway linking the
populated centres of Quebec, Trois-Rivières, Montreal, and Ottawa
by selling it to Canadian Pacific at a loss. The lesson went unheeded
as railway fever increased provincial and municipal debts faster
than the rails could reach the southern shore of the Gaspé (branch-
ing off from the hopelessly uncommercial route of the Intercolonial), into the Laurentians north and east of Montreal, and even, by
the end of the 1880s, joining Lac St. Jean to Quebec City. Almost
every small town on the south shore offered public enticements to
private railway companies in the hope that a passing railway
would bring permanent industrial development. Meanwhile, the
settlement of one of the more promising new agricultural areas of
the province, the Temiscamingue, had to await the construction
of a transcontinental railway. Once the Canadian Pacific Railway
(CPR) reached Mattawa in the mid-1880s, potential settlers had only
to scramble overland and by portage to the southern end of Lake
Temiscamingue; no rail line facilitated that trip until the end of
the century. By 1900, thirty-five hundred miles of railway—a seven-
fold increase in thirty years—tied the province together and facilitated the mobility of French Canadians. Nonetheless they rarely
moved to new colonization areas.

For all the government's talk of agricultural settlement, it gave
little concrete support. Fewer than seventy-thousand dollars a year
seem to have been earmarked in provincial budgets for colonization. With that amount the government could do little more than
acknowledge the existence of colonization societies, financed for
the most part by private donations, and regulate the establishment
of certain groups on new lands. It did disburse crown lands at
little or no cost to potential settlers and even offered one hundred
acres free to families with twelve children, a rare occurrence even
at a time of high birth rates. And it tried, rather unsuccessfully, to
mediate in the uneasy relationship between wood merchant and
settler. Each disrupted the life of the other and the government
never was able to solve the difficulties. The presence of settlers
meant that the wood merchants no longer had free run of the timber stands in a given area. A settler might even take a minuscule

hand in the trade himself: chop down his own woodlot haphazardly, sell the timber, and move on. At the same time the presence of wood merchants meant winter camps with temporary employment and an initial market for the agricultural produce of a new settlement. But while a young man was working in the woods, he was not clearing his own land and when a camp was the only market, it could name its own prices. Moreover, once a young man was accustomed to the work and the cash, he might well follow the wood trade ever north and west. French Canadian lumberjacks were in the woods of northwestern Ontario and even of Michigan long before the end of the century. Only with the development of hydro-electric power in the very late nineteenth century did the by then scrappy trees of the Quebec forest provide continuing jobs in Quebec in the new pulp and paper industry. In the meantime the provincial government acquired almost one-third of its revenues from the selling of timber lands and cutting rights to wood merchants; when the latter preferred not to be disturbed by the intrusion of new settlers, they usually had their way.

Suspecting or knowing from experience the difficulties of colonization, most French Canadians on the move chose the path of emigration. As they well knew and as politicians virtually admitted by their paltry sums and the clergy unwittingly revealed by their exhortations, colonization could not provide a sufficient living for the vast numbers of people needing sustenance. The answer lay in industry and until the 1880s and even later, most of that industry was elsewhere. While movements of people did take prospective farmers into the newly opening lands of the Canadian prairies, the American mid-west, or the closer areas of eastern and northern Ontario, emigration in the last third of the nineteenth century primarily meant the movement of prospective industrial workers to the factories of New England. By the hundreds of thousands they poured out of rural parishes, from the ones adapting to new dairy farming and even more often from those declining from self-sufficiency into poverty. Good year or bad appeared to make little difference to the numbers as people followed the railway lines and their relatives south. Sometimes they intended to return after a season or a few years, sometimes they made the move permanent. They went as single young women and men to live in boarding houses attached to factories in Fall River or Lowell, Massachusetts; they went as families to dwell in flats in tenement houses in Woonsocket, Rhode Island. Occasionally they came back for a visit. But even when their nostalgia was highly organized as it was in 1874 when the Saint Jean Baptiste Society brought special trainloads of Franco-Americans to Montreal for popular festivities, it was rarely sufficient to keep them in Quebec. Indeed they often returned to the States with several more relatives or parish neighbours in tow.

In the American factories, French Canadians acquired the unenviable reputation as the "Chinese of New England." They were prepared to work long hours at unskilled jobs for low wages and in poor conditions. They were content to have entire families in the employ of a textile mill; they even offered their family discipline freely to their employer and organized the rhythm of their lives around the seasons of cloth, brick, and paint production. They displaced native Americans for jobs and housing, and competed with the Irish for lowest spot on the socio-economic totem pole. And still they continued to arrive, their mobility testifying to their even more marginal economic existence in Quebec. By 1900 they formed ten percent of the population of New England with single young women outnumbering single young men just as in the cities of Quebec. And once there they followed jobs from town to town, the prospect of cash always luring them on.

Watching the flood of emigrants and only slowly coming to terms with the permanence of their mobility were a number of clerical and secular spokesmen. At the onset, they prophesied doom. French Canadians were surely going to the devil by following the infinitesimal glitter of gold among the spinning machines of New England. Many of them probably had the devil in them in the first place, to be tramping around the American states without any sense of place or purpose. Even the temporary migrants who promised to return did so with money jangling in their pockets and children used to urban living. The attraction for rural neighbours was immense especially since the factories offered combined family incomes of more cash in a month than many people ever saw in a year. Convinced that the money would be spent on luxuries, parish priests wrung their hands. Gradually, however, they decided that their presence among the emigrants would be more useful than their condemnation from afar. Unlike the many colonization movements which priests led, here they followed the French Canadians into "exile." They joined them in the "little Canadas" of the manufacturing centres of New England and added ecclesiastical and social structures to what they grudgingly admitted was a permanent presence beyond the borders of Quebec. By the end of the century they even began to find significance in that presence. Surely a population totalling three-quarters of a million in 1886 and doubling every twenty-eight years from the birth rate alone, without adding the continuing influx of immigrants from Quebec, must be destined to play an extraordinary role in America. Perhaps the hand of providence was at work after all, dotting the heathen landscape with compact groups of Catholics who treasured their familial customs and traditions.

Secular voices were only slightly more realistic. Rarely did government representatives openly contradict the clerical views of emigration as either diabolical or providential. But they did set commissions of enquiry to work investigating the reasons for the massive outflow of people. Some of the responses came from local clucking clerics: among the causes of emigration was a supposed love of luxury. Some too must have come from opponents of the government: ineffective policies chased French Canadians out of Quebec. Others suggested that gossip was the major source of American attractiveness: word-of-mouth was by far the fastest, if not always the most reliable, means of communication in rural areas. But most pinpointed very concrete causes for emigration: there were too many people on too poor land; they produced insufficient crops for an inaccessible market. The answer lay in industry. Only by promoting industry could Quebec hope to dam the flow of its people out of the province. Quebec politicians therefore supported wholeheartedly the protective aspects of the National Policy in 1879. As a result, Quebec textile, clothing, shoe, and tobacco industries were some of the first industries to benefit from the increased tariffs on imports. Still other secular voices romanticized the industrial experience of New England and offered it as a model for emulation by Quebec. Honoré Beaugrand, inveterate *rouge* and mayor of Montreal in the mid-1880s, produced a novel, *Jeanne la fileuse*, in 1878 to emphasize the economic necessity that took young people south. While the politicians were carving themselves comfortable niches in Confederation, French Canadian farmers were being driven deeper into debt and eventually into emigration. Once adapted to the working and living conditions of industrial towns, a process Beaugrand claimed took only three months, Canadian families prospered. Any attempt to bring them back to Quebec was a waste of time; any claim that miserable conditions in the United States prevented their return was a lie.

Industry required towns and there too French Canadians traced a pattern with their feet long before their political or spiritual elites sanctioned the move. Small towns had in fact developed from the spinoff of agricultural change in those areas where dairy farming was viable: people from the towns provided services for the farms. But unless a railway went through the town, there was little likelihood of industry. And unless a waterfall and, later in the century, accessible coal could provide motive force for machinery, there would be no industrial development. Finances, transportation, and construction all had to be assured. So too did workers. Spilling off the farms in search of jobs, any jobs, French Canadians filled up the towns and made possible a particular kind of industrialization.

Mostly they headed for Montreal. Already the metropolis of Quebec in terms of transportation, services, and finances, Montreal had every intention of becoming the metropolis of Canada. With the terminus of the new transcontinental railway locating in Montreal in the early 1880s, the CPR yards and machine shops were added to those of the Grand Trunk and to three American lines by the end of the century to make Montreal the production and repair centre for heavy transportation equipment in Canada. Skilled workers imported from Britain manned the shops; French Canadians slowly added their presence. The railways allowed Montreal to dominate the hinterland, drawing people into its di-

versified jobs and taking manufactured products out to a captive
market. In the last three decades of the nineteenth century, Montreal
grew from a modest commercial town of one hundred thousand to
a major industrial centre of close to three hundred thousand. Its
growth far exceeded that of Quebec or Canada as a whole and was
outpaced only by that of Toronto. The expansion of industries,
both new and old, appears to have been the major cause of the
growth. The influx of French Canadians provided the "hands"—
male, female, adult, child—for the new and the expanded industries and also turned Montreal into a majority French-speaking
city after 1870. People sorted themselves out by class and ethnicity,
sometimes even by skill, among the different wards of Montreal
and in its industrial suburbs, which were slowly taken over by the
expanding metropolis after the turn of the century. For those who
could afford it, horse-drawn trams carted them to work in the 1870s
and 1880s, and electric trams carted them home again in the 1890s.
Most working people, however, lived within walking distance of
factory or shop. If their job changed, so likely did their living quarters. They wandered as much within the city as in and out of it,
tracing a sometimes forlorn, sometimes hopeful pattern of supply
and demand.

The type of industry that developed in Quebec matched its mobile population. With farm families on the move or specializing in
commercial agriculture, they no longer could produce all they
needed to meet their ordinary requirements in terms of food or
clothing. Even less so did families installed in towns. Not surprisingly therefore food processing became the major industry in terms
of value of production throughout the last three decades of the
nineteenth century. Industrialized food processing both undermined
one of the traditional economic roles of women in the family and
attracted the surplus women to similar occupations now found in
factories. With the mechanization of much previous artisanal production, the factories in turn required only nimble fingers and
watchful eyes to tend to the machinery. Mechanization and the
presence of women and children also changed the nature of the
shoemaking industry although it remained in second place in terms
of value of production from 1870 to 1900. Wood and wood products also retained their ranking, in third place, across the entire
period; there too, only some of the specialized wood finishing
processes in furniture or sash and door production required skilled
labour. The mobile population with its attendant disruption of
rural families also created workers and markets for the clothing
industry which remained in fourth place between 1870 and 1900.
Even if the ranking of the various industries remained the same,
their value of production increased tremendously as Quebec captured the deliberately constructed markets of Confederation and
then maintained them thanks to the protective tariff. Those same
political conditions brought subsidized coal from Cape Breton to
the new steam powered plants of Montreal where mechanization

and a job-hungry population even made profitable the importing of raw materials such as cotton for the new textile mills. Both they and the new tobacco plants employed vast numbers of women and children. Only one new industry—pulp and paper—hinted at the technological innovations and attendant sexual changes in the labour force of the twentieth century. Yet even this industry, based on hydro-electric power and with an all male work force, demanded a mobile population, prepared to follow jobs to Chicoutimi, Trois-Rivères, or Hull.

For the people themselves, mobility had one serious drawback. People moving around, always on the lookout for jobs, and prepared to place all the members of a family in a single factory do not save money. The accumulation of capital, another prerequisite of industrialization, was therefore in the hands of a very few. English and Scottish names predominated among the factory owners; British, and increasingly American, borrowed capital and imported technology backed most of the enterprises. Scattered French Canadian names did appear among the industrialists: Sénécal and Lacroix in railways, Rolland in paper making, Dubuc in the lumber trade, Boivin in shoe production, and Parent in the early stages of hydroelectric development. But they all disappeared in the face of international movements of money and business in the early twentieth century. More numerous and more lasting were French Canadian names among the retail trades and in real estate development and promotion. Where the majority of French Canadian names predominated and remained, however, was among the factory workers.

Although Montreal was a major attraction for migrating French Canadians, it was by no means the only centre of industrial development in the province. Its size, location, and industrial head start as early as the 1850s did give it a decided advantage, but other towns also joined it on the industrial bandwagon of the 1880s. Textile industries in particular were spread out among the towns of the Montreal plain and the Eastern Townships drawing increasing numbers of people into Valleyfield, Chambly, St. Jean, Magog, Coaticook, and Sherbrooke. The larger textile mills remained in Montreal or its immediate suburb of Hochelaga and expanded sufficiently by the 1880s to begin the mergers that would be more characteristic of the Canadian economy after the turn of the century. Quebec City too drew people into its increasingly mechanized shoe trade. Montreal had in fact only ten percent of the fifteen thousand industrial establishments—a rather loosely defined census term—in Quebec in 1881 and the percentage declined to eight of twenty-three thousand by 1891. That fraction nonetheless employed almost forty percent of the eighty-six thousand industrial workers in the province in 1881. Montreal's industries were employing another five thousand "hands" by 1891, although their percentage of the total industrial labour force in the province fell to thirty-three. If the figures acknowledge the growth of industries throughout the province, they also indicate the heavy concentration in Montreal: with just under one tenth of the industries throughout the 1880s, the city harboured just over one third of the province's industrial labour force.

The presence of so many people, before they even entered the factory gates, created enormous problems for the city. Like other industrializing cities of the western world, Montreal had to cope with what appeared to be the evil effects of hundreds of thousands of people living in close proximity. Fire was a continuous hazard since workers' housing was constructed cheaply and quickly of wood and heated by wood-burning stoves. Sanitation was a daily concern and a periodic peril. Although new housing built after 1887 was supposed to have indoor plumbing, most of Montreal's working class housing had outdoor privies until well after the turn of the twentieth century. Garbage, particularly of a liquid sort, was often simply tossed into the streets, making walking hazardous and the wearing of a bonnet or cap a necessity. Montreal's drinking water was notoriously bad: a tourist guide in 1884 warned visitors to "avoid drinking largely of water on their first arrival. It is apt to cause diarrhoea when copiously drunk in hot weather". Such conditions guaranteed no immunity when diseases struck, as they did frequently. Throughout the 1870s and 1880s smallpox was a regular visitor to Montreal, carefully choosing its victims among working class French Canadians. Close to three thousand of them died in the epidemic of 1885, creating a more serious public stir than the reaction to the hanging of Louis Riel. More French Canadians rioted in the streets of Montreal to protest compulsory vaccination in the autumn of 1885 than did Métis on the banks of the South Saskatchewan River in the spring. While smallpox was the worst of the contagious diseases, there were many others that carried off old and young alike. Tuberculosis, diptheria, scarlet fever, and typhoid appeared to be largely urban diseases and, barring an epidemic of smallpox, were the major killers of the late nineteenth century. Added to infant mortality, which had tiny tots succumbing to gastro-intestinal ailments as a result of bad water and worse milk, the diseases made Montreal one of the worst places to live and the best places to die in the entire world.

In response to such evils, the city had to take on the role of physical guardian once reserved to the family. Housing, health, hygiene, and morality all became public concerns common to most North American cities in the 1880s and mediated somewhat in the French Canadian milieu by the presence of the Catholic church. Immense social services were beyond the church's capabilities or mission and they became public responsibilities. Transportation, streets, sewers, fire and water service, police protection, street lighting, garbage collection, even popular leisure activities in the all too few parks and the all too many taverns all came under the increasingly watchful eye of civic administrators. Pursued by journalists and upper class women advocating civic reform, municipal politicians were exposed and shamed into taking the necessary and expensive measures to make Montreal habitable. Many of the actual social services—hospitals and charities, daily assistance to the poor, the sick, and the old—were, however, left to the women, religious and secular alike. Such a male-female division of public labour, bolstered as it was by the organization of the Catholic church and by the notion of separate spheres, may well have obviated the need for any systematic critique of industrial society.

While reform took place outside the factory gates, inside, the workers had to assimilate the demands of the new industrial order. They had to acquire the rhythm of the work, a rhythm different from that of agricultural or artisanal production. Machines required steady and complete attention and factory owners or managers used various means to enforce the message and to discipline the workers. Fines for lateness brought workers scurrying into the factory on time, usually at six or seven in the morning. Fines also ticked off every case of inattention or misbehaviour. A noise, a laugh, a whistle, or a chat all meant a few cents off an already slim pay packet. So too did a smoke, a cheeky word to the supervisor, or badly done work whether it was the fault of the machine, the goods, or the worker. The hiring of entire families reinforced the discipline as father or elder daughter kept the younger children in line if they were all in the same workroom or, if they worked separately, parents enquired after the docked pay packet once everyone was at home well after six or seven in the evening. Sometimes physical force emphasized the lesson. Fortier's cigar factory in Montreal was notorious for its beating of employees, particularly children and young women. There was even a "black hole" on the premises, a windowless room in which youngsters could be placed until they consented to behave properly. When queried about the show of force by a royal commission enquiry at the end of the 1880s, neither Fortier nor the few employees who came forth to give evidence showed surprise or regret or revenge. Paternal behaviour was expected of the boss, just as docile behaviour was expected of the workers.

Wages were another means of ensuring docile behaviour. Paid at rates of one dollar a week for children or eighty cents to a dollar twenty-five a day for adults, they guaranteed regular assiduous work just to ensure that the family survived. Wages declined in the fall and winter even though employers knew that heating and food costs were higher at that time of the year; they justified the cuts by the excess numbers of workers looking for jobs. Needless to say those with jobs took the loss and attended to their work. The system of piecework payment, by far the most common in Canadian factories of the time, also ensured steady, diligent workers since they were paid by the number of items produced, rather than hourly or by the week. The practice of hiring entire families also permitted factory owners to pay each family member less; their communal needs would keep them in line. If not, the very hiring of women and children at lower wages than the men kept the men in line since they could be threatened with replacement by cheaper workers. With women constituting more than half the labour force in the light industries, the tactic was effective. If that did not work, employers often went outside the region, or even outside the country, bringing in contract labour from the Saguenay or from Europe to work for specified periods at rates lower than those paid to local labour. Even the one provincial law that in any way regulated labour relations, the Masters and Servants Act, reinforced the notion of proper behaviour on the part of the "servants": an employer could fire a worker without notice, but a worker wishing to leave had to give two weeks notice and was not always assured of receiving his wages during those two weeks. As a final inducement to correct factory behaviour, the very hours of work ensured a certain docility. Working ten to twelve hours a day, sixty hours or more per week, with only Sunday and a few hours Saturday afternoon off, workers had little time or inclination to ponder anything but work, food, and sleep.

The discipline was effective. It kept workers at the job in dreadful conditions and total insecurity. Factories were often either too hot or too cold, full of cotton dust or chemical fumes, badly ventilated and poorly lit. Some were three or four stories high without running water or toilets, to say nothing of fire escapes. Many of the machines lacked safety guards and easily caught fingers, arms, or legs and left the victims helpless for life. There was no protection against accident, sickness, old age, or death; insurance even if it was affordable was not yet available. There were no pensions and no vacations except for the forced ones of a factory closing. Montreal's industries followed the weather and the shipping: winter layoffs were common and seasonal closings to offset overproduction were normal. In such a setting, a single wage never sufficed. Even the earnings of three family members would barely bring the family above poverty level, given the insecurity of employment, the rising cost of living in winter, and the increased rents of the 1880s. And if an unhappy worker wished to register a protest, she or he could simply go elsewhere. There was always a newcomer to town ready to step into the job. Mobility itself kept many French Canadian workers docile. Numbers kept them cheap.

Against such odds, workers' attempts at self-protection were both vital and doomed. They never were enough: probably less than five percent of the industrial work force was unionized and those who were simply added one more hazard to their already perilous working conditions. Many employers required prospective workers to sign an agreement not to join a union. Others fired their workers once they knew of union membership. The royal commission enquirers examining labour in the late 1880s, although sympathetic to unions, were aware of employers' prejudices. "Are you a member of a workers' association?" and before the worker could reply, the commissioner added, "you need not answer that question".

Trade unions as associations of workers of the same skill were not new in the 1880s. As early as the 1820s, printers formed a union in Quebec City. Shoemakers in the 1860s hoped that a union might forestall the mechanization of their trade and the consequent influx of unskilled labour. Longshoremen in the 1850s and 1860s divided into Irish and French benevolent societies, forerunners of unions, whose purpose was to provide financial assistance to the family at the time of a worker's accident or death. Once trade unions acquired legal status in Canada with the passage of the Trade Unions Act by the federal government in 1872, they were able to take on more recognizable activities: protecting their members against employers by insisting upon higher wages and fewer hours of work. By the 1880s they felt the need for protection against other workers: unskilled or imported labour could be a threat to skilled workers. The trade unions tended to attract the elite of the working class, those with more education, more training, better pay, and a standard of living closer to that of the middle class. By 1886 they were numerous enough to form a national organization — the Trades and Labour Congress of Canada — and to begin making political demands.

Most workers in the 1880s, however, were unskilled. Those few with the time or energy to think about mutual protection against the living and working hazards of an industrial city had to find an association other than a union based on a skilled trade. *La Grande Association* in 1867 and *La Ligue ouvrière* in 1872 were early attempts to rally workers regardless of occupation or skill. But the major impetus came in the 1880s from the United States in the form of the Knights of Labour. Barring only lawyers, bankers, and sellers of whiskey from their membership, the Knights appealed especially to unskilled workers. They thus spread throughout Canada in the 1880s but were particularly numerous in Quebec. Like the unions organized by trades, their purpose was to provide mutual assistance, to improve working conditions by exerting pressure on employers, and, gradually, to take political action. Unlike the trade unions, the Knights displayed a somewhat more idealistic approach to labour relations. They believed a community of interest bound workers and owners and thus they preferred arbitration to strikes for solving disputes. They also urged legislative action as a means of improving not only working conditions, but society as a whole. As advocates of equal pay for women, temperance, co-operatives, and government control of railways and telecommunications, the Knights were much more politically radical than the trade unions. They believed in educating workers and many of their meetings took on the aura of a classroom. And, to the delight of members and the dismay of opponents, they also had the charming aspect of a secret society. Members were initiated by means of special rites; they swore secret oaths to—who knew what?

In spite of social and ideological differences between the two types of union in Quebec, they used a common weapon to express their unhappiness. Some two hundred strikes marked the industrial scene of the last three decades of the nineteenth century, seventy of them occurring during the 1880s. The demands, whether put forth by a trade union, an assembly of the Knights of Labour, or a spontaneous group of unhappy workers, were always the same. Low or inadequate salaries consistently topped the list of grievances. Of much less significance were the demands for shorter hours, the right to be a union member, better working conditions, fairer systems of payment, less mechanization, and the elimination of fines. Quite simply the workers did not have enough money. Protesting as they often did in an unorganized, incoherent manner, one factory at a time and for a short period, they usually lost. Industries using unskilled labour during a period of massive rural emigration were sure to win against sporadic union activity that rarely involved more than one hundred workers at a time.

And yet those very unions raised fears. Factory owners, journalists, politicians, and clergy, shuddered at the thought of workers demanding protection. That the state should protect employers by means of tariffs and assisted passage to contract labour seemed perfectly reasonable; but that workers should request similar assistance from the state seemed tantamount to revolution. Perhaps indeed it was, since the implication of social equality in the workers' demands was shocking to most nineteenth century minds. Even the liberal mind of Monseigneur Taschereau, the archbishop of Quebec who had been so unhappy with Monseigneur Bourget's intransigence only a decade before, could not encompass the union movement. He was particularly uneasy about the Knights of Labour. Their foreign leaders, secret rites, and tolerance of religious differences among the membership all disturbed his French Canadian and Catholic sensibilities. Their idealism, reformism, and pretension to a monopoly on the labour supply disturbed his liberal sensibilities. A group of workers had no right to put pressure on other workers much less on owners: freedom in labour relations meant individual contracts between worker and employer. Taschereau's aristocratic sensibilities may even have been piqued by a social movement inaugurated without the sanction of the church. In fact it would be another twenty years before the church took trade unions seriously enough to become actively involved in their formation and organization. In the meantime popular movements of workers looked too much like the next wave of European disturbers of the social order.

Taschereau's hostility to unions in general and the Knights of Labour in particular continued through the 1880s. He began with a veiled threat against union efforts to obtain higher wages: Catholics were not to constrain the individual's right to work for any wage. That many people disagreed with him is indicated by the very growth of unions in the decade. Even Taschereau's threat of excommunication was of little avail. In 1885 he went a step further and, arming himself with a papal decree against secret societies, he denounced the Knights of Labour. But still the numbers kept climbing; they reached twenty-five hundred in Montreal alone in 1887 when Taschereau, regretfully one suspects, gave up his battle and lifted the condemnation. His fellow bishops in Montreal and Ottawa had quietly ignored his directive; those in Ontario expressed their displeasure and an American cardinal who favoured the Knights noisily informed the pope of the folly of Taschereau's placing the church in opposition to workers. Four years later the pope in effect said so too. The encyclical *Rerum novarum*, "of new things," revealed the church's new found sympathy for the working class. The Knights of Labour, in the meantime, continued to gather adherents in Quebec throughout the 1890s until they lost out in inter-union rivalries within the Trades and Labour Congress in 1902.

By then, however, a number of union spokesmen had turned to active politics. In the late 1880s the first working class candidates began appearing in Quebec elections, both federal and provincial. In federal politics their particular concern was contract labour imported from Europe. They actually made sufficient public noise both in elections and in the hearings of the Royal Commission on Capital and Labour that the Conservative government of John A. Macdonald put a stop to the practice of importing labour under contract. But the involvement of workers in politics was not to everyone's liking. *La Minerve*, a Montreal Conservative paper, feared their presence would lead to class divisions and thereby undermine the existing parties. It did allow that on occasion workers might have a valid point of view to express; to permit them to do so the Liberals or Conservatives could on occasion let a labouring man slip into the parliamentary ring. Precisely that occurred in a federal by-election in Montreal East in 1888 when the Conservatives, by refraining from running, facilitated the election of the first worker candidate, Alphonse Lépine, member of the Knights of Labour and secretary of the Montreal Local Trades and Labour Council. No sooner was he in the House of Commons than he showed his gratitude to the Conservatives and earned the enmity of his working class colleagues in the union movement who claimed that he never said a word for labour in parliament. Perhaps he had already had his reward. At a banquet to mark Lépine's election, the secretary of state, Joseph-Adolphe Chapleau, praised the Knights of Labour, the National Policy, the royal commission enquiry, the Conservative party, and the strife-free nature of Canada's class relations all in one breath. Moreover, added the son of a stonemason now cabinet minister, there was room in Canada for upward mobility: "the industrious and honest man has a vast field open to him". Within four years Chapleau proved his point by becoming lieutenant-governor of Quebec; Alphonse Lépine vanished from public view in the federal election of 1896. Geographic, not social mobility, was the lot of Quebec's working class in the 1880s. And the problems of that class were the last thing on the minds of politicians, federal and provincial alike.

SELECT BIBLIOGRAPHY

Bélanger, Noel et al. *Les travailleurs québécois, 1851–1896.* Montreal: Les presses de l'Université du Québec, 1973.

Bonville, Jean de. *Jean-Baptiste Gagnepetit: Les travailleurs montréalais à la fin du XIXe siècle.* Montreal: L'Aurore, 1975.

Bradbury, Bettina. "The Family Economy and Work in an Industrializing City: Montreal in the 1870s." *Historical Papers/Communications historiques.* Canadian Historical Association, 1979. Pp. 71–96.

Chapleau, Joseph-Adolphe. *Discours prononcé au banquet des ouvriers à Ottawa.* (October 18, 1888). Pamphlet in the Public Archives of Canada.

Cross, D. Suzanne. "The Neglected Majority: The Changing Role of Women in 19th Century Montreal." *Histoire sociale/Social History* 6(1973):202–23.

Early, Frances H. "Mobility Potential and the Quality of Life in Working-class Lowell, Massachusetts: The French Canadians ca. 1870." *Labour/Le Travailleur* 2(1977):214–28.

Faucher, Albert, and Maurice Lamontagne. "History of Industrial Development." In *Essais sur le Québec contemporain.* Edited by Jean-C. Falardeau. Quebec: Les presses de l'Université Laval, 1953. Pp. 23–37.

Genest, Jean-Guy. "La vie ouvrière au Québec, 1850–1900: la réaction syndicale." *Protée* 2(1972):51–69.

Hamelin, Jean, Paul Larocque, and Jacques Rouillard. *Répertoire des grèves dans la province de Québec au XIXe siècle.* Montreal: Les presses de l'Ecole des hautes études commerciales, 1970.

Hamelin, Jean, and Yves Roby. *Histoire économique du Québec, 1851–1896.* Montreal: Fides, 1971.

Hamon, Edouard. *Les Canadiens-français de la Nouvelle-Angleterre.* Quebec: N.S. Hardy, 1891.

Hareven, Tamara K. "Family Time and Industrial Time: Family and Work in a Planned Corporation Town, 1900–1924." *Journal of Urban History* 1(1975):365–89.

Harvey, Fernand. "Les enfants de la révolution industrielle au Québec." *Critère* 25(1979):257–70.

Harvey, Fernand. *Révolution industrielle et travailleurs: une enquête sur les rapports entre le capital et le travail au Québec à la fin du 19e siècle.* Montreal: Boréal Express, 1978.

Kennedy, Douglas Ross. *The Knights of Labour in Canada.* London: University of Western Ontario Press, 1956.

Paquet, Gilles. "L'emigration vers la Nouvelle-Angleterre." *Recherches sociographiques* 5(1964):319–70.

Royal Commission on the Relations of Labor and Capital in Canada. Ottawa: Queen's Printer, 1889.

Silver, A.I. "French Canada and the Prairie Frontier, 1870–1890." *Canadian Historical Review* 50(1969):11–36.

Trofimenkoff, Susan Mann. "One Hundred and Two Muffled Voices: Canada's Industrial Women in the 1880s." *Atlantis* 3(1977):66–82.

RIEL

CHAPLEAU

MERCIER

LAURIER

10 The End of Empire

The last fifteen years of the nineteenth century shattered a number of political dreams. The Conservative party's dream of political longevity, based on its dominance of both federal and provincial politics in Quebec, came to naught among internecine quarrels in Quebec and Métis squabbles in the west. The ultramontane pretension to religious supremacy in civil matters collapsed in the face of political and social hostility. Confederation itself appeared doomed as neither the expected economic development nor the new nationality took form. The federal government's carefully laid plans for central control disintegrated under provincial assault. Even the old French dream of a Gallic presence across the continent, a tiny hope rekindled by some of the French Canadian makers of Confederation, turned to ashes under the gibbet of Louis Riel in Regina and in the law concerning Catholic schools in Manitoba. Canada's imperial connections, once a source of strength, now fostered ethnic animosity as appeals to the pope and appeals to the queen provoked mutual hostility between French and English Canadians. The male empire itself began to crack as female journalists, bicycle riders, and "typewriters" challenged male dominance of the public sphere. Surrounded by so many dissipating dreams, French Canadian politicians and intellectuals, like their English Canadian counterparts, began taking stock of Confederation and of Quebec's place in it.

The break-up of the Conservative party in Quebec was well underway before the ghost of Louis Riel consigned it to electoral oblivion. The party itself had always been a fragile alliance of Quebec *bleus*, Ontario tories, and scattered conservatives from elsewhere. If the alliance held sufficiently to ensure federal victories through the 1880s it was incapable of countering the rise of Liberals in the provinces. By the late 1880s every province had a Liberal government expressing regional grievances against the federal Conservative government. Even the always close connections between federal and provincial politicians—to the extent of trading places with one another when mutual advantage was to be derived—could not always ensure Conservative electoral victories at both levels of government. Moreover, ever since the death of George-Etienne Cartier in 1873, and long before Louis Riel met his fate at the hands of the federal Conservatives in 1885, the Conservative party in Quebec had been a fragile alliance of regional and ideological interests.

After Cartier's death, three men vied for his position as leader of the Quebec wing of the Conservatives. Joseph-Adolphe Chapleau, Adolphe Caron, and Hector Langevin brought to their rivalry differences of region as well as personality. Chapleau prided himself on being able to keep the Montreal area under his control. Caron paraded his electoral prowess in the Quebec City region and Hector Langevin did the same in Trois-Rivières. Each argued for place and prestige in the federal government on the grounds of the regional votes he could muster: each thought his claim more worthy than the other's. While they haggled among themselves, the ultramontane wing of the party plagued all three of them. Chapleau was the most upset by their presence, Langevin the most accommodating. Picking up on the nickname *castor* (beaver) which the ultramontanes had acquired, Chapleau derided them as nasty beasts who stirred up all sorts of mud to build their crude and destructive abodes and whose only value was in the selling of their skin. Gladly would Chapleau have skinned the Conservatives of the *castors*. He was even prepared to dismantle the party in order to dislodge them. In the early 1880s he approached those moderate Liberals that new political leaders like Honoré Mercier and Wilfrid Laurier were carefully cultivating. Perhaps an alliance might rid both groups of their radical fringe, the ultramontanes from the Conservatives and the *rouges* from the Liberals. Neither Caron nor Langevin was prepared to go that far nor, for the moment, was Mercier or Laurier. In fact, Chapleau's dickerings made him appear ever so slightly unreliable. In any case the rivalry between the three self-styled successors of Cartier, each contending that French Canadians could only have their rightful say in Confederation by uniting within one party behind one man—notably himself—probably did more harm to the Conservative party than the presence of the ultramontanes.

Louis Riel did of course play his part, if only as a dead man, in the shifting of political allegiances in Quebec from the Conservatives to the Liberals. The reaction to his hanging and to the federal Conservatives who brought it about in November 1885, did what Chapleau had been unable to do. It shook the ultramontanes loose from the "party of the rope." So angry were the ultramontanes over Riel's execution that they preferred the political company of one-time *rouges* saying we told you so about the repercussions of Confederation, of Liberals sensing an election issue, and of dismayed nationalists who saw in the hanging the end of any effective French Canadian presence in the west. The same anti-Conservative sentiments had united the same kind of people in 1871 over the New Brunswick school question, but the alliance then had been a momentary one, probably because of a lack of leadership. In 1885 such was not the case. Honoré Mercier, leader of the Quebec Liberals, although claiming his willingness to stand aside if Chapleau wished to become the man of the hour in Quebec by leading the popular hostility to the federal government's decision regarding Riel, had in fact been looking for such an issue for years.

Mercier had also been looking for a comfortable place in the political sun. Emerging from *rouge* country in the upper Richelieu, Mercier's early political attachments were to Cartier's *bleus*. As a young lawyer and journalist with the *Courrier de Saint-Hyacinthe* at the time of Confederation he was, however, more taken with the *rouge* criticism of the new political scheme. But he was also uneasy about the *rouge* lack of electoral success. He participated therefore in one of the early attempts to soften the *rouge* image; as secretary of the short-lived *parti national* in 1871, Mercier wanted the dissident liberals and conservatives who formed the new group to renounce their previous party allegiances and judge issues solely by national standards. Electoral success, however, remained just as elusive and Mercier had to don conventional Liberal colours to win a seat in the House of Commons in 1872. There his career was as brief as the life of the *parti national*. He took such a heated part in the debates over the New Brunswick school question and the Pacific railway scandal that the Liberals chose another candidate for his riding of Rouville in the elections of 1874. When he failed to win as a Liberal in St. Hyacinthe in the next federal election in 1878, he turned his attention to provincial politics.

There the scene resembled the French theatrical comedies of the late nineteenth century. Politicians came and went between Ottawa and Quebec, barely distinguishable one from another and almost all of them heavily involved in railway intrigue. In 1878 the lieutenant-governor, officially impartial but in fact a carefully chosen appointee of the Mackenzie Liberal government in Ottawa, got in on the act by dismissing a Conservative provincial government and replacing it with one more to his Liberal liking. Mercier quickly found himself a provincial seat and even enjoyed a few months as a provincial cabinet minister. But this Liberal government of Joly de Lotbinière was unable to maintain a majority in the legislature as Chapleau, now wearing a provincial cap, wooed some of its members to the Conservative side of the house. The action infuriated Mercier but also set him pondering a coalition with Chapleau. When nothing materialized, Mercier had to content himself with waiting out Chapleau's premiership, knowing that eventually Chapleau would go to Ottawa. He did so in 1882 and the next year Mercier took over the provincial Liberal party leadership from Joly. Through the 1880s, Mercier made speeches similar to that of Laurier in 1877, denying any connection between French Canadian liberalism and European revolutionaries. For all his efforts, however, he could command only a tiny group of fifteen or so in the provincial parliament of sixty-five seats. Mercier foresaw perpetual opposition.

But then Louis Riel came along, swinging from the gallows in Regina in November 1885. The federal cabinet ministers from Quebec, after much anguish, supported the government's decision not to pardon Riel or commute his sentence. The guilty verdict and the execution for treason were to stand. As federal cabinet ministers, Chapleau, Caron, and Langevin may have accepted John A. Macdonald's reasoning that the Conservatives had more to lose in Ontario by pardoning Riel than in Quebec by letting him hang. They may too have surmised that the public passion aroused at the time of the hanging—petitions, protests, and mass meetings orchestrated by known Liberals and ultramontanes—was just that, a momentary outburst that would soon blow over. They could even justify such a view since the Métis uprising itself in the spring of 1885 had been universally condemned in Quebec. Some ultramontanes did point to the grievances and unanswered petitions of the Métis in the west, but no one justified the taking of arms against legally constituted authority. Moreover there were French

Canadians among the troops sent west via the speedy new Canadian Pacific Railway to put down the rebellion. They were as convinced as any subsequent jury that the rebellion constituted treason. Come the autumn of 1885, however, many French Canadian Catholics in Quebec claimed the Métis leader as one of their own. They were not at all sure that Riel, religious fanatic that he admittedly was, bordering indeed on insanity, should pay with his life for the uprising and the various blunders and insensitivities of the federal government. The three Quebec federal ministers did not agree and Chapleau agonized over his decision to support the hanging. But their warnings of political havoc should Canada divide along racial and religious lines were drowned out in a chorus of protest. Directing the chorus was Honoré Mercier happily gathering up the protestors from the left of the Liberal party and the right of the Conservatives into a new *parti national.*

Mercier hoped that the new alliance would be more national and less partisan than its predecessor of fourteen years earlier. He also undoubtedly hoped it would lead him to the premiership of Quebec. It did both but not for long. The illusion of French Candian unity, pursued diligently by Quebec politicians since the 1840s, took on a semblance of reality as mass meetings were held to protest the hanging of Riel and to cheer Mercier's call to put aside partisan politics and unite in a national cause. Riel's death was a deliberate provocation of French Canada; he had gone to the gallows, claimed Mercier, because he was one of us. French Canadians must therefore use their provincial institutions to express their national protest. They must toss out Conservatives federally and provincially. The electorate, however, was more temperate. Neither then nor since did it sanction the national unity the leading politicians craved. In the provincial elections of 1886, in spite of the dangling of Riel's corpse before the nose of every elector, voters merely balanced the score by electing as many Liberals (many of them flying *parti national* colours) as Conservatives. Five conservative-nationalists then held the balance of power and it took a few months of parliamentary jockeying before Mercier was able to make his claim stick that a government formed by him would be a national and not a Liberal one. By early March 1887 the legislative majority swung slightly in his favour and Mercier became premier of Quebec.

Although the formation of the *parti national* and of Mercier's government actually favoured the Liberals in Quebec, federal Liberals were uneasy. Wilfrid Laurier shared the view of his Conservative colleagues from Quebec in Ottawa that a provincial party based on race and religion could have dangerous consequences. If imitated by French or English on the federal scene it could place French Canadians in a permanent and disabling minority position. Far better that they continue the pattern outlined by LaFontaine and Cartier by which political alliances rather than racial antagonisms form the basis of political parties. Only thus could French

Canadians be assured of any say at all in the government of the country. Laurier therefore refrained from moving too close to Mercier's *parti national*. But he did not stray too far away either. If successful provincially, as it turned out to be, albeit by a very narrow margin, it might provide a useful organizational base for defeating the Conservatives federally. For Laurier, it was merely a matter of playing his politics coolly. He was present at the huge public rally in Montreal the week after Riel's execution and told the crowd that he too would have shouldered a rifle had he been on the banks of the Saskatchewan. Fortunately from the benches of the federal opposition, all he had to do was fling words at the Conservatives for their inept and inhumane policies. He could even taunt the Quebec ministers for their unheroic stand, all the while sharing their views of the necessary political structures for a country such as Canada.

At the same time, Laurier carefully tended his own political connections outside Quebec. With the help of a strong Liberal presence in Ontario where premier Oliver Mowat had been waging battles for provincial rights since the 1870s, Laurier became the leader of the federal Liberal party in 1887. His very presence in Ottawa as the leader of a political party, the one forceful Quebec politician untainted by the Riel affair, gave the lie to Chapleau's complaint in 1888 that French Canadian influence in Ottawa was non-existent. As Laurier began sniffing electoral success in the wind, he also began to appear as the ultimate successor to Cartier, gathering moderates of all persuasions into his large Liberal fold. The death of Louis Riel certainly stirred up enough sentiment to shift some votes: in 1887 the federal Liberals from Quebec climbed from thirteen to thirty-two seats while the Conservatives dropped from fifty-one to thirty-three. But the real change came in the subsequent federal election of 1891 when the Liberals obtained a majority in Quebec. The death of Macdonald in 1891 may even have had more to do with the eventual dominion-wide Liberal victory in 1896, as the Conservatives searched desperately and unsuccessfully for a new leader of Macdonald's stature. The Liberals had their leader waiting, ready, and obvious. As Laurier well knew from the lessons he had learned from Joseph-Israel Tarte, a masterful political organizer then in the process of shifting his own political allegiance from Conservative to Liberal, elections were not won with prayers. But a good corpse could help and the Liberals had two.

There may have been more mundane reasons for the Liberals' growing presence on the provincial and federal scenes in the late 1880s. The Confederation promise of prosperity, population, and power was nowhere in evidence. Only the railways, crossing the country and crisscrossing the southwestern parts of the two central provinces, kept the dream of prosperity alive at all. They did bring industries to a number of towns and confirm the places of Montreal and Toronto in the urban hierarchy, but they also brought massive debts. And although they facilitated the transportation of goods and people, most of the people took the rail lines south to the United States. Feeble attempts at repatriation or attracting the exiled Canadians into the northwest came to naught. Immigration from abroad never did equal emigration from home. The National Policy appeared to give a boost to manufacturing in the early 1880s, but falling prices, imports, and exports later in the decade undermined even that hopeful respite. Moreover, industrialization entailed labour difficulties, both social and political, and some Canadians worried lest their dream of North American prosperity turn into a nightmare of European class warfare. Regional discontent also plagued the country as the Métis uprising in the west in 1885 was matched by the election of a separatist government in Nova Scotia in 1886. Intellectuals bemoaned the fate of Canada and even tempted politicians with their imperialist or continental panacea. In such a setting, changes in voting behaviour were perhaps not surprising.

Nor perhaps was Mercier's insistence on French Canadian unity. That the cry served political purposes was obvious: little else could bring Liberals and ultramontanes together. But it also may have served psychological purposes at a time of mass movements of population to the towns and to the United States. And in the face of growing English Canadian annoyance with things French and Catholic, the plea for unity may have been a natural defensive reaction. The difficulty with the plea was precisely what Quebec's federal politicians had claimed to see: it was bound to raise fears among those beyond its confines. Coincidentally many of those people happened to be members of the Conservative party in other parts of the country. Seeing the party disintegrate in Quebec as *bleus* sought political haven elsewhere, the Conservatives may even have raised their own politico-religious cry for electoral purposes. Certainly if the Conservative party were to survive the electoral changes in Quebec, it would have to strengthen its position in Ontario. What better way to encourage Conservative votes in Ontario than by stressing the English language and Protestantism? Popular prejudices thus fed on one another, the politicians sometimes quietly, sometimes noisily, reaping the profits.

Honoré Mercier certainly enjoyed posturing as a *chef national*. As premier of Quebec from 1887 to 1891 he kept alive the dangers confronting French Canada: opposition without and divisions within. With the latter he was quite familiar since his own rise to power had depended upon a coalition of quite diverse forces. Keeping them in line required a varied program and unifying slogans. Mercier had both. His electoral program and the flurry of activity undertaken by his government indicated his hope of satisfying everyone; they also gave the lie to his pretensions of national unity. For the Liberals, Mercier stressed decentralization, practical innovations in education, and economy in the administration. For the nationalists he emphasized provincial autonomy, and to keep the ultramontanes in line he reiterated his support for the existing clerical control of education and promised colonization and repatriation activities. To attract workers he proposed labour legislation to improve working conditions and he hoped to satisfy English-speaking voters by showing his respect for existing minority rights. "Cease our fratricidal strife and let us unite," cried Mercier as he paraded about the province and the world, as much the head of state in Lac St. Jean where he inaugurated the rail connection to Quebec City as in New York or Paris where he sought to borrow funds for his government's increasing expenditures. Mercier liked the taste and trappings of power.

The same motivations of money, power, and unity caused him to host the first interprovincial conference in Canada in 1887. He gathered the grumbling premiers of five of the seven provinces (three new provinces having joined the original four by this time: Manitoba in 1870, British Columbia in 1871, and Prince Edward Island in 1873) to Quebec City for a collective grievance session against the federal government. They all needed more money as provincial involvement in railway construction had sent their debts soaring beyond the niggardly sums of federal subsidies. They all wanted more power and objected strenuously to the federal right of disallowance which hung like a threat over all their activities. And they all thought provincial autonomy was just what their electorate, and their own political party, needed. With Nova Scotia threatening to secede from Confederation, Quebec unhappy over the Riel affair, Ontario embroiled in a series of court cases with the federal government over provincial jurisdiction, and Manitoba miserable about federal vetoes of its railway legislation, it was easy enough to have the guests at Quebec cry "Yes Yes" to a proposal of provincial rights. After all, argued Mercier, the federal government was a creation of the provinces and they should have more say in its functioning. For him that meant practical matters like the naming of senators; he left for his nationalist descendants the more thorough elaboration of the theory that Confederation was a compact between the federating provinces and the federating peoples—English and French.

No sooner had Mercier assisted the other provinces in tugging at Confederation than he raised a purely provincial issue which created a furor well beyond Quebec. The Jesuit Estates Act of 1888 was a proposal of the provincial government intended merely to resolve a complex dispute over the benefits from lands once held by the Jesuits in New France. The solution in fact created a worse stir as religious bigotry reverberated across Canada for another generation. Ever since the suppression of the Jesuit order by the pope in 1773, the lands had been crown property with their income used first by the governor and then by the assembly to support education. When the Jesuits regained papal sanction and reappeared in Canada as one of Monseigneur Bourget's imported religious orders in the 1840s, they staked their claim to the lands.

But to do so they had to compete with the Catholic church itself which now declared priority rights in education. The dispute embittered church-state relations in Quebec for almost half a century and it was only Mercier's coalition of Liberals and ultramontanes in the late 1880s that provided the impetus for and the necessity of finding a solution. The Act of 1888 proposed that the province buy out all claims to the properties for a sum of $400,000 with the sum to be divided among various Catholic groups involved in education. To satisfy Protestants who immediately protested provincial funds going to Catholic groups, the government attributed an additional $60,000 to the Protestant Committee of Public Instruction. The properties themselves were to remain crown lands. To satisfy ultramontanes and to avoid being caught in internecine religious squabbles, the appropriate division of the $400,000 among the various contenders was handed to the pope to decide.

At that, Protestants in Ontario bristled. What was the pope doing meddling in Canadian affairs? What was this appeal to a foreign power? What indeed was the Quebec government up to, riding to office on the coattails of a hanged traitor, currying favour with provincial premiers, and pretending to speak for, and even defend, minuscule French minorities beyond its boundaries? Could the cartoons be correct that showed Mercier replacing the name of every Canadian province with that of Quebec? And now the pope of all people in on some no doubt nefarious act. In the House of Commons, the "noble thirteen" or the "devil's dozen," depending on one's point of view, gathered behind Ontario Conservative MP D'Alton McCarthy to clamour for federal disallowance of the Jesuit Estates Act. Behind the demand seethed the bitterness of shattered illusions. Canada had not produced either the new nationality or the great nation that Confederation had promised. The fault surely lay with the Conservatives' catering to French Canadian sensibilities. Tolerance of language and religion had merely led to increased demands on the part of Quebec. Even Ontario was becoming soft, sheltering its Catholic separate schools, permitting the use of French in the primary schools, all because Quebec was so raucous. As for the French Canadians, they made no concessions at all. They refused to assimilate and as a "bastard nationality" they constituted the greatest danger to the Canadian confederacy.

McCarthy's outbursts were by no means those of an isolated fanatic. If he was unable to persuade the federal government to disallow the Jesuit Estates Act, he was able to arouse public opinion. In 1889, he and some Ontario Orangemen formed the Equal Rights Association to denounce the growing French presence in Canada. Was Canada to be French or English? The question should be resolved now, at the ballot box, before bayonets were required to make the decision within a generation. The Association's own proposal was to abolish separate (meaning Catholic) schools and to make English the sole language in Canadian schools. In the 1890s the same arguments were repeated by the Protestant Protective

Association, an American import that attracted fearful Ontarians bent on spying Catholic bogeymen in dark corners and public places. Even some intellectuals jumped on the racist bandwagon. For example, one of Goldwin Smith's implicit arguments for Canada's joining the United States was to provide a larger Anglo-Saxon pool in which to swamp the French Canadians. Canada itself, he argued, was an unnatural entity, a geographic, economic, and racial absurdity. The attempt "to fuse or even harmonize a French and Papal with a British and Protestant community" was sheer folly; a democratic Ontario and a clerical Quebec could never coalesce. Moreover, claimed Smith, for their inability and unwillingness to assimilate, French Canadians deserved the fate Durham had foreseen for them: factory hands in the employ of the English. Somewhat more generous, if ultimately just as supercilious, were the intellectuals of the Imperial Federation League, an organization established to promote a federal union of the British empire. George Parkin, George Grant, and John Bourinot all attempted to show that French Canadians could easily support imperial federation since they stemmed from the same Norman origins as English Canadians and had been relieved of the oppressive weight of religious and political absolutism by the Conquest. As unprogressive as they were, French Canadians, by the 1880s, could see the benefits that British political institutions had bestowed upon them. They ought therefore to be able to take the next logical step in the constitutional evolution of Canada, towards a closer integration of the British Empire. Only thus, thought Bourinot, could they survive at all. They would never last as part of the United States, much less as "an independent French nationality on the banks of the St. Lawrence." The Canadian Confederation was not even offered as an option, Bourinot and his colleagues seeming to have given up on it entirely. As for Honoré Mercier, he foresaw imperial federation leading to conscription for imperial wars.

In that setting of distrust, suspicion, and pessimism about the future of Canada, Manitoba delivered another blow to French Canadian equality in Confederation. In 1890 the Manitoba Liberal government abolished French as an official language in the province and ceased providing public funds for Catholic schools. Both were guarantees of the Manitoba Act, the federal law that created the province in 1870. Strictly speaking therefore, the action was both unconstitutional and illegal although it took the courts almost ninety years to say so. In the late 1880s few people had any such scruples. D'Alton McCarthy had been skulking about the prairie province making inflammatory speeches on the evils of Catholicism and the French language. The Manitoba government itself, still grating under the monopoly given by the federal government to the Canadian Pacific Railway and perhaps even looking for an election issue to turn the public eye away from its own rather dubious railway activities, may have thought it had a respectable provincial issue on its hands. It may even have surmised that the declining number of French Canadians in the province—from just under a half to less than one-tenth of the population in a mere twenty years—would be incapable of arousing much serious opposition. In fact, the Manitoba school question was a tinderbox which would prove to have the power to alight political, religious, racial, and linguistic animosities across the country for years to come.

Manitoba's Catholics began the protest and did not let up for almost seven years. Along the way they acquired momentary allies in both federal parties and among the clergy and politicians of Quebec, depending on the stage of their protest and often on the political allegiance of the ally. Unhappily accepting the abolition of French as an official language in Manitoba since there was no recourse short of an unlikely federal disavowal of the law, they were determined not to accept the virtual death of separate schools. They were of course free to finance their own schools privately, but they were not absolved from paying the provincial school tax as well, a tax which went to the support of non-sectarian schools only. On the grounds therefore that they were being doubly taxed for an educational right which was constitutionally theirs, the Catholics of Manitoba appealed, as Section 93 of the British North America Act permitted, to the governor general in council. They tried all three types of appeal: that the federal government disallow the Manitoba legislation; that the courts declare it *ultra vires*, that is, beyond the powers of the provincial legislature; and that the federal government intervene directly and restore the school rights of the beleaguered minority.

Only after a six-year struggle did the Conservative government in Ottawa agree to the last course of action. In the intervening years it wavered and wondered. It bought time, and thereby passed the one-year deadline for exercising its veto power, by financing the Manitoba Catholics' appeal though the courts all the way to the Judicial Committee of the Privy Council in London which eventually declared the school legislation quite within the powers of the Manitoba government. It pleaded internal difficulties as four prime ministers in as many years tried unsuccessfully to fill John A. Macdonald's shoes after his death in 1891. When badgered by the Manitoba Catholics to intervene directly, it delayed even more by asking the courts to clarify its right, quite clearly stated in the British North America Act, to do so. The highest Canadian court said no, the final court of appeal in London said yes. Even then the Conservatives, faced with an election in 1896, could not decide. They asked the grievers to present their case for federal redress and then requested that the Manitoba government submit its counter-argument. Only at the very last minute, early in 1896, when some kind of solution had to be presented to the electorate did the Conservatives make up their mind. A remedial bill would force Manitoba to reinstate public support for Catholic schools.

And then the battle began again, this time over provincial rights.

Laurier led the charge from the opposition benches in the House of Commons. Aware of the fine line he was tracing between provincial rights and minority rights, Laurier was also keenly conscious of the disarray of the Conservatives. With one eye on the forthcoming elections, he opposed the remedial bill. With another eye carefully scrutinizing the Catholic clergy both in Quebec and beyond who had petitioned the federal government for redress just a year earlier, Laurier promised negotiation, "sunny ways" rather than imposition. Compromise and tolerance were the only possible paths through the thicket of popular passions aroused by religio-linguistic disputes. Attaching those disputes to federal-provincial power struggles would only aggravate both. If the federal government could undertake to establish school rights in a given province, what could prevent it from attacking those same rights in another province? And what would be the reaction in other provinces if the federal government succeeded in passing the remedial legislation? Would Ontario, for example, be so angry as to turn upon its own separate schools?

Laurier also knew that opinion in Quebec was divided, no matter what the bishops might say, and he was hoping to take advantage of this in 1896. He had in fact carefully avoided committing himself on the Manitoba question throughout the 1890s. Although he had a federal Liberal majority behind him in Quebec, there was no longer a Liberal provincial government after Mercier succumbed to political disgrace due to a railway scandal in 1891 and the Liberals to defeat in 1892. Luckily for Laurier the smell of scandal hovered just as strongly around federal Conservatives as provincial Liberals. Hector Langevin had faced public exposure for railway and patronage deals in 1891 as well, even if both he and Mercier were exonerated by the courts. The only other political strongman the Conservatives had in Quebec, Joseph-Adolphe Chapleau, was twiddling his thumbs in the lieutenant-governor's mansion outside Quebec City. Chapleau had insisted on the passage of the Manitoba remedial bill before he would consent to rejoin the Conservative cabinet and, he assumed, save the party from certain electoral defeat in Quebec in the forthcoming elections. But the remedial bill died with the parliament and Chapleau remained quietly in Quebec; his silence eased the way for the federal Liberals. In June 1896, the electorate calmly ignored clerical threats of doom as a result of voting Liberal; as in the rest of Canada, where some Protestant ministers could also be heard invoking the penalties of judgment day on prospective Liberal voters, in Quebec the victory went to Laurier.

Sunny solutions to the Manitoba school question did not necessarily mean happy ones. Laurier carefully sent negotiators acceptable to the Quebec bishops to achieve a compromise with the Manitoba government of Thomas Greenway. But that did not guarantee the clerics' approval of the result. The single public school system was to remain; the Manitoba Liberals would not budge from that no matter how pleased they were to see Liberals in office in Ottawa. As a peace offering, they would allow religious instruction at the end of the school day if a certain number of parents requested it. Under the same conditions a Catholic teacher could be hired. And if ten pupils in any school district spoke a language other than English, the school was to provide bilingual teaching, in English and the other language. Nobody much liked the compromise: Quebec Catholics were unhappy with such meagre concessions, Ontario Protestants were disgruntled about the possibility of a revived French and Catholic presence in the west, and Manitobans begrudged what appeared to be an imposition of eastern Canadian feuds upon the west. While the Quebec bishops murmured their discontent, a papal envoy, sent once again to investigate the political bickering of the Catholic clergy in Canada, confirmed their uneasiness but argued that the path of compromise was the only one possible if Catholicism was to survive at all in Canada.

Shortly after the turn of the century, the gloomy and problematic nature of Laurier's sunny ways became apparent. The bilingual clause created havoc as immigrants from all over Europe filled up the schools of Manitoba and demanded bilingual schooling in every conceivable language. In 1916 the Manitoba government simply abolished that clause. By then of course Quebecois had other reasons for doubting the level of tolerance among English Canadians, but the lesson was just as obvious in the 1890s: French Canadians could enjoy their full religious and linguistic rights solely in Quebec; beyond that they constituted merely one minority among others subject, like the rest, to the whims of a majority. Because of that, the French-speaking minority outside Quebec was bound to be assimilated. The weight of numbers, the lack of legal protection, and the argument that the English language was necessary for national unity were bound to take their toll. In response Quebecois could only rally their own numbers in a restricted provincial place, legislate their own protection, and argue the necessity of the French language for national survival. The promised new nationality of 1867 dissolved into two nations, no longer even French and English Canada but Quebec and English Canada.

Nationalist intellectuals responded to the troubled times of the late nineteenth century and the debate over Quebec's place in Confederation has kept the press, the politicians, and the historians busy ever since. If few people now advocate Edmond de Nevers' solution of annexation to the United States, far more have adopted Jules-Paul Tardivel's open espousal of separatism. Like their English Canadian counterparts, the *fin-de-siècle* intellectuals were only able to envision a future for Canada elsewhere, in independence, in annexation, or in imperial federation. Only the federal politicians and perhaps the women, French- and English-speaking feminists allying easily, if only temporarily, within the National Council of

Women from the mid-1890s, seemed able to live with the here and now of the political and social problems that Canada encountered. The intellectuals preferred to project ideal political solutions as a confirmation of their nationalist sentiment of being apart or other.

Tardivel's separatism in fact predated the 1890s, but the Manitoba school question bolstered it. In his ultramontane newspaper *La Vérité* which he ran on a shoestring from his home in Quebec City, Tardivel began making separatist noises shortly after the Riel affair, in 1886. Ten years later he even claimed to his three thousand or so readers that the original purpose of his paper, founded in 1881, had been to convince French Canadian leaders of the providential destiny of Quebec to form an autonomous nation. But he was probably reading into his own past his immediate reaction to the Manitoba school question. The only options he envisaged as a result of the crisis were assimilation or separation. Compromise was impossible and Tardivel detested Laurier for attempting it. His political and religious ultra-conservatism may even have coloured his separatist message to later generations of Quebecois: even in the 1980s separatism has a connotation, for certain people, of right-wing intransigence. Tardivel would not have recognized the label. He considered himself free of all political and religious intrigue and would have appreciated the more sympathetic assessment that placed him at the origin of independent journalism in Quebec.

In 1895 Tardivel used a startling means to explore the separatist option. He wrote a novel, *Pour la patrie*, and filled it with all the political and religious intrigue which he denied in his journalism. He even felt he had to justify the literary form; his novel, unlike most, would be a force for good, a Christian tale of combat, a means of propagating the French and Catholic civilizing mission of French Canada in North America. Well he might attempt to justify his undertaking, for his novel was full of implausibilities. God and Satan intervened directly to perform miracles or dastardly deeds; the dead returned from heaven; and women acquiesced in their husbands' every demand. But the novel, set in the mid-1940s, was also an uncanny commentary on contemporary politics. Around a debate over Canada's future entailing the choices of the existing federation, a legislative union, or separation, Tardivel spun a tale of ruse and heroism leading to the divinely ordained and peacefully achieved separation of Quebec. Along the way he included all the pet peeves and passions of a late nineteenth century ultramontane separatist. He placed progress in the evil hands of Freemasons and revealed the anti-Catholicism of federalists. He had secret societies imported from Europe and acting in the name of liberalism to plot an end to the French Canadian nation. He portrayed conniving politicians supported by a servile press. And he had the state itself undermining religious and familial values by imposing free and compulsory education. To avoid such evils, Tardivel posited the intimate connection of religion and patriotism, the assurance of God's sanction for nationalist undertakings, the need for sacrifice and devotion, and the perpetual struggle.

Quite different was Edmond de Nevers' analysis of the ills of and remedies for French Canada. De Nevers had an even smaller audience than Tardivel, having spent most of his adult life in study in the universities of Berlin and Paris in order to escape the "intellectual indolence" of his native land. In 1896 he published *L'Avenir du peuple canadien français* privately and somewhat timidly, sending it to select people for comment and urging them not to release any of it to the press. He even slyly sent a copy to Goldwin Smith, whose annexationism he shared, inscribed "from a French Canadian who would make a very poor factory hand."

The French Canada that he portrayed, unlike Tardivel's beleaguered nation under the perpetual assault of evil forces from the outside and treacherous collaborators within, was apathetic and unprogressive. The people wandered aimlessly to town and factory, betraying their decadence by their attraction to the materialistic and English language wonders of the American giant to the south. The more educated among them wandered equally aimlessly towards politics, discarding their adventuresome past and their cultural mission in North America and limiting their intellectual curiosity to the intrigues of politicians jockeying for place. A handful of competent administrators could easily accomplish the tasks of the three hundred or so people involved directly or as aspiring hangers-on in the game of politics. Meanwhile French Canada desperately needed engineers, agronomists, physicians, chemists, and properly trained teachers instead of student priests who served as mere monitors to bring an enlightened patriotism to bear on the practical questions of education, colonization, repatriation, and the development of natural resources. Where was the internationally renowned university, the conservatory of music, the library, the school of fine arts, and the polytechnic that a city such as Montreal should have? It was time for French Canadians to recognize that they were ignorant and mediocre and that a reputation for joviality and hospitality could not long cover the fact. In the great judgments passed upon peoples, warned de Nevers, French Canadians would be found negligent in their economic and intellectual contribution to the progress of mankind.

Perhaps for that reason de Nevers predicted their ultimate fate in annexation to the United States. Whether he saw there greater scope for the intellectual endeavours he urged or happier circumstances for the exercising of the linguistic and cultural mission that characterized French Canadians is not clear. Certainly he saw no future in imperial federation where French Canadians would always be a thorn in the side of Anglo-Saxon unity. Canadian independence from Great Britain was just as far-fetched as long as the present generation of English Canadians was so doggedly opposed to sharing the country equally with French Canadians. As for separatism, de Nevers dismissed it as ridiculous: an independent Quebec would be like a South American republic where greed, ambition, vanity, corruption, mediocrity, and intolerance reigned. Thinking about separatism was a waste of time. French Canadians should concentrate instead on developing their intellectual resources so that they could join the United States at the appropriate time as an ally. The presence of so many French Canadian emigrants in the northeastern states had already prepared the way; de Nevers' passing interest in repatriation turned to an admiration for the qualities of independence, energy, and perseverance displayed by Franco-Americans. Far from having left the country, they had in fact enlarged it. Once the entire continent was American, there would be so many natural and cultural differences that no one would dare impose any uniformity of language or customs or traditions.

De Nevers' wistful and Tardivel's providential future for French Canada, although quite different, both reveal the extent of unhappiness about Confederation in the 1890s. None of the dreams of the 1860s had materialized; most of the risks emphasized by the *rouges* had come true. A kind of intellectual separatism in both French and English Canada recorded the demise of empire and the lack of enthusiasm for the present. Even the feminine women whom de Nevers thought were a distinguishing feature of French Canada were hopping on bicycles and riding resolutely away from family enclaves. Only the Liberal politicians were betting on Canada and they were to have the luck of economic prosperity after 1896 to support them. No sooner had Quebec given the federal nod to Laurier in 1896 than it did so a year later to the provincial Liberals. They in turn promised obedience to the French Canadian prime minister. A new political empire was in the making revealed by the provincial Liberal's co-operation in dismissing, at Laurier's request, a provincial plan for the creation of a ministry of education. So too was a new economic order as the provincial government prepared to finance the economic development of Quebec with foreign funds. With a little help from the Americans and only the occasional admonition from the intellectuals, the twentieth century might belong to Quebec.

SELECT BIBLIOGRAPHY

Berger, Carl. *The Sense of Power: Studies in the Ideas of Canadian Imperialism, 1867–1914.* Toronto: University of Toronto Press, 1970.

Bourinot, Sir John George. *Canadian Studies in Comparative Politics.* Montreal: Dawson Brothers, 1890.

Bourinot, Sir John George. *Canada During the Victorian Era.* Ottawa: J. Durie and Sons, 1897.

166   THE DREAM OF NATION

Clark, Lovell, ed. *The Manitoba School Question: Majority Rule or Minority Rights?* Toronto: Copp Clark, 1968.

Clippingdale, Richard. *Laurier: His Life and World.* Toronto: McGraw-Hill Ryerson, 1979.

Cook, Ramsay. *Provincial Autonomy, Minority Rights and the Compact Theory, 1867-1921.* Ottawa: Queen's Printer, 1969.

Crunican, Paul E. "Bishop Laflèche and the Mandement of 1896." *Historical Papers/Communications historiques.* Canadian Historical Association, 1969. Pp. 52-61.

Désilets, Andrée. "La succession de Cartier, 1873-1891." *Historical Papers/ Communications historiques.* Canadian Historical Association, 1968. Pp. 49-64.

Désilets, Andrée. *Hector-Louis Langevin: Un père de la Confédération canadienne (1826-1906).* Quebec: Les presses de l'Université Laval, 1969.

Flanagan, Thomas. *Louis 'David' Riel: 'Prophet of the New World.'* Toronto: University of Toronto Press, 1979.

Girard, Mathieu. "La pensée politique de Jules-Paul Tardivel." *Revue d'histoire de l'Amérique française* 21(1967):397-428.

Miller, J.R. *Equal Rights: The Jesuits' Estates Act Controversy.* Montreal: McGill-Queen's University Press, 1979.

Neatby, H. Blair. *Laurier and a Liberal Quebec: A Study in Political Management.* Toronto: McClelland and Stewart, 1973.

Neatby, H. Blair, and John T. Saywell. "Chapleau and the Conservative Party in Quebec." *Canadian Historical Review* 37(1956):1-22.

O'Sullivan, J.F. "D'Alton McCarthy and the Conservative Party, 1876-1896." Unpublished M.A. thesis, University of Toronto, 1949.

Parkin, Sir George Robert. *The Great Dominion.* London: Macmillan, 1895.

Rumilly, Robert. *Mgr. Laflèche et son temps.* Montreal: Editions du Zodiaque, 1938.

Rumilly, Robert. *Honoré Mercier et son temps.* 2nd ed. 2 vols. Montreal: Fides, 1975.

Silver, Arthur. *The French Canadian Idea of Confederation 1864-1900.* Toronto: University of Toronto Press, 1982.

Smith, Goldwin. *Canada and the Canadian Question.* Toronto: University of Toronto Press, 1971 (Hunter and Rose, 1891).

". . . million dollar mush"
La Tuque Pulp Company, 1916.

11 The Twentieth Century Belongs to Quebec

Sir Wilfrid Laurier, the Liberal prime minister, greeted the new century in the name of Canada, expecting it to bring to the nation on the northern half of the continent the population, prosperity, and prestige that the United States had experienced in the nineteenth century. Simon-Napoléon Parent, the Liberal premier of Quebec, welcomed the new century for the provincial economic development it promised, expecting investment and education to float the province and its people to prosperity and thus stem the tide of emigration. Laurier hoped to consolidate Confederation and to heal the estrangement between French and English. Yet almost everything he touched turned to nationalist rancour in Quebec. Parent and his successor Lomer Gouin assumed that favourable circumstances and liberal policies would ensure popular contentment;

they too had to confront a fierce nationalist critique while strikes across the province hinted at popular unhappiness. The nationalists themselves spoke loudly of autonomy for Canada, Quebec, and the economy, but they could rarely manage their own and frequently found themselves caught in political conundrums. Even when they limited their criticism to social and cultural affairs, they ran into competition from feminists and clerics. Nonetheless, all of them embraced the new century with enthusiasm and optimism.

From the opening of the century until his political defeat in 1911, Laurier constantly stoked the optimism that fired the press and the politicians of Canada. Whether inside the country or abroad, he flaunted the prosperity that the world economic upswing at the end of the 1890s heralded for his northern nation. At the periodic colonial conferences in London, Laurier acted as master of ceremonies for great Canadian shows featuring himself, the first French Canadian prime minister of Britain's oldest Dominion, knighted by Queen Victoria in 1897, accompanied by troops of mounted police and colourful Indians. He murmured pleasantries about Canadians taking their places in the parliament of Westminster and surveyed the British press for favourable coverage of Canada. Good reports meant immigrants and investments to fill the plains and trains of Canada. Laurier even took on the role of advertising agent for his own wild railway scheme to develop two new transcontinental lines in addition to the existing Canadian Pacific. In London he drummed up business for them by using the language of imperialism to praise a round-the-world route of imperial trade passing by the lines and steamships of Canada's booming transportation companies. He flaunted the rising international importance of his country after a particularly enterprising engagement by Canadian soldiers in the South African war. Independence might even be Canada's destiny, especially if Britain continued to cater to the Americans as it did in a dispute between Canada and the United States over the boundaries of the Alaskan panhandle. In the meantime, as a sign of national prestige if not yet independence, Canada could well afford its own navy, even if, as Laurier stipulated, it was to be available to Britain in time of need.

All the while Laurier expected French Canadians happily to follow suit, drawn by and contributing to the "magnet of the civilized world" that Canada was sure to be for the next hundred years. Many of them did. Provincial Liberals, rarely working at cross-purposes with their federal counterparts and electorally just as successful through most of the twentieth century, shared Laurier's excitement about the times. So in fact did the budding nationalist movement, although it often disputed ways and means. Laurier attempted to harness the enthusiasm of French Canadians with a trickle of French immigration, a transcontinental railway through northern Quebec, a valiant struggle for separate schools in the new western provinces of Alberta and Saskatchewan, a "tin pot" navy, as his Conservative opponents dubbed it, some of it to be constructed in Quebec shipyards, and of course his own charisma, similar to that of Pierre Trudeau in the late 1960s. But it did not always work.

One of the earliest difficulties appeared on the very eve of the new century. Britain's involvement in the South African war in 1899 raised the question of Canadian participation. Although a similar British venture into Egypt in the 1880s had merely aroused John A. Macdonald's sarcasm, by the late 1890s the climate of opinion in Canada had changed dramatically. Laurier had fierce English Canadian imperialists to contend with, some of them in his own party. They were enchanted by the final fling of British imperialism in the late nineteenth century and, for reasons both emotional and economic, they had drawn closer to Britain. Some of them even expected to bring the entire country into a political, economic, and military embrace of empire. They argued their case on nationalist lines claiming the ties of a common past, common social and political traditions, a literary and legal culture distinct from and superior to that of others, and a mission to spread the good word, along with British deeds, to all parts of the globe. In English Canada itself, all the elements of popular culture spread the imperial word: school books and church sermons, parades and public holidays. A special version of God Save the Queen—"Far from the motherland/Nobly we'll fall or stand/By England's Queen" —accompanied many Canadian anniversary celebrations of Queen Victoria's sixty years on the throne in 1897.

From that vantage point Canadians reacted with alarm when British troops were unable to bring a quick halt to the war between Britain's Cape Colony and the Boer republic of the Transvaal in the southern tip of Africa. Ever since the establishment of the Transvaal independent of the Cape Colony in the 1830s, Britain had unsuccessfully claimed sovereignty over the area. At issue in the late 1890s was the alleged ill treatment by the Boers of British subjects spilling north from the Cape Colony into both the Transvaal and the neighbouring Orange Free State. English Canadian newspapers dutifully reported the "liberal" justification for British entanglement and clamoured for Canadian involvement in defence of the rights of the English settlers. That those settlers were perhaps the unwitting outriders for certain interests in the Cape Colony—British entrepreneur Cecil Rhodes among them—anxious to acquire easy access through the Boer territory to the diamonds and gold in the lands to the north was lost on most Canadians. One who did register the fact, however, was the young Liberal MP Henri Bourassa.

The grandson of Louis-Joseph Papineau, Bourassa added to his grandfather's rebelliousness vast historical knowledge, a deep appreciation and understanding of British constitutional principles and practices, and a Catholicism bordering on ultramontanism. Like many other nationalist spokesmen he had had an education somewhat different from the norm, never having attended a classical college. His erudition and oratorical talents were impressive and Laurier was much taken with the young man until they came to blows over the question of Canadian participation in the South African war. Bourassa was absent from the Commons one day in the summer of 1899 when a unanimous resolution of sympathy was expressed for Britain's efforts to obtain full rights for its subjects in the Transvaal. And the House was not in session in October 1899 when Laurier decided, the day after the outbreak of the war, that an order in council was sufficient for the raising of a few thousand volunteers to be sent at minimal expense to join the imperial troops in South Africa. Only a few days earlier he had declared the impossibility of sending Canadian soldiers, legally constrained by the Militia Law to the defence of Canada on Canadian territory; moreover, since the Canadian parliament was not sitting, there was no way to obtain funds for an expedition of any sort. But Laurier changed his mind, apparently at the request of Britain and certainly in the midst of an imperialist clamour in Canada.

Laurier's decision along with everything else about the South African war angered Bourassa. He interpreted the war as one of commercial conquest, part of the final fling of the rapacious imperialism of the late nineteenth century. There was nothing liberal about it and Laurier was abandoning his own liberalism by pretending that it was a just war. As for Britain's claim to sovereignty in the Transvaal, it was historically invalid; moreover, its call for colonial assistance in the war was politically outrageous. The ties of empire should be as loose as the ties of federalism, Bourassa argued: autonomy and decentralization should characterize them both. Certainly Canada's ties to Britain should not be subject to the passing passions of English Canadians. Who knew what that blind emotionalism might lead to? It was so vague and so imprecise and yet so powerful that it could well change Canada irrevocably. Already Laurier had provided the precedent for Canadian participation in future imperial wars. The next step might well be a consolidation of imperial ties. Before Canadians knew it and before they even had a word to say on the matter, they might find themselves trapped in an imperial federation. There they would have no more voice than the Canadian parliament had had in the sending of soldiers to South Africa. Bourassa registered his personal protest by resigning his Commons' seat; his electors confirmed his views by returning him by acclamation in the following by-election.

Bourassa's opposition made him a popular figure in Quebec. He never did sanction some of the more volatile reactions to Canadian participation, one of which drew parallels between the situation of the Boers and that of the Quebecois crushed beneath Britain's imperial weight. But his reasoned claim for Canadian autonomy caught the attention of press and people alike. If it made little difference to the federal election results in Quebec in November 1900 when

Laurier's prestige and organization maintained almost all of the Quebec seats for the Liberals, that was because there was no alternative. Bourassa, re-elected in 1900, was not yet ready to make peculiar alliances with even more imperialist Conservative politicians. That gamble would come later in the decade when a larger nationalist movement had gathered strength. In the meantime young people began hovering around Bourassa, hanging on his public words, feeling electrified by his speeches, and preparing to make of him a *chef*. The immediate result was the formation of the *Ligue nationaliste* in 1903 and the founding, in 1904, of the newspaper *Le Nationaliste*, edited by Olivar Asselin. Both the *Ligue* and the newspaper advocated Canadian autonomy within the empire, provincial autonomy within Confederation, and the rational development of Canadian resources.

If the South African war created a nationalist movement in Quebec, the influx of immigrants helped to give it a popular base. Just how would French Canadians fare among the hundreds of thousands of newcomers pouring into Canada annually by the turn of the century? When the immigration boom came to an end in 1914, it was clear that English speakers predominated, having come primarily from the United States and Great Britain. French Canadians expected that. But they also expected French and Belgian immigrants and wondered vaguely why the federal government put so little effort into attracting them. More than two hundred agents of the Canadian government scoured Britain for potential emigrants; two such people covered France and Belgium. European countries might be loath to see their citizens depart, but French Canadians were not convinced that the federal ministry of the interior, responsible for immigration and headed by Manitoban Clifford Sifton, did all it could. Barely one thousand French speakers arrived per year at the turn of the century; even at two thousand per year thereafter, they were hardly perceptible in the annual influx that passed four hundred thousand in the peak year 1913. More French speakers would come, the agents assured the government, if Canada did not restrict its intake to agricultural immigrants. Those who did come, the ministry in turn assured parliament, were properly received: there were French Canadian officials in Montreal, Mattawa, and Ville-Marie facilitating their move west or into Temiscamingue. There were even French Canadian agents of the federal government in the United States hoping to encourage French Canadians to move back to Canada. The one in Michigan used all the tricks of the Canadian trade, making speeches and sending letters, distributing articles and pamphlets, competing with the magicians and the Salvation Army for the attention of the Saturday night crowds in mid-western American towns. The agents worked on commission and there is no evidence that anyone made a fortune.

By far the most visible of the immigrants were those who spoke neither French nor English. They flowed into the ports of Quebec and Montreal, their language and their dress loudly proclaiming their difference. They lingered in both towns waiting for trains to take them west. There, and all along the route, they returned the stares of the inhabitants, French and English alike, impassive faces all round masking the uneasiness that everyone felt. Few openly voiced the fear. But it was evident in the writings of Olivar Asselin and Henri Bourassa watching the stream heading west from Montreal and of J.S. Woodsworth, a Methodist minister engaged in social work among immigrants in the north end of Winnipeg. Could such strange looking people really contribute to the strengthening of Canadian nationhood, one of the aims of the *Ligue nationaliste?* Would they not more likely upset the delicate balance between French and English, so painfully constructed over the last century? Were they not also likely to deprive Canadians of jobs? And who knew anything about their standards of health or morality? French Canadians had long memories of the gruesome connection between immigrants and disease. Why moreover did they receive favoured treatment from the Canadian government and pay less to cross the Atlantic and the continent than French Canadians did to go west from Montreal?

Asselin and other nationalists had few answers to their questions, but they did expect some action on the part of government officials. They suspected collusion between the railway interests and the ministry of the interior and demanded that the provinces have more of a say and more of a financial stake in immigration which, after all, was a joint federal-provincial responsibility. They also suggested that a larger French Canadian presence in the Canadian west might facilitate the assimilation of the newcomers by making the dual nature of the country and its institutions more apparent. But financial difficulties kept French Canadians confined to eastern Canada; they could only afford to move into eastern Ontario or drop off the new National Transcontinental in the Quebec and Ontario northland. A few vague voices, clerical mostly, even began to sanction this pitiable movement of poverty by dreaming of a bridge of French Canadian settlement from Quebec to the west across the harsh land of the Canadian shield. The nationalists of the early twentieth century, however, were much more hard-nosed than their clerical contemporaries: they insisted that French Canadians receive some of the financial assistance going so lavishly to the new immigrants.

The nationalists had good reason to be hard-nosed for they were far outnumbered by voices denying the dual nature of Canada, particularly in the west. The rapid settlement of the Canadian west necessitated carving two new provinces and enlarging the boundaries of another out of the Northwest Territories. Both the creation of Saskatchewan and Alberta in 1905 and the extension of Manitoba north to Hudson Bay in 1912 raised the school question once again. Was there to be duality in the institutions of the new west? The North West Territories Act of 1875 had stipulated that the minority of either religion, Catholic or Protestant, had the right to its own schools directed by people of its own faith and funded by its proportion of the general school tax. In the intervening thirty years, however, schooling in the Territories had evolved towards a much more unified system with the introduction of a common curriculum and administration and with restrictions on the establishment of new Catholic schools and on the teaching of religion. The Manitoba school question had also occurred in the interval, leaving little doubt about the hostility of westerners to separate schools. And in the context of massive immigration, the hostility became rigidity: the west needed a unified school system if it was to assimilate all those foreigners.

Neither a Liberal federal government in 1905 nor a Conservative one in 1912 was able to satisfy French Canadian demands for a dual school system in the west with both public and separate schools financed from provincial revenues. Laurier attempted in vain to reinstate the provisions for minority education rights found in the Northwest Territories Act of 1875 into the autonomy bills that created Alberta and Saskatchewan. The effort cost him both western supporters infuriated by his eastern presumptions and French Canadian supporters dismayed by his ultimate compromise. And yet Laurier's concern for separate schools was as great as theirs. He considered religious teaching in the schools to be one of the bases of social stability. Unlike his western Liberal colleagues, he had no faith in the American system of "national" schools. Far from creating a nation, their religious neutrality, Laurier believed, gave rise to all the social ills of contemporary American society. Nonetheless, all he could impose upon the new western provinces was the continuation of existing separate schools now to be under the single administration and control of the newly established provincial governments. Even in 1912, when needled by French Canadian nationalists who had assisted it to power in 1911, the federal Conservative government of Robert Borden, did no better. Manitoba would not hear of school legislation different from its own in the newly added northern territory of Keewatin and in that it had the backing of Wilfrid Laurier, now leader of the federal opposition. Borden leaned that way too in spite of severe criticism from his nationalist allies. His compromise was to arrange some minor modifications to the original Laurier-Greenway agreement of 1896. But by 1912 Quebec nationalists had a school crisis right next door in Ontario to contend with to say nothing of imperial war clouds gathering over the Atlantic.

Indeed the early signs of those clouds had brought nationalists and Conservatives together in the first place. From opposing points of view, they both objected to Laurier's plan of 1910 to develop a Canadian navy which could be handed over to the British admiralty in case of emergency. Henri Bourassa felt so strongly about what he saw as the latest threat to Canadian autonomy that he began a newspaper, *Le Devoir*, to denounce Laurier. Canada must not commit itself in advance and without any popular consultation to participation in whatever international scrape Britain might choose to call an emergency. The spectre of automatic Canadian involvement in British wars haunted Bourassa once again. Laurier countered with the legal maxim that as a colony Canada was at war whenever Britain was: Bourassa retorted that such an affront to Canadian autonomy had not been seen since before the days of responsible government. In the meantime the Conservatives were drumming up opposition to Laurier's naval bill in Ontario. A Canadian navy would be so small and take so long to develop that it would be of no use to Britain. What was required was an immediate grant of money as a gesture of imperial solidarity. Such an argument was hardly one that the Conservative leader in Quebec, Frederick Debartzch Monk, could use. He in fact sounded more like the nationalist Bourassa, arguing that the money required for a Canadian navy would be better spent on internal transportation development and claiming that the offer of the tiny navy to Britain constituted a change in imperial relations which required at least the sanction of a plebiscite. Monk wondered indeed why Canada should contribute so freely to imperial defence and yet have no say in imperial policies. The more nationalist and autonomist Olivar Asselin contended that with a navy of its own Canada was taking on the burdens of nationhood; it should therefore become independent and cease to "drag the fetters of colonialism."

Certainly, nationalist and Conservative, autonomist and imperialist all spotted the navy as an issue which might be used against the ageing Laurier government. And when a nationalist candidate defeated a Liberal in a federal by-election in 1910, they all became very friendly. Conservative organizers appeared at nationalist meetings, gauging the temper of the anti-navy, anti-imperialist, and, gradually, anti-conscriptionist crowds and speeches. Conservative money was even said to be financing *Le Devoir*. When Laurier called a general election for September 1911 on the entirely different issue of reciprocity with the United States, thereby hoping to to defuse the naval question, the Conservatives and nationalists hid their differing economic views and combined forces for the electoral fray in Quebec. Where one had a chance to win, the other refrained from presenting a candidate. Uniting them in public was the proposal for a plebiscite on the navy and the demand for a Canadian voice in imperial policies if there was to be Canadian assistance in imperial defence. Privately many Conservatives doubted the wisdom of the former and many nationalists that of the latter. But they kept their doubts to themselves long enough to add sixteen seats to the Conservatives' eleven from Quebec which, combined with a much stronger swing away from the Liberals in Ontario, contributed to the Conversative victory.

Once in their Commons' seats in Ottawa, the nationalists discovered the peculiarity of their position. They were insufficiently numerous to make any dent upon Conservative policies and only the more conservative of them received any of the plums of office. They had to swallow the new government's announced intention to make an immediate monetary contribution to the British admiralty and they had to accept western desires for the school system in Keewatin. By 1914 they even agreed to Canadian participation in a major British war in Europe. Decidedly the alliance was a fiasco.

Long after, Henri Bourassa continued to blame the nationalist members of parliament: they had been bought off by the Conservatives. But where was he in the heyday of the alliance? He had chosen not to run even though his paper carefully reproduced a campaign song that praised his leadership qualities to the tune of O Canada. And where was he right after the election? He had chosen not to be available for consultation and had disappeared from Montreal. He might have had a say in the selection of cabinet ministers from Quebec; had he run he might have had one of the positions himself. He could have had a voice in Conservative policy and the course of Canadian activity during the years of the First World War might have been very different. But Bourassa was a better political critic than actor.

Of course some of his attention had already turned to the provincial field. From 1908 to 1912 Bourassa sat as an independent member of the Quebec legislature for the riding of St. Hyacinthe. There he voiced much of the nationalist critique of the economic and industrial boom that Quebec, like the rest of the country, was experiencing in the early twentieth century. As concerned about the economic autonomy of Quebec as he was about the political autonomy of Canada, Bourassa attacked the Liberal government of Lomer Gouin for giving the province away to foreign investors.

The Liberal government of Quebec from 1897 until the mid-1930s naturally saw things in quite another light. For premiers Félix-Gabriel Marchand, Simon-Napoléon Parent, Lomer Gouin, and Alexandre Taschereau the promise of the twentieth century was the industrial development of Quebec. They even used a vaguely nationalist argument to herald it: new industries would provide jobs in Quebec and French Canadians would no longer have to emigrate in search of them. To that end they were prepared to ease the way for foreign investors and foreign companies willing to set up shop in Quebec. In fact, liberal philosophy as much as nationalist sentiment guided their behaviour: they believed the role of government to be minor in the economic life of a people. Like nineteenth century liberals elsewhere they assumed that each individual's rational pursuit of economic betterment would automatically benefit the entire community; the state simply maintained order. To that basic philosophy they added the Canadian practice of state aid in the creation of an economic infrastructure. In the nineteenth century that aid went to railways; in the early twentieth century it built roads. No one—Liberal, Conservative, or nationalist—

contested the obligation of the province to construct and maintain roads. But the increasing costs, particularly after the appearance of automobiles, demanded increasing revenues. To obtain more funds, the Quebec government, ever shy of imposing direct taxes, employed the only two means available to it. It insisted on more funding from the federal government either by increased subsidies, as in 1907, or by a new arrangement of conditional grants, as in 1913. And it increased its own revenue within the province by selling off water, wood, and mineral rights on crown lands to private companies. Only gradually, and then only under pressure from the nationalists, did the Quebec government begin leasing rather than selling such rights and even imposing, as in 1910, restrictions on the export of cut pulpwood.

Water, wood, and minerals were to mark Quebec's economy for the entire twentieth century. Together they increased the complexity of industrialization in Quebec by adding industries based on natural resources to the light industries employing masses of cheap labour that had developed in the late nineteenth century and continued in the twentieth. The addition integrated Quebec's economy even more into that of North America and rendered it in fact more similar to the entire Canadian economy in that primary resources, with minimal processing, were exported for final production elsewhere. The immediate benefits seemed obvious: vast numbers of labouring jobs for an unskilled and largely masculine work force; resources so plentiful that even the minimum royalties imposed by the government filled provincial coffers. The long-term effects, only hinted at by the nationalists in the 1900s and again in the 1920s, were the same for Quebec and Canada: an underdeveloped manufacturing sector and the exploitation of the natural and even the industrial wealth of the country by foreign, mostly American, companies. To argue that such has always been the pattern of the Canadian economy since the days of New France may ease a few consciences, but it was a handful of Quebecois intellectuals and journalists who were among the first to point to the peculiarity and the inappropriateness of the pattern.

Only in the very late nineteenth century could technology harness the wild rivers of Quebec to provide the new power of the second industrial revolution. Unlike coal—the fuel for the steam power of the first industrial revolution—hydro-electricity was potentially limitless and much more easily transported. Moreover, Quebec had rivers galore tumbling out of the Laurentian shield, whereas coal was always a cumbersome import from the Maritimes. The very number and variety of rivers determined the type of hydro-electric development. In contrast to Ontario, where a single massive site at Niagara summoned a unified and publicly-owned hydro commission as early as 1906, Quebec's far-flung rivers and distances attracted individual companies serving regional markets in different ways. Each company bought or leased rights to the waterfalls from the Quebec government on terms that were always very generous.

Before the turn of the century the Shawinigan Water and Power Company was already established on the St. Maurice River above Trois-Rivières to service the growing pulpwood industry. Gradually it extended its lines and customers across both shores of the St. Lawrence from Montreal to Quebec City and even into the Eastern Townships to electrify the mining operations at Asbestos and Thetford Mines. The company also acted as a magnet to industry by offering cheaper rates close to the source of supply. Quebec's aluminum and carbide industries were drawn to Shawinigan before the First World War and expanded tremendously because of the readily available power. Older industries, such as textiles, also felt the tug to the St. Maurice valley where labour was as cheap as the power and just as tractable. The Shawinigan Power Company soon was indistinguishable from the town of the same name, designed to be a model manufacturing community and harbouring 11 000 people by 1915.

A much smaller company served different purposes in Montreal. The Montreal Light, Heat and Power, beginning in 1901 and using the St. Lawrence itself as its source, had a captive market in Canada's largest city. Far from aggressively attracting new companies into its network of consumers, as did the Shawinigan company, the Montreal firm concentrated on ensuring its monopoly position. Intimate connections between the company's directors and the economic and political elite of the time facilitated the task. The company had then merely to wait until Montrealers literally saw the light. That they gradually did from the electrified street lamps and street cars of the 1890s to the businesses, industries, and then, trickling down by class, the homes of the city in the 1900s. Profits were reaped less by expansion than by the monopolistic setting of rates. So keen in fact was the Montreal Light, Heat and Power to keep potential competitors out of its territory that it used its economic and political pressure to prevent hydro-electric developments north and west of Montreal on the Ottawa and the St. Lawrence. As the economist John Dales hints, such activity may have hindered industrial development on the island of Montreal and in western Quebec generally.

Tinier still and different again was a third company operating in the western part of the Eastern Townships. The Southern Canada Power Company serviced from 1910 the agricultural regions of southwestern Quebec. With only minor rivers as a source of supply, the company was not interested in attracting huge consumers of electricity such as aluminum, chemical, or pulp plants. To do so would have necessitated purchasing the extra power from Shawinigan and reselling it, at minimal profit, to the heavy industrial consumers. Rather the company preferred to concentrate on the much more lucrative domestic market for electricity. For that it needed a growing population with ever-increasing consumer re-quirements. Such a population was the result of a certain kind of industrialization, one in which light industries used proportion-ately more labour than power. A population like that would con-gregate in towns and would demand municipal electric services and then gradually, with a bit of prodding from the electric com-pany, would insist on ever more sophisticated electric appliances for the home. Like the Shawinigan company but with a different plan, the Southern Canada Power Company aggressively attracted industry into its electric domain. Only during and after the First World War did towns like Sherbrooke, Drummondville, or St. Hyacinthe really catch the electric and industrial fever, but St. Jean was already there as a model by the 1900s with canneries, food processing plants, textile mills, clothing factories, small metal in-dustries, and the huge Singer Sewing Machine Company which opened in 1904 and employed one-third of the labour force. Elec-tricity may well be one of the reasons almost half of Quebec's population of two million lived in urban centres by 1911.

Electricity was certainly connected with the other major innova-tion on the economic scene in the early 1900s. Wood, long a staple of the nineteeth century economy, produced a new resource tied at the Quebec end to hydro-electric power and at the urban and in-creasingly American end to the insatiable demand for newsprint. The scrub trees left aside in disdain during the nineteenth century scramble for oak timber and then pine planking finally came into their own, modest producers of million dollar mush. In the first few years of the century a lot of the wood itself was exported directly by the American firms that held forest concessions by pur-chase or lease from the Quebec government. But after 1910 an em-bargo on the export of pulpwood cut from crown lands succeeded in encouraging American pulp manufacturers to establish plants in Quebec. Those plants required immense amounts of electricity to fire the vats that changed wood to pulp and then to press and dry it to a transportable state.

Canadians in the field had already begun the process and in-deed pushed it a step further. Alfred Dubuc was producing pulp at his mills in Chicoutimi in 1897 and then even further inland in the western Lac St. Jean region at Val Jalbert, St. Amédée, and Desbiens. Company roads and railways took the pulp to Port Alfred on the Baie des Haha for direct export by ship to Britain and the United States. Nearby, William Price, the third generation representative of a lumbering family in the Saguenay, opened paper mills at Jonquière in 1909 and Kenogami in 1913. Export by rail of the much more compact paper product eliminated the problems of bulk and season that the shipping of dried pulp by river and sea en-tailed. Both Dubuc and Price had their own source of electric power, harnessing affluents of Lac St. Jean and of the Saguenay for the private needs of their companies. In 1911 the American reduction of import duties on paper persuaded American newsprint manufacturers to complete more of the production process in Quebec. Along with most of the profits, the newsprint was exported to the United States where by the early war years it supplied one-quarter of American needs; less than fifteen years later it furnished two-thirds of that market.

If hydro-electricity and pulp and paper contributed to the regionalization of Quebec's economy, the bulk of the economic activity and the industrial presence in Quebec stayed concentrated in Montreal. The city continued its nineteenth century role as trader to the nation, taking out almost half Canada's exports and bringing in more than a third of the imports. It supplied transportation, financial, and commercial services for half a continent as well as for a city and a province. With the startling development of the western prairies after the turn of the century Montreal's command of the sinews of Canadian trade increased. The light industries characteristic of the 1880s now became the necessary suppliers of consumer goods for newly established western farmers. Sugar, shoes, tobacco, biscuits, dresses, shirts, caps, stockings, and dry goods plain and fancy headed west in a non-stop flow along the rail lines whose engines and cars were made and repaired in the huge machine shops of the city. With the exception of electrical goods, none of the industries was new, but each blossomed under the sun of heavy demand, easy transportation, and the federal protective tariff. The expansion entailed modernization as companies electrified their operations, merged into giant corporations, or constructed new and enlarged plants away from the city centre. They continued to hire vast numbers of employees: more than five thousand each in cotton, tobacco, and sugar production alone. Men, women, and children, in spite of repeated legislative attempts to curb the employment of youngsters under the age of fourteen, flocked to the factories from the city and, as in the 1880s, increasingly from the countryside. Their needs and those of their relatives heading for the smaller towns of the province or the suburban municipalities around Montreal constituted a construction boom: houses, apartments, factories, offices, churches, municipal buildings, waterworks, and schools covered the growing urban landscape as fast as workers and the weather permitted. With more people living in towns, more of the population worked in the manufacturing and service sector of the economy. The number of women in the public labour force grew faster still and capping it all was the value of production, increasing at an even greater rate. These were boom times and Montreal was the centre of it all.

The city's working class, however, was far from the centre of the prodigious wealth produced in the 1900s. Indeed, the living and working conditions of the vast majority of ordinary people deteriorated during the period, giving the lie to the liberal dream of prosperity for all through industrial development. The dream in fact never took account of the distribution of the benefits of economic development. Liberals and Conservatives alike took for granted a hierarchical social structure whose ordering was a result of individual merit and effort. Some of them even posited the necessary presence of the poor in order to develop the equally necessary charitable instincts of the rich. A very few voices, mostly among the nationalists, timidly suggested that the suffering of the working class was perhaps abnormal, far beyond that which religion prescribed as part of the human condition.

From both the concerned and the indifferent came the panacea of education. Thereby workers, particularly male ones, could improve their lot. The early twentieth century in fact produced all manner of educational schemes and institutions from technical schools to industrial schools to night classes for adults and higher commercial training for the elite; for girls the innovation was domestic science training. Except for the domestic training, few of the educational changes trickled down to youngsters in the urban slums. Their attendance at school rarely lasted more than three or four years: the wages of the lads required to supplement the family income, the babysitting services of the girls to release mothers for paid work outside the home. Moreover, schools still required fees, albeit minimal; only the ultra-radicals, effectively silenced by the milieu, advocated free education. Even the tax and administrative structure of the school system ensured poor schooling for Montreal's working class children. The Catholic and Protestant sectors divided the school taxes between them not in proportion to the number of pupils but rather to the size of the contributions. Since the large industrial firms, more often than not headed by English-speaking Protestants, contributed the largest number of tax dollars, the Protestant school commission received the largest piece of the educational pie even though there were fewer Protestant than Catholic children in the schools of Montreal.

Schooling in fact was probably the least of the concerns of a working class family at the opening of the twentieth century. Paying the rent on a five-room flat likely without running water or indoor conveniences in a dusty or muddy street close to the horse stables of the city's livery business was the first item of family business. To it, all members contributed. When they could not manage, as the cost of living rose faster than wages, they moved into dingier or more cramped quarters. Or they cut into the second essential item of a working class budget, food. But this too succumbed to the rising cost of living and there was little room for financial flexibility let alone physical sustenance in a diet made up increasingly of bread and potatoes. Nor surprisingly, sickness took its toll particularly among infants and children at a time when the milk from Montreal dairies was frequently below the standard set for human consumption. Sick or well, however, the family still had to be clothed and this third task of the family economy fell largely to the mother and daughters who made most garments. Even the wives of the most skilled workers with steady incomes rarely wore store-bought dresses. But still, no one made boots or shoes at home and their purchase required cash. So too did fuel, the fourth demand on the meagre resources of the family, coming at a time of the year when the budget was even more constrained by seasonal unemployment. Firewood in fact constituted the major product of Quebec's wood trade, far surpassing that of sawn lumber or pulpwood. If there were any pennies left over for pleasure once the family had met its minimum requirements of shelter, food, clothing, and warmth, the hundreds of bars that were never more than a few doors away in working class districts offered the closest outlet and the quickest solace.

In such conditions, factory work, obviously a necessity, may even have been preferable to family life. Certainly many young women, much to the chagrin of their social betters in the middle and upper classes, preferred factory work to domestic service, the only other occupation available to them. And certainly the working class accepted without much audible public grumbling the conditions of factory work. As in the 1880s they still worked sixty hours a week for irregular salaries in grim factories along Montreal's Lachine canal. Even with increasing numbers of women in the industrial labour force, women still earned only half of the wages paid to their male co-workers. Where they were present in an industry, they constituted the largest number of waged as opposed to salaried workers. Women also made up forty percent of the recorded sweated labour in the garment trade, doing piece work at home. Far more of them never declared such activities to any official enquirer. All workers were subject to industrial accidents to such an extent that the Liberal government was shocked into legislating a form of workmen's compensation in 1909. Like child labour laws, however, this legislation remained largely inoperative, just as it was in other parts of North America experiencing the same economic boom.

Those few workers who did react to their working and living conditions joined unions and went on strike. If they were skilled workers for one of the national transportation companies they even had a chance of catching the attention of the federal government. Such was the case among the maintenance workers of the CPR in 1901, the machinists of the Grand Trunk in 1905, the machinists and carmen of the CPR in 1908, the conductors and trainmen of the Grand Trunk in 1910. Sometimes these nation-wide strikes boomeranged with the closing of local shops and factories, adding to the perpetual hazard of insecure employment. Even with that threat, however, other workers persisted in using the one weapon at their disposal in a very uneven struggle for better wages, fewer hours of work, and, on occasion, union recognition. The longshoremen of Montreal tied up the spring opening of the port in 1903; members of building trades slowed construction through the late spring of 1904. Textile workers tried repeatedly with different methods to protest low or lowered salaries and to gain the right to form a union. They disrupted work at almost every mill in the province:

at Magog, Montmorency, and Valleyfield in 1900; at Valleyfield again in 1901 and 1907; at Hochelaga and St. Henri in Montreal, and at Valleyfield once again in 1908. Women were among the militant strikers and constituted the majority of the members of one of the early unions—the Federation of Textile Workers of Canada. In 1912 Montreal clothing workers, forty-five hundred strong, protested their working conditions. Sometimes the labour trouble began with the employers as occurred in the lockout in the boot and shoe industry of Quebec City in the autumn of 1900 and again in 1903. Sometimes it surfaced in non-industrial activities: sawmill employees in Buckingham struck in the autumn of 1906; Gaspé fishermen at Rivière-au-Renard in 1909 protested the feudal hold of the big fishing companies over the people of Gaspé. Few of the strikes were successful since neither the unions nor the working class could claim the same solidarity they encountered among their opponents. Moreover, given the existing working and living conditions and the easy availability of replacements, few workers could afford to go on strike.

The few public murmurings of discontent did, however, reveal the darker shades of the dreams of the early twentieth century. When federal and provincial politicians waxed eloquent about possessing the century, they were a long way from working class reality. But so too was working class reality far removed from the South African war, prairie schools, or federal subsidies to the provinces. Perhaps only the terrain could equal the expansionist dreams: real estate promotion in urban areas built model towns and modest fortunes for a French Canadian middle class and the very borders of Quebec stretched north in 1912 to touch Hudson Bay and east to embrace Ungava and Labrador making the province the largest in Canada. Certainly the layers of public existence in Quebec rarely intersected as different groups assumed their interests were the interests of all. Even the nationalists, acting as critic on both the federal and provincial stage and thus able to pretend to a certain integrating function, sometimes played the fool. They spotted the danger of imperialist ideology floating in the Canadian air and of economic colonialism anchored in Quebec, but by their politicking they may have dealt a blow to a dream which they in fact shared with Laurier—that of a united but dual French-English nation increasingly autonomous from Britain. Hinting at a more activist role for the provincial state, the nationalists were only able to engage in intellectual action themselves.

SELECT BIBLIOGRAPHY

Ames, Sir Herbert Brown. *'The City Below the Hill': A Sociological Study of a Portion of the City of Montreal, Canada.* Montreal: Bishop Printing, 1897.

Asselin J.F. Olivar. *A Quebec View of Canadian Nationalism.* Montreal: Guertin Print, 1909.

Brandt, Gail Cuthbert. " 'Weaving It Together': Life Cycle and the Industrial Experience of Female Cotton Workers in Quebec, 1910–1950." *Labour/ Le Travailleur* 7(1981):113–26.

Brown, Robert Craig, and Ramsay Cook. *Canada, 1896–1921: A Nation Transformed.* Toronto: McClelland and Stewart, 1974.

Clippingdale, Richard. *Laurier: His Life and World.* Toronto: McGraw-Hill Ryerson, 1979.

Copp, Terry. "The Condition of the Working Class in Montreal, 1897–1920." *Historical Papers/Communications historiques.* Canadian Historical Association, 1972. Pp. 157–80.

Copp, Terry. *The Anatomy of Poverty: The Condition of the Working Class in Montreal, 1897–1929.* Toronto: McClelland and Stewart, 1974.

Corcoran, James I.W. "Henri Bourassa et la guerre sud-africaine." *Revue d'histoire de l'Amérique française* 18(1964):343–56; 19(1965):84–105; 229–37; 414–42.

Dales, John Harkness. *Hydroelectricity and Industrial Development: Quebec 1898–1940.* Cambridge, Massachusetts: Harvard University Press, 1957.

Hamelin, Jean, and Jean-Paul Montminy. "Québec, 1896–1929: une deuxième phase d'industrialisation." In *Idéologies au Canada français, 1900–1929.* Quebec: Les presses de l'Université Laval, 1974. Pp. 15–28.

Jamieson, Stuart Marshall. *Times of Trouble: Labour Unrest and Industrial Conflict in Canada, 1900–1966.* Ottawa: Task Force on Labour Relations, 1968.

Levitt, Joseph, ed. *Henri Bourassa on Imperialism and Biculturalism, 1900–1918.* Toronto: Copp Clark, 1970.

Linteau, Paul-André. *Maisonneuve ou Comment des promoteurs fabriquent une ville.* Montreal: Boréal Express, 1981.

Neatby, H. Blair. "Laurier and Imperialism." *Annual Report.* Canadian Historical Association, 1955. Pp. 24–32.

Rouillard, Jacques. *Les travailleurs du coton au Québec, 1900–1915.* Montreal: Les presses de l'Université du Québec, 1974.

Rumilly, Robert. *Henri Bourassa: la vie publique d'un grand canadien.* Montreal: Editions Chantecler, 1953.

Schull, Joseph. *Laurier: The First Canadian.* Toronto: Macmillan, 1965.

". . . the nationalist argument that the French Canadian family had some peculiar essence . . ."
Miller and his wife at Val Jalbert, 1910.

12 Feminism, Nationalism, and the Clerical Defensive

In the early 1900s, the social repercussions of industrialization dawned upon three distinct groups among Quebec's elite: feminists, nationalists, and clerics. Similar conditions in the 1880s had raised scarcely a murmur; now they produced a veritable chorus of concern. The difference appears to have been one of quantity rather than quality. The sheer number of industrial workers, the physical expansion of cities and towns, the commercial boom of metropolitan Montreal could no longer be ignored. Quebec was obviously shedding its nineteenth century agricultural skin and the process seems to have been more difficult for certain elite groups who had been urban dwellers for generations than for the rural emigrants. Feminists, nationalists, and clerics, all went about their self-imposed task of protecting the family from urban ills with varying methods and prescriptions, sometimes in co-operation and sometimes in conflict with each other. Right up to the First World War when nationalists and clerics ganged up on the feminists to remind them of their rightful place in society, the three performed an intricate dance to the tune of their individual interests and their mutual sympathies.

Of the three, feminism was the newest on the Quebec scene. It was both a result of and a commentary upon the social turbulence of the time. The presence of so many women and children in the industrial work place upset many notions of social propriety. How could one maintain a strict demarcation of the species by sex, function, and location in the burgeoning factories of town and city? How could one ensure proper family formation when so many young women appeared to be discovering new ways of earning a living? By the end of the nineteenth century, they appeared in increasing numbers as salesclerks in shops, particularly in the newfangled department stores, and in offices where they were so closely associated with the typewriter that they actually acquired the same name. Even so the notion of separate spheres may have continued to plague them as female clerical workers took over and at the same time devalued the young male occupation of clerk. The same thing had long since happened in the elementary teaching profession and by the late nineteenth century some young schoolmistresses even dared to insist upon greater training either in normal schools or universities. Some English Protestant women went so far as to demand access to professional careers as nurses, doctors, professors, or lawyers, but their demands were seldom echoed by French Canadian women for whom the avenues to most professions were closed.

Newspapers and the women's associations informed the public of the many social changes involving women. By the end of the nineteenth century almost every large city daily had a female journalist contributing a regular column or editing an entire woman's page. One paper in the 1890s, *Le Coin du feu*, edited by Joséphine Marchand Dandurand, was intended solely for women. Most of the female journalists hid their identity, as if their work was somehow inappropriate. The women's pages themselves, by their segregation from the rest of the paper, indicated the force of the ideology of separate spheres; however, interspersed among the patterns and the novels, the recipes and the advice columns were discussions of feminism and of the women's movement in English Canada, the United States, France, and Great Britain. Higher education and votes for women were in the air and also in the press. Moreover, many of the journalists were members of, or close sympathizers with, the National Council of Women, a Canadian federation of women's organizations dating from 1893. There they discussed and passed on to their readers issues such as women's work, education, health, duties, and even, on occasion, women's rights. National and international meetings of women's organizations and the participation of individual French Canadian women at such gatherings as the Chicago World's Fair in 1893 or the Paris Exposition in 1900 brought reports to the Quebec press of the ever-increasing murmurings of women throughout the western world. It took only the burst of nationalism that accompanied the opening decade of the twentieth century to have French Canadian women form a feminist organization of their own.

Nationalism followed a similar path in the early twentieth century. Older than feminism, at least in Quebec, it was even more isolated and individualistic until the turn of the century. It had provided the language of revolutionary rhetoric in the 1830s and of the politics of survival in the 1840s, but it took varying forms thereafter. In the 1860s it could be discerned among both the proponents and opponents of Confederation; some clerics even attempted to hitch it to an ultramontane star. It gained a martyr in Louis Riel and the occasional journalist used it to predict a particular future for French Canada. But always it remained a thin thread of intellectual flirtation, a source for set speeches expected of orators at annual Saint Jean Baptiste festivities. Like feminism, it required an international climate of opinion to turn it into an organized, semi-political force. In the early twentieth century, the optimism of economic progress and the pessimism of imperial entanglements gave birth to a new form of Quebec nationalism, more public, more vociferous, more self-assured, and more critical than before.

The clerics were the oldest of the three elite groups troubled by the social scene of the early twentieth century. They were also the most experienced, used to adept manoeuvres to acquire and maintain a privileged position in Quebec society. In the early nineteenth century, religion had been insufficient to guarantee their social pre-eminence; they added education and then social work, filling a vacuum left by an indifferent state. Some of the bolder among them had even claimed a virtual clerical right of veto over all secular activities, including those of the state. But if the ultramontanes eventually retreated into largely intellectual corners, the church itself had no intention of giving up its acquired rights or status. It certainly had the bargaining skill and the political finesse to make its point. For example, the bishops apparently came to an agreement with Laurier over his compromise solution to the Manitoba school question: they would tone down their criticism if he would ensure that Quebec's Liberal government abandoned its intention to establish a ministry of education. Now, in the opening years of the twentieth century, the clerics were not about to give ground, in education or social concern, to feminist or nationalist upstarts. Or so they thought.

The three groups actually had much in common. They all saw themselves as guardians of the social order although each sometimes wondered about the other. The implications of feminism in particular concerned both clerics and nationalists, and the feminists spent a lot of time reassuring them. The nationalists meanwhile fancied themselves as the advance guard, ever attentive to the least sign of danger to the nation. They all suspected that most of the dangers centred around the family and they all claimed a public right to protect it. The feminists thought that as women they had a special insight. Who could know more about housing, infant mortality, parks, schooling, or the cost of living than mothers? They thereby attached their own desire for a recognized place in public life to their maternal concern for the everday problems of families. The clerics on the other hand believed that they, as upholders of morality, had the most to offer families surrounded by promiscuity and licentiousness in large anonymous cities. The nationalists in turn thought that they had the most lessons to teach to the family. And yet few of the protectors knew the object of their attention at first hand. Class, education, and social status made them elites, removed from the households of Montreal's or Quebec's "city below the hill." Together they approached their self-appointed task with a decided air of *noblesse oblige.*

All three shared a dedication to the preservation of the family. They all believed that the family provided the foundation for religion and morality; they all regarded the state as an enlarged family. None of them could conceive of a social organization without the family at its centre. And each of them repeated the nationalist argument that the French Canadian family had some peculiar essence that rendered it inherently superior to English-speaking neighbours down the street or across the continent. That of course was just where the difficulty lay. Industrialization in Montreal did not really look very different from that in Chicago or Toronto or London or Paris: the same slums, the same illnesses, the same unemployment. In the large cities of North America, the family's private problems, hung out with the wash for all to see, were culturally and linguistically indistinguishable. Only by responding to those problems in a particular way could the distinctions be maintained. And thus feminists, nationalists, and clerics alike developed their own institutional responses to the social and familial ills they observed. Sometimes they collaborated willingly, working together in the same associations; sometimes they were reluctant companions and only the force of circumstances or the magnitude of the task forced them to collaborate. Just as often they were competitors: the educational interests of both the feminists and the nationalists worried the clerics; the feminist implication of sexual equality disturbed cleric and nationalist alike; while the clerical assumption of social righteousness troubled both feminists and nationalists. Their complex three-step through the opening years of the twentieth century did, however, succeed in alleviating some of the social ills of the time and also in giving a distinctive colour to the Quebec scene.

In 1907 the women's committee of the Montreal Saint Jean Baptiste Society formally constituted a new organization, the *Féd-*

ération nationale Saint-Jean-Baptiste. Modelled on the National Council of Women, the *Fédération* was to be a co-ordinating body for the innumerable women's associations and clubs that proliferated throughout Quebec in the 1890s and 1900s. If women spoke with one strong, organized voice instead of whispering in a thousand tongues, they might have some public impact. Moreover, the *Fédération* could provide a secure public platform for opinions that might otherwise be discounted as individual idiosyncracies. The family connections of the founders certainly helped: Marie Lacoste Gérin-Lajoie and Carolina Dessaulles Béique came from and married into impeccable upper class, wealthy, and political families. Their interest in education and charitable work was part of what was expected of young women of their class, although it was also assumed that they would undertake such tasks in conjunction with the church. But they were already pulling against that stricture when Béique established a secular domestic science school in Montreal in 1907 and sent two of the instructors off to France for training. Gérin-Lajoie's sister, Justine Lacoste Beaubien, did the same by founding Montreal's Ste. Justine hospital for sick children the same year. Gérin-Lajoie herself had tugged at male prerogatives by her unusual interest in law. To occupy herself after a convent education and before marriage, she dipped into her father's law library and was shocked to discover the legal status of women in Quebec as mere adjuncts of their husbands with no personal, financial, or civil autonomy. She even considered turning down a marriage proposal in order to spend her life improving the conditions of women. But the proposer, a liberally minded grandson of Etienne Parent, persuaded her of his sympathies for such activities as long as she did not neglect her wifely duties. Gérin-Lajoie eventually wrote a legal handbook, the *Traité de droit usuel* in 1902, all the while keeping an eye on small children. Her legal expertise benefited both the National Council of Women with whose local council in Montreal she was closely involved and the fledgling *Fédération nationale Saint-Jean-Baptiste* whose first steps she guided.

The initial handicap of the new organization was the stigma of feminism. A term of ridicule throughout most of the western world, much like "women's lib" in the 1970s, feminism was particularly odious to many French Canadians. Anything that risked taking women out of their proper sphere was frowned upon as both a social and national peril. The women of the early twentieth century seeking socially useful roles beyond the family and outside the church appeared to be calling into question the very bases of French Canadian society. No wonder the early feminists trod warily. In 1901 Joséphine Marchand Dandurand defined feminism so broadly as to include everything that women did, even giving it a moral tinge with which she expected no one to disagree: feminism required of well-to-do women some action to help alleviate social distress. She deliberately avoided any criticism of the ideology of separate spheres that confined middle and upper class women to inactivity or mere social whirls. And although she approved of higher education for women, she justified it by the improved wives and mothers (of sons) that it would produce. As for votes for women, Dandurand thought them unncessary. Women could exercise their civic spirit sufficiently by doing good deeds and influencing their husbands to vote wisely. Dandurand's careful skating around the danger signals of feminism is a clear indication that like the Liberals and even the Knights of Labour before them, early feminists had to find a niche in hostile terrain and camouflage themselves to maintain it.

The feminism in the new *Fédération* was, according to Carolina Dessaulles Béique, feminism of a particular kind. Rather than revolutionary feminism, a European or North American variety that pulled women away from their homes and their proper roles, the *Fédération nationale Saint-Jean-Baptiste* harboured Christian feminism which anchored women in their rightful duties and obligations towards others. Marie Lacoste Gérin-Lajoie was more specific but just as circumspect: the new organization was to be a centre for Christian women to aid themselves and to advance their own moral development, vocations as wives, duties as mothers, and their philanthrophic or religious works. Both women, thoroughly familiar, one suspects, with the history of the *Institut canadien*, sought and secured the sanction of the bishop of Montreal for their new organization. The bishop, Monseigneur Paul Bruchési, himself offered a definition of feminism as the "zeal of woman for all those noble causes in the sphere to which Providence has assigned her." He even gave some examples: temperance, the education of children, domestic hygiene, fashions, and the problems of young working girls in factories. Through them all, he expected the laywomen to support the existing activity of religious communities.

On the whole, the undertakings of the *Fédération* were well within the prescribed norms. The largest number of affiliated associations were in fact charitable groups controlled by nuns. Whether this raised internal difficulties or whether the nuns were actually feminists in disguise is an open question. Certainly the larger, secular *Fédération* was able to do fund raising for its membership on a scale that its religiously run affiliates could not manage. Within the *Fédération* the next largest group was made up of professional associations, some of the early and tentative alliances of women engaged in similar occupations. Associations of domestic servants, store employees, teachers, business women, and factory employees each found a place and support in the umbrella organization. The associations appear to have been as much social and cultural clubs as mutual benefit societies for particular kinds of workers. Middle class women worked through the *Fédération* organizing classes in commercial, technical, and household science subjects, delivering literary lectures, or sponsoring musi-

cal *soirées* in the various associations. For the factory employees
they established a sickness fund, employment bureaus, boarding
houses, and even country homes where working girls could go for
inexpensive holidays. If their concerns were as much moral as economic, they were little different from those of feminist doers of
good deeds in other North American cities. They also probably
served to open a number of middle class eyes to the extent of urban
poverty, although as late as 1913 journalist Henriette Dessaulles
St. Jacques, writing under her pseudonym Fadette, commented
benignly in *Le Devoir:* "Dear readers, you wouldn't even believe
such ugliness existed." Quite removed from any ugliness was the
third and smallest group of affiliates to the *Fédération:* cultural
associations varying from book clubs and literary societies to
musical and artistic guilds.

The *Fédération* sanctioned all the groups, created a network
among them, and offered its annual meeting as an educational
seminar for them. In 1909 for example members discussed the
problems of alcoholism, infant mortality, popular education, housing for workers, and the implementation of homemaking courses
in the schools. By 1914 the *Fédération* was particularly pleased
with its public endeavours: it claimed the credit for the doubling
of women teachers' pensions, the naming of a female factory in-
spector (actually it was the National Council of Women that had
convinced the Quebec government to name two such inspectors in
1898), better lighting in factories, chairs for women clerks in stores,
a reduction in the number of taverns, and the improvement in infant feeding by the establishment of pure milk depots which also
offered courses in domestic hygiene and child care. The ubiqui-
tous classes in domestic science, in both English and French, were
designed to improve the lamentable state of knowledge about diet
and housekeeping and, just perhaps, to improve the quantity and
quality of young women available for domestic service in the
spacious homes of Sherbrooke Street.

In those homes were other young women frittering away their
time in pointless inactivity. The daughters of a number of the
women associated with the *Fédération nationale Saint-Jean-
Baptiste* needed more education if they were to continue their
mothers' public tasks. A convent education might provide a good
secondary education, although some women were dubious even
about that, but it was virtually a dead end. As indeed it was intended to be: only those young ladies obliged to earn their living
were directed to the teacher training sections of the Ursuline convent in Quebec City or the *Congrégation de Notre-Dame* in Montreal. Young women without such an obligation were sent home at
age seventeen or eighteen to prepare for marriage. Since access to
universities was via the classical colleges and no such college
existed for girls, the path to higher education was effectively blocked.
In 1900 Laval University did consent to permit women to join the
public audience for some of its faculty lectures in rhetoric or

literature, but they were not to register for a degree, nor were any academic exercises required of them. There was no question of permitting them access, even as auditors, to the professional faculties of law and medicine. At the same time then that the *Fédération* was supporting domestic science training it was also urging the opening of a classical college for young women.

A combination of daring and discretion created the *Ecole d'enseignement supérieur pour les filles* in Montreal in 1908. Female journalists in the 1890s had demanded such an institution; the feminists of the 1900s exercised the pressure of their class and wealth upon certain sympathetic ears in the *Congrégation de Notre-Dame* to achieve it. Even the dubious bishop overcame his reluctance when he discovered that two other women journalists intended to establish a secular *lycée* on the French model. If young ladies really had to have higher education, and Monseigneur Bruchési was not at all convinced, they should at least acquire it within the proper religious framework. But it was all to be very discreet. The new *Ecole*, run by the nuns of *Notre-Dame*, was not even to have the title of college, something which it would only acquire in 1926 when it became the *Collège* Marguerite Bourgeoys. And it was expected to be self-supporting, student fees and the religious community providing the sole financing; neither church nor state intended to sanction this temerity of women. Laval did provide accreditation and the students took the same examinations as in the men's colleges, but the university also sent along its vice-rector to stress to staff and students alike the limitations placed upon the young female students. They might follow the same program as their brothers, but they were not to think that their futures would in any way be altered: they were to be submissive and graceful wives, not doctors, lawyers, accountants, or pharmacists. The *Ecole* dutifully added piano recitals, poetry readings, and afternoon teas to its heavy academic program. It also hid its chagrin at seeing no public announcement from Laval of the scholastic achievement of one of its first students. Marie Gérin-Lajoie, the daughter of one of the school's promoters, placed first among all the classical college students of the province. By then the school had also organized study circles to initiate young women students into the intellectual and practical aspects of contemporary social problems. In the 1920s some of the graduates joined Marie Gérin-Lajoie in forming the *Institut de Notre-Dame-du-Bon-Conseil* to provide a religious framework for their social work; others remained in secular life and exercised their activism through the *Fédération nationale Saint-Jean-Baptiste*.

The connection between schooling and social questions was not lost upon the nationalists either. Unlike the feminists, however, they tended to approach the question in a more intellectual manner. For them it was not just particular groups of people who needed practical or academic training, but rather an entire society that required an approach to learning that stressed secular, scientific, commercial, and industrial education. One expression of this point of view can be found in Errol Bouchette's series of writings in the 1900s: *Emparons-nous de l'industrie, Etudes sociale et économique sur le Canada,* and *L'indépendance économique du Canada français.* Fascinated by the economic development promised and delivered early in the new century, Bouchette was concerned that French Canadians play a prominent role in it. To do so they had to destroy an old myth of their being unfit for commerce and business, and they had to become aware of the effect of the new industrial order in Europe and the United States, so that Canada could extract the benefits and avoid the problems.

Such undertakings required education, training, and appropriate legislation. Bouchette was not at all convinced that the graduates of classical colleges had the necessary stuff to face the economic challenge of the new century; rather he suspected that many of the colleges perpetuated the notion of French Canadian commercial ineptitude. He rejected the idea of national characteristics and argued that knowledge could overcome all problems. But that knowledge had to be planned, organized, and integrated into the economy. Drawing on contemporary reports of industrial education in Europe, Bouchette suggested that government and employers co-operate in designing specific programs for schools and factories in order to increase the technical competence of industrial workers. The result would be not only a more skilled labour force but also a solidarity of interest between employers and employees. Education would thus guarantee social peace. The university too, while maintaining a theoretical approach, could play its part by expanding more into the pure and social sciences. Montreal's polytechnical school, a rather moribund institution established in the late 1870s, should attract students aggressively; it ought to house a bureau of scientific and industrial research as a source of information for the state's economic planning. The elementary school system should also be remodelled along French lines with the senior levels preparing youngsters for practical occupations in the work place and the lower levels at least attacking the shameful problem of illiteracy which, according to Bouchette, was greater in Quebec than in any other Canadian province. And the entire educational system should be free, co-ordinated and directed by the state.

Bouchette justified his ideas on nationalist grounds. Without decent education, young people were bored, handicapped, and discouraged; their subsequent poverty forced them to emigrate to the United States. There at least they proved their industrial competence. But still they were lost to Canada. In a revealing analogy Bouchette argued that education protected industry the way an army protected a frontier or a parliament a constitution. Education, in short, was not only the key to industrial progress but also to national survival. The three were indissociable. By championing industry, French Canadians would be continuing the mission of their forefathers. Unlike other North Americans who came to the new land in search of subsistence or conquest or religious freedom, French Canadians arrived with civilization in their pockets and it behooved them to be at the head of economic progress in North America. To fail in such a noble goal would be unpatriotic; to undertake it meant working for the salvation of an entire people. Such a blatantly nationalist argument also had a twist to it, peculiar to the optimism of the early twentieth century. Bouchette insisted that French and English co-operate in the industrial endeavours of the new century. Together the two people could create a distinctive North American community.

Bouchette's views were shared by his contemporaries in the *Ligue nationaliste*. Like the feminists, they were aware of international currents of opinion and they took many of their social cues from the American progressives. Like them, and indeed like most of their contemporaries, the nationalists were fascinated by the economic progress so visible in the early years of the twentieth century. But they were vaguely uneasy about the possible consequences. They wondered about the fitness of politicians to guide the state; they queried the moral rectitude and actual behaviour of the upper classes who were supposed to be models for society; they worried about the apathetic public spirit of their contemporaries; and they found the materalism that accompanied prosperity somewhat distasteful. They were not at all sure that a distinctive French and Catholic society could survive in the face of all that.

The *Ligue* itself, established in 1903, was still quite young when two nationalists engaged in a rather peripheral debate over its political orientations. Jules-Paul Tardivel, never a member of the *Ligue*, and Henri Bourassa, its inspirer, revealed that differences of opinion could divide nationalists as much as mutual sympathies joined them. Tardivel took the *Ligue* members, mostly from Montreal, to task for their Canadian as opposed to French Canadian nationalism. He published the program of the *Ligue* in *La Vérité* but complained that its desire for provincial autonomy within Confederation did not go far enough. French Canadians should be clearly defined as a distinct nationality in Confederation with their own patriotic aspirations, their own ideals, rights, and duties. Tardivel had once argued that the historical effort to preserve the language, institutions, and nationality of French Canada made no sense unless an independent nation was the eventual outcome. Now, with that same end in sight, Tardivel argued that the effort demanded the preservation of French Canadians themselves by means of agriculture, colonization, an end to infant mortality, and the creation of barriers against Protestant, Anglo-Saxon, and American infiltration.

Without denying any of the contemporary social or ideological evils that threatened French Canada, Henri Bourassa defended the new *Ligue*. He was not ready to admit that Quebec alone constituted French Canada. Nor was he convinced that Confederation was an impossiblity. Rather, by strengthening French Canadian minorities beyond Quebec, the position of Quebec itself in Confederation would be strengthened. Bourassa shared Tardivel's passion for Catholicism, but he also justified the *Ligue*'s very toned down expression of it. Montreal was not at all the same city as Quebec; young people were already exposed to every conceivable idea through the popular press and the younger nationalists were not particularly religious at all. Far better to praise them for undertaking social and political action for the betterment of Canada than to condemn them for some ideological lapse. For Bourassa and the *Ligue*, the imperial question and the social question were of far more significance.

In bringing social issues to public attention, the nationalists of whatever political persuasion emphasized the powers and obligations of the Quebec government. In that, they went beyond both feminists and clerics who were content to see social problems remain the prerogative of concerned individuals, albeit increasingly organized ones. The nationalists were suspicious of the growing number of mergers among large firms in the province; the benefits were surely not accruing to French Canadians. Nor did they approve of the co-operation, open or veiled, between the state and large-scale business concerns. Instead of providing generous subsidies to such firms, the state should become a shareholder in them. That way it would have some voice in the economic exploitation of the province. As it was, the government appeared almost anxious to give away land and forest, rivers and mines, even throwing in a railway or two, to private companies for very small fees. And its activity was trumpeted by the newspapers, in the pay of one or other of the political parties, as the normal course of events. The consequence, argued the nationalists, was that French Canadians exercised little control over their economic resources. The government could not even offer colonization as an escape for urban workers locked into soulless industries because it had abdicated its control of lands, and hence any possibility of rational development, to large and mostly foreign companies. Moreover the government shared the hostility of industrial firms to any legislative or even trade union protection for workers. The nationalists of the early twentieth century feared the outcome: the political minority that the nineteenth century had made of French Canada was about to become an economic minority as well.

Some of the nationalist criticism actually struck a responsive chord in the government. Henri Bourassa's stint in the provincial legislature from 1908 to 1912 may even have helped. Although he was in opposition and an independent at that, he had an increasing public following and he was a formidable debater. Whatever his influence, by 1910 the province was leasing rather than selling water, forest, and mining rights; it was prohibiting the export of pulpwood cut from its lands; it was tentatively approving minimal labour legislation; and it was preparing to assist settlers heading into Abitibi. It was even scrutinizing and adapting some aspects of the educational system. Night schools and technical schools appeared in urban centres; agricultural classes were added to the program of rural schools. A graduate commercial school, the *Hautes Etudes commerciales*, began in 1907 with government backing to offer classical college graduates an alternative to the still too tempting literary, legal, and medical faculties of the university. The goverment also gave its guarded approval to a federal royal commission investigating industrial education between 1910 and 1913 on the condition that there be no question of the province's retaining exclusive control.

The increasing interest of feminists, nationalists, and even the state in education was sure to raise clerical suspicions. Much of the clerics' claim to social prestige was based on their educational activities. As long as education was primarily a matter of elementary instruction for the masses and elite schooling for the select few, church and state were able to agree on clerical administration in return for low costs. But the new century's accent on more advanced and more practical training prodded the state into action. The new technical and commercial schools, for example, were not placed under clerical control. The priests argued in vain that they had been teaching a commercial program in sixteen of the province's twenty-one classical colleges for years, but they could not stop the growing secular interest in education. Many of them in fact considered it part of the times. If the church were not to be totally discarded in an urban world of industrial disrespect for religious holidays, of bars being more numerous than churches, of alienation between priest and people, it would have to react. If no one else was going to defend the church's rightful place in the new industrial order, the church would have to do so itself.

Although launched to protect the clergy's places of power in society, the clerical defensive had a positive connotation—and name—in the early twentieth century. "Catholic action," similar in many respects to the social gospel movement within certain Protestant churches, lent a moral tone to all manner of practical undertakings by clerics all over the world. Supporters of Catholic action assumed that the social question that so agitated feminists and nationalists was above all a religious and moral question and hence required clerical intervention. In the French Canadian context they added the national question to the equation and again came up with necessary social action by priests.

The priests were certainly everywhere to be seen, organizing and encouraging numerous forms of Catholic action. At Laval in 1902 they fostered the *Société du parler français* to protect the French language from the corruption of a technical, urban environment. In the classical colleges in 1904 they grouped pious young men into the *Association catholique de la jeunesse canadienne-française*, a province-wide network of study circles and discussion groups to plan domestic and public Catholic action. After 1906 individual priests lent their local support to the fledgling *caisses populaires*, savings and credit institutions that were to be French Canada's alone. In 1907 the Quebec diocese gave its support to a newspaper appropriately titled *L'Action sociale* and just as appropriately retitled eight years later, *L'Action catholique*. In 1910 still other priests arranged to have the Catholic spotlight of the world on Montreal at the international eucharistic congress where nationalist speaker Henri Bourassa publicly rebuked a visiting bishop from Britain for his association of Catholicism and the English language in North America. To ensure that at least college students if not foreign bishops knew their history, the priests introduced the teaching of Canadian history into the curriculum. Among the teachers scrambling to prepare courses without textbooks was *abbé* Lionel Groulx, then teaching at Valleyfield but shortly, at the instigation of Henri Bourassa, to take up the first chair in Canadian history at Laval University's Montreal campus. Within a few years he, and not Bourassa, was the undisputed *chef* of a new generation of religiously oriented nationalists. In the meantime priests had also shaped that generation through the *Ecole sociale populaire*, begun in 1911 to publicize the Catholic response to social problems. And the clerics clearly established their linking of language and nationalism when Laval hosted a huge *Congrès de la langue française* in 1912, attracting delegates from all over North America. The priests were literally everywhere.

They even tried their hand at more specifically economic activities. Both bishops and local clergy, notably those outside the large metropolitan centres, were enthusiastic promoters of business enterprises and road and railway schemes. Depending on their location, they would advocate a cheese factory or a pulp mill, a foundary or a brickyard and harangue investors to initiate them. In small centres they acted as intermediaries between industrialists and the local population. In Quebec City the archbishop arbitrated a labour dispute between shoe manufacturers and some four thousand workers in 1900. The result of Monseigneur Nazaire Bégin's intervention was a clear statement by the church of the workers' right to join unions.

The type of union which the clergy advocated was, however, another matter. Few of the clergy were content with existing unions. They either saw them as unnecessary restraints on individual workers or as flags marking an unacceptable division of society into warring classes. Most of the unions crossed over ethnic and religious lines and frightened the clergy with the spectre of loss of faith. Moreover, the majority of them were affiliates of international unions and thus brought American norms to Quebec. Even the early national unions, most of which were in Quebec but were expelled from the Trades and Labour Congress of Canada in 1902 precisely because of their lack of international affiliation, were suspect. Although they favoured conciliation and even harmony between employers and employees and thus ought to have found favour with the clergy, their very presence testified to the rivalry and hostility among workers that clerics found so abhorrent. Besides, neither national nor international unions would tolerate clerical intervention in their affairs. And yet their numbers were growing. Unless the church could stake a claim to a presence within the union movement, vast numbers of French Canadians would exercise social relations quite divorced from religion. The church was quick to point out the evil consequence; it was more circumspect about the possible threat to the clerical position in Quebec.

The claim not only to clerical presence but to clerical leadership in unions came out of Chicoutimi in 1907. *Abbé* Eugène Lapointe was determined to organize the forestry and industrial workers of the region, but he wanted neither a company union in the pocket of employers nor an industrial or trade union directed by organizers from elsewhere. Rather he hoped to organize the workers on a confessional basis and to have the social doctrine of the church inspire his *Fédération ouvrière de Chicoutimi.* His union would teach respect for the rights of workers instead of class warfare and its interests would be broader than mere material benefits for its members. The workers, however, needed a lot of convincing. Lapointe had to overcome their scepticism not only about his union with its obligatory chaplain, temperance, Sunday observance, and retreats but also about his friendship with the major employer of the region, Alfred Dubuc. Gradually he won his point so that by 1912 a larger formation emerged from the forest lands of the Saguenay-Lac St. Jean, the *Fédération ouvrière mutuelle du nord.* Thereafter the movement grew as new unions were initiated by priests, or former national unions in Hull, Trois-Rivières, Sherbrooke, or St. Hyacinthe became Catholic ones. They never equalled the international unions in size or number, but they did grow sufficiently through the years of the First World War to form the *Confédération des travailleurs catholiques du Canada* (CTCC) in 1921. From then until their secularization as the *Confédération des syndicats nationaux* in 1960, priests continued to play an active role in one strain of the union movement in Quebec.

Of the three groups initiating social action in Quebec in the early years of the twentieth century, the clerics had the upper hand. Their longer past and more formal position in Quebec society undoubtedly guaranteed that. But an unofficial alliance between male clerics and nationalists against the feminists may also have helped. No formal grouping linked the two, but they often found themselves on the same critical side of the social or political fence. They collaborated on newspapers and in nationalist and Catholic action groups. Occasionally, in fact, they were the same people. But in spite of all the good deeds they willingly credited to certain groups of women, they were uneasy with the very concept of feminism. Unlike the women, they had the resources, in pulpit, press, and platform, to make their views known.

Sometimes the women themselves provided the occasion for expressions of male hostility. In 1913 while all the world watched British feminists battling with police and engaging in hunger strikes in prison in order to gain political equality by means of the vote, French Canadian feminists invited priest Louis Lalande to address the *Fédération nationale Saint-Jean-Baptiste*. The topic was the very one that had inaugurated the *Fédération:* the two kinds of feminism. Fearful lest Canadian women be attracted toward the worst kind and start demanding political rights themselves, Lalande denounced it for its shrill bitterness, as violent and brutal as the men it purported to despise; it could only lead to unnatural demands, the defiance of authority, and ultimately the break-up of the home. In contrast, Lalande pointed to the good works, particularly the moral protection of young workers, accomplished in the name of religion and feminine dignity and in the acceptance of authority and natural inequalities. The constrast could hardly have been more pointed. But if the members of the *Fédération*, well aware that the National Council of Women had openly espoused votes for women in 1910, had any misgivings about Lalande's portrayal, they kept them to themselves.

Nor did the *Fédération* ever respond publicly to Henri Bourassa's virulent attack on feminism in *Le Devoir* that same spring of 1913. According to Bourassa, the ultra-Catholic editor of the nationalist Montreal daily, feminism was a foreign import, another Protestant infection, bound to poison the French Canadian family and through it French Canadian civilization. Women in fact were the guardians of all that made for French Canadian cultural superiority in North America: they held the key to the survival of religion, morality, education, and the family. If they stopped behaving in the prescribed manner, if they ceased to embody all the ideal characteristics not only of French Canada but of humanity itself, they would bring down the social order in ruin about their heads. Drawing on religion and logic, biology and politics, propriety and ridicule, Bourassa lashed feminism with a vehemence that indicated more the febrile state of his imagination than the reality of Canadian feminism.

That reality was actually much closer to the ideal image of women that nationalists and clerics concocted for their own convenience. Canadian feminists, French and English alike, accepted the notion of separate spheres; they acknowledged, as eternally given, the social distinctions that stemmed from sexual distinctions; they agreed that they had a particular mission in life to be cultured, morally uplifting, soothing, and healing. Bourassa had only to read the columns of his own female correspondent, Fadette, in *Le Devoir* or even those of Colette (Edouardine Lesage) in the rival *La Presse* where an entire front page was given over in 1913 to depict the three types of women in the public eye. Dominating the page and contrasted both with the moderate suffragette, mistaken in her desire for the vote but permitted nonetheless to express her views, and with the violent suffragette, a fury who had discarded all her femininity, was the real woman, devoted solely to her maternal mission, the ornament of her family, the object of everyone's adoration. French Canada, *La Presse* was relieved to note, had only the last kind of woman. The feminists thought so too. When they took on public tasks beyond the home, they did so to protect the home. They were merely enlarging their maternal sphere for the benefit of society. If their entrance into the public arena of education and social welfare was in fact a criticism of the extent of the industrial mess men had created or of the efficacy of religious institutions to cope with it or even of the stifling role that the ideology of separate spheres thrust upon them, few of them said so. The clerics' and the nationalists' ability to spot danger where in fact none existed deprived Quebec women of the right to vote in provincial elections until the 1940s. In the second decade of the twentieth century it was easy enough to direct women into knitting socks and bundling bandages for soldiers overseas while the nationalists and the clerics, harbouring more ambiguous views about the First World War, fought the "Prussians" next door.

SELECT BIBLIOGRAPHY

Babcock, Robert. "Samuel Gompers and the French-Canadian Worker, 1900–1914." *American Review of Canadian Studies* 3(1973):47–66.

Dandurand, Joséphine. *Nos travers.* Montreal: Beauchemin, 1901.

Danylewycz, Marta. "Changing Relationships: Nuns and Feminists in Montreal, 1880–1925." *Histoire sociale/Social History* 14(1981):413–34.

Drolet, Jean-Claude. "Mgr. Eugène Lapointe, initiateur du syndicalisme catholique en Amérique du Nord." *Rapport de la Société canadienne d'histoire de l'Eglise catholique* (1966):47–56.

Dumont-Johnson, Micheline. "Histoire de la condition de la femme dans la province de Quebec." In *Tradition culturelle et histoire politique de la femme au Canada.* Ottawa: Information Canada, 1975. Pp. 1–57.

Dumont-Johnson, Micheline. "Les communautés religieuses et la condition féminine." *Recherches sociographiques* 19(1978):79–102.

La Fédération nationale Saint-Jean-Baptiste célèbre le cinquantenaire de sa fondation. Souvenir issue of *La Bonne Parole,* 1956–1958.

Lavigne, Marie, and Yoland Pinard, eds. *Les femmes dans la société québécoise: Aspects historiques.* Montreal: Boréal Express, 1977.

Levitt, Joseph. *Henri Bourassa and the Golden Calf: The Social Program of the Nationalists of Québec (1900–1914).* Ottawa: Les editions de l'Université d'Ottawa, 1972.

Levitt, Joseph. *Henri Bourassa: Catholic critic.* Ottawa: Canadian Historical Association, 1976.

Rouillard, Jacques. *Les syndicats nationaux au Québec de 1900 à 1930.* Quebec: Les presses de l'Université Laval, 1979.

"... the appeal of patriotism ..."
Recruitment poster, World War I.

13 The Prussians Are Next Door

Nationalists in Quebec have never forgotten the First World War and Liberal politicians have been a close second in reminding voters of its political ravages. For many nationalists the war years turned French Canada into Quebec. For many Liberals the blunders of federal Conservatives during the same years provided electoral ammunition for generations to come. To some French Canadians, the war revealed the basic incompatibility of Canada's two people: alien cultures finally exposed, in total disagreement over the demands of imperialism, the force of nationalism, and the logic of feminism. For other French Canadians, the crises of the war years —from Ontario schools to conscription to votes for women—were just that, temporary aberrations from the Canadian norm of compromise and forbearance. The difference of opinion within French Canada troubled the nationalists as much as English Canadian hostility although no one seemed unhappy to see the momentary reference to separatism disappear from the headlines as quickly as it appeared late in 1917.

Certainly separatist thoughts were far from anyone's mind in the summer of 1914. Even the vaguely voiced notion of Canadian autonomy from Britain was swept aside in a wave of enthusiasm for European military adventures. The British declaration of war on Germany in early August bound the entire empire, if not to actual participation, then to a legal state of war. In fact no one lingered over legal niceties: there was no questioning of Canadian support for and participation in the British war effort. Crowds in the cities of Quebec vied with those in other Canadian centres to express their emotion. The Quebec government was as generous as that of the other provinces in offering an assortment of Canadian agricultural products freely to Britain. Four million tons of Quebec cheese thus made its way across the Atlantic accompanied by the salmon, hay, cattle, apples, and potatoes of the Canadian cornucopia. Only Henri Bourassa wryly commented upon the supplementary freight trains required to haul all the generosity to Canadian ports and the likelihood of much of it rotting on the quays of Liverpool before it could be distributed and consumed. But even he, although acknowledging no constitutional obligation to be involved in Britain's wars, admitted to a moral interest in the outcome for the two European countries with which Canadians had historical and emotional ties.

Canadian assistance and support was easy enough to offer when no one knew the extent or the demands of the war. Wilfrid Laurier, leader of the Liberal opposition in the House of Commons, offered his entire support to the Conservative government of Robert Borden. From the Liberals would come no questioning, not a word of reproach, as long as there was danger on the European front; the friends and foes of Great Britain should know that Canadian hearts and minds were united. Such magnanimity was as shortly lived as it was eloquently expressed. But in the spirited summer days of 1914, this political co-operation enabled the Canadian government to pass the War Measures Act which sanctioned extensive controls over the lives and economic activities of Canadians. In Quebec the lieutenant-governor offered all the resources of the province for the defence of Canada; Sir Lomer Gouin, the premier, indicated that Quebec government employees could enlist and continue to receive full salary. The archbishops of Quebec and Montreal spoke of the sacred duty of Canadians to aid Great Britain. Only later in the war were appeals made in the name of Canada's two "mother countries"; in the early months some French Canadians seriously wondered whether the war was not divine retribution for a France that had strayed from the path of true religion. The mayors of Quebec City and Montreal joined the chorus of assistance to Great Britain and the popular press followed suit. After all, the war was only supposed to last a few months; those few Canadian soldiers who were likely even to go overseas—as volunteers, the prime minister carefully assured the country—would be home for Christmas after a pleasant European tour.

The recruiting stations were barely open when some French Canadians began wondering just where the real battle was. Indeed, a number of nationalist leaders were being recruited, not to the Canadian Expeditionary Force—although there were some there such as Olivar Asselin, a military enthusiast ever since his participation in the Spanish American war at the end of the nineteenth century—but rather to assist their French-speaking compatriots in Ontario. There, the Prussians were not across the Atlantic but across the street, the trenches held not by allied forces but by mothers armed with hatpins. The military analogies in the exaggerated language of Ottawa's *Le Droit*, a paper begun in 1913 to speak for the growing number of French Canadians in eastern Ontario, revealed both an ignorance of the horror of European trench warfare and the depth of the hurt occasioned by the Ontario school question. The intermingling of the war's demands with English Ontario's implacable hostility to all things French dampened French Canadian enthusiasm for the war effort and created a new breed of nationalist.

The increasing number of French Canadians in Ontario seems to have been at the origin of the dispute over bilingual schools that began in 1912. By that date, one-tenth of Ontario's population was French-speaking as newcomers moved in from Quebec to join well-established communities in southwestern Ontario, to add to the newer settlers in the north along the lines of the National Transcontinental, or to swell the French presence in Ottawa and the counties of eastern Ontario. Their arrival complicated the lives of English-speaking Catholics, particularly in the schools, and raised fears among English-speaking Protestants, always suspicious of Catholicism and even more so when it was linked to the French language. Moreover the concentrated presence of French Canadians in three distinct areas of the province also had political implications for the Conservative provincial government. When many of them also showed signs of imitating their Quebec relatives by organizing formal interest groups, English-speaking Ontarians became distinctly hostile. In 1910, for example, the *Association canadienne-française d'éducation d'Ontario* held its first conference in Ottawa. Twelve hundred delegates from French-speaking areas of the province voiced their concern for the twenty-five thousand youngsters attending bilingual primary schools in the province: they wanted their children properly taught by competent teachers with legislative grants for their schools.

Other Ontarians had similar worries but for quite different reasons. Bilingual schools had no legal existence in the province; they had simply developed along with the French-speaking population, usually as part of the Catholic separate school system constitutionally guaranteed since 1867, but sometimes, if a given district had no separate school, within the public school system. Administrators in the ministry of education had nightmares about the complexities and the very thought of a third school system with multiple demands for classrooms, teachers, inspectors, and programs. Where would one find competent seventeen-year-olds able to teach the entire primary program in both languages and frequently in a single classroom for the scant hundred dollars annual salary offered by most school boards? Should French be encouraged at all when Ontario's industrial future, and the youngsters' place in it, was assuredly English? Like Manitobans of the late nineteenth century, English-speaking Ontarians could only measure progress in English terms.

Quebec nationalists always had difficulty with the fact that the school question surfaced because of the complaints of a Catholic bishop. The ideological connection that had been developing since the late nineteenth century, thanks largely to ultramontane logic, between language, religion, and nationality could not quite hold in the face of bitter Irish-French disputes in Ontario. The villain was supposed to be clad as an Orangeman; instead, in his first appearance, he wore the cassock of a priest. Monseigneur Fallon, the bishop of London, complained to the Ontario government and the press that the bilingual schools in his diocese were producing poorly trained children, inferior to those in the English language separate schools. The public controversy that swirled around Fallon's remarks induced the provincial government to investigate the bilingual schools of the province and, once the investigation confirmed the accusations, to pass regulatory measures. On the assumption that a single language would cure all the practical problems which the investigator, Dr. Merchant, spotted in certain of the bilingual schools, the ministry of education added Regulation XVII to its decrees for elementary schools. Beginning as a mere directive in 1912, the regulation, slightly modified in the face of Franco-Ontarian opposition, became law in 1915. By then its purpose was hopelessly enmeshed with the Canadian war effort, as nationalists from Quebec fanned the flames of resentment between English- and French-speaking Ontarians.

To both Quebecois and Franco-Ontarians, Regulation XVII implied the end of French language teaching in Ontario. Its stipulation that French could be used as a language of instruction only in the first two years of the primary program, after which pupils were expected to know enough English to continue their schooling in that language, and that French as a subject of study should be limited to one hour a day, raised all the old fears of assimilation. In vain, and indeed not very loudly, did the Ontario government protest that the regulation only applied to an annually construed list of bilingual schools where English was inadequately taught or where the teachers lacked the proper qualifications. In vain did it tinker with the inspection system of the regulation: no one within the ministry of education or outside knew precisely how the regulation was to work or just what it intended. French Canadians, ever fearful, and increasingly sensitive to the question of language as the early twentieth century tumbled people together, believed the regulation meant their demise.

Little during the war years was to relieve their anxiety. While the Ontario government threatened to cut off provincial funds from schools that did not obey Regulation XVII, fanatical Protestants in the province urged even more severe restrictions. The Orange Order, claiming to defend British principles and therefore the English language, urged the abolition of all bilingual schools since they were agents of French Canadian infiltration into the province. Worse still for the Orangemen was that those French Canadians were probably disloyal, given their poor showing in the enlistment figures for the war. Just as unsettling for French Canadians was the feud with their fellow Catholics. Prompted by Monseigneur Fallon, English-speaking Catholics, with a population three times that of the French in Ontario, argued that the senseless struggle over language risked endangering the much greater principle of Catholic education. If the French Canadians annoyed the Ontario government to such an extent that it decided to turn on separate schooling itself, where would Catholics be then? The two groups of Catholics came to legal blows in Ottawa when the English and French sections of the Ottawa separate school board disputed the majority French section's defiance of Regulation XVII. While lawyers contested the validity of the regulation and of the government's means of enforcing it, French-speaking children and their mothers defended the schools and the teachers of their choice. A Laval University student newspaper cheekily remarked that the real threat to French civilization in the world was no longer in Flanders but in the schools of Ottawa.

Although the school question was to assist them in doing so, French Canadians had not yet drawn a frontier along the provincial boundary. Those in Quebec gladly lent their ideological and financial support to *Le Droit* and the *Association canadienne-française d'éducation d'Ontario.* The Franco-Ontarian leaders were all relative newcomers and they called upon intellectual and nationalist sustenance from their home province. Nationalist spokesmen from Quebec visited Ontario and reported on the struggle to their colleagues in Montreal and Quebec. Henri Bourassa was a favourite guest at Ontario gatherings; his powers of logic and persuasion were solace to the embattled minority. Bourassa in fact saw the French-speaking minorities in the rest of Canada as the outposts of Quebec: their defence against the attacks of a bigoted majority assured Quebec's own survival; if they succumbed, Quebec would be next. Bourassa's paper *Le Devoir* thus gave full coverage of the events in Ontario. Nationalist associations in Quebec held fund raising campaigns to assist the Ontarians in their educational and legal defiance of Regulation XVII. Quebec bishops encouraged the campaigns and approved clerical ones launched from the pulpits of parish churches. The Catholic school commission of Montreal voted funds to assist the bilingual campaign in Ontario. Even the Quebec government, gingerly stepping on the mine field of interference in another province's affairs, passed a motion regretting the divisions over the bilingual school question in Ontario. It also permitted municipalities in the province to make financial contributions to patriotic, national, or educational causes, the latter intended to cover the Franco-Ontarian situation. Businesses even began to register the cost of French Canadian unhappiness as Quebec clients refused to place orders with Toronto firms. Through it all, the force of numbers became increasingly obvious, although seldom openly admitted. French Canadians were only safe in numbers and only in Quebec did they have the numbers.

Quebec's federal politicians would never make such an admission, but they too had to swallow much of the bitterness of the school question. Indeed, with some of the more dramatic episodes of the struggle taking place within shouting distance of Parliament Hill, they could hardly avoid the issue even if they had wanted to stay on the neutral terrain of education being a provincial matter. The tattered remains of the nationalist alliance with the Conservatives in 1911 rallied sufficiently to have cabinet ministers Pierre-Edouard Blondin, Thomas-Chase Casgrain, and Esioff-Léon Patenaude request that prime minister Borden refer the entire question of the status of the French language in Canada to the Privy Council for clarification. Borden refused on the grounds that the British North America Act was perfectly clear: French had a legal existence in the debates and recordings of the federal parliament, in those of the Quebec provincial legislature, and before the federal and Quebec courts. He refrained from adding "and no further" that many Conservatives then and since have muttered. Nor would he, along with most English Canadians, accept an argument for French based on natural right or even on the legally imaginative grounds that French Canadians, in Saskatchewan for example, required education in French in order to be able to take a case to a federal court in that province in their own language. In fact none of the defenders of bilingual schools in Ontario denied the necessity of learning English; they simply wanted their children taught in French as well.

But when such views were expressed in the federal parliament, they encountered a blank and sometimes hostile wall. Borden refused a petition from senator Philippe Landry and most of the

Quebec bishops requesting federal disallowance of Regulation XVII; in the background some of his Conservative colleagues began to grumble about French Canadian participation in the war effort. In May 1916, the MPs voted down an intricately worded resolution from Ernest Lapointe, Liberal member for Kamouraska, requesting that the Ontario government not infringe upon the linguistic privileges of French-speaking school children. The Liberal leader, Laurier, barely kept his Ontario members in line for the vote as westeners openly balked and voted with the Conservative majority. Behind the defeat, legitimate enough on the grounds of federal non-interference in provincial matters, was also the grim sentiment expressed by the former western Liberal MP, Clifford Sifton: the Franco-Ontarian agitation was criminal and unpatriotic at a time of national crisis. For Sifton and many English Canadians the real national crisis was on the European battlefield; for many French Canadians it was in the linguistic heart of Canada. When *abbé* Lionel Groulx, six years later, placed the federal debate over the school question at the centre of his novel *L'Appel de la race*, he barely mentioned the war. But he did sanction the dissolution of a marriage—a personified Confederation—on the grounds of linguistic and racial incompatibility.

In 1916, however, the war could not be forgotten. Canadian involvement was about to produce a clash between French and English that would make the Ontario schools question pale in comparison. Rumours of compulsory military service were already touring the country when some of the signs of appeasement appeared in the bilingual schools dispute. The courts left no doubt that Regulation XVII was quite within the power of the Ontario government although the learned law lords in London confessed to finding the language obscure, the effect difficult to ascertain, and some of the methods of enforcement dubious. But they also decreed that the Ottawa separate school board was overstepping its jurisdiction by defying the regulation. The pope also had a word to say on the matter. Responding to the appeal of different groups of Canadian Catholics, he advised moderation and tolerance. The unity of the Canadian Catholic church was essential and he was not at all sure that Quebec clerical involvement on behalf of the Franco-Ontarians was serving that cause. While a few French Canadian priests wondered privately about the power of the Irish in Rome and Henri Bourassa pointedly refrained from any comment in *Le Devoir*, the papal directive did in fact carry some weight in calming emotions. Among English-speaking Ontarians, some soothing voices began to be heard as Liberals and businessmen invented *bonne entente* in an effort to repair the broken bridges of politics and commerce. Meanwhile the Ontario government found its regulation increasingly difficult to enforce and ultimately abandoned it in 1927. Only the Orange Order was left to fulminate against separate schools themselves, but even its fury abated when conscription offered a more exciting battleground for denouncing

French Canadians. Although the schools question trailed off somewhat ignominiously, its stark lesson of numbers, reinforced by the implication of brute force in the conscription issue, was not forgotten.

By late 1916 the war that had been expected to be brief had become an endless bloodbath. It sucked up men, munitions, and supplies and buried them all in the trenches and then the mud of western Europe. Ever since the initial heroic send-off of one hundred thousand Canadians in the early autumn of 1914 from the final training camp at Valcartier near Quebec City, the numbers of enthusiastic recruits had steadily declined. There were only so many able-bodied recent British immigrants in the western provinces; they had been the first to respond to the imperial summons. In contrast, native born Canadians held back, their tie to empire easily calculated by the number of generations their families had been in the country. The appeal of patriotism and religion, used effectively in both French and English Canada, began to wear thin as God appeared quite indifferent to the slaughter. Moreover the war was economically beneficial to Canada: western farms and eastern industries competed much more effecitvely for man and woman power than did the Canadian Expeditionary Force. But as the number of casualties rose and the number of recruits declined, the murmurings began. Population figures alone meant that English Canadian familes were receiving more of the dreaded beige telegrams announcing death; the lists of wounded, missing, and demised were automatically longer in the English language newspapers. But when the murmurings turned into a slogan—"equalization of sacrifice"—then people began watching the enlistment figures and pointing to that part of the country producing the fewest recruits.

Naturally, Quebec was at the bottom of the list. As the oldest Canadians, Quebecois had the least interest in the war; no emotional tie pulled them to Britain or France. Besides, they had never found a comfortable place in the Canadian military service. Even the frequent presence of a French Canadian as minister or deputy minister of the department of the militia could not camouflage the essentially alien character of the institution for French Canadians. Few of the higher officers were French-speaking. Only a tiny fraction of the cadets at the Royal Military College in Kingston, the training school for military officers, was French Canadian and all the instruction was in English. Being an officer meant being or becoming English. The senior officers of the permanent, as distinct from voluntary, militia tended in fact to be British and they shared imperial enthusiasms. They had neither time nor patience for developing military attachments among French Canadians. The suggestion that a distinctive uniform, modelled on that of the Zouaves, might add to the attractiveness of the military for young French Canadians was vetoed at the very time when some English Canadian regiments were permitted to don the equally foreign and much less practical kilt. Not surprisingly, by 1912, there were only twenty-seven French Canadian compared to two hundred and twenty-seven English Canadian permanent officers in the Canadian militia.

Furthermore, nothing during the war years made French Canadians any more welcome in Canadian military ranks. The language of instruction and command remained English. The difficulty of raising and maintaining French-speaking units without having them dispersed to reinforce others was obvious in the amount of political pressure required to form and sustain the French Canadian Royal 22nd Battalion. There at least French Canadians were able to develop an outstanding military force of their own, envied indeed by English Canadians. But elsewhere, appointments or promotions of French Canadians to the higher ranks of the military were few and far between. Even the minister of the militia during the early years of the war, Sam Hughes, could not hide his hostility: he particularly did not wish to have French-speaking military units accompany Catholic popular processions. And he was careful to keep the one French Canadian general, François-Louis Lessard, busy in Canada instead of sending him overseas. Also, his own department established crude enlistment quotas based on a simple proportion of the total Canadian population. With twenty-eight percent of the population, Quebec should be producing twenty-eight percent of the recruits. Proportionately to the other regions of the country, however, Quebec had fewer men of military age, fewer bachelors, fewer casual labourers, and fewer British born, all of whom tended to be first in line at the recruiting stations. No statistics measured the impact of the Ontario school question or of Henri Bourassa's increasingly virulent anti-war tirades in *Le Devoir*. Although dead silence greeted Armand Lavergne's outburst in the Quebec legislature early in 1916 that every penny spent on recruitment in Quebec was money stolen from the Ontario minority, the mass circulation *La Presse* placed the controversy over bilingual schools in Ontario at the head of its list of reasons why French Canadians did not rush to enlist. Given so little encouragement to do so, it is perhaps surprising that as many as thirty-five thousand French Canadians found their way into Canada's armed forces by 1918 at all (approximately half of them before conscription and half after).

By early 1917 conscription was more than just a rumour. Prime minister Borden was determined to raise the number of Canada's soldiers to half a million, a figure he had set a year earlier. But the task became all the more difficult as the number of recruits no longer kept pace with the increasing casualties. The war itself was particularly bleak, the outcome no longer sure, and the end nowhere in sight. Russia withdrew from the allied cause into revolution and civil war; the United States had not yet rallied its forces; the French army was fed up and mutinous; successful submarine warfare sapped the strength and morale of Britain. All of that

Borden absorbed in a visit to England in the spring of 1917. At the same time he admitted that volunteers were no longer forthcoming in Canada. Neither national registration nor the idea of a home defence force early in 1917 succeeded in producing new recruits. National registration in fact raised more suspicion than enthusiasm. This country-wide registration of talent and availability for various wartime jobs also recorded the number of military prospects and French Canadians were not alone in suspecting a trap. Both the Liberal press and labour organizations across the country joined them in wondering about the political motives of the enquiry. At the same time, employers and unions alike resisted the government's suggestion that more female labour be hired in order to release men for military service. In last minute efforts to attract men, the military itself consented to lowering its medical standards while recruiting agents took to haranguing crowds lined up for Saturday night entertainment. French Canada's one general attempted his own campaign for volunteers in Quebec. But the indifference was constant and it was all across the country. The people who were by then shouting so loudly for conscription clearly were not the same people as those who were supposed to sign up.

One of the first victims of conscription may have been in the House of Commons itself where the Military Service Bill proposing conscription was introduced in June 1917. Sir Wilfrid Laurier, far too old for military service, may yet have felt most severely the brunt of compulsion in the bill. During the debate over the government proposal to raise one hundred thousand recruits from various categories of male British subjects aged between twenty and forty-five, Laurier was forced to preside over the disintegration of the Liberal party. His westerners had already balked over the Lapointe resolution a year earlier; now they were adamant supporters of the government's conscription bill. Some of them were already dickering with the Conservatives about a possible "Union" government that would unite all right-thinking Canadians in a thorough prosecution of the war effort. Laurier himself wavered just long enough to sense that any co-operation on his part in imposing conscription would send Quebec voters in droves into the nationalist embrace of Henri Bourassa. He therefore drew back from the temptation to join a Union government. But the various votes on the conscription bill carried off many of Laurier's followers from Ontario and the Maritimes, voting with their western colleagues in favour of conscription. To his remnant of French Canadian Liberals from Quebec was added a handful of one-time nationalists from the Conservative benches. Laurier was thus forced to abandon his concept of national unity and to take on the leadership of one group only, a group primarily defined by language and race. In opposing conscription Laurier was also forced to discard his own promise of 1914 of a united war effort; Canadian hearts and minds were far from united on this question and he could not pretend otherwise. Given that stand, Laurier was then forced to pursue his opposition to conscription all the way to a federal election. No unanimous consent was forthcoming to prolong the life of parliament as had happened in 1916 to avoid the disruptions of a wartime election. Unanimity no longer existed and the disruptions would have to take their course. That they did, and very bitterly too, in the federal election of December 1917.

Laurier's reasoned parliamentary opposition to conscription was a careful translation of the emotional opposition seething in Quebec. Laurier argued from law and precedent and politics: none of them sanctioned conscription. The government had no mandate to impose compulsory military service on the country. Some Liberals even accused the Conservatives of digging up conscription as a popular cause to cover up a moribund government. Certainly the measure was part of an increasing number of controls exercised by the federal government over the lives of ordinary Canadians. Justified by the war and facilitated by the War Measures Act, various controls from rationing to price fixing, from decrees against hoarding to those against loitering, probably overwhelmed the civil service more than anyone else, but they did indicate the state's willingness to go beyond persuasion to actual coercion in directing the activities of its citizens. Provincial governments—all except Quebec's—had also imposed restrictions, most notably in supervising the drinking habits of people by means of prohibition; the federal government would follow suit in 1918, although none of the laws lasted very long. Even the votes and incomes of Canadians came under close scrutiny by the federal government. By means of the Wartime Elections Act in 1917, the Conservatives carefully disfranchised certain Canadians of European background and just as carefully enfranchised the female relatives of soldiers. And in the same year the government introduced the income tax, thereby controlling the revenues of all Canadians, supposedly as a temporary measure to meet the mounting costs of the war effort. In such a context conscription was hardly an unusual idea. To Laurier, however, the setting could be no excuse: conscription was an illegitimate ploy on the part of a flagging government. The least it could do was hold a referendum on the question. Laurier may have expected the government to lose such a referendum, given the opposition of the working classes and of French Canadians to conscription. And if it won, well there would at least be some democratic justification for the measure.

The difficulty was that the democratic numbers game on such an issue was racially fixed. On the whole, English Canadians supported conscription and were easily able to silence the protests of farmers and workers in western Canada; French Canadians virtually unanimously opposed it. It was all very well for French Canadian Liberal politicians in Ottawa or Quebec to follow Laurier's lead and claim that Quebec would accept a Canadian verdict in a referendum; they really could not be sure. The issue cut too close to the bone: it was a majority of a different language and culture imposing military service for a foreign war upon a minority. In that light democracy could be an instrument of force. No one spoke of rape, Canadians of the time being much too prudish; but many people did recall the Conquest. No one in the eighteenth century had asked permission for that use of force; no one was likely to do so in twentieth. Laurier's amendment to the Military Service Bill, that it be submitted to a popular referendum, was soundly defeated.

With the passage of the Military Service Bill, popular passions over conscription intensified throughout the summer and early autumn of 1917. While Henri Bourassa wrote in *Le Devoir* of national suicide for a foreign cause, the *Globe* in Toronto referred to conscription as fresh dedication to the cause of liberty. Mass meetings in Quebec filled the Sunday air with protest. Some federal Conservatives from Quebec hastily resigned from the government; others, remaining and even voting for conscription, knew that their political days were numbered. Young men took off for the woods, preferring to camp out in hiding than risk the legal intricacies of the exemption process. Senior students in classical colleges suddenly sported clerical garb and earnestly declared their intention to become priests, an occupation exempt from conscription. A last minute attempt at voluntary recruiting netted a grand total of ninety young men in the province. In some minds, the possibility of civil war loomed as a logical, perhaps even a deserved, consequence of the government's insensitivity. The Ontario schools question surfaced again, tangled with the conscription debate in the Commons, and left French Canadians profoundly uneasy about their place in Confederation. Attacks on their language and their faith were crystallizing in the imposition of military service. Henri Bourassa claimed that the conscription law, enacted early in August 1917, was an open invitation for a popular uprising.

The uprising, such as it was, occurred in the form of a federal election. The Conservatives took no chances on the outcome. They lured conscriptionist Liberals from the west into a Union government and ensured even more western backing by exempting twenty year old farm workers from their military obligations. They even wooed the women with the strange beginnings of federal woman suffrage in Canada. Assuming that the wives, daughters, and sisters of Canadian soldiers would vote Conservative in order to bring their men home sooner, the government accorded them the vote. It also organized the overseas military vote in such a way as to favour Conservative candidates. The government hardly needed the popular press to fan passions and prejudices, but that was precisely what the elections of 1917 did. Of the many issues confronting the country from profiteering and the cost of living to immigration and the nationalization of the railways, the press preferred the sensationalism of Quebec's opposition to conscription and English Canada's reaction to it. The English language press quoted Henri Bourassa's arguments against the war and treated him, and by extension all French Canadians, as a traitor. A vote for Laurier would be a vote for Bourassa, for Quebec control of the entire country, for withdrawal from the war, and for the imposition of bilingual schools throughout the land. Quebec was the spoiled child of Confederation and should be compelled to do its share for the war effort. A map of Canada depicted Quebec in black, the "foul blot" on the country. Surrounded by such images, Unionist candidates in Quebec could hardly open their mouths. They were heckled, shouted down, pelted with rotten eggs, and threatened with revolver shots. No paper would carry their message to French-speaking voters. The nationalists, less of an organized political force than in 1911 but holding a much more volatile issue, urged support for Laurier, a mere six years after they had turned on him as a traitor. They insisted upon the suspension of the Military Service Act while Laurier stated more vaguely the Liberal policy of maintaining Canada's war effort by voluntary means. The result was predictable: all the ridings but three in Quebec voted Liberal; all the ridings but twenty in the rest of the country returned Unionist candidates. No one took heart in the mere three hundred thousand popular vote difference between Unionists and Liberals since the parliamentary composition was much more striking: Quebec in opposition and English Canada in power.

The first response came from the Quebec legislature. A rather sorrowful motion, introduced by Joseph-Napoléon Francoeur, raised the question of separatism. If Quebec was so despised, perhaps it should opt out. Although a few students and an obscure clerical paper trumpeted the power of an independent Quebec with its control of rail and shipping routes, Francoeur was much more despondent and the assembly greeted his motion in the same way. A rather desultory debate never even came to a vote on the dreary proposition that:

> This House is of the opinion that the province of Quebec would be disposed to accept the breaking of the Confederation pact of 1867 if, in the other provinces, it is believed that she is an obstacle to the union, progress and development of Canada.

With the onus put upon the rest of Canada, few Quebecois presumed to read the minds of their English-speaking compatriots, minds that had spoken all too clearly in the recent elections.

Neither the election nor the hint of separatism put a stop to French Canadian opposition to conscription nor even to government blundering in its relations with Quebec. Only in January 1918 were the first men requested to report for military induction and most of them successfully claimed exemptions. Conscription ultimately produced some eighty thousand soldiers in Canada, about a quarter of whom were from Quebec but not all French Canadians. Few of them went overseas, let alone to the battlefront, before the end of the war in November 1918. The numbers were minimal for the hostility aroused and the symbolism created. Few French Canadian families would forget English-speaking agents ferreting out their young men. Few young men would forget the months in hiding to escape the law or, for those enrolled, the low status of a conscript especially if he spoke French. More dramatic, because more public, were the anti-conscription riots in Quebec City in the early spring of 1918. Sparked by mounted police rounding up presumed defaulters and fed by popular discontent over wartime prices and rationing, the unrest boiled around the provincial capital for three days. True to form and no doubt fearing complicity between rioters and French Canadian troops, Borden had English-speaking soldiers from Toronto sent to assist in quelling the disturbances. Well might some Quebecois wonder just where the war was being fought.

For other French Canadians an even greater threat to the social order was issuing from Ottawa. Relegating Le Devoir's commentary on the Quebec City riots to his second-in-command, Henri Bourassa took on what he obviously considered a much more serious problem, that of suffrage for women. By 1917 all of the provinces west of Quebec had introduced the suffrage and the women involved had no intention of limiting their voting to the provincial sphere. They argued their special interest in matters of social reform, from prohibition to public health. They pointed to their wartime activities in fund raising, support to the troops, and actual military service as nurses. Speaking though the National Council of Women, various women's associations convinced prime minister Borden to enlarge his peculiar precedent of 1917 and introduce total woman suffrage for federal elections. The bill was progressing through its various stages in the Commons at the very time of the anti-conscription riots in Quebec City. Meanwhile, Bourassa was exposing in Le Devoir all the ill effects of woman suffrage. Once women had the vote they would no longer marry since they would be engaged in fearsome competition with men. The family would thereby disintegrate, the education of children would be abandoned, and the privileged position that women now merited because of their maternal functions would disappear. Social degradation would follow woman's degradation.

For Bourassa, the suffrage, like feminism, was one more foreign import threatening the social structure of French Canada. It was a direct consequence of the individualism of Protestant religions; perhaps it suited Anglo-Saxon women who had long since lost their ability to influence society by feminine charm and natural means, but it was quite alien to French and Catholic women. The latter, Bourassa was convinced, did not want the vote; they were surely glad to be free of the civil and military duties that accompany a say in public affairs. Nor would they wish to take part in the cabals and base intrigue of political warfare. Their place was quite literally in the home; only by staying there could they aspire to any social role at all let alone one claiming superiority. To step into the public sphere was to defy their sex, to deny the family as the basic social unit, to disrupt all notion of hierarchy and authority, to destroy the subordination of rights to duties. In spite of the feminist argument that the vote was a mere means of bringing women's moral and social concerns to bear more directly on society, Bourassa spotted the radicalism of the measure. Once women had the vote they would be in a position of equality with men in terms of their relationship to the state. That relationship would no longer be mediated by men and who knew what the social consequences of that challenge to the natural order might be? Expressing what the Montreal *Gazette* termed "mouldy ideas," Bourassa and some of the French Canadian opponents of the woman suffrage bill in the House of Commons—none of whom was able to stop the bill's passage—thought they knew what suffrage would lead to and they did not like the prospect at all. French Canada would be irretrievably changed, and for the worse.

A number of clerics added their amen to the views of Bourassa and the politicians. The theologian Louis-Adolphe Paquet, surveying the world from within the walls of the Quebec seminary where he taught candidates for the priesthood, also foresaw the evil of women in competition with men as a result of the suffrage. With Saint Paul, Saint Thomas, and the current pope, Benedict XV, on his side, Paquet could safely condemn the challenge to authority, the family, and society that lay behind feminist demands. But he was not as sure as Bourassa that the demands were foreign. Rather he feared that much in contemporary French Canadian society actually spawned feminism: the education of young girls was much too similar to that of boys; too many young women defied parental authority in their clothing and their behaviour; the economic necessity of jobs in industry and commerce, which Paquet acknowledged, took women out of their homes, tossed them together, and facilitated their developing new aspirations. Paquet would have girls carefully educated for their maternal and religious role, differentiating their training not by talent but by class. No matter whom they married, all young women would have the same basic function—to develop the virtue of their sons and sustain the faith of their husbands, although depending on whether their husband was a farmer or a judge, their station in life would be different and would require special training. The cardinal archbishop of Quebec, Monseigneur Bégin, echoed Paquet's views by carefully culling papal antipathy to woman suffrage and passing it on to his priests. In their teaching and preaching, they were to keep in mind that neither the interests of society nor natural law justified votes for women. The Catholic press dutifully followed suit in opposing suffrage for women.

The major feminist organization in Quebec, the *Fédération nationale Saint-Jean-Baptiste*, also followed the clerical directive and subordinated its early interest in the suffrage. Instead it concentrated on preparing women for the proper exercising of the vote. Working as closely as it did with clerical groups, the *Fédération* perhaps could not avoid the intense hostility the male hierarchy of the church evinced towards the idea of legal equality for women. Sharing similar views about the roles of women in the family, in society, and in the preservation of French Canadian culture, the women of the *Fédération* may have been just as sensitive to the enormous wounds the war years delivered to French Canada. Those wounds in turn may have reinforced the feminists' compulsion to soothe rather than disrupt. Certainly the journalist Fadette, writing in *Le Devoir*, thought Quebec women would exercise their new found and unasked for federal political right with more moderation than English Canadian women: she was half-pleased and half-alarmed to see the Montreal Women's Club, a member of the local branch of the National Council of Women, split over the issue of conscription. Once women entered politics, she surmised, all their endeavours would be contaminated.

The fear of contamination coloured many French Canadian reactions during the years of the First World War. The English Canadian association of imperialism and nationalism was fraught with dangers (notably that of fighting in distant wars) for French Canadians who associated nationalism with anti-imperialism. The French Canadian link between language, religion, and nationality had proven to be tenuous when confronted with co-religionists who spoke another language and compatriots who professed another religion, all of whom tied the future of a quite different Canadian nation to the English language. And in the face of a determined majority on the conscription issue, an equally determined minority could only succumb: conscription does not permit compromise. When that same majority went beyond trampling on the national sensitivities of French Canadians to threaten a fundamental notion of social order in the family by granting women the vote in 1918, the minority could only withdraw into self-protection, nursing its differences in an alien world. With Prussians in various guises on all the frontiers, it was time to shore up the defences.

SELECT BIBLIOGRAPHY

Armstrong, Elizabeth H. *The Crisis of Quebec, 1914–18.* New York: Columbia University Press, 1937.

Barber, Marilyn. "The Ontario Bilingual Schools Issue: Sources of Conflict." *Canadian Historical Review* 47(1966):227–48.

Bourassa, Henri. *Femmes-hommes ou hommes et femmes?* Montreal: Le Devoir, 1925.

Durocher, René. "Henri Bourassa, les évêques et la guerre de 1914–1948." *Historical Papers/Communications historiques.* Canadian Historical Association, 1971. Pp. 248–75.

Granatstein, J.L., and J.M. Hitsman. *Broken Promises. A History of Conscription in Canada.* Toronto: Oxford University Press, 1977.

Gravel, Jean-Yves. *L'armée au Québec: un portrait social, 1868-1900.* Montreal: Boréal Express, 1974.

Morton, Desmond. "French Canada and the Canadian Militia." *Histoire sociale/Social History* 3(1969):32-50.

Morton, Desmond. "French Canada and War, 1868-1917: The Military Background to the Conscription Crisis of 1917." In *War and Society in North America.* Edited by J.L. Granatstein and R.D. Cuff. Toronto: Thomas Nelson and Sons, 1971. Pp. 84-103.

Paquet, Louis-Adolphe. "Le féminisme." *Le Canada français* 1(1918): 233-46.

Prang, Margaret. "Clerics, Politicians and the Bilingual Schools Issue in Ontario, 1910-1917." *Canadian Historical Review* 41(1960):281-307.

Rumilly, Robert. *Henri Bourassa: la vie publique d'un grand canadien.* Montreal: Editions Chantecler, 1953.

Trofimenkoff, Susan Mann. "Henri Bourassa and 'The Woman Question'." *Journal of Canadian Studies* 10(1975):3-11.

Willms, A.M. "Conscription, 1917: A Brief for the Defence." *Canadian Historical Review* 37(1956):338-51.

Lionel Groulx, professor, 1920s. "
Courtesy of Fondation Lionel Groulx.

14 Abbé Groulx Sounds the Alarm

In the 1920s a new generation of Quebec nationalists examined the place of French Canada in an urban, industrial society and in Confederation. They were not at all sure they liked what they saw. As intellectuals, they were largely removed from the material concerns that continued to prompt their fellow French Canadians to adapt rural roots to urban settings. And as nationalists, thanks to the repeated blows of the First World War, they were much less optimistic than the prewar nationalists about the future of Canada or even the economic promise of the new industrial order. The voices of the earlier nationalists faded in the 1920s and Henri Bourassa's waning star lost out to the rising one of the priest-historian *abbé* Lionel Groulx. Between the two men stood an insuperable barrier created by Groulx's evocation of separate political institutions for a Quebec on the defensive. Separate cultural institutions already existed, but neither Groulx nor his sympathizers in the *Action fran*çaise believed the French language, Catholicism, or the family strong enough to guarantee the survival of a distinctive French Canada. Each required bolstering in the disturbing social, economic, and political setting of the postwar decade.

The nationalist blend of religion, language, and the family was hardly new in the 1920s. Groulx's contribution to the ideology was to render the three indissociable, virtually indistinguishable. Because of that he was personally never capable of disentangling the elements and rendering one more important than another. Nor could he ever understand accusations by his opponents that such categorizing might be necessary in order to ensure religious or even political orthodoxy. Groulx's nationalism was an integrated whole, an organic blend of all good things French Canada had been in the past and all promising things it might be in the future. The continuity, however, required vigilance: in a North American, increasingly urban setting, growth was not guaranteed; it might even be stunted by foreign manners and mores. The most public of Groulx's endeavours in the 1920s to tend to the appropriate development of his nation were his teaching of history and his direction of the periodical and the nationalist organization of the same name, *Action fran*çaise.

Part of Groulx's ability to integrate religion, language, and the family stemmed from his own background and personality. Born in 1878 near Vaudreuil, he was the fourth of an ever-enlarging farm family that survived poverty, illness, and death because of an intense emotional and religious solidarity. Groulx's mother was at the centre of that solidarity and she provided him with unforgettable lessons in determination, endurance, and fidelity to the task at hand. She also ensured that young Lionel received more schooling than the few years she had been able to wrench from her own parents. Groulx's classical college training was an immense financial sacrifice for the family but it developed his literary, oratorical, and pedagogical talents and directed him, as his mother had hoped, towards the priesthood. But the emotional wrench from the family was severe. Geographical and then religious distance may well have caused the sensitive young student priest to romanticize his own family and subsequently, by abstraction, the nation itself.

Groulx's clerical costume by no means restricted him to religion. Although he frequently said masses, directed retreats, and occasionally tended a parish for an absent friend, his real vocation lay in teaching. There he combined literary interests with religious and patriotic ardour. As a young teacher-priest at Valleyfield in the 1900s he directed a college circle of the *Société du parler fran*çais; the students busily corrected their own French, that of their fami-

lies, and even that of local businesses. Groulx was also one of
the initiators of the *Association catholique de la jeunesse canadienne-française* that encouraged young people to study and apply
their religion to the concrete social setting of French Canada. All
the while Groulx taught French literature, kept a journal, penned
letters to former students, and wrote poetry, short stories, and
later novels; in 1912 he spoke on the French traditions of Canadian literature to the immense audience of the *Congrès de la
langue française* in Quebec City. Three years of study in Europe,
from 1906 to 1909, temporarily interrupted his growing talent for
inspiring young people with religious and secular zeal. On his way
to or from theological studies in Rome and literary ones in Fribourg
where he toyed with starting a thesis on the French language in
Canada, he experienced the official ostracism of religion in France.
Anticlerical laws, secular schooling, even the mocking of priests
in public were all, according to Groulx, signs of the decadence of
France. And they occurred in a country safe behind numbers and
the cultural homogeneity of language. Groulx tucked the lesson
away for future reference in Canada.

By the end of the First World War, French Canada was in need
of the lesson and Groulx in a position to deliver it. He might indeed have gone on inspiring adolescent crusades, as the title of his
first book in 1912 dubbed the young student movement, had Henri
Bourassa not begun a public campaign in *Le Devoir* for the teaching of Canadian history in Montreal's Catholic university. In 1915
he made his point, the chair was inaugurated, and Groulx summoned to fill it. For more than thirty years he stamped firm history lessons on the thousands of students passing through the
Arts faculty of the University of Montreal, independent from Laval
as of 1920. From the past he extracted reasons for pride in a French
Canada (Groulx's preferred *"petit peuple"*) charmed by providence
but doomed by history to the status of ever-vigilant minority.
Groulx's first lectures, unlike the writings of his few predecessors
among French Canadian historians, gave only a passing glance at
New France, the time for the birth of a people. They then passed
quickly to the British regime where Groulx revived a view of the
Conquest as disaster and extended Garneau's notion of perpetual
struggle to include the period of the Union and of Confederation.
Groulx was in fact one of the first Quebec historians to look criti-
cally at Confederation and he chose the fiftieth anniversary year
to do so. With Canada in the midst of the conscription crisis,
Groulx calmly dissected the Confederation pact and hinted that it
would last only as long as its guarantees held for the contracting
parties. Although he thought French Canadian interests had elevated the Confederation debate above the materialism displayed by
others, he was not sure that Quebec's politicians had shown either
the necessary vigilance or foresight. As for those since Confederation, the less said the better. Groulx believed they had all too frequently sacrificed minority rights to party solidarity. If he occa-

sionally flung a barb at English Canadians, most of his work was designed for the present edification of French Canadians, not for the denigration of their English-speaking compatriots. Indeed French Canadian politicians, past and present, constituted one of Groulx's favourite targets, much to the delight of a perpetually iconoclastic student body. His history lessons were all intended for present consumption, the past a constant reminder of what had been done and what could be done.

As for what should be done, Groulx had a hand in that too. Incapable of limiting his activities to the lecture hall or the history book, Groulx took on the leadership of a nationalist movement in Montreal, the *Action française*. His presence in the city and the breadth of his interests facilitated the transformation of the tiny *Ligue des droits du français*, formed as a result of the *Congrès de la langue française*, from an association for the preservation of the French language to the *Action française*, an organization for the preservation of French Canada. Groulx completely dazzled the small group of journalists, lawyers, and priests who were hovering protectively over the increasingly minor place the French language occupied in the urban world of commerce and industry. He convinced them that compiling lists of technical terms in French and nagging businesses to send their bills, advertise their wares, or even label their products in French was only one of the tasks, and a minor one at that, confronting an increasingly threatened French Canada. What was required was action on all fronts—historical, contemporary, futuristic, economic, political, social, linguistic, educational, literary, and religious—in short French action, *action française*. The name, attached first to the monthly periodical begun in 1917, and then to the organization itself in 1921, recalled the literary and intellectual panache, if little else, of the French *Action française* in Paris. The flimsy link was nonetheless dangerous by the late 1920s when the French group came under papal censure for subordinating religion to nationalism, but by then the Montreal group had begun to disintegrate anyway.

For more than ten years, however, it put up a public front of intense activity. The periodical focussed on every imaginable issue of concern to French Canada in the postwar decade. As editor, *abbé* Groulx organized the annual year long enquiries into various topical questions, chased collaborators, encouraged subscribers, invented literary competitions and yearly pilgrimages to historic sites, and wrote many of the lead articles under a variety of pseudonyms. In the name of the periodical, its publishing house, and the organization, Groulx also spoke everywhere, to groups of French Canadians in the Canadian west, the American northeast, all over Quebec, and in the classical colleges of the province. Only a dozen or so people kept the *Action française* alive, but more than a hundred different writers contributed to the review and subscriptions reached as many as five thousand. Teachers and clerics extended the audience even further by commenting upon articles and using them as the basis for classroom lessons in the colleges. Moreover, many of the misgivings of the *Action française*, particularly those of a social and economic nature, were also voiced by others during the decade. The political interests of the group, more far-fetched at the time, began to appear both sensible and desirable to many Quebecois half a century later. Taken together, they reveal more about nationalist worries than popular reality, but they do hint obliquely at many facets of Quebec society in the 1920s.

The first worry was one of numbers. A minority not only had to preserve its numbers but somehow also have them count for more than their mere arithmetical total. *Abbé* Groulx and the *Action française* were not at all convinced that the location or the activities of Quebecois ensured either. Carefully they scrutinized the statistics of the federal census of 1921 to sound the alarm about the decreasing number of French Canadians compared to the rest of the Canadian population. From thirty-one percent at the time of Confederation, the proportion had now declined to twenty-seven. What of the future? Mathematics alone could easily predict eventual extinction and in the meantime the small numbers accounted for much of the powerlessness that the war had revealed. Had the nationalists been demographers they might have taken heart at the provincial birth rate, consistently higher than that in other provinces, and even more so in exclusively French Canadian areas of Quebec. But they were better worriers than statisticians. They only saw that the birth rate was on the decline, particularly in the major cities and most noticeably in Montreal, the home of the *Action française.* The number of births per one thousand people in the population (the crudest of demographic measures, omitting as it does the age and sex distribution of the population) had fallen in the city from thirty-four in 1916 to twenty-seven in 1923. If there were fewer births in the cities than in rural areas, there were also far more deaths as Montreal continued to be one of the most dangerous places in the world in which to be born, particularly if one chose to be born French Canadian. Glossing over the poverty that later studies confirmed as the major cause of infant mortality, the nationalists of the twenties tended to place the responsibility on mothers, poorly educated for their task of nurturers to the nation. What the *Action française* did not point out was that it was almost as dangerous to be a young woman in the childbearing years as to be an infant, the death rate for woman between twenty and forty-four being higher than that for men in spite of the fact that contagious diseases, notably tuberculosis, attacked the adult population indiscriminantly. Death was in fact more a determinant of family size than deliberate limitation of the number of births, a practice purportedly only just beginning in Quebec in the 1920s and then only in the large cities. The *Action française* denounced it with oblique references to voluntary sterility and abortion inducing angel-makers, two of the urban evils that attacked the family and ultimately diminished the numbers of French Canadians.

The location of the numbers worried the nationalists even more. Harbouring a notion of social equilibrium based on a balance of rural and urban activities and hankering somewhat for the social virtues supposedly sown with the spring crops, *abbé* Groulx and his allies, not unlike the western progressives at the time, bemoaned the decided urban shift in the population. Again they watched the census. Already in 1921 it recorded the urban imbalance: sometime during the war years the cities had attracted enough rural inhabitants to make Quebec fifty-six percent urban. By 1931 sixty-three percent of Quebec's population was living in urban areas. Those areas were more varied than in the late nineteenth century: hydro-electricity and aluminum created overnight model towns such as Arvida; hydro-electricity and chemicals attracted newcomers to established centres such as Shawinigan; hydro-electricity and pulp and paper did the same for La Tuque and Kenogami; gold and copper produced a string of mining towns along the Cadillac fault in Abitibi; regional administrative services increased the drawing power of Sherbrooke, Chicoutimi, and Roberval. But Montreal continued to be the major urban magnet. Its port, its industries, and its Canada-wide services drew migrants and immigrants by the thousands every year. Although the extension of its boundaries helped, the population growth was nonetheless remarkable: two hundred thousand more people became Montrealers between 1921 and 1931, representing an urban growth rate of thirty percent. By the end of the 1920s, Montreal housed almost the same percentage of the entire population of Quebec and almost half of its urban population. Anxious to have all of Quebec equal to more than the sum of its parts, Groulx and the *Action française* often mistook one of the parts for the whole. Awed by, and afraid of, the burgeoning metropolis, they frequently read moral lessons to Quebec based solely on their reaction to Montreal's urban reality.

In that they revealed another of their fears. Cities bred standardization, homogeneity, and ultimately, they suspected, assimilation. With too many people engaged in too many activities of rather dubious worth, the city could hardly nourish the values of French Canada; it might even toll their demise. Using a vivid rural simile, *abbé* Groulx compared the crowding of people into cities to that of apples in a barrel: they would all soon rot because of a few bad spots. In fact the bad spots in a city were far more visible. Besides the declining birth rate and the high death rate, which the *Action française* attributed to overcrowded housing conditions, the city undermined family solidarity in other ways. Sunday movies showed American melodramas with dissolute characters; the popular press aped the worst American papers by making heroes of sordid criminals; the dance halls jumped to the barbaric tones and lewd embraces of American jazz; the arenas foisted American baseball on huge crowds willing to pay for their own passivity. And, perhaps worst of all for the symbolic gesture of independence implied by the action, young women cut off their hair and their skirts and presumed to move about the world as freely as men. All of the activities fostered an individualism that would surely be the ruin of families. The father, no longer enjoying his rightful paternal authority, spent more time in the tavern, an easy prey for sinister influences. The children, no longer under mother's watchful eye, drifted from one sordid attraction to another. And if the mother was also earning a living outside the home, the family lost its centre of gravity. Divorce would be the obvious result.

Abbé Groulx's was far from a moralistic muttering in the urban wilderness. Both press and pulpit echoed his fears and decried the moral decrepitude associated with urban activities. Even though newspapers earned their living from those activities and the advertising revenues they generated, they nonetheless devoted many editorials to clucking over popular behaviour and urban ills. The priests, whose major role was to organize the ethical behaviour of their parishioners, found the task increasingly difficult in urban centres where the jumble of newcomers and the annual spring search for cheaper living quarters constantly threatened the carefully constructed bounds of parish stability. The association of stability with decency was easy enough in a city like Montreal where movement, be it of cars or films or the airwaves of radio and popular music, seemed to announce decadence. Various novelists also shared Groulx's condemnation of great pagan cities. They spotted thievery, drugs, and prostitution in Canada's metropolis with little civic effort at control. They spoke openly of the white slave trade, venereal disease, and abortionists. They wondered why Montreal was such as centre for rum-running into the nearby United States, prohibitionist since 1919. Behind all the social worries of nationalists, journalists, clerics, and novelists lay more than the disdain of intellectuals for the assumed vulgarity of popular behaviour; rather they nursed a great fear that the city might be the ultimate assimilating force. By turning urban French Canadians into French-speaking Americans, the city appeared to wreck all the religious and social patterns that had characterized and protected French Canada.

According to *abbé* Groulx, the *Action française*, and other nationalist sympathizers, the economy of the 1920s posed just as many risks for French Canada as did the city. The two indeed went hand in hand: increasing industrialization attracted more rural Quebecois to the city; the city in turn extended its urban mores ever further into the rural hinterland. Fully aware that the process could not be reversed, Groulx and his allies nonetheless worried about a potential imbalance. Too much industry was as bad as too little agriculture. The one would surely produce too many goods that no one could consume and the other insufficient food for the ever-increasing urban population. If the economic analysis was hardly sophisticated, it had an eery ring of prophecy in the light of the depression years of the 1930s. Moreover the nationalists differed little from other Canadians in the 1920s in their moralistic reaction to the economy. All across the country the decline of agriculture was viewed with alarm. Canadian society was rooted in the land and in the special virtues of independence and self-reliance that it supposedly nourished. In contrast, the machines and concrete of an exaggerated industrial order could only produce proletarian pygmies, cowering and dependent.

Needless to say, the economy of Quebec in the 1920s was somewhat more complex than the nationalists made out. The war years had artificially bolstered the demands on Quebec agriculture; the slump of the early 1920s was merely an exaggeration of the changes since the latter half of the nineteenth century. Farmers' movements might protest all they wished, and in doing so they sounded much like western progressives, but they could do little to alter the fact that, by 1920, agriculture provided only one-third of the total value of production in Quebec. And its relative position went on declining throughout the decade. Far from providing a balance in the economy, let alone constituting the basis for it, agriculture could not even hold its own during the 1920s. New mining in Abitibi, new forestry in the Saguenay, and new hydro-electric installations to accompany mushrooming pulp and paper industries in the Saguenay, St. Maurice, and Gatineau valleys did provide huge local markets for the farms in the vicinity, but they also produced more wealth with fewer people. In the Richelieu area, long a weather vane of the state of Quebec agriculture, farmers went on producing hay for a horse-drawn urban and military market that no longer existed in the increasingly motorized cities of the 1920s. The problems of overspecialization, overproduction, and indebtedness for the acquisition of land and machinery, common to much of Canadian agriculture, struck the region south and east of Montreal long before the disaster of the 1930s.

Other sectors of the economy added to the complexity which the nationalists tended to gloss over. One was manufacturing which, like agriculture, constituted only one-third of the total value of production in 1920. As it rose during the decade, agriculture declined and thereby fuelled the worries of Groulx and the *Action française*. Certainly more people were attracted to manufacturing during the decade, the want ads of newspapers alone indicating the great demand, particularly for young women. By 1929 Montreal housed sixty-three percent of all the manufacturing in the province. But for all the fear that industry gave rise to in the minds of the nationalists, the real change of the 1920s was not taking place there. Rather it was in the increased exploitation of Quebec's natural resources: the forests, the mines, and especially the hydro-power. Each attached Quebec ineluctably to the export markets of North America as well as opening the doors to massive development capital, coming primarily from the United States in the years

after the war. This the nationalists did spy, with a kind of unerr-
ing instinct for the presence of foreign bodies in the nation. A
sector of the economy they rarely analysed was the increasingly
large area of services required by an industrial society. During the
1920s more people found employment there than in manufacturing or in primary production. If the relative importance of services
is an indication of level of industrialization, Quebec was a highly
industrialized province by the 1920s.

While the social implications of industrialization troubled Groulx
and the *Action française*, so too did the national overtones. By the
1920s French Canadians were increasingly rare among the economic
innovators and directors in the province. They were present,
massively, at the lower end of the occupational and income scale
in the manufacturing industries, in the retail stores and offices,
and along the communication links from rural general stores to
urban suppliers. They held their own at the middle level of urban
services in small shops and construction businesses, in real estate
and the provision of intellectual goods through schools, newspapers,
notarial, legal, and religious offices. But among the economic elite
they were imperceptible, partly because of the Canadian entrepreneur's penchant for obscurity but mostly because they simply were
not there. Rodolphe Forget may have pulled many of the strings of
the Montreal Light, Heat and Power and other companies and Alfred
Dubuc cut a swath through the pulp forests of the Saguenay, but
they were few and far between and Dubuc did not survive the
increased competition of the decade. Most of Quebec's development
during the 1920s was financed from the States as American money
poured into pulp and paper, aluminum, chemicals, textiles, and
asbestos mining.

The absence of French Canadians from both the direction and
the financing of the large enterprises of economic control in Quebec
left Groulx and his colleagues perplexed and ill at ease. French
Canadians were beginning to look all too much like the hewers of
wood and drawers of water that Lord Durham had predicted for
them so long ago. What troubled Groulx even more was that his
contemporaries seemed to acquiesce in their own relegation to second class status. Government, the press, and the people grovelled
before the American presence; those who could not profit from it
in the province followed its glitter to the States as emigration once
again reduced precious French Canadian numbers. What might it
all mean for French Canadian survival, wondered the *Action
française*, aware that economic power meant political power and
yet fearful lest the dictates of an industrial society mean the
assimilation of French Canada.

To offset the dangers *abbé* Groulx hoped to inspire a number of
social overseers to organize the defences of French Canada. He
spread his net much wider than did the nationalists of the prewar
generation and he had specific tasks for all his potential allies.
They were to personify the abstract traits that distinguished French

Canada and they were to fortify those traits in Quebec society. They were to develop special institutions tailor-made for a French Canadian urban and industrial world and were thus to ensure survival. If they succeeded, French Canada might well count for more than the sum of its parts. Certainly it would move beyond the incantation of religion—language—family as a kind of three-part magic spell sure to render French Canadians safe. Groulx of course was not immune to incantations himself; his own religious, historical, and patriotic rhetoric was full of them. He always claimed that his work was the formulation of a doctrine by which French Canadians could live in harmony with their past and serenely with their future. Nonetheless his history books were peppered with real people organizing real resistance to the many forces of assimilation that had surrounded them since the eighteenth century. He expected his *Action française* to encourage French Canadians to do the same in the present.

Groulx's nationalist allies and his companions in the *Action française* were ready to use their intellectual talents in talk and in print wherever there were French Canadians willing to listen or read. The names of Joseph-Papin Archambault, Joseph Gauvreau, Omer Héroux, Anatole Vanier, Philippe Perrier, and Antonio Perrault reappeared in the pages of the monthly magazine, along with those of just about every aspiring nationalist or literary talent in Quebec. Collectively they assumed the task of guardians and organizers of the nation, pointing out the omnipresent dangers and urging a vigorous response. Groulx's own remedy was to instill pride: if French Canadians were conscious of their own heritage, their cultural distinctiveness, and their collective strength they would not barter it away lightly for a mess of American pottage. His history lessons, his pilgrimages to historic sites, his creation of popular heroes such as Dollard des Ormeaux (soldier and supposed saviour of Montreal from Iroquois attack in 1660) and his guiding hand in the annual investigations by the *Action française* of such topics as the national strengths of French Canada, the economy, the political future, Catholicism, and bilingualism all had an intensely practical purpose: to rally French Canadians to the defence of their nation. Some of his colleagues concentrated on specific lessons in linguistic pride. They offered their services to businesses that dealt far too much in English; they badgered politicians who did the same. They claimed responsibility for Montreal's bilingual telephone system and for its first bilingual street signs. They may even have been responsible for Canada's first bilingual stamps in 1927. Other activists with literary talents took to writing novels, still considered a somewhat vulgar form of literature. Jean-Charles Harvey invented a French Canadian industrialist, *Marcel Faure*, and Harry Bernard read moral lessons to young women captivated by city manners in *La Maison vide* and *La Terre vivante*. Groulx himself tried the genre to show how a self-seeking lawyer in *L'Appel de la race* could be transformed into a political patriot by the renewal of ancestral ties. Later, in *Au Cap Blomidon*, Groulx indicated that even the long lost terrain of Acadia might be reclaimed by French Canadians prepared for work and sacrifice. Groulx also had friends and contacts in the nationalist, Catholic, and independent press in Quebec. *Le Devoir, L'Action catholique*, and *Le Courrier de Saint-Hyacinthe* often reprinted articles from *L'Action française*, reported many of its public endeavours, and shared with it the self-assigned role of national conscience. If most other papers, particularly those with strong political affiliations, found the nationalists somewhat self-righteous, they were increasingly unable to ignore them. Groulx had created a numerous and avid following among the intellectual elite of Quebec.

He also counted on his clerical allies as overseers and organizers of French Canada. They too were willing and eager. Groulx's close colleague, *père* J.-P. Archambault, inaugurated the *Semaines sociales* in 1920 as a kind of travelling university. Hosted each year at the end of the summer in a different city of Quebec and bringing together lay and clerical elites from the area, the *Semaines sociales* sponsored a series of public lectures and discussions on given social topics. The intention was to arm participants and audience alike with the weapons of social Catholicism. The clerics learned to apply Catholic doctrine to concrete social problems of family and industrial relations, urban living conditions, and popular behaviour; the lay people learned to take responsibility for those very problems and to work with clerics in designing specifically French Canadian solutions. No one missed the message that what characterized French Canada and thus ensured its survival was the indissociable tie between religious and secular matters. Throughout the 1920s the *Semaines sociales* applied the Catholic viewpoint of harmonious social relations based on mutual rights and obligations in a hierarchical but organic, family-based society to such varied topics as capital and labour, the family, the economy, and the city. At a time when the social gospel among Protestant clergy and lay people was losing much of its prewar force in the increasingly secular and disillusioned world of the 1920s, social Catholicism was being strengthened and added to the arsenal of defence for French Canada.

Another activity of priests touched the economic concerns of the working class even more closely. Clerical inspiration and organization of unions for workers and farmers came to fruition in the 1920s with the *Confédération des travailleurs catholiques du Canada* (CTCC) in 1921 and the *Union catholique des cultivateurs* (UCC) in 1924. Both were attempts not only to offset the attraction of "foreign" organizations—American affiliated unions or English Canadian united farmers—but also to create protective institutions for workers, farmers, and the nation. The CTCC united some twenty thousand workers in varied industries and occupations in construction, railway yards, machine shops, shoemaking, textiles, clothing, pulp and paper, and breweries. The UCC brought together some thirteen thousand notoriously individualistic farmers across the province to share their problems and find common solutions. Neither organization ever attracted a majority of workers or farmers and in each the tension between the moral and patriotic interests of the clerical instigators and the economic concerns of labourer and farmer was evident. So too, however, was the mutual interest. Clerics knew full well the economic need for and force of unions, but unless they took a hand in organizing them, the priests risked being shunted aside. Perhaps for that reason, gala religious observances began to accompany the annual Labour Day festivities in 1922. At the same time, labourers and farmers recognized the trained leadership, the extensive networks, and the good press that sympathetic priests could provide. Moreover the message of nationalism and social Catholicism bound them. All remembered the wartime hostility to French Canadians and the rural exodus that alarmed clerics also worried those farmers bound to the land by family and tradition. And yet harmony did not always reign in the two organizations. Disputes over tactics, finances, personalities, and even the power and responsibilities of the associated clerics sapped energies while classically organized strikes belied the altruism the priests wanted desperately to evoke. The pages of Groulx's *Action française* tended to camouflage the difficulties but always they were present.

Groulx did not invent nationalist and clerical activity in defence of the nation in the 1920s. Only his spirited combination of the two, fanned by his energy and conviction, distinguished him from earlier self-styled guardians of the nation. What he did add to an existing formula was that the family, particularly the woman of the family, and the government should be in on the act of organizing the defences of Quebec. Unfortunately for Groulx, both were more hesitant than his nationalist and clerical allies. Easily enough could he indicate what was expected of women and of the state; less easily could he cause it to be done. Disappointed by what appeared to be the wilful elusiveness of two of his key agents of national redemption, Groulx retaliated by weaving a dream around each of them: the woman as survival and the state as independence.

Young women, in fact, were providing the most visible sign of social change in the 1920s. Unlike factory and farm lasses, properly raised middle class girls had been carefully confined to home and convent. Now they were emerging, demanding of parents and society a few years of independence between schooling and marriage. And they did so with a flair of fashion and behaviour all the more disturbing to conservative minds because it was so visible. Just what the connection was between short skirts and short morals has never been determined, but Groulx, his associates, and his sympathizers in the *Action française* suspected the worst. Given their tendency to place most of the responsibility for the maintenance of the social order upon women, these self-appointed guardians of the nation feared that as female behaviour changed, so would society. As one deteriorated, so would the other. The greatest need therefore was to remind young women of their divinely ordained role in the family and the intimate connection between that role and the survival of the nation. The first caused few problems at the time; the second required greater effort. How was a young mother to know that the songs, toys, and parties she provided for her toddlers could be the thin edge of the wedge of assimilation? How was she to discern the potential danger of her shopping habits, her meal planning, her own occasional frivolity of tea or bridge?

Groulx and his friends undertook to tell her. Some of the advice was practical: avoid Santa Claus and patronize French Canadian merchants; object to proposals for provincial suffrage and do as the man of the family decides in any federal vote; encourage domestic science even in the new classical colleges for women; join campaigns against divorce and protest any change in the legal status of married women. Much more of the advice was of a symbolic nature. Women were to live up to an image Groulx harboured all his life and that he probably drew from his mother. She in fact appeared in many guises in his historical writing: he recognized her among the pioneer women of New France and among the religious innovators of education and social work. And when she became increasingly invisible among the celluloid and marshmallow figures of femininity that pranced about the urban world of Groulx's adult life, he summoned her spirit to infuse the entire nation. French Canada needed the inexhaustible strength and energy, the courage, the religious conviction, the sense of duty and mission, the will to survive, and the very assurance of continuity across time that only women could provide. Only with such feminine qualities, so sorely lacking in the 1920s, could Groulx's *petit peuple* survive the urban and industrial world of twentieth century North America. Women had to embody the qualities and teach them to the nation.

The political plan Groulx added to his feminine framework for French Canada required the provincial government to act as a major social overseer, along with nationalists, clerics, and women. In spite of an expressed antipathy to politics, probably based on the recognition of a minority's lack of power, Groulx and the *Action française* were aware of the potential of a government where French Canadians formed the majority. In that they merely echoed the advocates of Confederation who had argued just such a possibility in the 1860s. But the potential had rarely been tested let alone realized. Behaving much like its North American counterparts, the Quebec government had shied away from social or economic intervention, much less direction. Even when it did venture to regulate the financing of public charities, as in 1921, or to specify adoption procedures, as in 1924, the nationalists were not always happy. But more often, what feeble economic muscle governments chose to display was for the benefit of business interests with whom politicians and even premiers had very close ties. That those interests were largely, if not entirely, in American and English Canadian hands only added to the nationalists' ire. They would have the Quebec government be much more careful in its handing out of water, mineral, and forest rights. They would see more stringent controls on foreign exploitation of Quebec's natural resources. They would have the government study, organize, and plan the rational development of agriculture, resources, and industry. They argued for colonization and against emigration and expected the government to follow their advice. And they dismissed their critics who had visions of the Russian Revolution at the least sign of state intervention. To the handful of nationalists in the 1920s, the state was supposed to be what it became in the 1960s, a tool of national defence and development.

For a brief moment in the early 1920s, Groulx and the *Action française* toyed with the idea of a separate state as the ultimate defence against external threats. In 1922 the British empire gave every sign of imminent collapse: it had lost its financial supremacy to the United States and its colonies in all parts of the world were clamouring for autonomy. Canada was one of them and it too appeared to be disintegrating. Wartime crises involving schools and conscription had broken Canada into its constituent racial parts. Postwar labour unrest presaged class divisions of irreparable proportions. The surprising appearance of so many western progressives in the federal election of 1921 revealed agrarian unhappiness and hinted at the regional dissolution of the country. Certainly there was no ideological coherence as Canadians quarrelled incessantly over autonomy, imperialism, free trade, protectionism, and American materialism. Canada was surely a spent force. To that analysis of contemporary politics, Groulx added a historical critique of Confederation: not only had it undermined French Canadian rights, but it had been a mixed marriage from the beginning and hence an error. For good measure Groulx tossed in the old ultramontane definition of a nation: on the grounds of common origin, language, religion, territory, customs, and history, only French Canada formed a nation. The result was a thinly disguised evocation of a separate state. Hedged in ifs, buts, and maybes, the separate state was to provide the final response to the dangers Groulx saw all around. Its geography was never clear, its politics even less so, but the ideal was there for the pondering. One day the future might be arranged to suit French Canadian tastes; political institutions, a nation state itself might be shaped in conformity with French Canadian genius. An independent French state on the banks of the St. Lawrence, Groulx speculated, could be the best defence yet.

Groulx never did convince the politicians, let alone many of his contemporaries. His ties with Henri Bourassa broke irrevocably over the issue and Groulx was so disappointed that he took to calling Bourassa mad. But after a year-long analysis of various facets of the future state in the pages of *L'Action française* in 1922, the group rarely mentioned it again and Groulx spent the rest of his life denying that he was a separatist. Neither the British empire nor the Canadian Confederation collapsed in the 1920s and French Canada continued its worrisome way to an acceptable form of survival. Groulx's powerful voice was heard along that way in the postwar decade when many French Canadian ears were attuned to alarm bells. Out of the original ingredients of French Canadian nationalism—religion, language, and family—Groulx spun a heady myth centred largely on Quebec. His history lessons and his *Action française* provided the drama, the romance, the personae, the tasks, and the ideal to furnish French Canadians with one of their more carefully etched dreams of nation. At the same time he made of nationalism a public force which politicians could no longer wish away. Of course none of Groulx's planned defences prevented the world from turning topsy-turvy in the 1930s. But largely thanks to him, well-armed nationalists, often in alliance with others, could attempt to set at least the Quebec portion of it straight again.

SELECT BIBLIOGRAPHY

Dupont, Antonin. *Les relations entre l'Eglise et l'Etat sous Louis-Alexandre Taschereau 1900–1936*. Montreal: Guérin, 1972.

Groulx, Lionel. "Henri Bourassa et la chaire d'Histoire du Canada à l'Université de Montréal." *Revue d'histoire de l'Amérique française* 6(1952): 430–39.

Groulx, Lionel. *Mes mémoires*. vols. 1, 2. Montreal: Fides, 1970 and 1971.

Montreuil, Claude. *La vérité choque*. Montreal, 1923.

Robertson, Susan Mann (Trofimenkoff). "Variations on a Nationalist Theme: Henri Bourassa and Abbé Groulx in the 1920's." *Historical Papers/ Communications historiques*. Canadian Historical Association, 1970. Pp. 109–19.

Rouillard, Jacques. *Les syndicats nationaux au Québec de 1900 à 1930*. Quebec: Les presses de l'Université Laval, 1979.

Senese, P.M. "Catholique d'abord! Catholicism and Nationalism in the Thought of Lionel Groulx." *Canadian Historical Review* 60(1979): 154–77.

Trofimenkoff, Susan Mann. *Action française: French Canadian Nationalism in the Twenties*. Toronto: University of Toronto Press, 1975.

Trofimenkoff, Susan Mann. "Les femmes dans l'oeuvre de Groulx." *Revue d'histoire de l'Amérique française*. 32(1978):385–98.

Vigod, B.L. "Ideology and Institutions in Quebec. The Public Charities Controversy 1921–1926." *Histoire sociale/Social History* 11(1978): 167–82.

*"Cities provided relief payments to the unemployed . . .
and . . . attempted to exact work in return."*
Relief men pruning trees, St. Helen's Island Park, Montreal, 1937.

15 The Search for Equilibrium

In many ways Groulx's warnings and even his remedies rang true in the 1930s. Industrial overproduction pulled Quebec, along with the rest of the western world, up short after the frenzied years of economic speculation and prosperity of the late 1920s. The weight of urban manufacturing tipped the scale not just away from Groulx's aesthetic notion of a balanced economy but also from the liberal economists' dream of a growing distribution of wealth by means of increased industrial expansion. It all ground to a halt, leaving a million miseries in its wake. While urban worker and farm labourer bore the brunt of the economic turmoil, the intellectuals and politicians feared for the collective security of French Canada. Like their English-speaking counterparts in the rest of the country, they foresaw social upheaval in the bread lines, the soup kitchens, the tar paper shanties, and the garbage dumps of the decade. A sprinkling of their more extreme colleagues even promoted that upheaval. But most thought that a collective and reasoned response was the only cure for the evils of the Depression. Curiously enough, they pointed to the same two actors Groulx had hoped to use in the 1920s. If women would provide an element of social stability and the state some aspect of political change, Quebec might discover the necessary equilibrium to survive this latest onslaught.

The tendency to interpret the Depression as another foreign invasion was natural enough. As far as Groulx's intellectual allies in the *Action nationale*, a revived form of the *Action française* in the 1930s, or his clerical friends in a host of organizations devoted to social Catholicism could see, the Depression was a result of overindustrialization. And that industrialization was associated with foreign capital: American, British, or English Canadian. The capital, in turn, had had easy access to Quebec because of the lax policies of the provincial Liberal government. According to nationalists, the Depression gave the lie to a notion of endless prosperity and limitless jobs by means of massive concessions to foreign investors. That the investors were capitalists and the Depression a crisis of capitalism was only of secondary concern. Quebec's intellectual and clerical elite looked askance at an English Canadian and socialist critique of capitalism in the Co-operative Commonwealth Federation (CCF) and even more fearfully at a European critique in the form of communism. Both were as foreign as the investors and potentially even more evil. The only acceptable foreign source was the pope and early in the decade he had roundly condemned both the individualism of liberal economic theory and practice and the class conflict inherent in collectivist critiques of the crumbling economic order. But the pope never witnessed what Quebec nationalists saw every day: English-speaking owners tossing French Canadian workers out on the street. Groulx was astute enough to acknowledge that a mere replacement of English by French in the upper echelons of the economy would not solve all the social evils of the decade, but it would at least eliminate the emotional aggravation. If the economy were in French Canadian hands, somehow things would be different.

The nationalist analysis remained far removed from the reality of the Depression for hundreds of thousands of Quebecois. Across the province the hard times hit at different moments and with varying severity. Overproduction of pulp, paper, and even hydroelectricity closed down mills in the Saguenay as early as 1927. The end of horse-drawn transportation spelled doom for hay farmers in the Eastern Townships by 1929. A decline in trade and manufacturing began the spiral of urban unemployment in Quebec City and Montreal in 1931; tumbling prices for cod undermined the livelihood of Gaspé fishermen by 1932. Only the mines of Abitibi continued the production of gold and copper, but the number of jobs in mining had always been small. Within each region the hurt spread out to bruise the surrounding area. Single industry towns might have half the population out of work and take stores, services, and specialized agricultural suppliers in the vicinity down with them. Only the farms that had few urban contacts managed to hold their own, but subsistence farming had never been an enviable occupation. Neither the farmers of Lac St. Jean nor the fishermen of the Gaspé could supplement their dwindled income in the traditional manner with a season in the lumber camps since the forests themselves were now worthless. In short order the farmer's credit with the local store, the implement dealer, the mortgage company, and the tax office was equally worthless. Farmers even joined the unemployed when they lost cattle, machinery, and the farm itself to the bill collector.

Nor was there any escape. The traditional routes of economic improvement, if not salvation, were all blocked. Emigration to the United States came to a halt as the American government closed its doors. Migration to rural areas demanded capital, stamina, and available land. All the good will of clerics and back-to-the-land enthusiasts—and there were many of both—could not turn Quebec's mostly inarable land into fertile farms. The cities themselves no longer beckoned. Indeed they positively spurned rural migrants for fear that they would add to the already overwhelming number of unemployed. All municipalities established residency requirements of up to two years for anyone wishing financial assistance from local coffers. Occasionally a young woman from the country could retrace a well-worn path towards domestic service in the city and thus assist her family, but the low pay and long hours as often lured her into prostitution or condemned her to the tuberculosis sanatorium. Even the number of religious recruits declined. So too did the possibility of teaching or even schooling for younger members of rural families as numerous school commissions simply closed the schools when they could not pay the two hundred dollar a year salary for the schoolmistress. With no escape in sight, most of Quebec's rural inhabitants—only slightly more than a third of the total population—were at least able to keep from starving.

Such was not always the case among urban dwellers during the Depression. Henri Bourassa shocked the comfortable members of the House of Commons and his deskmate J.S. Woodsworth, the founder of the CCF, by revealing that seventy-five thousand Montrealers were living in conditions unfit for animals. Other cities managed to conceal their truly destitute although both Hull and

Valleyfield had rat- and disease-infested shanty towns on their out-skirts. Where a town's scrap heap provided insufficient sustenance, homeless young men wandered the streets, outcasts from family and adrift in the cross-country search for non-existent work. They combed the gutters for cigarette butts or a stray penny, they queued for a cup of soup and again for a bed for the night in a hostel, a warehouse, or a railway car. And the next day they began again. Should they chance upon a local relative, the greeting was likely to be hostile. In Montreal in 1933 (the worst year of the Depression), close to three hundred thousand people, more than one-third of the population, were reduced to accepting hand-outs from the city and they had neither room nor welcome for a drifter from afar. Indeed, entire families of the unemployed also drifted. Every spring, in a futile attempt to match their increasing poverty to the falling prices of the Depression, they sought cheaper accommodation in ever more squalid dwellings. Rent never did fall as much as the cost of food and relief payments never covered either totally. To meet the difference fathers took whatever temporary work they could find for whatever pittance was offered. They knew that any complaint could lead to their being reported to municipal authori-ties and removed from the city relief rolls. Mothers knocked on the doors of middle class homes begging for day work as house clean-ers. Daughters took cuts in pay and hours just to keep a semblance of a job in a cheap retail store. All the while the pallor and list-lessness of undernourished children haunted parents and public alike.

While the urban poor bore the physical and emotional brunt of the Depression, the municipalities shouldered the expense. City officials had to pick up the bill when private charitable organiza-tions were swamped by unending demands, when hard-nosed com-pany presidents refused, even with a promise of tax reductions, to keep their plant open, and when the provincial government was determined to avoid a deficit and the federal government convinced that unemployment was not its responsibility. Municipal politi-cians, after all, had to face elections every two years; the others did not. Moreover, most of them were convinced that social stability was at stake. According to the estimates of Camillien Houde, Mont-real's populist mayor during most of the 1930s, some fifty thou-sand unemployed in Montreal were ready to revolt at a moment's notice. Easily enough therefore did local politicians persuade them-selves and others that theirs was the thumb in the dike of social revolution. In response they let their budgets skyrocket in a des-perate attempt to buy social peace. Cities provided relief payments to the unemployed for food, fuel, and lodging. Later in the decade they picked up the tab for electricity and medical expenses as well. They attempted to exact work in return for relief and offered slight-ly higher payments, varying from city to city and depending on local conditions, for casual labour in the maintenance of parks, playgrounds, streets, and public buildings. And they howled so loudly about their mounting costs that the federal government be-grudgingly renewed, but only on an annual basis through the decade, an accord with the provinces and municipalities for a tripartite division of relief costs.

Even then the cities sank further into arrears. The growth of ur-ban services in the 1920s had left a burden of debt that threatened to bury municipal governments in the next decade. In Montreal's case, it had acquired suburban debts along with its annexation of suburban municipalities. Throughout the decade mayor Houde tried to relieve the financial pressure by arguing that unemploy-ment was a federal responsibility, but until a royal commission on dominion-provincial relations said so too in 1940 he was wast-ing his breath. The federal government would provide emergency funds only. For a while it also agreed to house some of the wander-ing unemployed in emergency relief camps such as the one at Valcartier, an existing military base. But it would go no further in acknowledging responsibility. In the meantime Montreal's ebullient mayor tried to convince the provincial government to join the fed-eral old age pension plan which dated from 1927 and provided pensions to the needy elderly. That at least would remove seven thousand old people from the city's relief charges. Before the prov-ince agreed to that in 1936, it had already come to the rescue of some seventy-five municipalities bankrupted by the Depression. Montreal held out until 1940 when it began defaulting on its close to four hundred million dollar debt. The province then put the city's administration under its wing and added the costs to its own mounting debt.

As the numbers of unemployed climbed, the fear of social un-rest increased. With almost four hundred thousand people in a population of three million—more than one-third of the public labour force—out of work in the worst years of the Depression, public officials felt justified in predicting the worst. They eyed mass meetings with suspicion. They frowned on public demonstra-tions. They shuddered at the appearance of an American labour organizer or at the very thought of the communist inspired Workers Unity League. But the spectre of social revolution was more in the minds of certain elites than in the heads of Quebec's unemployed or working class population. Most of the latter had seldom known much different; the Depression was just a prolongation of the sea-sonal, occupational, health, and housing hazards they had known for generations. For some of the unemployed, indeed, the Depres-sion actually improved their chronic state of joblessness by pro-viding assured, if minimal, relief. Moreover, like other Canadians, Quebecois accepted the notion of work as an individual responsi-bility. If there was none, the fault was their own, not that of soci-ety. Most of them too, whether Catholic or Protestant, accepted a social hierarchy that placed the poor deservedly and perpetually at the bottom of the heap. For many, a reward in heaven was much more likely than any earthly improvement in their lot.

Nevertheless there were signs that all was not well. Among the mere twelve percent of the labour force that was unionized, rumblings of discontent could be heard. Whenever the Depression showed the least sign of alleviation, as in 1934 and again in 1937, working class protest emerged. Sometimes it took the form of inter-union rivalry with the internationals claiming to offer more security than the Catholic unions. Although the two often had tacit geographic and sectorial agreements to leave mining in the northwest and construction in the cities to the international unions and logging in the north and textiles in the regional towns to the Catholic unions, neither was content with limited jurisdiction. The Catholic unions often attempted to attract workers from heavy industry, largely dominated by the internationals. Employers too had their preferences: if they could not avoid unions entirely, many of them preferred to deal with Catholic ones, on the assumption that they would be more docile. But the unions recognized the threat from employers and occasionally they joined forces to fight not only for the recognition of unions, but also for the sole right of one or the other to represent and bargain collectively for the workers in a given industry. That this sense of protection should supersede salaries or working conditions as the dominant motive of the multitude of strikes in 1937 is a small indication of the helplessness that workers felt throughout the decade. Whether the strikers were longshoremen in Montreal, aluminum workers at Arvida, asbestos miners in the Eastern Townships, paper makers in Trois-Rivières, shipbuilders in Sorel, or the ten thousand textile hands in nine different plants of Dominion Textile and its subsidiaries across the province, their purpose was the same: self-protection. If the unions were not able to provide the protection, as the church and government mediated settlement of the textile strike suggested, the workers abandoned them.

The growing presence of women in existing unions and in the formation of new ones in the 1930s is another small indication of the despair provoked by the Depression. Yvette Charpentier answered the call of the International Ladies Garment Workers Union in 1937 and persuaded her co-workers in Montreal's dressmaking industry to do so too. Like Charpentier, many of them had worked since childhood in the factories of the trade, eking out a living on wages paid according to production and hours extending to seventy a week. By 1937 they were ready to protect themselves by strike action. Meanwhile Laure Gaudreault was organizing the first rural teachers' union in Quebec in Charlevoix county, northeast of Quebec City. She too had been teaching since the early twentieth century in the rural schools of the county, rarely earning more than one hundred and twenty-five dollars a year. By the summer of 1936 she was willing to take on the provincial government. A *Fédération catholique des institutrices rurales* might hold the government to its promise to raise the minimum salary for teachers to three hundred dollars a year. Certainly a teachers' union rather than an individual young schoolmistress could more effectively combat a parsimonious school commission that claimed even salaries of two hundred dollars would bankrupt them. The school teachers waited another generation before imitating other workers in the use of the strike but their very association, like other new unions in the 1930s, suggested that many people were no longer willing to submit quietly to the dictates of the economy.

Women refusing to submit may have been one of the greater shocks of the topsy-turvy world of the 1930s. Their very presence in the public labour force, let alone among strikers and union organizers, became an affront to a natural order that had somehow gone awry. One of the more radical women even took on organizing men: Jeanne Corbin, an organizer for the Workers Unity League, stirred up lumber camp workers in Abitibi sufficiently to have them strike and descend upon Rouyn in protest in 1933. More typically, the submissive and yet dauntless Maria Chapdelaine of the backwoods of Peribonca had become the wayward and cheeky Florentine Lacasse of Montreal's St. Henri. Only the employers appreciated the transformation since it enabled them to obtain bargain-priced workers. But most other male Quebecois were decidedly uneasy. Politicians, clerics, and nationalists all feared for the stability of the family and hence of the nation as women appeared to be drawn away from the private sphere into the public domain. The process had of course been underway for decades, but the danger it posed really only became clear in the 1930s. Women appeared to be the cause of much of the social dislocation. If they could be convinced to remain true to the ideal men had of them, they might also provide the cure.

During the Depression, a number of measures were actually proposed to limit women to their proper sphere. In 1932 a few Quebec politicians sported suits made of homespun cloth. Their garments, they said, were a protest against expensive imports, high tariffs, and excessive urbanization; in fact they were advocating the refurbishing of the domestic spinning wheel and weaving loom and the return to unpaid female labour in the home. A more direct attack on paid female labour in the work place occurred in the Quebec legislature in 1935. The politicians debated the merits of a bill to limit access to the labour market to only those women who had an attestation of their financial need from a responsible (meaning male) person, such as the *curé*, the mayor, or an alderman. Although the bill was defeated, both sides in the debate expressed the same suspicion: women's presence in the paid labour force might well be the cause of high unemployment for men. Meanwhile many members of the clergy and religious orders were working with young women students to reinforce the notion of woman's role as unpaid social benefactor not only to the lower classes but to the nation as a whole. In 1937 *abbé* Albert Tessier took on the task of upgrading domestic science schools, making them into special secondary schools for the training of "wonderful wives". The provincial government lent a hand and for more than twenty years funded what were to become the Family Institutes, all the while refusing grants to the women's classical colleges. And throughout the decade the same people, politicians and clergy alike, put up a steadfast and successful defence against the greatest symbol of women's public equality: the vote. Year after year, the legislators, of whatever political persuasion, rebuffed delegations of women demanding the suffrage even if the delegations were led by the upper class and well connected Thérèse Casgrain. In effect, her suffragette activities placed her on par with the popular singer Mary Travers, "La Bolduc," whom the elite considered vulgar: both, in quite different ways, were challenging a surely natural division of social responsibilities by sex.

Quebec's elites were convinced that social stability depended upon that division. To reinforce it would thus bolster resistance to the Depression. Even the institutional responses that intellectuals, nationalists, clerics, and politicians dreamed up were based on an image of the family in which the woman was both an integrating force and an illustration of individual submission to the good of others. Each of the three Cs that took the fancy of Quebec's intellectuals in the 1930s — colonization, corporatism, and cooperatives — promised social regeneration and each spun its promise around an image of woman.

As a solution to the Depression, colonization always was more a matter of nostalgia than numbers. It was supposed to restore Quebec's rural-urban balance and recreate the rural family in which women and men were economic partners in a common enterprise. The revived rural family would rediscover the natural hierarchy lost in the individualism of the city and both women and children would fall into a divinely ordained place, subservient to and dependent upon the master-father. Actually, colonization made the greatest demands upon women as, for example, along the road to Abitibi, young urban women and even those from established rural parishes had to discard fashionable shoes and flimsy dresses, store bought bread and medical assistance, neighbourly advice and family support. This may indeed have been the greatest obstacle to colonization. Certain politicians, however, were sufficiently enamoured of the idea of colonization to produce a federal plan in 1932 to move some nine thousand urban poor off city relief rolls and into Quebec's northwest; one of the appropriately named destinations was Rivière Solitaire. A provincial plan followed in 1934 and by the end of the decade some forty-five thousand people, new settlers or former farmers, had been moved into areas such as Abitibi, Temiscamingue, northern Lac St. Jean, the Rimouski region, and the Gaspé. As many as two-thirds of them did not stay permanently, unable to turn the clock back as easily as certain elites imagined. The provincial government's own doubts about the validity of colonization were reflected in its expenditures. Only a fraction of its annual expenditures of approximately one hundred million dollars each year between 1930 and 1939 went directly to the back-to-the-land movement. In contrast, public works and direct relief absorbed most of the budget. Colonization never was a paying proposition.

Even less practised was another panacea advocated by certain elites. Corporatism, as a theory of economic organization, filled the pages of periodicals like *L'Action nationale* and *L'Actualité économique*, the lecture halls of *Hautes Etudes commerciales*, and the debating rooms of classical colleges. It had the blessing of the pope, always useful for the advocates of certain political ideas in Quebec. But its real attraction lay in its promise of economic regeneration and stability by mirroring the family structure in the economy. That structure was both hierarchical and harmonious, the woman again being the symbolic key, acknowledging the hierarchy and achieving the harmony by a constant subordination of her individuality to the good of the whole. As it was done in the family so it could be achieved in industry. Workers and employers in a given area of production would harmonize their interests in a corporation rather than institutionalize their differences in workers' unions or manufacturers' associations. The various corporations from different sectors of the economy would then combine to form an economic council to work in conjunction with the government to plan and regulate economic policy. It was even suggested that such an economic council replace Quebec's existing legislative council. Nothing ever came of any of the ideas, but the dream was there: a means of organizing and perhaps even controlling the economy according to a social structure purportedly peculiar to French Canada.

A more realistic response to the Depression was the co-operative movement. More limited in ambition, it in fact achieved the most concrete results. Recognizing the isolation and powerlessness of the small primary producer, whether farmer or fisherman, and sometimes of the ordinary consumer too, as saver or spender, the advocates of co-operatives urged a combining of individual effort into collective strength. Again the family served as a model, less in this instance for its hierarchical structure than for its communitarian practice. The woman's devotion to the common good taught children in particular the benefits of familial co-operation and her contacts with other women in village and church organizations formed the basic lines of social support. On such principles, savings and lending co-operatives had existed since the early twentieth century in the *caisses populaires*. Farmer's co-operatives too had begun in the 1920s as rural producers joined forces to control more of their income from sales and their outlay for supplies. In the 1930s both the financial and the farmers' co-ops expanded while urban consumers and Gaspé fishermen formed additional ones. Involvement in a co-op was not always easy since the major private companies always had the means to tempt a wavering individual away from a nascent co-operative where the benefits were long term and collective rather than immediate and personal. But precisely because the benefits were collective, the co-operatives enjoyed the support of powerful spokesmen. Nationalists, clerics, and academics not only spoke and wrote but also acted and organized on behalf of co-operatives. Laval University's school of social science which was to produce so many of Quebec's secular elite in the 1950s was founded in 1938 and incorporated a chair in cooperation. The director, Georges-Henri Lévesque, a cleric deeply involved in Catholic social action, proceeded to organize a provincewide federation of existing co-ops and to produce a periodical to advertise the movement, *Ensemble*. By the end of the decade co-operatives boasted more members than colonizers and corporatists combined.

The search for social stability by means of specially tailored institutions led inevitably to politics. Legislative sanctions were needed to maintain traditional roles for women. Colonization demanded legislative monies. Corporatism implied a totally different relationship between politicians and businessmen. Co-operatives needed the support that only a favourably inclined government could grant. In order to reinforce the social order therefore, politics themselves might have to be changed. Some very shrill but nonetheless isolated voices did cry out during the decade for separatism, communism, fascism, or socialism. The latter three all found more adherents in parts of Canada other than Quebec. Separatism itself had some youthful enthusiasts and some ardent theoreticians, but no one really knew what *abbé* Groulx meant when he proclaimed to a wildly exuberant crowd in Quebec City in 1937: *"Notre état francais, nous l'aurons"* (we shall have our French state). Most people wondered more seriously about reform than about revolution. And most of the electorate, like other voters across Canada, merely awaited its chance to toss the government out.

To prod the provincial government into any action at all was a major undertaking. The assembly only met about three months of the year and during that time it avoided controversial legislation. Ministers of the crown casually accumulated directorships of companies—premier Taschereau himself had ten—and seldom legislated against their benefactors. The occasional piece of social legislation acquired significance more by its rarity than its substance. A minimum wage act for women dated from 1919 but was rarely enforced. From 1921 on, provincial funds assisted private and church-run social welfare institutions on a definite basis. As of 1934 the results of collective bargaining in one regional location involving a majority of workers in a given industry were to be extended automatically to the same workers in other regions. But there were no old age pensions until the eve of Taschereau's resignation in 1936 and no unemployment insurance. Even the palliatives demanded by the Depression were given grudgingly. The government, like others in North America, had neither weapon nor will to combat the fall-out from foreign companies, especially when those companies had been attracted in the first place by government largesse.

When the legislature was not in session, members and ministers alike engaged in their own form of social action. Through their law firms or business and professional connections they spread the good word, and more often the good deed, of the Liberal government. The distribution of patronage was in direct proportion to a member's power and a county's electoral fidelity. The system was finely tuned: large companies in expectation or receipt of lucrative government contracts casually contributed to the party's electoral fund; the fund in turn greased many a palm, directly or indirectly, all the way to the voting booth. Premier Taschereau's many relatives who handled government affairs could attest to his vast knowledge of the tricks of the political trade. To anyone keen enough to watch but not to challenge, Taschereau, who served sixteen years as premier, could provide many a lesson in political longevity. As of 1933 he was in fact under the attentive and ambitious eye of the new Conservative leader, Maurice Duplessis, sitting among his eleven followers in the perpetually lopsided assembly. While awaiting the opportunity to challenge, Duplessis learned all he needed to know about patronage and paternalism. Taschereau was a fine teacher and Duplessis an apt pupil.

Duplessis' chance came less from the Conservative party than from the Depression and the intellectual and political ferment it produced. The party in fact laboured under the double burden of continuing electoral defeat since the 1890s and conscription imposed by its federal colleagues in 1917. Nor did it profit from the two favourable signs the federal Conservatives had to their credit in Quebec. Neither the Conservative-nationalist alliance of 1911 nor the Conservative defeat of Mackenzie King in 1930 spilled over into political capital for the provincial party. Successive leaders attempted in vain to rekindle the nationalist commitment of 1911, but nationalists remained far too skittish to tie their emotions to a political party. Nor was Camillien Houde, leader of the provincial Conservatives from 1929 to 1932, able to bring to the party the populist fervour he aroused as mayor of Montreal. The Conservative program did begin to hint vaguely at issues of growing concern in the 1930s—agricultural problems, foreign domination of the natural resource industries, the electricity trust—but the debate on such questions was much more fervent outside political circles. Students, teachers, nationalists, clerics, study groups, professional associations, writers, and journalists all discussed the miseries and the dangers of the Depression. Some of them suggested local scapegoats such as the Jews, a growing presence in Montreal's retail trade since the 1920s; some spied communists behind every steeple while others longed for a regenerating leader; still others pondered a cultural reformation through modernized Christianity. But at the same time they were all appalled by the political practices and policies of the provincial Liberals. No matter how much some of the critics may have resisted the idea, their notions of social salvation all pointed in a political direction. Along that path, carefully on the watch for potential allies, was Maurice Duplessis.

The allies came from two major sources. One was a group of laymen and clerics involved in Catholic social action; the other a gathering of critics on the fringes of the existing political parties. The first had a long-standing institutional framework for their ideas in the *Ecole sociale populaire* dating from 1911 and inspired by the indefatigable *père* Joseph-Papin Archambault. The second emerged in the early 1930s as an uneasy presence within the Liberal party; in 1934 it openly labelled itself a third political force under the banner of *Action libérale nationale*. By then the *Ecole sociale populaire* had already launched a program of social restoration to adapt papal teaching to the Quebec scene and provide a Catholic alternative to socialism. The *Programme de restauration sociale* was in fact designed as a response to the CCF. It proposed the restoration of agriculture by means of colonization and easy credit for farmers, the restoration of workers by means of social legislation, notably family allowances, the restoration of public finances through government ownership of the utility companies, and the restoration of politics by the elimination of corruption and patronage. The program was silent on the mechanics of any restoration, but it could count on the sympathetic ear of a host of clerically inspired youth groups, student activists, workers' unions, farmers' associations, and co-operatives. More concretely, the individuals already discussing political reform within the Liberal party endorsed the program and urged it upon Paul Gouin, son of a former Liberal premier and leader of the dissident *Action libérale nationale.* The aims of the group were indeed similar to those suggested by the *Ecole sociale populaire* except that they were directed specifically at the Liberal party. The party should be purged of its corrupt electoral and governing practices; it should take social problems much more seriously and it should exercise more control of the province's economy. The specific measure to guarantee that control was the nationalization of hydro-electric companies, particularly the private monopoly that squeezed Montreal's industries and residents alike—the Montreal Light, Heat and Power. "Down with the trusts" became the watchword of political reformers. If premier Taschereau showed no inclination to listen, perhaps Maurice Duplessis would.

In fact, Duplessis, once the *Action libérale nationale* declared its intention to combat Taschereau from outside the Liberal party, did prick up his ears. Alone, neither the *Action libérale nationale* nor the Conservatives stood much of a chance of storming the Liberal electoral fortress. Together, they might just make an impact. In preparation for the provincial election of November 1935, therefore, the Conservatives carefully emphasized those aspects of their program which most closely resembled the *Programme de restauration sociale*. And in the meantime Duplessis wooed Paul Gouin. Neither had much to lose and within three weeks of the election each in fact thought he had much to gain. They agreed to join forces under the banner of *Union nationale*. The name conjured up the old dream of French Canadian unity free of party divisions and strong in the face of Anglo-Saxon hostility.

The reality was less promising but electorally more viable. The new party combined long-time Conservatives, English and French, born-again Liberals with a radical streak, and nationalists enamoured of both the economic and ethnic potential of government control of monopolies. Behind the three groups were the not always compatible financial, ideological, and clerical backers of each. But the combination was sufficiently strong to give the Liberals a bad fright. In the election the *Union nationale* took forty-two of the ninety seats in the assembly. Duplessis swallowed his pride over the fact that his allies had won twenty-six of the forty-two and pressed his advantage. Under his constant harassment and revelation of one scandal after another, the Liberals collapsed and Taschereau resigned in June 1936. Even an untainted Adélard Godbout could not hold the crumbling government together. By the end of August another election installed the *Union nationale* in power with seventy-six seats and fifty-eight percent of the popular vote. The alliance had paid off.

Duplessis, however, had no intention of honouring it. Before the election of August 1936 he had already quarrelled with Paul Gouin; as the much stronger personality and politician, Duplessis had won. After the election he gave the same treatment to Gouin's followers. There was not to be a majority of cabinet positions for former members of the *Action libérale nationale* as the original agreement of 1935 had stipulated. There was no question of Duplessis sharing power with anyone. Nor did he feel bound to the electoral program of the alliance. Personally he had promised clean government; if others had rashly foreseen nationalization of electricity or a revamped legislative council to provide some planning for and control of the economy, that was their problem. So sure was Duplessis of his power that he did not even bother to invite the few die-hards of the *Action libérale nationale* to caucus meetings. While some of them howled publicly about treason, others willingly bartered their silence for a taste of power.

And yet Duplessis did garner more than just the premiership from his momentary alliance. The nationalists had popularized a number of their fears and Duplessis grasped the political potential of them. He picked up the concern for provincial autonomy and began fulminating against the least federal initiative. He objected to the centralizing intent of the Rowell-Sirois Commission on Dominion-Provincial relations and he formed a chummy alliance with Ontario's premier Hepburn in addled hostility to prime minister Mackenzie King. Duplessis gave provincial autonomy a political power it had never known before. He did the same with anti-communism, another of the nationalist bugbears of the decade. In 1937 Duplessis' Act Respecting Communistic Propaganda, popularly known as the Padlock Law, permitted the police to close any place suspected of harbouring communist or bolshevist literature, personnel, or ideas. The vagueness of the charges alarmed civil libertarians in the rest of Canada but left the much more favourable impression among the provincial electorate that Duplessis was seriously protecting Quebec from foreign threats.

Duplessis slipped easily into the role of protector. His own conservative temperament and background nurtured a respect for authority, a concern for social stability, and a fear of change. He moulded his government in the same image. While he insisted on cabinet ministers cutting their ties with corporations, his purpose was to protect each from the undue influence of the other. He had no intention of straying any farther into the economic realm. The state's role was to maintain favourable conditions for business enterprises to flourish. He might insist that foreign companies have provincial charters to exploit natural resources in the province or that a provincial hydro-electric commission be created. But these were relatively harmless devices to protect Quebec's patrimony and calm certain *Union nationale* voters; they did nothing to change the pattern of economic development in the province. Duplessis' grants to the aged, to widows, orphans, and needy mothers was a paternalistic means of cutting them off municipal relief rolls. He even saved the state from condoning immorality when he removed unwed mothers and unmarried couples from the lists of relief recipients. And he attempted to protect the unemployed from the debilitating effects of public handouts by inaugurating more public works programs. Roads, parks, and civic centres improved morale and embellished the province; if carefully located they also improved the temper of the electorate.

The same considerations shaped Duplessis' concern for rural dwellers. While he actually believed that farmers best assured social stability, he also knew that they controlled more than their fair share of votes. Since the *Union nationale* had in fact captured more of the urban than the rural vote in 1936, Duplessis had every incentive to turn his attention to the countryside. The budget for colonization increased immediately; rural roads sprang from nowhere and some of them were even kept clear in winter. Agricultural schools attempted to train youngsters in scientific farming methods and also to persuade them to stay on the land. Much talk but few wires dangled the promise of rural electrification before the eighty-seven percent of Quebec farms without it. Of more immediate benefit was a government sponsored system of agricultural credit. With government guarantees, an Agricultural Credit Bureau permitted farmers to borrow up to seventy-five percent of the value of their land in long-term, low interest loans. The economic purpose was to revive agriculture; the moral purpose was to keep large families on the land. In either case Duplessis believed he was protecting the foundation of society.

The protection of workers was a little more complicated. Some of them already had their own protective organizations and they looked to the *Union nationale* government for favourable legislation. For example, almost all unions, of whatever affiliation, wanted legal guarantees for the closed shop. But Duplessis was less interested in working with existing organizations than in showering his paternalism on individuals. To him, the closed shop contradicted notions of freedom in the work place. His early labour legislation effectively prohibited the closed shop by fining employers who interfered with their workers' membership or non-membership in a union. At the same time Duplessis promised to protect non-unionized workers with his Fair Wage Act: a government board would determine salaries and working conditions for certain categories of workers. The Act also put an end to Taschereau's provision for the extension of collective agreements. According to Duplessis, a mere majority of union members ought not to impose their settlement on all sectors or regions of a given industry; rather all unionized workers should negotiate their own contracts. If no settlement was possible, the Fair Wage Board would impose one. The unions, both Catholic and international, were immediately suspicious, fearing that the entire collective bargaining process was being undermined. Their suspicions were confirmed in 1938 when the huge Dominion Textile company refused to bargain with its unionized workers but was quite willing to have the Fair Wage Board study possible settlements. And in the meantime the government had excluded its own contracted work from the provisions of the Fair Wage Act. From the unions' point of view, the government could set wages and then undermine them itself. But the unions constituted only twelve percent of Quebec's waged workers and an even smaller proportion of all voters. Duplessis knew that too.

As in the rest of the country, the electoral system provided the outlet for many of the frustrations of the 1930s. There was no social upheaval, no revolution, and very little flirting with foreign ideologies. The skilful politician—a Bennett in Ottawa or a Duplessis in Quebec—was even able to make political capital out of contemporary fears. But most social miseries were lived in isolation, in the shuffling breadlines, in the crowded slum, or on the distant farm. The few collective responses were filtered primarily through male voices and attempted to adapt religious and familial values to a secular society run amuck. Woman's position in public remained precarious, even illegitimate, because others' dreams had placed her elsewhere. The state took on a purely defensive role because the dream had conjured up a protector. And neither would change much for another generation. Possibly the internal equilibrium had been found. The external world, however, had the real answer to the economic problems of the Depression. And with it, the Second World War flung another nationalist challenge at Quebec.

SELECT BIBLIOGRAPHY

Black, Conrad. *Duplessis.* Toronto: McClelland and Stewart, 1976.

Casgrain, Thérèse F. *Une femme chez les hommes.* Montreal: Editions du Jour, 1971.

Desbiens, Jean-Paul. *Sous le soleil de la pitié.* Montreal: Editions du Jour, 1965.

Dumas, Evelyn. *The Bitter Thirties in Quebec.* Montreal: Black Rose Books, 1975.

Dumont, Fernand et al. *Idéologies au Canada français, 1930–1939.* Quebec: Les presses de l'Université Laval, 1978.

Durocher, René. "Taschereau, Hepburn et les relations Québec-Ontario, 1934–1936." *Revue d'histoire de l'Amérique française* 24(1970):341–56.

Grignon, Claude-Henri. *Un homme et son péché.* Montreal: Editions du Totem, 1933.

Groulx, Lionel. *Mes mémoires.* vol. 3. Montreal: Fides, 1972.

Hughes, Everett C. *French Canada in Transition.* Chicago: University of Chicago Press, 1963.

Lapalme, George-Emile. *Le bruit des choses réveillées.* Montreal: Leméac, 1969.

Lavigne, Marie, and Yoland Pinard, eds. *Les femmes dans la société québécoise: aspects historiques.* Montreal: Boréal Express, 1977.

LeFranc, Marie. *La rivière solitaire.* Montreal: Fides, 1957.

Lemelin, Roger. *Les Plouffe.* Quebec: Bélisle, 1948.

Lévesque, Andrée. *Virage à gauche interdit.* Montreal: Boréal Express, 1983.

Miner, Horace M. *St. Denis, a French Canadian Parish.* Chicago: University of Chicago Press, 1939.

Neatby, H. Blair. *The Politics of Chaos: Canada in the Thirties.* Toronto: Macmillan, 1972.

Quinn, Herbert F. *Union Nationale: a Study in Quebec Nationalism.* Toronto: University of Toronto Press, 1963.

Report of the Royal Commission on Dominion-Provincial Relations. Ottawa, 1940.

Ringuet (Philippe Panneton). *Trente arpents.* Paris: Flammarion, 1938.

Roy, Gabrielle. *Bonheur d'occasion.* Montreal: Beauchemin, 1945.

"Steel, rubber, chemicals, asbestos, radio and radar equipment were all produced ..."
Woman war worker operating an asbestos carding machine, Asbestos, 1944.

16 Ottawa's War

One week after the British declared war on September 3, 1939, the Canadian government followed suit. Some French Canadian members of parliament muttered their unhappiness, but the one outspoken voice of opposition was not that of a French Canadian at all. Before parliament even met, the federal government refurbished the old War Measures Act from the First World War and prepared to don the mantle of organizer of the nation. Both the wartime circumstances and the government's assumption of control worked wonders for the Canadian and Quebec economy. But for any sense of nation they did the opposite. Not only did certain Quebecois contest the idea of a Canadian nation, but they also argued that Ottawa's actions were detrimental to the true nation in Canada, French Canada. A far off war, with the Canadian response directed from Ottawa, appeared to be yet another external threat to French Canada.

The war was indeed distant in September 1939. If the French Canadian press sympathized with Britain and France, many people doubted the wisdom of Canadian participation. That English Canadians should jump so immediately and emotionally to Britain's side was perhaps predictable but not always understandable. Where was all the hard won autonomy of the inter-war years? What was the real meaning of the Statute of Westminster that had supposedly sanctioned Canadian independence in 1931? And what of the statements of prime minister Mackenzie King and his major French Canadian colleague, justice minister Ernest Lapointe? Since 1935 they had been saying that Canada ought not to become involved in foreign wars. Did they know all along that for the majority of Canadians Britain was not foreign? In the parliamentary debate on Canadian participation in early September 1939 Lapointe acknowledged that sentiment but argued more from a juridical standpoint: Canada could not remain neutral because a series of legal commitments bound the country irrevocably to Britain. Still, even those people convinced by reason or sentiment that Canada had to become involved thought the fighting would be far away and short-lived. Germany's strength was a mere show and would soon collapse; Canadian participation would be in supplies rather than manpower. And it would all be voluntary.

Few people waited to be convinced. Much to the dismay of certain youth, nationalist, farmer, and labour groups, young French Canadian men flocked to the recruiting stations as soon as the doors opened. For some there was genuine interest; for others a genuine job. The army's basic pay of $1.30 a day, to which food, clothing, housing, and even physical training were added, was a boon to the poor and the shabby, the homeless and the hungry of Quebec's urban unemployed. By the end of September two French Canadian regiments in Montreal, the *Maisonneuve* and the *Fusiliers de Mont-Royal*, were the first in Canada to complete their mobilization. There was even a waiting list. By Christmas, French Canadian regiments, among them the Royal 22nd, were part of the first Canadian division en route to Britain. By the end of the war, in 1945, French Canadians numbered close to one hundred and forty thousand of the seven hundred and thirty thousand Canadian soldiers. Along the way they served in the air force and the navy, constituting approximately fifteen percent of the former and five percent of the latter. In all the services, they encountered the same problems as their fathers did during the First World War. Officers were primarily English-speaking, military schools had few French language textbooks; efficient training and then promotion often depended upon a knowledge of English. The navy and the air force operated solely in English. Apart from the forestry crews, the specialized services of the military offered few places for French Canadians. But still the numbers were there and until the federal Conservatives went desperately looking for a political issue late in 1941, no one suggested they were too few.

In the autumn of 1939 Maurice Duplessis decided to make a political issue of the war itself by calling an election. The Canadian commitment was barely two weeks old and Duplessis hoped to garner all the uneasiness in Quebec about a foreign war and to turn it to the advantage of his *Union nationale* government, itself barely three years old. He claimed that the War Measures Act would involve excessive centralization; the autonomy of the provinces was at issue. Worse still, conscription was probably lurking in the minds of the centralizers. After all, it had been a logical consequence of Canadian participation in the First World War only a generation ago; why should things be any different this time? Only the *Union nationale* could guarantee Quebec's autonomy; only Maurice Duplessis could keep conscription at bay. By constrast, Duplessis asserted, a Liberal government in Quebec would simply play into the hands of the Liberal government in Ottawa.

The federal Liberals had other ideas. Considering Duplessis' election a direct affront to the fledgling war effort, they intervened in full force in the provincial election. Liberal Ernest Lapointe and his two Quebec colleagues in the cabinet, Arthur Cardin and Charles G. Power, respectively minister of public works and postmaster general, presented themselves as the real protectors of Quebec's interests. Quebec needed a strong voice in Ottawa; without it the conscriptionists would indeed have their way as they had in 1917. But to be truly strong that voice needed not just federal votes in Quebec but provincial ones as well. Lapointe, Cardin, and Power threatened to resign from the federal cabinet if the Quebec electorate returned the *Union nationale.* They thereby flung the conscriptionist threat back in the face of Duplessis: if he won and they resigned and Canada abandoned voluntary recruitment, he would be responsible. The convoluted reasoning and the political threat were effective. The Liberals hardly needed the additional help of some of the War Measures but the federal politicians were not taking any risks: censorship emerged from the mothballs of the First World War just in time to affect the election campaign. No political speech could be aired on radio unless it was presented to the studio ahead of time for censoring; no live broadcasts of political meetings were permitted. Adélard Godbout, the provincial Liberal leader, dutifully submitted his speeches; Maurice Duplessis did without the radio. His government also did without some funds as the newly created foreign exchange control commission insisted on vetting all borrowing outside the country by individuals, municipalities, or provinces. Even Duplessis' electoral fund may have diminished as potential donors calculated greater benefits from federal promises of war contracts to industries in localities that voted the right way. Needless to say, the voters chose the path of least resistance: they reversed their preferences of 1936 and gave the Liberals seventy seats and the *Union nationale* fourteen. If some people protested Ottawa's calculated manipulation of Quebec voters, others carefully noted the pact that the election had sealed between Ottawa and Quebec: in exchange for Liberal votes, there was to be no conscription.

Caught in the middle was the new premier of Quebec, Adélard Godbout. An agronomist from Ste. Anne de la Pocatière, he owed his victory to his federal colleagues and they seldom permitted him to forget it. He had also made a personal pledge to fight them if they mobilized any French Canadian against his will. More than that, Godbout was a moderate reformer and had an electoral program that included woman suffrage and compulsory education. Both were highly suspect to certain nationalists who nevertheless supported him in 1939 because of their bitter disappointment with Duplessis in 1936. Some of those same people were still advocating the nationalization of the hydro-electric industry in Quebec and Godbout was inclined to listen to them. And then there was the labour vote, also disappointed by Duplessis. Even if Godbout had possessed the self-assurance and the aristocratic presence of Taschereau or even the bravado of Duplessis, he still would have had difficulty at the best of times manoeuvring among such diverse currents.

Nonetheless Godbout was able to legislate a number of reforms during his almost five years in office. Perhaps his rural stamina enabled him to succeed where others had failed. Or perhaps the very diversity of his political allies permitted him to bargain with each for the pet project of the other. Certainly he withstood the continuing opposition of the church to votes for women, as expressed by Cardinal Rodrigue Villeneuve of Quebec City, and he convinced the Liberal caucus to do so too. Based on the presumed threat of the suffrage to family solidarity and female modesty, the opposition was beginning to make Quebec look rather peculiar in the western world. Moreover it was also an insult to the socially prominent women who had been urging it for years. Both houses of the Quebec parliament passed the suffrage bill in the spring of 1940 with scarcely a murmur. The significance of its passage may well lie less in the political equality it accorded women than in the public rebuke it delivered to the Catholic hierarchy: the state alone was competent to judge.

On matters of schooling the situation was reversed. There the Catholic church had the upper hand. The provincial government was welcome, indeed obliged, to provide financial assistance, but the church alone was competent to judge. Over the years, however, the state had established a number of schools, totally divorced from the clerically controlled Committee of Public Instruction, offering technical, commercial, and other specialized training. But the government had never been able, much less willing, to go beyond this. It had persistently bowed to clerical and nationalist opposition and shied away from legislating compulsory education for the elementary schools, a demand of the more radical provincial Liberals and a commonplace in every other Canadian province since at least the early twentieth century. The very idea raised fears of secularization, of state interference in the divinely ordained right of parents to educate children as they chose. And yet, in the early

1940s, Godbout was able to assuage the fears. His government not only passed a compulsory education bill in 1943 to make schooling free and obligatory up to age fourteen, but it did so with the consent of the Committee of Public Instruction and the blessing of Cardinal Villeneuve. Villeneuve may now have been convinced that the moral dangers were greater for the close to four hundred thousand school-age children who were not in school than for the general population being told by a government what to do.

During the same years Godbout tackled a powerful section of the Montreal business community. Flanked this time by some nationalist allies, he took on the electricity trust. Except for a few small municipally owned generating stations, most of Quebec's hydro-electric power was in the hands of private companies. In the 1930s nationalists had succeeded in branding those companies as the symbol of Quebec's economic exploitation. In the 1940s they argued that rates could be reduced and industrial expansion encouraged if the natural resource belonged to the people of Quebec rather than to a small group of privileged individuals. By 1944 the government of Quebec was ready to establish a provincially owned hydro-electric network. Hydro-Quebec began with the nationalization of the Montreal Light, Heat and Power Company and one of its earliest activities was to inaugurate a system of rural electrification. Godbout may have been persuaded to act because of the presence of a new political force in the province, the *Bloc populaire*, that advocated just such a measure. But whether from conviction or persuasion he nonetheless fashioned an instrument of economic power, one of the few in the hands of Quebecois, that, once completed twenty years later by the next Liberal government in Quebec, would provide a major source of economic development and nationalist pride in the 1960s.

In the 1940s nationalist pride took a number of heavy blows and Godbout was associated with them as well. He paid his political debt to the federal Liberals on numerous occasions during the war years and each time the nationalist temper in Quebec rose slightly higher. Whether the issues were constitutional, financial, military, or social, they aroused the sensibilities of certain Quebecois. To them Ottawa seemed to be fashioning Canadian behaviour and Quebec appeared to acquiesce. Monitoring it all, while he cured himself of various political and physical ailments, among them alcoholism, was Maurice Duplessis. Eventually he was to regain the premiership and be the winner in the multiple tug of war between Ottawa and Quebec.

In the early 1940s Ottawa attempted to solve some leftover constitutional questions from the 1930s. An amendment to the British North America Act in 1940 finally acknowledged some federal responsibility for unemployment by instituting an Ottawa-organized system of unemployment insurance. Premier Godbout timidly suggested the possibility of joint federal-provincial legislation, but in the face of Mackenzie King's opposition, he gave his assent to the federal plan. No one, it seems, paid any attention to the views of one Quebec economist, even though they had appeared as an appendix to the Rowell-Sirois Report recommending federal unemployment insurance, that this insurance would simply make the conditions of urban workers all the more attractive and hence contribute to further rural depopulation. The report itself was the subject of a two day dominion-provincial conference in 1941. There Godbout quietly let his Ontario, Alberta, and British Columbia counterparts demolish it. None of them was willing to accept the report's recommended redistribution of financial powers (all, they thought, in favour of Ottawa) and the report was shelved.

By 1942 Ottawa's direction of the war effort required massive amounts of money. If the provinces would not agree to a constitutional rearrangement perhaps they would accept a temporary wartime shuffling of accounts. Again Godbout acquiesced by relinquishing succession duties, personal income tax, and corporation taxes to Ottawa in return for a lump sum payment. Duplessis fumed, but it was Godbout who signed the agreement to last until one year after the end of the war. During all the various intergovernmental negotiations, Ottawa also orchestrated a vast public relations campaign in favour of the war and financial backing for it. Although few French Canadians manned the planning offices of this campaign in Ottawa, they were present everywhere in Quebec, in the press and the pulpit, on the radio and among the politicians and businessmen, urging their compatriots to subscribe to war loans by purchasing Victory bonds. The campaigns were immensely successful, the people of Quebec more willing, it seems, to part with their money than their sons.

Perhaps this was because there was more money to part with. The war brought an industrial boom to Quebec and there were jobs aplenty as war industries, under contract to the federal government, sprang up all over the province. Even the wartime controls which Ottawa imposed under the War Measures Act on prices and wages, quantity and quality of consumer goods, and labour relations did not dampen the industrial ardour. On the contrary, war industries were assured of materials and markets as boards and commissions housed in Ottawa regulated the supply, production, and distribution of everything from agricultural goods to steel, timber, oil, chemicals, and power. If private industry with all that prodding could not produce the necessities of war in record time, the federal government itself established crown corporations to do so. In Quebec, armaments, airplanes, and ships were among the products of federally controlled companies. If an occasional voice complained that Ontario was benefiting more from the war-inspired federal generosity, the tramp of feet to the factory gates and the roar of machinery inside effectively muffled it.

With Canada supplying much of the allied war material between the fall of France in the spring of 1940 and the entry of the United States into the war in December 1941, Quebec's industries worked overtime. Day and night shift workers in the urban areas of the Saguenay shared jobs and even housing without ever meeting. The aluminum plant at Arvida, an immense factory constantly being expanded, produced more aluminum in 1942 than had been manufactured in the entire world in 1939. While the businessmen of the area dreamed of making the Saguenay the industrial heartland of postwar Canada, they also had to find alternative routes for importing bauxite to make aluminum. The St. Lawrence was no longer safe as German submarines were spotted in the gulf and as far upriver as Matane. The bauxite was therefore hauled by train from Portland on the Maine coast. In turn, trains and ships took Arvida's aluminum overseas and to the burgeoning aircraft manufacturing plants in Montreal. The trains themselves, both for domestic and overseas service, were built in huge plants in Montreal and Quebec City. The same plants retooled to make military equipment as well: trucks, tanks, and heavy guns. Ships to carry the material across the Atlantic sprang overnight from shipyards in Montreal, Sorel, and Lauzon. At Sorel, the Simard family used its political connections with federal minister Arthur Cardin to obtain munitions as well as shipbuilding contracts for Marine Industries, the family firm. The largest explosives factory in the empire took form at St. Paul l'Ermite, just north of Montreal, while the plant at Beloeil on the Richelieu expanded from a minor producer of commercial explosives to a major contributor to the allied arsenal. The Canadian army itself had armaments factories in Quebec City and munitions depots in Montreal. Steel, rubber, chemicals, asbestos, radio and radar equipment were all produced as fast as the agent for Quebec's commerce and industry ministry could pry the contracts out of Ottawa. Even the more traditional industries supplied the war: tobacco, boots, shoes, and textiles made in Quebec soothed, shod, and covered millions of allied soldiers.

In turn, the industries created jobs. As a munitions factory opened its gates, the municipality closed the relief office. Towns in fact squabbled among themselves in their pursuit of war contracts and new industries. And the workers came off the bread lines, away from the soup kitchens, and into the factories. Settlers from the various colonization schemes of the 1930s happily found their way back to urban employment. Munitions factories in Quebec City alone employed more than ten thousand people while more than twenty thousand moved into the industrial region around Chicoutimi seeking jobs. The industrial labour force doubled in the first four years of the war and the economic spinoff was felt throughout the province.

So was a social spinoff felt since thousands of the new workers were women. Store clerks, domestic servants, young girls from the countryside and, most disturbing of all, married women from the home dropped their ill paying tasks and headed for the factories. In those where textiles, tobacco, knitted goods, shoes, and rope were being made, the newcomers joined a female labour force almost one hundred years old. In others, such as aircraft, aluminum, chemical, munitions, and steel plants, in metallurgy, smelting, and tool manufacturing, they were the first women on the assembly lines. Some of them recalled a mother or an aunt who had done similar work in the First World War, but most of them were initiates to heavy industry. By the fall of 1943 they constituted one third of the industrial work force in Montreal, Quebec City and indeed in the province as a whole.

Both government and industry facilitated the presence of women in the paid labour force. The provincial government suspended some clauses of its labour legislation to permit women to work at night. The federal government used tax incentives to lure married women out of the home: as long as their income was from war-related employment, their husbands could continue to claim them as a tax deduction. Industries established flexible hours and part-time jobs to attract married women workers. They organized day-care centres on their own premises to attract the mothers of young children. The two governments and industry collaborated on advertising campaigns that emphasized the charm of overalled, spanner-wielding young women. Yet once the war was over, they dismantled the laws, the incentives, the child-care centres, and the advertisements. The women faded away as quickly as they had come, although few of them returned to rural areas or to domestic service, at least not as maids.

To the opponents of women's industrial war work, their presence in the labour force was a disaster. Women were abandoning their sacred duties in the home to scurry after the excitement and the cash of vulgar jobs in industry. They were exposing themselves to moral and physical dangers: the road to prostitution wound inevitably from the promiscuity of the factory to that of the brothel. Those who narrowly escaped that fate nonetheless bore the traces of industrial health hazards. Their strength was undermined and their constitution poisoned. What kind of children would they produce? And what about the ones working mothers had already engendered? Those children left to their own devices, at best in the hands of strangers, at worst to wander the streets, would soon be juvenile delinquents. The fate of the French Canadian family and hence of the nation was thus sealed in the oil-stained hands of young women and mothers in the munitions plants. The periodical press lamented "The conscription of women" and "The great sorrow of the family." "What will become of them?" "Bring the mothers back home," they wailed, "Children need their mothers." The Catholic bishops of Quebec and the other provinces listed women's war work along with all the moral disorders of the time: blasphemy, alcoholism, Sunday work, and communist propaganda. The male legislators of Quebec passed a unanimous resolution requesting the federal government not to intensify its recruitment of women for war industries and thereby destroy the soul of the Canadian home. The labour unions camouflaged their uneasiness with a similar plea for the family: woman's role was in the home bringing up children. It certainly was not in the work place in competition with men, nudging them towards the army and undermining the strength of their unions. In all the reaction to women's war work, the villain was clearly identifiable. The war had imposed an unnatural state of affairs upon Quebec and the war was Ottawa's doing.

Among those unnatural affairs was an increase in labour unrest. In the 1930s the lack of work had caused fear for social stability; the surfeit of jobs in the 1940s appeared to be even more volatile. Unions fought each other to sign up new members and to achieve the closed shop among paper makers, aluminum workers, shipbuilders, and municipal service employees. The Catholic unions in particular saw the war as their opportunity to expand into heavy industry; but there they encountered the hostility of yet another international rival, the Congress of Industrial Organizations. Union membership in fact jumped dramatically during the war. But many workers did not wait for unions to protest rising costs, fixed wages, and the lack of housing and consumer goods. On numerous occasions, non-unionized workers took the initiative in strike action. One of the most dramatic was the five day work stoppage by five thousand aluminum workers, supported by another four thousand in construction, at Arvida in July 1941. Only a tiny minority of the workers was unionized and the strike took the union itself by surprise. Because of the importance of the product to the war economy, the federal government immediately dispatched an English-speaking conciliator from Ottawa, and, for good measure, troops from Valcartier. A subsequent royal commission found no trace of saboteurs, only poorly paid workers unhappy about the conditions in the plant. Elsewhere, women's clothing workers demanded a twenty percent wage increase, aircraft workers insisted upon a retroactive cost of living bonus, munitions workers complained that their Ontario counterparts earned more money, tramway operators in Montreal tied up urban transit with their inter-union rivalry while police and firefighters in the same city struck just to have a union at all. The federal government put a stop to strikes in shipbuilding in Quebec City and Lauzon in 1943 by creating its own company, Quebec Shipyards Limited, to oversee construction. The provincial government hoped to call a halt to union rivalry and strikes when in 1944 it legislated the negotiation of collective agreements between employers and whichever union represented sixty percent of the workers. If the two sides could not agree, they would have to proceed through a conciliator and finally an arbitration commission. Only if the latter failed could a strike legally take place. As for provincial government employees, firefighters, and police, there were to be no unions and no strikes. If the number of strikes is any indication, both the federal presence and the provincial legislation soothed the troubled labour scene: one hundred and thirty-three strikes in

1942 declined to one hundred and three in 1943 and forty-four in 1944.

By 1944, however, Quebec's male population was living under a much greater menace than that of provincial regulation of industrial and labour disputes. Since 1940, the federal government had been holding the threat of conscription over the heads of Canadian men. Prime minister Mackenzie King claimed, however, that there was no threat. Had he not manoeuvered among all the conscriptionist sharks of the Canadian military and the Conservative party, to say nothing of traitors in his own caucus, to stay the spectre of conscription? He did not need to be told that the spectre had haunted French Canadian imaginations since 1917. After all, it also haunted his own Liberal party, and King had no intention of ending his days a broken political leader like Sir Wilfrid Laurier with the Liberal party in tatters around him. Except for politically active Liberals in Quebec, however, no one was particularly concerned about Mackenzie King's political premonitions. Conscription for overseas duty, imposed by a hostile majority and for a foreign war, was nightmare enough.

It all began in 1940. The fall of France in June put an abrupt halt to the notion of a short-lived war and a militarily inept Germany. It also darkened the promise, so loudly proclaimed by federal Liberals during the Quebec election campaign in the fall of 1939, that there would be no conscription. Now Britain was standing alone. Canada had fully expected to be a major supplier of materials, now the country was almost the only supplier. Perhaps the number of men would have to be increased as well; more troop ships might have to join the supply ships heading east in convoy across the Atlantic.

In preparation, the federal government passed the National Resources Mobilization Act (NRMA) in June 1940. An inventory of men and materials was the justification; the creation of an army of conscripts for the defence of Canada was the major result. Few people objected to defending Canada; more were troubled by a department of labour regulation that ordered employers to check the NRMA registration cards of their workers. Montreal's mayor, Camillien Houde, denounced the Act as disguised conscription. He did not intend to register and he publicly recommended that others follow suit. For his pains he spent the next four years under arrest in a federal detention camp. Others too, and not only in Quebec, slipped off to be married and thereby escape the celibate status that marked them as available for war service. But many more tramped just as cheerfully to the first training sessions of the home defence army for thirty days in the countryside away from their regular work. The camps were in fact a boon to the local economy and businessmen and politicians clamoured to have one established in their district. The extension of the training period in 1941 to four months and then to continuous service, irked some farmers and occasioned some desertions, but still there were few voices of dissent. According to the law, the NRMA soldiers, "zombies," as they came rather cruelly to be called, could not be sent overseas. They were home defence soldiers and French Canadians had always said they would be the first to defend their homeland. The NRMA troops, about forty percent of whom were French Canadian by 1944, were of course prime targets for persuasive and sometimes aggressive recruiting agents. Would they voluntarily change their status to that of general service soldiers available for action anywhere in the world? Some would. Most would not.

Actually the need for any kind of military persuasion was minimal until late in 1944. Canada's regular soldiers saw relatively little action until the invasion of Sicily in the summer of 1943 and then of Europe from Normandy in June 1944. Most of them were in camp in southern England taking advanced training and awaiting the expected German invasion. When it came, the air force, not the army, called its bluff. Canadian soldiers were also among the foolhardy British troops holding Hong Kong against the Japanese at Christmas 1941; all two thousand Canadians were killed or taken prisoner. Almost twice that number died or were wounded on the beaches of Dieppe in August 1942. But until the last months of the war, Canadian soldiers, like the politicians back home, grumbled more than they fought: where was all the action?

Thus, when conscription tugged at the public conscience again early in 1942, it did so as a political, not a military question. The war had by then taken on its global context with the United States and Japan having entered the fray in December 1941. But except for a few frights on Canada's Pacific coast, the enlarged war did not mean an increased military role for Canada. Some Conservative politicians, however, thought it should. They even launched a second career for their leader from the 1920s, Arthur Meighen: he would take on the federal leadership once again and he would urge conscription. The Conservatives suspected they might even ferret out some closet conscriptionists from among the Liberals. Moreover, the great French Canadian barrier to conscription in the Liberal cabinet, Ernest Lapointe, had succumbed to cancer late in 1941. Who now would counter the Conservative statistics, based on the figures for Ontario, that Quebec was contributing only half of its proper share of enlistments? Mackenzie King, with his finger up to the political wind, did not savour the atmosphere at all. It threatened storms of sentiment, of race, and, worse still, of politics. With the blithe assumption that the stability of Canada depended upon the stability of the Liberal party as the unchallenged and, if possible, undivided party of government, King determined to head off the Conservative cry for conscription. He would request the opinion of the electorate although not in a general election for that was neither legally necessary nor politically wise. Rather he would stage a referendum, an unusual political practice in Canada. He would, he announced via the speech from the throne opening parliament in January 1942, "seek from the people, by means of a plebiscite, release from any obligation arising out of any past commitments restricting the methods of raising men for military service." King expected Canadians to vote in favour of releasing the government from its earlier promise of no conscription. The Conservatives heard the wind go out of their sails and French Canadians felt betrayed.

The sides were quickly drawn for the April plebiscite. French Canadian members of the federal cabinet relaxed under King's assurance that there was to be no conscription, no matter what the outcome of the vote. They even agreed to campaign in Quebec for a YES answer to the question. King solidified their intention by bringing into his cabinet a prestigious lawyer from Quebec City, Louis St. Laurent. The lot of them misread the Quebec electorate. Had they listened to the former Liberal, now independent MP, Maxime Raymond, or even to some of their own backbenchers, they would have been prepared for the massive rejection. Raymond warned them of Quebec's reading of the agreement of 1939: wartime participation and even wartime Liberal votes in return for no conscription. To request that the entire country now release the government from its promise to one part of that country was unjust.

Raymond muttered dark thoughts about separatism but proceeded to organize the NO campaign by forming a League for the Defence of Canada. With supporters and organized sections throughout Quebec, the League argued that Canada had already given its fair share of men and materials to the war, that voluntary recruiting was in fact producing more men than were required. Conscription therefore was totally unnecessary. The message was heard more in Quebec than in Canada; indeed the airwaves of the CBC were denied to the League. Instead it counted on the nationalist network of organizations, discreet clergy, and key individuals to convince Quebecois that the excessively wordy plebiscite was really a simple question of YES or NO for conscription. Old people like Henri Bourassa said so; youngsters like Jean Drapeau and André Laurendeau said so; *Le Devoir* said so. *Abbé* Groulx wrote manifestoes behind the scenes; young people in the streets sang *"A bas la conscription"* (Down with conscription) to the tune of God Save the King. Maurice Duplessis announced he would vote NO; Cardinal Villeneuve carefully avoided any pronouncement and premier Godbout sat unhappily on the fence.

They all foresaw the results better than Mackenzie King. The prime minister had actually expected a YES vote from Quebec; after all, he had said that the vote did not mean conscription. Instead he had to watch moodily as a great roar of NO swept over Quebec on April 27. It was loudest in the purely French-speaking areas of the province—as high as ninety-seven percent—and a clear French-English division occurred in the mixed French and English districts. All of Quebec voted seventy-one percent NO and the rest of Canada eighty percent YES. Quebec's vote was all the more startling given the massive wartime propaganda and censorship directed from Ottawa. King pondered Lord Durham's one hundred year old description of Canada as two nations warring in the bosom of a single state. Jubilant Quebecois nonetheless wondered what was next.

King's answer was a tiny amendment to the National Resources Mobilization Act. His ministers and the public were pressing him from all sides: one could not simply hold a referendum and then do nothing. The majority YES vote in the country was surely an indication of the acceptability of conscription. But the majority NO vote in Quebec was an equal indication of the hostility to conscription. Almost no one accepted King's ruse that this was not a question of conscription at all. But still he persisted. Bill 80, introduced into the House of Commons early in May 1942, merely removed the brief clause of the Mobilization Act of 1940 which prohibited the sending of the NRMA soldiers overseas. Nevertheless, proclaimed King, there would be no sending of anyone anywhere: if and when an occasion should arise, parliament would decide, later. For all the weaselling, perhaps even because of it, King lost one minister on the grounds that conscription was now a reality and almost lost another because conscription seemed not to be a reality. Public works minister Arthur Cardin resigned because Bill 80 seemed to undermine all the assurances he had given his compatriots when urging a YES vote in the plebiscite. Meanwhile defence minister James Ralston threatened to resign because he felt Bill 80 blocked rather than facilitated an ultimate imposition of conscription. He actually sent a letter of resignation to King who hung on to Ralston by promising cabinet rather than parliamentary action should the enactment of conscription ever become necessary. But King also pocketed the letter; it might become useful. For the moment Ralston's presence was more important even though Cardin's absence might conceivably provoke a political realignment among Quebec Liberals and nationalists.

By the summer of 1942 such a realignment was a distinct possibility. Most French Canadian members of parliament had voted against Bill 80. But were they unhappy enough to leave the Liberal party? If so, Maxime Raymond, planning a means to consolidate the NO vote from the plebiscite, would welcome them. With Cardin and his many supporters, Raymond might succeed in enlarging the League for the Defence of Canada into a new political party. Raymond never did win over Cardin but he did manage to tie together into the *Bloc populaire* an odd combination of disenchanted federal MPs, unhappy provincial Liberals, new born nationalists of the anti-conscription campaign, and one-time *Action libérale nationale* people, still smarting from Duplessis' rejection in 1936. As in the case of the *Union nationale*, the name again was revealing. Behind the *Bloc* was a nationalist and a populist dream. French Canadians should form a solid block of opposition to English Canada's centralizing and dominating tendencies in Ottawa. At the same time they should insist upon legislation for the people of

Quebec: labour laws, family allowances, slum clearance, nationalization of electricity, gas, and telephones. In the early 1940s the
dream was not at all fanciful and despite endless wrangling over
personnel, policy, and strategy among the *Bloc* leadership, it
succeeded in marking the political map, if only temporarily. In
1943 a *Bloc* candidate won one federal by-election in the Eastern
Townships and came second to a communist winner in another in
Montreal's working class district. In the provincial election of 1944
the *Bloc* took fifteen percent of the popular vote (André Laurendeau
was among four winners of seats) and may even have given the
election to Duplessis by doing so. On the other hand the two federal seats it won in 1945 did nothing to dent the Liberal domination of Ottawa.

By then of course Mackenzie King could say that the domination
was justified. He could point to multiple occasions when he had
held out against conscription. No Conservative would have done
so well, he intimated. Even though he did give in, under tremendous pressure and only at the last minute in the fall of 1944, he
had agreed to only a limited form of conscription. And at that
point there was indeed some question of military necessity. Defence minister Ralston had seen first hand the state of Canadian
troops, then in the front lines of northern France. They needed to
be reinforced, and quickly. Now, claimed Ralston, was the time for
conscription; the government must impose it or he would resign.
The Conservatives agreed, and gave their press a free hand to make
comments such as that of the *Globe*: "The government is wickedly
sacrificing young men's lives to retain its governing power in Quebec." Many people wondered why the required fifteen thousand reinforcements could not be found among the two hundred thousand
general service soldiers available in Canada or Britain. Was it so
imperative that they come from the NRMA soldiers? Even so, King
resisted. He surprised his cabinet by accepting Ralston's two year
old letter of resignation and replaced him with a retired army general who would continue to seek volunteers. General McNaughton
received more rotten eggs than candidates for overseas duty and
he gave up the effort after three weeks. King however needed even
more persuasion before imposing conscription. The senior army
officers, McNaughton informed the prime minister, were about to
revolt. That was more serious than any cabinet crisis and King
carefully told only one person of the supposed plot. Louis St.
Laurent would be the key figure in persuading Quebec that King
had done his best. And so, by order in council, late in November
1944, the federal government ordered sixteen thousand of the home
defence soldiers to prepare for duty overseas. Anyone could see it
was not total conscription. With a bit of imagination and by ig-
noring the four thousand soldiers, half of them from Quebec, who
disappeared when they heard the announcement, one might even
think it was not conscription at all.

But perhaps the die was already cast in Quebec. When the

provincial Liberals had lost that summer to Duplessis and the
Union nationale, federal Liberals had stepped gingerly around
that election. Godbout had not been keen to have them at all and
they may have thought of throwing him to the wolves and thereby
saving their own skins for the federal election due in 1945 at the
latest. Whether deliberately or not, they succeeded in both.
Mackenzie King may even have arranged the release of Camillien
Houde the week after the *Union nationale* victory in August 1944
as another occasion for the crowds to let off steam. By November
he could only count on the Liberal press in Quebec to reiterate
his contention that the limited Liberal conscription was preferable
to what the Conservatives would have imposed. Even the independent *Le Devoir*, appalled by the political ploys, had to admit a
grudging admiration for King who somehow slid successfully, if
not always elegantly, among Conservatives, militarists, nationalists,
the English Canadian press, and his own Liberal conscriptionists.
Nonetheless, Louis St. Laurent thought the federal Liberals would
lose all their seats in the province. The few Quebec MPs who
supported the vote of confidence, in effect sanctioning the conscription decision, claimed they would not dare show their faces
in their ridings for fear of being stoned. But six months later the
Quebec electorate gave the federal Liberals eighty-one percent of
the popular vote. And it went on doing so, in spite of the gloomy
prediction of an English Canadian MP from Quebec, C.G. Power.
One of the self-styled barriers against conscription back in 1939,
Power resigned from the cabinet to protest its imposition in
November 1944 and predicted that although English Canada would
forget, French Canada would not.

In any case, Ottawa had not yet had its final word in the direction of Canada's war effort. The economy had felt the federal hand
and now the military as well. Politics was always a bit more hazardous but allowing for the occasional provincial aberration—
Union nationale in Quebec and CCF in Saskatchewan—even that
might be manageable. Especially if the left-wing ideas of social
security, increasingly so popular, were incorporated into a vast
plan for postwar reconstruction. By the mid-war years civil servants in Ottawa and Liberal politicians in the House of Commons
were drafting proposals for a federally devised and directed good
life for Canadians after the war. Supplementing the earlier established unemployment insurance program would be health insurance, universal old age pensions, family allowances, housing, and
job training. Was it not the federal government's responsibility to
prevent a postwar depression, to retool industry for peacetime production, to find jobs for former soldiers and for the employees of
war industries? Used to planning for war, Ottawa now intended to
plan for peace.

For financial and cultural reasons Quebec objected. Ottawa's
plans would mean financial centralization. If Godbout had been
willing to hand over major tax sources to the federal government

for wartime purposes in 1942, Duplessis was not going to do so for peacetime purposes in 1946. Indeed, neither Ontario nor Quebec would agree to Ottawa's plans for a continuation of the wartime tax rental arrangement. Moreover, for Quebec, the social planning was being undertaken by a vastly expanded civil service in Ottawa which employed few French Canadians. The very best of plans therefore would be "foreign" in conception and execution. Not that planning itself was the problem, although the electorate never really sanctioned it in Quebec until the 1960s. The *Bloc populaire*, the co-operative and the labour movement, the old *Action libérale nationale*, and on occasion the *Action française* and the old *Ligue nationaliste* from the turn of the century had all hinted that economic and national conditions in Quebec would be improved if the government did some serious organizing and planning. But those groups had the provincial government in mind and they never succeeded in convincing it or the electorate. What they did manage to do was to persuade many people that the federal government was somehow foreign and perhaps even inimical to the best interests of Quebec.

Family allowances provide the best illustration of the fears and even the ambiguities that such a position entailed. The federal government announced the plan for 1945 as a means of maintaining postwar purchasing power and thus avoiding an expected recession. Less publicly did it hope that the allowances would induce women to leave the paid labour force. Nationalists in Quebec could hardly say no to either purpose. And yet to them, the measure appeared to be treading on the constitutional toes of the provinces. Duplessis denounced it as such, but he did not challenge it in the courts since the popular appeal of family allowances was undeniable. But for all their popularity, some people also saw them as an affront to paternal responsibilities. The state was insulting the father by suggesting he could not provide for his children and undermining his authority by paying the cheques to the mother. The federal government was thus destroying the French Canadian family. So vociferous was the complaint that Mackenzie King wavered and was prepared to have the allowances for Quebec residents paid to the father. Only the personal intervention of Thérèse Casgrain, using all her political and social prestige, convinced him otherwise. And through it all, Conservative opponents of family allowances in the rest of Canada flung abuse at Quebec by stating that the money was just a Liberal scheme to buy the votes of the notoriously huge French Canadian families. Some nationalists in Quebec thought so too and thus found the plan degrading. True family allowances should be attached to salaries in industry and not come as handouts from the state. Moreover Quebec should be devising its own social legislation in conformity with its own ideals. Nationalist economist and writer François-Albert Angers suggested that Quebecois not accept the cheques. He was one of the few to take his own advice.

The uneasiness over family allowances was a reflection of the changes the war had wrought in Quebec. By 1945 there was not much left of the nationalists' traditional defences of French Canada. Agriculture and colonization spewed their surplus population into war industries. Families sent their young women and sometimes their mothers in the same direction. Young men went off to a foreign war, sometimes willingly, sometimes pressured by economic circumstances or political propaganda. And the church, or at least its highest authorities, encouraged them to do so. So too did the state as provincial and federal Liberal politicians from Quebec more or less quietly acquiesced in Ottawa's war. But 1944 marked a change. Since then the political party in power in Quebec has almost consistently differed from that in Ottawa; before then it had almost as consistently been the same. Just what that difference would mean, what other kind of defences might be constructed, who would contribute to and profit from them were still open questions. Throughout the 1950s the debate would rage and by the 1960s Mackenzie King's wartime fears for Canadian unity seemed almost imaginary.

SELECT BIBLIOGRAPHY

Auger, Geneviève, and Raymonde Lamothe. *De la poêle à frire à la ligne de feu. La vie quotidienne des québécoises pendant la guerre '39–'45.* Montreal: Boréal Express, 1981.

Black, Conrad. *Duplessis.* Toronto: McClelland and Stewart, 1976.

Chaloult, René. *Mémoires politiques.* Montreal: Editions du Jour, 1969.

Dawson, Robert MacGregor. *The Conscription Crisis of 1944.* Toronto: University of Toronto Press, 1961.

Dumas, Evelyn. *Dans le sommeil de nos os: quelques grèves au Québec de 1934 à 1944.* Montreal: Leméac, 1971.

Granatstein, J.L. *Conscription in the Second World War 1939–1945.* Toronto: Ryerson Press, 1969.

Granatstein, J.L. *Canada's War. The Politics of the Mackenzie King Government 1939–1945.* Toronto: Oxford University Press, 1975.

Granatstein, J.L., and J.M. Hitsman. *Broken Promises: A History of Conscription in Canada.* Toronto: Oxford University Press, 1977.

Jamieson, Stuart Marshall. *Times of Trouble: Labour Unrest and Industrial Conflict in Canada 1900–66.* Ottawa: Task Force on Labour Relations, 1968.

Lapalme, Georges-Emile. *Le bruit des choses réveillées.* Montreal: Leméac, 1969.

Laurendeau, André. *La crise de la conscription 1942.* Montreal: Editions du Jour, 1962.

Pickersgill, John W. *The MacKenzie King Record.* vols. 1, 2. Toronto: University of Toronto Press, 1960 and 1968.

Quinn, Herbert F. *Union Nationale: A Study of Quebec Nationalism.* Toronto: University of Toronto Press, 1963.

Thomson, Dale C. *Louis St.-Laurent: Canadian.* Toronto: Macmillan, 1967.

". . . the flag proclaimed in 1948 what nationalists had been saying for years . . ."
Union Nationale youth marching in favour of the fleur-de-lis, Montreal, 1948.

17 Rally Round the Flag

In 1948 the government of Quebec adopted the fleur-de-lis flag as the province's distinctive banner. At the very time when Quebec was partaking of North America's postwar economic development, it unfurled its own flag. While everything in the economy emphasized North American integration, the flag emphasized Quebec's difference. Old time nationalists were ecstatic. They had been demanding just such a symbol for years. Newcomers to the nationalist fervour of the war years were just as delighted. They had all applauded the motion of an independent member of the assembly who had first raised the subject in 1946. And they had orchestrated a vast publicity campaign to convince a divided legislature and an even more dubious premier of the popular support for a distinctive flag. Maurice Duplessis, for all his interest in provincial autonomy, had hesitated over the specificity of the flag and the symbolism of its raising. Once adopted, however, the flag and its meaning became part of his political arsenal for the rest of his life. Its symbolism was to colour the constitutional studies of the Tremblay commission in the mid-1950s and denote the close collaboration of much of the Catholic church throughout the postwar period.

Flags had been part of Quebec reality since the days of New France. A white cross, a royal fleur-de-lis, the standards of aristocratic families, and the colours of different regiments of French soldiers had consecutively and sometimes concurrently marked the French presence in North America. With the Conquest, the various French flags disappeared, but different groups of French Canadians kept adopting or designing ones of their own. The *patriotes* paraded bands of green, white, and red in the 1830s; the *Institut canadien* waved the French revolutionary tricolour in the 1840s. In the late nineteenth century, religious processions were resplendent with banners, pennants, and streamers. So forceful indeed was the religious influence that in 1903 a sacred heart was added to the centre of a long-lost fleur-de-lis flag purportedly to have graced the French defence of Carillon in 1758. The *Carillon-Sacré-Coeur* was then bandied about by various nationalist groups. With the removal of the heart and the straightening of the fleurs-de-lis, accompanied by some parliamentary footwork by Maurice Duplessis, it became the official flag of Quebec in 1948.

The contemporary symbolism rather than the historical origin of the flag meant more in mid-twentieth century Quebec. One could of course read specific historical lessons into the cross and stylized lilies of the pendant: religion and France had formed Quebec and by implication should go on doing so. One could even deduce qualities of purity and grace from the stark white on sky blue. But for all its crispness of colour and design, the flag in fact fluttered over a hazy realm of emotions and sentiment. It assumed a unity among the inhabitants of Quebec, some common denominator of attachment to land or language, to family or fortune, to tradition or temerity. Rarely was that unity articulated, much less acted upon. It hovered in the unconscious and the unspoken and may have taken as many as four million different forms in 1950. Yet the very planting of the flag bolstered convictions. A flag delimits a territory and hints at the will, if not the power, to protect it. Beyond that territory lies something else, perhaps not alien but decidedly different. In many ways therefore the flag proclaimed in 1948 what nationalists had been saying for years, but what politicians would not utter until the 1970s: Quebec was a separate place, a community, a homeland, distinct from the rest of North America.

Unfortunately for the hoisters of flags, very little in Quebec's postwar economy confirmed their beliefs. On the contrary, almost every indicator of economic activity, development, or well-being suggested that Quebec was very similar indeed to the rest of North America. Factory workers, union members, and housewives had in

effect been saying that for years, but few people listened to them;
now they took advantage of the glimmer of prosperity promised
by the war years and the economic boom of the 1950s to emphasize their point. They struck for higher wages and they spent more
of those wages on consumer goods. They produced more children,
moved to suburbia, and entertained themselves and their kids in
American cars, at American sports, and by means of American radio
and television. Scarcely one-quarter of their compatriots lived in
rural areas and fewer still actually earned their living from agriculture. Mechanization and electrification pushed the surplus population off the remaining farms and most of the migrants headed
for Montreal where the population doubled to two million in the
twenty year period 1941 to 1961. Even the old agricultural stand-by
of seasonal labour in the lumber camps disappeared as mechani-
cal saws and logging roads transformed the once isolated, labour
intensive, and temporary nature of the wood trade. In such a setting, colonization died a natural death. Its mourners had always
been safely ensconced in cities in any case.

In those cities were all the other signs of industrial development.
The wartime heavy industries of iron and steel, transportation
equipment, aircraft manufacture, petroleum, and aluminum production led the way in the unexpectedly smooth transition to a
peacetime economy and continued to dominate the industrial scene
of the 1950s. An expanding construction industry serviced them,
built new plants for the older textile, leather, and pulp and paper
industries, and also catered to a huge consumer market for housing. In terms of numbers of workers, construction was in fact the
largest single industry, employing some one hundred and fifty
thousand people in 1957. Although forty percent of them were
working in Montreal, others built the company towns for new
mining, hydro-electric development, pulp and paper, and aluminum
production in a band across Quebec's northland from Abitibi in
the west to Ungava on the east. Chibougamau, Baie Comeau, Sept-
Iles, Schefferville way to the north, and even Murdochville in the
Gaspé all sprang to life in the postwar period, charmed into existence by American capital and new-found or newly exploitable natural resources. Some of the resources supplied local industry, but
most were extracted for processing in the American mid-west. Indeed, it was the iron ore of Ungava, so much in demand by the
steel plants of the United States, that finally encouraged the Canadian and American governments to complete the much talked of
St. Lawrence seaway by the late 1950s. The politicians spoke of
international co-operation; American investors knew they were
dealing in integration. So did almost everyone else.

The integration, however, did have some peculiarities in Quebec.
If American investment there was massive, it was even more so
in the rest of Canada. When American companies decided on subsidiaries north of the border they looked first to Ontario before
considering Quebec, so much so that some Canadian companies

followed suit, their exodus from Quebec in the mid-1950s camouflaged by the exceptional development in other sectors. The disparity nonetheless appeared in lower salaries, lower productivity,
and higher unemployment in Quebec than in Ontario. Again the
overall prosperity cushioned the impact. The contrast with the dark
days of the 1930s was sufficient to silence many objectors, but
still the difference was known and pondered. Was it a result of
psychological characteristics peculiar to Quebecois? Or was it the
outcome of a different demographic and industrial structure? With
a higher birth rate, Quebec had proportionately more young people and thus fewer workers, male and female, in the labour force.
Quebec also had more workers than Ontario in the traditionally
low-paying industries of textiles, tobacco, and shoes. And what of
the continuing lack of a French Canadian presence in the upper
echelons of most Quebec industry? No one knew for sure what
caused the disparity and no one seems to have asked the question
of whether the disparity was in fact real in terms of cost and standard of living in the two provinces. Certainly no one knew how to
overcome it or whether a solution might not lead to still further
integration. Behind that worry lay a philosophical debate that
rankled throughout the 1950s: whether difference entailed dispar-
agement or distinction. Flag wavers of course thought the latter.

In Maurice Duplessis they had a political ally. Or so it seemed.
Duplessis spotted so many dangers all around and spent so much
energy posing as the protector of French Canadians that he must
surely have thought there was something worth protecting. Actually his nationalism was very poorly developed; his political an-
tennae, on the other hand, were very finely tuned. He did wave the
Quebec flag in front of Ottawa politicians as a reminder that they
had not yet devised a similarly distinctive sign for Canada. But at
the same time he was not anxious to break the tie to Britain if it
meant, as it did in 1949 for example, that the federally appointed
Canadian Supreme Court was to become the final court of appeal
and the ultimate interpreter of the Canadian constitution. He taunted
his political enemies with communism, but while doing so he resembled more the American hangers-on of United States senator
Joseph McCarthy than he did conservative Quebecois. He flaunted
his attachment to all things French Canadian and then slipped
happily into the crowds at Yankee Stadium in New York to enjoy
his only non-political passion, American baseball. He painted
glowing pictures of a rural Quebec as the basis for social stability
and economic progress but spent hours on the telephone or in his
Chateau Frontenac suite charming American and English Canadian
businessmen into multiplying their industrial investments in the
province. He claimed to champion the workers and then sent the
provincial police to ensure the docility he had promised the foreign investors. Since the ambiguities actually reflected much of
Quebec society, they alone may explain his four election victories
from 1944 to 1959.

If Duplessis' activities suggested a shrewd awareness of the integration of Quebec into North America, they also reflected values associated with a distinctive Quebec. Old time nationalists had long tried to ignore the fact that Quebec was in America; they had convinced themselves by reference to language, religion, and superior habits of mind and behaviour. Duplessis was a product of such beliefs and he may have harboured them himself although he did not always display them. His political opponents frequently sneered at the vulgarity of his language and the ostentation of his religion; they may even have wondered about his celibate status. But Duplessis did reveal the conservatism of a society with strong rural and religious roots. He acknowledged the power and hierarchical structure of the Catholic church as both necessary and proper social values. He duplicated priestly paternalism and stood no affront to his own prestige as secular leader. He bound people to him with what were basically ecclesiastical and familial ties: personal largesse, immense good humour spiced with the occasional fit of pique, vast storing and selective sharing of intimate knowledge about individuals, marks of favour, emotional blackmail, and a dose of fear. He was the *chef* among his colleagues and the father among his people. If only slightly over fifty percent of the electorate accepted the beliefs or the tactics sufficiently to vote *Union nationale*, they nonetheless gave him the opportunity to revel in his role with a huge number of seats (varying in the 1950s from sixty-eight to eighty-two) in the ninety-two seat provincial assembly.

Duplessis used that majority to perfect a political idea that was at least seventy years old in Quebec: provincial autonomy. Although this notion was not peculiar to Quebec, its popular appeal definitely was. Liberal leader Georges-Emile Lapalme, struggling against impossible odds, groaned as he realized the depth of public sentiment Duplessis had sounded with it. Provincial autonomy meant many things to many people and Duplessis' opponents frequently claimed that his version meant next to nothing. But behind the slogan and the echoing of its presumed hollowness was the shape of a Quebec different in language, culture, and values from the rest of Canada, a Quebec uneasy about the power and the intentions of an English Canadian majority seated so comfortably in what Lapalme referred to as the Anglican cathedral on Parliament Hill. Although the Quebec electorate returned most of its federal seats to the party in power, it just as consistently accused members of parliament of being the handmaidens of Ottawa. Either way Duplessis came out the winner.

There was in fact more to provincial autonomy than nationalist dreams or political name-calling. Money and power kept Duplessis, for one, constantly intrigued with it. Ottawa's wartime financial and political supremacy had both irritated him and provided him with the means of returning to the provincial premiership in 1944. Thereafter he consistently refused overtures from Ottawa. He would not agree to a continuation of the tax-rental scheme of the war years; he would not sell, rent, or loan the province's right to direct taxation in return for a paltry sum from a bureaucracy in Ottawa. He rejected federal plans for joint undertakings, suspecting that Ottawa's offers were both carrot and stick to force the provinces to do what the federal government wanted. And he opposed Ottawa's initiatives in areas that were quite clearly of provincial jurisdiction. There would be no federal monies paving Quebec roads even if the particular road was intended as a trans-Canada highway. There would be no Ottawa dollars dangled over the heads of provincial universities on the grounds that graduates were a national asset. There would be no federal financing of health insurance in the name of pan-Canadian standards of health care. Much of Ottawa's financial supremacy, Duplessis argued, stemmed from the federal government's picking provincial pockets; it should not then use its ill-gotten gains to trod on provincial toes.

The difficulty with saying no, however, was that it cost money. Like the other provinces Quebec had spiralling costs for roads, education, and health services. Unlike the others it had a major social institution, the Catholic church, shouldering much of the financial burden of education, hospital care, and social assistance. In many ways, therefore, thanks to the Catholic church, Quebec could afford provincial autonomy. But for all its appearance, the church was by no means self-sufficient and the costs kept mounting. The universities in particular saw their counterparts in other provinces grow fat on federal cash. Quebec did accord them a special grant but even that annoyed Duplessis since the increased expenditures were a reaction to Ottawa's initiatives. In 1954 Duplessis gambled on a solution to the dilemma by instituting a provincial income tax. His Liberal opponents thought they had an easy target: surely no Quebec voter would accept double taxation and willingly pay an income tax to Ottawa and to Quebec. Moreover they were assured by their colleagues in Ottawa that the federal government would not alter its income tax as a consequence of a Quebec one. Duplessis could sink or swim. As they all should have known, Duplessis was a strong political swimmer. Within a year of the creation of the provincial income tax, he was able to negotiate an arrangement with Ottawa by which the federal income tax for residents of Quebec was reduced. The provincial Liberals retired to their corner, cowering, recognizing that Duplessis had won a major, and this time tangible, battle for provincial autonomy.

Some of Duplessis' other battles entailed considerably more shadow boxing. He presumed to place Canada in the very centre of the Cold War with Quebec as the bastion against communist hordes. He accused any political opponent of communist sympathies and smeared *Le Devoir*, after the paper turned against him in the early 1950s, as a bolshevist rag. He even found the Quebec Liberals guilty by association: their Ottawa colleagues voted monies for the farmers in southeast Asia—all communists surely—but would offer none to the farmers of Quebec. He pounced on "communist" eggs on the Quebec market and thereby denounced certain illegal Canadian trade practices. He actually had some people believing that saboteurs had caused the collapse of the Duplessis bridge in Trois-Rivières one bitterly cold night in January 1951. He guarded the Polish art treasures, which had been transferred to Canada for safekeeping during the war and housed in Quebec convents and then the provincial museum, from precipitous return by Ottawa to the now communist regime in Poland. At a time when there was no more than a handful of communists in the entire province of Quebec—and most of them changed their minds after the Russian invasion of Hungary in 1956—Duplessis postured as the protector of Quebec against communism, materialism, atheism, and class warfare.

He maintained that posture quite effectively in some very real battles against organized labour in Quebec. By playing on the notion of Quebec as a family, Duplessis could allow a squabble or two but no open confrontation of generations, siblings, or sexes. Indeed, any questioning of the ordered hierarchy of family, society, and the state must necessarily be the work of foreign agitators. Duplessis actually located a communist or two in 1946 organizing strikes of textile workers in Valleyfield and miners in Noranda. He intended to stamp them out and he expected the law and the agents of law enforcement to assist him. Only thus could the social stability necessary to attract the investment that created jobs and improved living conditions for the working people of Quebec be ensured. Duplessis expected gratitude and in large measure he received it. But for the minority of unionized workers and sometimes only for the tinier minority of union leaders, doubts began to grow. Duplessis' much vaunted social stability appeared to be synonymous with their exploitation.

Few of the major strikes of the postwar period were open declarations of class warfare. Most entailed the usual elements of working class unhappiness: low salaries, long hours, miserable working conditions, and the lack of union recognition. Whether the strikes were in Quebec's traditional industries such as textiles at Louiseville in 1952, in more modern ones like mining at Asbestos and Thetford Mines in 1949, at Noranda in 1953, and at Murdochville in 1957, or even in retail clerking at Dupuis Frères department store in Montreal in 1952 and whether the unions involved were Catholic or international, they all displayed the same workers' desire for income and job security. The asbestos strike initiated a complaint much more current in the 1970s, that of pollution. The high level of asbestos dust was causing so many fatal diseases that the local union leader claimed the cemetery itself could be mined for the mineral. Each of the strikes was uncommonly long, reflecting a postwar pattern of fewer but longer work stoppages than during the strike-ridden years of the Second World War. The length, varying from three months at Dupuis Frères to eleven months at Louiseville, revealed, if not class conflict, the determination of both workers and owners. And yet only one of the strikes was a clear victory for the workers —that involving the retail clerks, mostly women, at Dupuis Frères. The others resulted in a draw or an outright loss.

The major reason was Duplessis himself. Both his laws and his behaviour created a climate of uneasiness for unions. Labour laws hemmed them in, checked their expansion, their activities, and even the moral qualities of their leaders. Procedures were lengthy and cumbersome, both for the certification of unions and for the conciliation and arbitration that were necessary before a strike could be legally declared; many workers were convinced that the procedures were biassed in favour of companies. When unhappy workers, despairing of the legal process, simply ignored it and commenced a strike, they were easy prey for Duplessis' kept press. An illegal strike was illegal. The provincial police were then justified in intervening—which they did; in fact they appeared outside Associated Textiles in Louiseville and Dupuis Frères in Montreal although even by Duplessis' rigid interpretation of his own laws those strikes were legal. In every instance the police made their sympathies clear. They protected the property of the company. They escorted strikebreakers in and out of mine, plant, or store. They hassled strikers on the picket lines, union organizers at strike headquarters, and workers' families in their homes. Their presence probably heightened the potential class conflict Duplessis so wished to avoid; it certainly emphasized the class collaboration between government and employers. Duplessis may have won his point and most of the strikes, but he also planted and nurtured the seeds of political opposition.

While Duplessis lived, however, he managed to keep that opposition carefully curtailed. The electoral map itself helped since it favoured the rural counties at the expense of the much more populous urban ridings. Thus a rural population dwindling through the 1950s from thirty-three to twenty-five percent of the total elected more than half of the seats in the provincial assembly. The single ballot, simple majority voting system also gave an enormous advantage to a party that just slipped by with fifty percent of the popular vote. Duplessis of course did not change either the electoral map or the voting system. He simply tinkered with the voters. Roads, schools, hospitals, and hydro lines graced the countryside of sympathetic counties, their appearance and their extent timed to the electoral calendar. The task of most cabinet ministers was to spread provincial funds in the most electorally profitable way. The *Union nationale* also had a distinct, and immense, campaign chest, filled by everyone who had benefited or hoped to benefit from a government contract, a leasing of territory, or an easing of taxation. Duplessis' campaign organizers dipped into the chest for three million, five million, then nine million dollars to cover the incidental expenses of the elections of 1948, 1952, and 1956. Even then the chest kept expanding; at the time of Duplessis' death in

1959 it contained some eighteen million dollars. In contrast, the
Liberals could barely scrape up a million in 1952. *Union nationale*
funds paid for the Americanization of Quebec electoral practices:
massive radio and newspaper advertising, tracts and posters, popular
amusements free of charge, showers of small gifts from lighters
and ash trays to nylon stockings. The funds paid bills for indigent
voters, furnished houses with consumer goods from radios and
refrigerators to the Trojan horse of television. Through it all
Duplessis could blithely argue that the real electoral battle was
that of Quebec struggling to maintain its rights, its freedom, and
its prerogatives.

What exactly that was supposed to mean Duplessis left to certain intellectuals to fathom. In 1953 he appointed the Tremblay
Commission to enquire into Quebec's constitutional position. The
initiative was not his; indeed anything so precise was not characteristic of Duplessis. Rather it came from a number of Chambers
of Commerce across the province whose members had been questioning the distribution of revenues within the province. Some of
them complained that the federal, provincial, municipal, and school
commission slicing of the tax pie made for incoherent administration and insufficient funding for key areas such as education. But
the Tremblay Commission took the criticism and effectively buried
it in a massive document detailing the philosophical, sociological,
even theological reasons for Quebec's distinctiveness and thus for
Duplessis' cherished provincial autonomy. Over every page of the
five books of the Commission's report in 1956 wafted the fleur-de-
lis flag.

Like other flag wavers, the Tremblay Commission apprehended
threats to French Canada on all sides. The pace of industrialization raised the fear of final assimilation. The more French Canadians lived in urban settings with factory jobs and ready cash for
the consumer goods of America's mass production, the more they
were likely to speak, think, and behave like Americans. Unhappily
acknowledging a process that had been going on since the Conquest when French Canadians were confronted with foreign political institutions, the Tremblay Commission declared the 1950s to
be the culmination of the threat of industrialization. Menaced as
it was with foreign social institutions, French Canada's survival
was a now or never proposition.

Adding to the threat of assimilation by industrialization, the
Commission emphasized, was the threat of centralization. Ottawa
had been slowly eating away at Quebec's constitutional rights since
at least 1917 with the introduction of the income tax. The Depression of the 1930s permitted even more federal interference. Even
though very little had resulted from the Rowell-Sirois Commission
in the late 1930s, its very enquiry and report indicated federal
designs for national norms at provincial expense. Then the Second
World War added military and social justification for those designs
now being pursued by Ottawa in the 1950s. The English-speaking

provinces might be prepared to accept such centralization; the Tremblay Report would not allow Quebec to do so. As the only province with a French-speaking majority, Quebec had to stand firm in the face of external threats. It could only do so by drawing on its vast reservoir of distinctiveness. History, religion, language, traditions, culture, and patterns of social behaviour all characterized French Canadians and differentiated them from others in North America. They could no more conform to the "foreign standards" of social services proposed by Ottawa than they could deny their religion. Moreover, that religion had given them a mission in North America: theirs was the cultural gift to alleviate the burden of materialism borne by the rest of the continent. French Canadians had a civilizing role to fulfil and they could not cast it off to cater to mediocrity. Thus like many nationalist intellectuals before them, from Bishop Laflèche in the nineteenth century to *abbé* Groulx in the twentieth , the members of the Tremblay Commission covered up their uneasiness with a heightened sense of disdain for their surroundings.

What they proposed in much more precise terms than any of their predecessors was a constitutional confirmation of the differences. Significantly, the proposal was a return to the past, the past of true federalism in 1867. Confederation, according to the Tremblay Report, had been an agreement between provinces and a pact between peoples. Both the division of power—economic to the federal government and socio-cultural to the provinces—and the financial resources had been well defined. Now it was time to return to that definition, make the necessary adjustments, and ensure that the provinces controlled and administered social welfare and cultural development and had sufficient funds to do so. To the provinces therefore should go income and corporation taxes and succession duties; to Ottawa, excise, sales, gasoline, and tobacco taxes. Such a division of powers and resources would permit Quebec at least to cope with the admittedly serious problems concerning education, rural life, and social welfare, in ways unique to Quebec. In short, federalism should sustain rather than undermine the genuine differences between provinces and peoples.

Like the federal government's examination of constitutional questions in the late 1930s, nothing very specific came of the Quebec government's investigation in the 1950s. And yet both the Rowell-Sirios Report in 1940 and the Tremblay Report in 1956 rather uncannily indicated the nature of future federal-provincial relations. The federal commission hinted at increased direction by Ottawa; the provincial commission registered increased provincial resistance. Duplessis may have found both distasteful since he shelved the Tremblay Report, without even reading it some say, as easily as he had dismissed the Rowell-Sirois investigation. The provincial Liberals, on the other hand, began studying the report. By 1960 they had transformed its conservative philosophy into progressive plans for financial negotiations with Ottawa. Some of the Tremblay Commission staff even found their way into the upper echelons of the civil service after the Liberal victory in 1960, guided perhaps by one of the implications of the Tremblay Report. If it were so that the threats to French Canada were of an economic, social, and especially political nature, then perhaps only a political entity could provide the necessary protection. The boundaries of French Canadian defences were thus increasingly assimilable by those of Quebec. According to the Tremblay Commission, French Canadians constituted a distinctive people and only Quebec appeared to have the potential political power to protect them.

Before the Quebec government could take on that role, it had to remove from centre stage another social institution with the same pretension. The Catholic church had always claimed to protect and differentiate French Canada. No other group in North America could claim the divine assurance and the institutional presence that the Catholic church brought to French Canadians. Since the Conquest that church had allied itself carefully if not always comfortably with the political power in the land. At the same time it had provided spiritual solace and secular assistance to the people. Its very presence as much as its power in schools, colleges, and universities, in unions and youth groups, among the poor, the old, and the orphaned gave the distinguishing mark to French Canada. Indeed, only someone's sense of heraldry and perhaps the church's own sense of propriety had removed the sacred heart from the centre of the proposed flag for Quebec. Not that it needed to be there. The cross of a church spire and the glint of a church roof were as characteristic of Quebec as any flag.

In the 1950s, however, the church found it increasingly difficult to be all things to all people. Its multiple activities demanded more personnel, yet potential recruits, particularly among the men, began seeking and finding secular careers of equal status and interest. As a result, lay people had to be invited in to staff expanding schools and social welfare agencies. They could hardly be asked to take on the religious and spiritual work of *curés* in parishes, but there too numbers began to tell. As an indication of the multiple and perhaps overextended roles of the clergy, fewer than half of Quebec's priests were resident *curés*; in contrast France had eighty percent of its priests in that category. Moreover, the religious personnel were unevenly distributed across the landscape with more of them than warranted by the population in rural areas. Even there the clergy ran into conflicting lines of power and communication: local bishops wanted the parish and the diocese to remain as bases for clerically inspired activities; youth groups, professional associations, and co-operatives, all with clerical contacts if not direction, envisaged instead provincial networks through colleges, unions, and businesses. The bishops themselves rarely presented a common front since their regional concerns varied so greatly one from another. And after the death of Cardinal Villeneuve in 1947, there was no one with his personal supremacy to unify them.

All the cracks in the clerical armour benefited Maurice Duplessis. After the disappearance of Villeneuve, Duplessis rarely gave the nod of deference to any individual, but he played favourites with all who came calling. And most of the bishops did. They needed funds for a school or a hospital, they solicited larger provincial grants for a college or a sanatorium. Each of the dependencies tightened Duplessis' hold. Usually he came through with the money, but often he kept the requester waiting, sometimes to the brink of bankruptcy for a given institution. He rarely assured the funds on a regular basis: each grant increased the gratitude; each announcement was an advertisement for the generosity of the government. Duplessis knew of course that the grants were infinitesimal compared to the costs of state-run education, health care, or welfare services. Vows of poverty kept salaries low for religious personnel and affected those of their lay colleagues; all that was to the government's advantage. Duplessis also knew that the church's fears of secularization were greater than any monetary concern. He could easily watch the budget with one eye and grace his clerical visitors with a gleam of piety in the other. That the rather unhealthy collaboration between church and state may have tarnished the church irrevocably was left for later generations to ponder.

To many Quebecois of the 1950s, however, that collaboration reinforced the notion of French Canada as a distinct community. Family, church, and state shared the same ideals and the same structure. Each practised co-operation and preached devotion within a hierarchical, even patriarchal, framework. Each exercised a division of labour within its ranks and among each other. Ostensibly based on merit and capacity, the division was as often based on sex and, in the higher levels of government at least, on ethnicity. Each division presupposed and at the same time reinforced common assumptions about the natural roles of individuals and institutions. The family reproduced the nation; within it the father exercised the authority of the breadwinner, the mother demonstrated the dexterity of the housekeeper. The church taught and healed the nation; within it bishops and priests furnished moral and spiritual direction while the nuns instructed the children, nursed the sick, and served the priests. The state administered the nation; within it male politicians determined priorities, with an English Canadian almost always looking after finances, and female secretaries took dictation. Linking all three was the direct and public behaviour of men and the diffuse and private behaviour of women. But the only really distinguishing feature was the presence of the church. The rest was a replica of the norms of North America, indeed of much of the western world.

Perhaps for that reason the school system was such an important instrument in clerical hands and recognized as such by most

French Canadians. It permitted the church to spread the religious and social message of French Canadian and Catholic community in North America. It also provided the church with an immense and presumably continuing place of social prestige and power. The state therefore collaborated with rather than dictated to the church in its direction of schools. Through the provincial secretary, a member of the cabinet, the government provided funds and administrative services for the schools of the province. Through the Catholic Committee of Public Instruction, on which all the bishops of the province sat, the church defined the subject matter, the programs, and the textbooks for all the Catholic schools of Quebec. A similar Protestant committee did the same for the English language and largely Protestant schools of the province. Although religious personnel formed less than half the public school teachers at the elementary and secondary level, their presence counted for more than their numbers because of their prestige. Moreover, most local school boards had the resident priest at least as a member if not as the chairman. Clerics also controlled the training of teachers, either as principals of the provincial normal schools or as teaching sisters in the special programs in convents. At the higher levels of the educational system, both in terms of scholastic attainment and of prestige, the clergy was omnipresent. Clerics formed ninety percent of the teaching staff in the forty-five private, fee-paying classical colleges for boys and young men. The figure was probably even higher for the nuns guiding the instruction in numerous convents and in the sixteen classical colleges for girls. The three French language universities—Laval, Montreal, and Sherbrooke (begun in 1955)—all had priests in the major administrative and teaching positions. Each was defined as a Catholic university and their programs and course content reflected that. Access to the university was almost solely from the classical colleges, although some science and engineering faculties did accept the relatively few students who requested entrance from the last year of the public secondary schools. No one in Quebec could acquire an education, no matter how limited, without encountering a priest, a nun, or a teaching brother.

The criticism that such a system began to evoke in the 1950s was directed more to administrative and academic incoherence than to clerical direction. There were so many different kinds of schools, each with different requirements; there was so little connection between them and the specialized technical, craft, or occupational schools operated directly by the state. And as the number of schoolchildren rose, thanks to the compulsory education law of 1943 and the prosperity of the 1950s, so too did the need for schools, teachers, books, and facilities. But even with the expansion, fewer youngsters in Quebec than in Ontario actually completed any secondary education. The privileged went to prestigious classical colleges after elementary school; the state recognized the prestige and added to the favouritism by providing annual grants, for the boys' colleges alone. The graduates rarely encountered those from public secondary schools since the few from either source who went on to university were strictly segregated by faculty. Small wonder, claimed the critics, that law, medicine, and the priesthood continued to be the prestigious occupations when what was required in a highly industrialized milieu were engineers, scientists, and businessmen. To acquire them the school system would have to place far more emphasis on science, technology, and commerce. Even the Tremblay Commission, with its philosophical penchant for all things peculiarly Quebecois, stated that education was the major problem confronting Quebec in the 1950s.

One peculiarity did stand out in the debate over education although it was the institution and not the argument that was special to Quebec. The concern for matching educational training to a modern industrial economy was for boys alone. For girls industrialization was presented as a threat rather than a challenge. The great risk was that girls would be distracted from their future roles of wives and mothers. Their education must therefore be different. It had to prepare them for a pre-ordained role rather than expose them to new and varied opportunities. Beginning in the late 1930s, the church had upgraded many of the domestic science schools in the province into what came to be known in 1951 as Family Institutes. The postwar expansion of the schools—there were forty-four by the mid-1950s—was a response to the fears raised by the Depression and the war: when few jobs existed, men should have them; wartime employment should spare married women; postwar jobs should be reserved for men. By the 1950s there was clearly a sufficient number of jobs; there was also sufficient prosperity to permit most married women to stay out of the paid labour force. But to keep them happily at home, their domestic occupation had to be raised to the level of a profession.

The Family Institutes trained its students to be "professional wives." In a two to four year secondary program, the Institutes taught femininity and domesticity. The schools were private, fee-paying institutions, run by nuns, sustained by the benevolence of bishops and, much to the chagrin of the far fewer girls' classical colleges, accorded annual grants from the government. All the subjects, whether graced with scientific names or not, specified the girl's future role in the home. A bookkeeping lesson displayed a household budget; a chemistry class analyzed food; biology examined child development; psychology stressed the innate differences between men and women; history demonstrated the role of women in the maintenance of families and of religion and hence of civilization. But mostly the girls studied cooking, sewing, religion, and French with a sprinkling of etiquette, hygiene, crocheting, weaving, and music appreciation. They read specially prepared textbooks and they organized their classmates into simulated families. After graduation, the occasional student might pursue training as a nurse or teach domestic science in the elementary schools.

But all were equipped, and most only inclined, to spend their lives cheerily, neatly, competently, and submissively with a man to whom they looked for guidance and direction and for whom they would found families. Those families in turn would assure social stability to French Canada. Only with such professional wives would contemporary society be spared the plague of divorce and juvenile deliquency so evident in the United States. Specially trained women would ensure the survival of familial virtues and thus of the nation. Flag waving was to be a domestic affair.

Like Duplessis, the nationalist philosophers of the Tremblay Commission, or the alliance of church and state, the Family Institutes did not survive long past the 1950s. Unable to withstand the criticism of irrelevance and intellectual shallowness, the schools fell victim to the rush of rationalization of the early 1960s. By then Duplessis himself had died, the contradictions of his own stances pathetically evident in his demise at Schefferville, site of one of the major foreign investments in the province. For all his posture as a defender of French Canada, he may even have given nationalism and the church a bad name by appropriating much of their fervour to a political party that engaged in dubious electoral practices and that provided the only concrete manifestation of nationalism in a rather hollow, but electorally successful, notion of provincial autonomy. Certainly he alienated people both to the right and the left. In spite of the Tremblay Commission's assurances that separatism was not one of the options for Quebec, a tiny group on the nationalist right formed one of the early separatist associations, *L'Alliance laurentienne* in 1957 with the motto *Dieu, Famille, Patrie* (God, Family, Country). A larger group on the clerical and intellectual left questioned Duplessis' hostility to labour. In fact the dream of nation conjured up by the blue and white fleur-de-lis flag enveloped only part of French Canadian reality in the 1950s. Much of the rest was visible through and symbolized by another medium whose presence in Quebec households was often the result of Duplessis' electoral generosity: television.

SELECT BIBLIOGRAPHY

Archambault, Jacques, and Eugénie Lévesque. *Le drapeau québécois.* Quebec: Editeur officiel, 1974.

Black, Conrad. *Duplessis.* Toronto: McClelland and Stewart, 1976.

Brookwell, Sherene H. "The Instituts Familiaux of Quebec." Unpublished M.A. thesis, University of Ottawa, 1979.

Brown, Evelyn M. *Educating Eve.* Montreal: Palm, 1975.

Chaloult, René. *Mémoires politiques.* Montreal: Editions du Jour, 1969.

Confédération des syndicats nationaux. *En grève! L'histoire de la C.S.N. et des luttes menées par ses militants de 1937 à 1963*. Montreal: Editions du Jour, 1963.

Daigneault, Richard. *Lesage*. Montmagny: Libre expression, 1980.

David, Hélène. "L'état des rapports de classe au Québec de 1945 à 1967." *Sociologie et société* 7(1975):33–66.

Falardeau, Jean-Charles, ed. *Essais sur le Québec contemporain*. Quebec: Les presses de l'Université Laval, 1953.

Gagnon, Mona Josée. *Les Femmes vues par le Québec des hommes*. Montreal: Editions du Jour, 1974.

Hamelin, Jean, Jacques Letarte, and Marcel Hamelin. "Les élections provinciales dans le Québec." *Cahiers de géographie de Quebec* 7(1959–1960):5–209.

Jamieson, Stuart Marshall. *Times of Trouble: Labour Unrest and Industrial Conflict in Canada 1900–66*. Ottawa: Task Force on Labour Relations, 1968.

Lapalme, Georges-Emile. *Le vent de l'oubli*. Montreal: Leméac, 1970.

Laporte, Pierre. *Le vrai visage de Duplessis*. Montreal: Editions de l'Homme, 1960.

Lavigne, Marie, and Yolande Pinard, eds. *Les femmes dans la société québécoise: aspects historiques*. Montreal: Boréal Express, 1977.

Lemieux, Vincent, ed. *Quatre elections provinciales au Quebec 1956–66*. Quebec: Les presses de l'Université Laval, 1969.

"Quebec Today." Special issue of *University of Toronto Quarterly* 27(1958).

Quinn, Herbert F. *Union Nationale: a Study in Quebec Nationalism*. Toronto: University of Toronto Press, 1963.

Rumilly, Robert. *Maurice Duplessis et son temps*. 2 vols. Montreal: Fides, 1973.

Tremblay, Louis-Marie. *Le syndicalisme québécois: idéologie de la C.S.N. et de la F.T.Q., 1940–1970*. Montreal: Les presses de l'Université de Montréal, 1972.

Trudeau, Pierre Elliott, ed. *The Asbestos Strike*. (1956). Toronto: James Lewis and Samuel, 1974.

Voisine, Nive et al. *Histoire de l'église catholique au Quebec, 1608–1970*. Montreal: Fides, 1971.

"The combination of television and the French language created an immense stage for artistic talent."
Drama for CBC television, Montreal, 1952.

18 Ici Radio-Canada

Just as in the rest of Canada, television spread rapidly across Quebec in the 1950s. In 1952 one household in ten tuned in to the first Canadian programs; three years later almost half of them did so and by 1960 eighty-nine percent of the homes in Quebec boasted a television receiver. Much more rapid than the extension of telephones and radios, creeping across the Canadian and Quebec landscape at a snail's pace since their inception in the 1880s and the 1920s, the rate of television acquisition reflected the greater prosperity of the 1950s and, in the case of Quebec, the greater ingenuity of electoral bribery. But it also revealed, both visually and symbolically, the faster pace of integration into the North American world of consumer technology. Advocates of that integration sprang up almost as fast at the TV sets themselves, although never so numerous. Fascinated by the medium and scornful of flag wavers, new social groups urged an adaptation of Quebec not just to the technology of North American society but to its entire ethos. They were joined in their reformist critique and excitement by certain people within the church and others within the Liberal party. In their eagerness few of them pondered the ultimate implications of adaptation.

In the early days of television the American influence was pervasive. American channels were the only ones available in the late 1940s and one had to be rich, very close to the border, and English-speaking to catch them on the few TV sets in the province. But they set the fare for the initial programming of Canadian television with a mix of westerns, variety, domestic comedy, and sports shows. Indeed, their continuing presence as an alternative in the border areas of Canada ensured that English language broadcasting at least would not be very different. Finances also dictated the importing of American films and television broadcasts to complete the limited production in Canada. The fascination of American offerings even leaped over the language barrier as French-speaking youngsters switched from an overly serious children's program on *Radio-Canada* to the guns and horses of an American western. But no one seemed particularly concerned. Only the budding Canadian nationalists of the Massey Commission on Arts, Letters and Sciences in 1951 or of the Fowler Commission on Broadcasting in 1957 raised some doubts. Canadian television and radio, they said, ought to be different; it ought to introduce Canadians to each other and present the world to them in a Canadian light. And yet it could not be too different from American programming or it would lose a good part of its audience. Nationalists never did resolve the dilemma; the CBC always walked a narrow line and TV watchers, where they had the option, continued to switch channels at their pleasure.

When television was inaugurated in Quebec, practical concerns, rather than Canadian nationalism or even English Canadian enlightenment, dictated an early experiment in bilingualism. The CBC's CBFT began broadcasting on channel 2 in Montreal in September 1952, the first Canadian station to take to the airwaves and the only one in both French and English. Construction of studios and designing of programs had been underway for almost two years; in 1951 the Duplessis government had finally added its permission to that of Montreal's, granted seven years earlier, for the placing of a transmitter on Mount Royal. Even then, the forty-mile range and the cost of a television receiver kept the expectations about the size of the audience to a minimum. Besides, there was the question of talent, money, and sponsors: would there be enough of any of them to fill even the limited programming of four and a half hours a day? The initial solution was to divide those hours in half again, with French and English taking turns. The language varied according to the type of broadcast; sometimes, French commercials were simply slotted into an imported American show in English. Everyone complained and sponsors were scarce. When only the beer companies could be found to back hockey and other sportscasts in French, Montreal wags dubbed CBFT the Canadian Breweries French Television.

Within a few years, however, both demand and daring altered television dramatically. In 1954 the experiment in bilingual television ended with the establishment of two CBC channels in Montreal. CBMT operated solely in English on channel 6 and CBFT continued as *Radio-Canada* solely in French on channel 2. Private television companies were kept at bay in the metropolitan area until 1961. Elsewhere in the province, the CBC did permit private companies, mostly connected with local press and radio, to operate as affiliated stations. They thereby beamed certain CBC programs into most corners of Quebec from television stations in Quebec City, Rimouski, Sherbrooke, Jonquière, Rouyn, and Chicoutimi. Most of the programs came from CBC studios in Montreal and by 1957 television production there was third in the world to New York and Hollywood and second to none in French. Gone were most of the badly dubbed American films or the ancient French ones. In their place were made-in-Quebec variety shows, quiz programs, news and sports broadcasts, drama, concerts, and serialized novels.

The rapid development of television in Quebec had startling results. On the one hand, television brought the world, no longer filtered by press, priest, or politician, into Quebec's kitchens and living rooms. Some of that world actually did look as frightening as the interpreters had said it was: in 1956 communists were in fact crushing popular unrest in Hungary; British and French imperialists really were protecting their interests in Suez. And yet much of that world also seemed surprisingly familiar and the similarities and contrasts invited comment and consideration. Through a medium of pictures and words, of animation and specifics so different from the vague, diffuse sentiment that surrounded the flag, the message was clear: Quebec was perhaps not so different after all. In terms of consumer tastes, leisure activities, and way of life, Quebecois appeared to be very similar indeed to other North Americans. But at the same time, television in Quebec magnified the tiny world of a Laurentian village, a lower town Quebec, or a local hockey arena into a provincial possession. *Un homme et son péché* came off the library shelves and, transformed as *"Les belles histoires des pays d'en haut,"* captured the understanding of everyone watching TV on a Monday night. *"Les Plouffe"* kept writer Roger Lemelin occupied for years spinning segments of his novel into a television series for an insatiable audience on Wednesday night. The same audience, just as faithful to and enraptured by *"La soirée du hockey"* on Saturday night would not permit the displacement of *"Les Plouffe"* for a hockey playoff. If television's integrating force created a global village, as Marshall McLuhan has suggested, its distinguishing force also gave the village national stature. In Quebec, television did both, in French.

The combination of television and the French language created an immense stage for artistic talent. Where Quebec had once hidden away its artists—shunning the popular ones, exiling the ambitious or the outspoken, tolerating only the safe decorators of churches or painters of landscapes for the narrow walls of the *Ecole des beaux arts*—now it put its artists on parade. To the delight and astonishment of viewers all over Quebec, television produced a seemingly endless stream of home grown entertainers. Actors were perhaps the favourites and they and their characters fast became family friends. But there were musicians as well, composers, performers, poets, and singers. Even the commentators of sports, news, or public affairs revealed a stage presence of language, poise, and artistry: René Lévesque performed as he informed the audience of his current affairs program *"Point de mire."* And behind them all were the directors, producers, and technicians, as remarkable as they were invisible.

All of the talent reflected both the integrating and distinguishing facets of television. Writers, actors, producers, and composers revelled in an ultra-modern medium that placed them in skilful competition with the best talent in the world. Many of them already had or now acquired links to that world, whether North American or European, but few felt the old need to go elsewhere in order to be in the world's cultural limelight. Indeed, part of that light was now focussed on Montreal and even attracted French language talent from Europe. Even so all of the new talent was increasingly conscious that its creativity was French in an English-speaking environment. The tension may even have been a source of the artistic effervescence. In any case by 1959 those very people had made television into something special for French Canada: a purifier of language, a provider of education, an outlet for talent. In short, in the eyes of its makers, television had become an essential part of French Canadian culture.

Most of the artists, intellectuals, professionals, and union leaders who became so visible in the 1950s welcomed the television rays that illuminated the integration of Quebec into North America and they advocated even more of it. By doing so, they all, deliberately or implicitly, criticized many of the facets of contemporary Quebec society. Their own futures of course depended upon that society's making room for them and much of it had to alter to do so. They seldom acknowledged the changes that had already occurred and which produced them in the first place. Rather they demanded that both church and state adjust to their presence. Only belatedly did this newly self-conscious middle class realize what most members of the working class had always known: room at the very top was reserved for people of another language. Challenging that barrier would require far more solidarity among themselves and a far more powerful use of the state than many of the individualists of the 1950s would allow.

Two artists in 1948 set the tone for much of the following decade. Paul-Emile Borduas and Gratien Gélinas, different in personality, temperament, and medium of expression, shocked their contemporaries in a surprisingly similar manner. The solitary painter Borduas, after a conventional training and career as church decorator and teacher of drawing, began experimenting with surrealism in the early 1940s. His notion of painting that flowed freely from the unconscious without form, composition, order, tradition, or connection with reality caught the fancy of students and colleagues. Together, this fledgling group of unconventional artists, known as the *automatistes*, extended their artistic theories to society. Freedom, they declared in a forthright manifesto *Refus global* (total rejection) required the similar unfettering of society from the traditional and formalized hold of politics and religion. Borduas' outspokenness cost him his job at the *Ecole du meuble* and he gradually exiled himself first from Montreal, then from Quebec, and finally even from North America. But his artistic and social message echoed through Quebec in the 1950s as increasing numbers of artists and intellectuals wielded free-flowing brushes and pens. Some of the latter pounced upon the first performances of playwright Gélinas' *Tit-Coq* in 1948 and saw in it a subtle criticism of the family, the church, and the state in Quebec. The gregarious Gélinas, actor and popular comedian of the 1940s, denied then and since any purpose other than that of telling a humorous and pathetic love story. But what was one to make of the tale of an illegitimate lad denied a normal life by the familial, ecclesiastical, and political upholders of proper behaviour? Gélinas suggested greeting it with laughter and tears; many of his younger contemporaries argued for action, even if they only meant intellectual action.

Intellectuals were hardly a new species on the Quebec scene in the 1950s. Both the church and the nation had commanded their services and accorded them stature for generations. Few indeed had been able to survive, ideologically or financially, without that support. Their task had always been to come to terms with the present in the light of certain unquestionable givens: the appropriateness of Catholicism to French Canada and the importance of nationalism to survival. Many such intellectuals continued to thrive in the 1950s. The Tremblay Commission attracted them; *abbé* Groulx gave them his blessing. Groulx had even trained a variation upon them in the secular historians Guy Frégault, Maurice Séguin, and Michel Brunet at the University of Montreal. They traced the contemporary ills of French Canada to the Conquest: a military defeat by an alien people had warped the normal development of Quebec. One of the results was a powerful church and these historians, unlike most of their predecessors, did not like it at all.

But still, it was not French Canada's doing: an omnipotent church was a consequence of conquest.

Other intellectuals stepped farther afield in order to pinpoint the problems within. Writers for *L'Action nationale* and *Le Devoir* such as Gérard Pelletier and André Laurendeau moved beyond the usual bounds of nationalist rhetoric and began arguing for economic, social, and political reforms to modernize and purify Quebec. The school system needed overhauling to ensure access and coherence; Montreal's politics needed cleansing to rid the city of graft, corruption, and immorality. Joined by academics and other critics, the writers consulted companions in France and colleagues in English Canada; they took notes, kept files, and concluded that Quebec was backward and French Canadians were responsible. Some of them did cling to provincial autonomy or wonder about cultural survival with so much American TV, but mostly they urged a great questioning of Quebec's social institutions on the grounds that they did not conform to the dictates of an industrial society. That society itself they embraced with boundless enthusiasm. Other intellectuals went farther still and, writing mostly for themselves, filled the pages of a new periodical *Cité libre* after 1950 with criticism of everything that had even the faintest odour of tradition or authority. Among the group was Pierre Elliott Trudeau, lawyer and gadfly intellectual, sporting inherited wealth and an international education. They all delighted in taking issue with Quebec's past and present. The institutions and ideas of the past were a dead weight upon the development of Quebec as a modern industrial and democratic state. Most of the people of the present, notably the politicians, were little different. And the responsibility could not be placed upon others. French Canadians had to shoulder that burden themselves; only they could lighten it.

Much of this type of criticism suited the purposes of the new professional people in the 1950s. For unless Quebec used North American norms to define itself, there would be little place for the businessmen, architects, engineers, chemists, social scientists, lay teachers, and professors emerging from Quebec's professional schools or returning from post-graduate training abroad. The industrial and business opportunities of the war had given some a boost: financier Jean-Louis Lévesque, for example, began a rags-to-riches career selling Victory bonds. The continuing prosperity of the 1950s embellished the promise. Some of the newly trained went off to Ottawa for careers in the federal civil service and some of them even pondered the nationalist heresy of a highly centralized Confederation to cope efficiently with the economic and social planning of a modern economy. Others bemoaned the lack of similar ideas in the Quebec civil service, still run like a patronage filled family enterprise. Meanwhile newly trained academics began carving their own niche in society by turning the modern light of social science research on contemporary Quebec. They made such a splash doing so that they attracted the attention of English Canadian scholars, for most of whom Quebec was a discovery. They all relished and promoted an urban, industrial, diversified, and secular society; their own positions in fact depended upon just such an open, expanding, and pluralist milieu.

The vision of such a milieu attracted many members of the union movement in Quebec. Some of the leaders in fact looked more like the new intellectuals or professionals than they did industrial workers. Gérard Picard, a journalist and militant unionist, and Jean Marchand, a social science graduate and union organizer, became respectively president and general secretary of the *Confédération des travailleurs catholiques du Canada* (CTCC) in 1946. They brought with them a much more secular approach to union activities than had ever been in the head of previous leader Alfred Charpentier. Their arrival in fact coincided with and contributed to the gradual shunting aside of the clerical presence, let alone influence, in the Catholic unions. Since 1943 union chaplains could no longer exercise a veto, affiliated unions could discard the word Catholic from their titles, and non-Catholics could become members. Through the 1950s the trend continued: while the CTCC acknowledged the inspiration of Catholic social doctrine it also eyed potential recruits in Montreal's heavy industry where religious and cultural pluralism abounded. From just such a source—the metal workers—came the proposal in 1956 that the CTCC discard its confessional character which hindered expansion and efficiency. By 1960 a change of constitution and name to the *Confédération des syndicats nationaux* (CSN) capped the process and signalled the completion of another aspect of Quebec's absorption of North American norms.

Quebec's international unions had always been closer to those norms. By their very presence and numbers the internationals had implied a sense of North American worker solidarity free of the barriers of nation or culture. And yet there was little solidarity within Quebec. Provincial federations of international unions had never been very successful since affiliation was voluntary and the central body inadequately financed and staffed. Since the early 1940s, moreover, the internationals harboured a serious split between trade unions and industrial unions. The trade unions were the more numerous, the industrial unions the more brash and the rivalry between them often bitter. So deep was this rift that when talk of union integration was in the air throughout North America in the 1950s, an alliance of industrial unions with the CTCC seemed more natural than one with the trade unions, especially since the CTCC was taking an increased interest in radical politics. Eventually, however, Quebec's international unions accepted the pattern designed in the United States and emulated in Canada. Just as the American Federation of Labor linked itself to the Congress of Industrial Organizations with a hyphen in 1955, the Trades and Labour Congress and the Canadian Congress of Labour amalgamated with a new name, the Canadian Labour Congress (CLC), in 1956. The *Fédération provinciale du travail du Québec* and the *Fédération des unions industrielles du Québec* followed suit in 1957 to form the present *Fédération du travail du Québec* (FTQ). Quebec's Catholic unions, slowly casting off their religious affiliation, resisted the temptation to follow suit. They wanted a distinctive status within the Canadian Labour Congress and the fledging amalgamation was not prepared to accord that. The FTQ was to be the provincial wing of the CLC and the CTCC would remain independent.

The different adaptation to North American norms was indicative of the now contrasting, now complementary activities of the union centrals in Quebec. Rivalry among the unions continued throughout the 1950s although it was generally less vicious than during the mid-war years. Union membership remained relatively stable through the decade, hovering around twenty-five percent of the work force after a jump just after the war from nineteen percent and another in 1955 to twenty-nine percent. The actual number of union members increased simply because the labour force itself increased. Membership in unions affiliated to the CTCC passed the one hundred thousand mark in the mid-1950s; closer to two hundred thousand workers carried international union cards. They accused each other of currying favour with the government and then hurled the favourite term of opprobrium, that of communist, at each other. They worked out different forms of political strategy, the CTCC moving towards a radical critique of contemporary politics and society, the FTQ timidly apolitical until the CLC declared its intention to assist the CCF in forming a new political party. And yet they also joined forces on occasion, supporting each others' more dramatic strikes at Asbestos in 1949, Louiseville and Dupuis Frères in 1952, and Murdochville in 1957. The Murdochville strike even rallied the traditionally individualist FTQ unions to the support of one of their largest affiliates, the Quebec locals of the United Steelworkers of America. But the centrals were not able to agree among themselves, let alone convince their membership, to stage a general strike in sympathy with the textile workers at Louiseville or the miners at Murdochville. Nor would they march together on the Quebec legislature in 1954 to protest the latest addition to Duplessis' oppressive labour legislation. Some of their activities indeed suggested a gulf between militant leaders and apathetic members as wide as that between the central themselves.

The gulf between union leaders, new professionals, and radical intellectuals was decidedly less pronounced. Two incidents in the 1950s illustrated their mutual sympathy and even gave cohesion to it. One was the publication of a book in 1956 about a strike; the other was an actual strike in 1959. Because of the authors, the approach, or the participants, both *La Grève de l'amiante* (*The Asbestos Strike*) and the strike of television producers at *Radio-Canada* startled contemporary Quebec. They also added to the critique of society that was burbling through the decade.

La Grève de l'amiante emerged from the presses of *Cité libre* in 1956, edited and introduced by Pierre Elliott Trudeau. In four hundred pages, a series of young authors drawn from unions, the press, the church, and the new academic professions of economist and sociologist dissected the strike in the mining and asbestos processing towns of Asbestos and Thetford Mines in the Eastern Townships in the late winter and spring of 1949. Trudeau's lengthy introduction set the tone. According to him, Quebec's past was gloomy, conservative, and authoritarian, closed to economic reality in general and to the working class in particular. The other authors took the cue and detailed the strike and reactions to it as a welcome sign of enlightenment on the part of Catholic unions, workers, and the church. Here, surely, was the working class claiming its place in the sun, the elite's recognition of Quebec as an industrial society, and the alliance of government and company, cemented by police power. The book emphasized precisely what its authors wanted to see, not just in the strike but in Quebec society as a whole: union solidarity, clerical sympathy for workers, and popular hostility to political repression. It justified the illegality of the strike by the immorality of Duplessis' labour legislation. As part of the critique of contemporary society the book may even have been more important than the strike itself.

Ten years after the strike and three years after the book, a very different kind of labour confrontation took place. Neither the church nor the working class in its traditional sense of skilled or unskilled manual labour was anywhere in sight around the television studios of *Radio-Canada* in downtown Montreal in late December 1958. Rather the producers, a group of professionals which had not existed ten years earlier and which CBC management considered part of itself, went on strike to back their demands to form a union and to negotiate a collective agreement. No one might have noticed the strike by some seventy producers had not the whole of Quebec become used to seeing their programs every evening on television. Moreover the strikers were backed by writers and performers who withdrew their services from *Radio-Canada* and by technical and office staff, already unionized, who refused to cross the producers' picket lines in the cold of a January winter. CBC directors scrambled to import French feature films and endured the hostility of local cinema owners. They also maintained their refusal to recognize a union for producers, an unheard of demand on the part of professionals. For more than two months the strike continued while the producers experienced first-hand all the intricacies of union activity, public hostility, and even police harassment. The federal government allowed the negotiations to drag and even to stop altogether, and the occasional French Canadian voice could be heard wondering aloud whether Ottawa would have permitted the continuation of such a strike on the CBC's English language network. Did anyone at the top of CBC really care if French language television died? By March 1959, press and people cared, in part because the Montreal *Canadiens* refused to play in any televised hockey playoffs if the strike were not settled. Public pressure thus forced the CBC to agree to a union for its producers. But there was to be no question of affiliation to a union central, especially not the radical CTCC now with Jean Marchand as its president. Through the entire strike neither side even considered the church as a possible mediator, something which had been a natural recourse only ten years earlier. Instead, an industrial relations expert, from McGill University at that, was to resolve any unsettled issues.

Where indeed was the church in the intellectual and social questioning of the 1950s? Certain elements stood back in dismay; others enthusiastically promoted the social criticism. Some bishops, priests, and members of religious orders foresaw every kind of evil from materialism to positivism and socialism, all of them of course entailing secularization, in the least concession of the church or of Quebec to North American norms. Others fervently believed the only way religion, let alone Quebec, would survive was to be in the forefront of social change. In fact the church, albeit unwittingly, had actually prepared a number of young people for the critical questioning of the 1950s. Various youth organizations in the 1930s had argued their way out of a close alliance with nationalism. The *Jeunesse ouvrière catholique* and the *Jeunesse étudiante catholique* had not only pulled away from the older *Association catholique de la jeunesse canadienne-française* but had even disputed that group's pretensions to an overall direction of young people. Partly the problem was one of divorcing Catholicism from nationalism; partly it was a desire to separate social questions from national ones. By the 1950s that split was public and many graduates of the Catholic youth groups of the 1930s appeared among the new intellectuals and social critics. They also emerged from the co-operatives and the unions with which the church was closely involved.

Much more deliberate was the systematic effort by certain members of the church to develop a lay elite in the new social sciences. That undertaking also went back to the late 1930s with Laval University's school of social science which became a separate faculty in 1943. The Dominican dean, *père* Georges-Henri Lévesque, had to struggle for years to convince his academic colleagues and his clerical and political sponsors that training students to be economists, sociologists, or political scientists was a worthwhile endeavour. What would they do? How were they being taught? Indeed what were they being taught? Lévesque's critics sniffed secularization. He had insisted on distinguishing the practical courses of scientific social study, research, and methods from the theoretical ones of Catholic social doctrine. By the time some of his graduates such as Jean-Charles Falardeau, Maurice Lamontagne, Fernand Dumont, or Léon Dion had returned from graduate study in the United States or Europe to teach in the faculty, they and the students were prepared to scrap the theoretical courses entirely. But the scepticism about social science did not abate. In the early 1950s critics wondered about *père* Lévesque's chumminess with English Canadian intellectuals as a member of a highly dubious federal enquiry, the Massey Commission on Arts, Letters and Sciences; they also thought his students were absorbing far too many statistics and not enough encyclicals. Opponents even carried their objections to Rome, hoping to have Lévesque denounced as a heretic. His precious social sciences would next be undermining the clerical presence in unions and then in schools. Lévesque may even have thought it would be a good idea. He was certainly not alone in thinking religious authorities should withdraw a bit from their customary high public profile. Perhaps Rome agreed; in any case it did not act upon the complaints against Lévesque.

Certainly a high public profile could on occasion be hazardous. Clerical involvement in the asbestos strike in 1949 undoubtedly opened many eyes, both religious and secular, to the reality of social forces, but it also dealt a blow to the church in the forced resignation of Monseigneur Charbonneau, archbishop of Montreal. As the strike lengthened through the spring of 1949, many clerics became increasingly sympathetic to the workers. Neither local *curés* nor distant bishops could stand aside while a Catholic union engaged in a protracted defiance of government and company in order to achieve minimally decent working conditions and while families of strikers were prepared to go hungry for the same elementary cause. "If I were a miner, I'd be on strike too," declared the *curé* in Asbestos. "The working class is the victim of a conspiracy." Monseigneur Charbonneau announced, "it is the duty of the church to intervene." While Charbonneau and the other bishops urged and organized collections at church doors for the strikers, both sides in the strike asked Monseigneur Roy, archbishop of Quebec, to act as mediator. Six months after the settlement of the strike in July 1949, Monseigneur Charbonneau left the archbishopric and went into premature retirement in British Columbia.

Just why he disappeared remains a mystery. His sympathizers saw the evil hand of Duplessis striking down an enemy who had dared cross wills with the premier over the strike. The gesture was certainly not out of character. Whether Duplessis actually had the papal creators and dispatchers of bishops in his pocket is another matter. Charbonneau's detractors, on the other hand, from both within and outside the church, claimed that he had erred. His sympathy for the asbestos strikers was symptomatic of a mind too attuned to the secular trends of contemporary society. He believed that Catholics should co-operate with non-Catholics in professional and charitable organizations. He wanted the Catholic University of Montreal to operate like a North American university and avoid the Laval difficulties of attempting to annex the new social sciences to Catholicism. According to his critics, Charbonneau had simply gone too far. More neutral commentators simply pointed out that Charbonneau was a bad administrator, an outsider to Montreal's ecclesiastical complexity. The different interpretations of Charbonneau's departure became part of the very debate of the decade over the appropriate place of the Catholic church in an increasingly pluralist society. Ultimately, his withdrawal may have symbolized that of the church itself from a highly public, almost political, social role. The church, however, took another fifteen years to complete the process and in the meantime Charbonneau was perhaps another of the signals of the integration of Quebec into North America.

Only a few weeks after Charbonneau's retirement, the church signalled the same message. Quebec's bishops signed a collective pastoral letter analyzing the question of labour in the light of Catholic social doctrine. Gone was the notion that only on the land could people find salvation; the city, an industrial milieu, could be just as conducive to spirituality. Gone too was the moralistic clucking over workers; they had a right to material improvements in their living and working conditions. It was their duty to join unions. They should even pursue notions of worker participation in the ownership, management, and profits of industry. And what was more, they should do it by themselves. No longer should chaplains of Catholic unions take on active leadership roles. While the bishops openly declared their sympathy with organized workers, they were also preparing an escape route for the church from any direct participation in labour relations. Over the next ten years the church followed that path and by 1960 it was easy enough to break the tie officially with the Catholic unions.

The path of disengagement could on occasion be rough. Shortly after the provincial elections in 1956 an English Canadian paper in Toronto acquired a private critique of political morality in Quebec. Two priests, *abbés* Gérard Dion and Louis O'Neill, had prepared a document for clerical eyes only in their diocese of Quebec. The intention, it seems, was to weigh the church's recognized role as overseer of private morality with its increasing reluctance to speak out on political issues. But the commentary hit the press across Canada and then appeared as a pamphlet in Quebec. The furor was so great that Duplessis simply withdrew for a time from the nosy eyes and pens of journalists. The English Canadian press used the Dion-O'Neill document to decry similar political practices elsewhere in Canada; the French Canadian press seemed more shocked by the fact that the authors were clerics than by their revelations.

As the two priests themselves remarked, everyone knew what was going on at election time and in between. The problem was that the public accepted the buying of votes, the distribution of bribes, the impersonation of voters, the false witnessing, the corruption of electoral officers, the threats against opponents, and the actual violence. And after selling their votes without the slightest twinge of conscience for the payment of a hospital bill or a pair of shoes, electors were quite prepared to accept the political falsehoods that Duplessis circulated. Too many people, recipients of refrigerators or televisions at election time, willingly believed the slogans bandied about in the interval: social security was the first step towards marxism; health insurance sabotaged the religious communities; assistance to underdeveloped countries impoverished Quebec and encouraged communism. It was all a great lie and vast numbers of people, some of them even within the church, participated knowingly in it. By doing so they were destroying the respect for truth, justice, liberty, and integrity, in short all Christian moral values. They could hardly then flaunt their superior Catholic virtues.

Four years later, and anonymously this time, another cleric claimed the demise of cultural virtues as well. *Les Insolences du frère Untel* (*The Impertinences of Brother Anonymous*) denounced the education French Canadians received and the language they spoke. Both were corrupt. The school system lacked direction, guidance, even awareness of what was going on in the world. Teachers were ignorant, unprepared for their task, and unwilling to break out of a traditional mould. They all deferred to authority, whether of a religious or political nature, and they instilled in their pupils their own sense of fear. Where were the inquiring minds and the intellectual excitement that ought to characterize the schools? *Frère* Untel claimed they had long since been stamped out by the mediocre minds on the various committees of Public Instruction at the provincial level. As for the language, the impertinent brother advocated shooting anyone who spoke *joual*, a popular idiom in accent, pronunciation, syntax, and grammar named for the common slurring of the word *cheval*. Even if the school system were able to encourage youngsters to think straight, how could they do so when their tongues were in such a muddle?

Frère Untel's own tongue was soon silenced, but the damage had already been done. His religious community shipped him off to safer endeavours abroad while his book sold hundreds of thousands of copies. In the late 1960s he reappeared as journalist Jean-Paul Desbiens, no longer a cleric, and quite at home in the much more secular society he had heralded. His critique stirred the schools, particularly those run solely by clerics, to their roots; Georges-Emile Lapalme, Liberal leader through most of the 1950s, referred to it as nitroglycerine. It delighted the growing number of social critics in the decade and revealed, even if anonymously and with penalties for the author, that the church itself could be the butt and the source of angry young men.

Such people the Liberal party in Quebec would dearly have loved to attract during the 1950s. Lapalme tried democratizing the party in an effort to cut its ties from Ottawa and from large financiers. He pondered advanced social policies only to have Liberal hesitancy and *Union nationale* denigration continue to defeat him. Without money he was unable to charm the customarily bought press. Without a large presence in the legislature, he was easily overshadowed by the *Union nationale.* And without Duplessis' outgoing and popular personality, he could not attract individual loyalty. He faced the television cameras timidly during their first electoral coverage in 1956, but even the new medium was not for him.

Admittedly, his task was monumental. There were so many tangled strains of economic, political, and social criticism in the decade. The unions were increasingly unhappy with *Union nationale* labour legislation, but they were not convinced the Liberals would do any better. Autonomists disliked the shallowness of Duplessis' anti-Ottawa tirades but feared the Liberals' still close ties to their federal counterparts. Economic critics looked unhappily at the continual concession of Quebec's natural resources to foreigners but were not sure the Liberals would do anything very different. Partisans of public morality committees prided themselves on beginning the cleansing of Montreal civic politics with the election of Jean Drapeau in 1954 but were dubious about the Liberals' ability to do the same on a provincial scale. The various threads of political criticism fluttered around the Liberals, supported by *Le Devoir*, in the election of 1956, but they may have been more of a hindrance than a help since the Liberals dropped a percentage point in popular favour, to forty-five, and lost three of their twenty-three seats.

For the rest of the decade the various critics continued to develop in their own isolated way. As prosperity turned to economic difficulties after 1957, both union centrals began urging a more direct role for the state in the economy. Private enterprise, stated the FTQ, would never furnish the planning and direction so necessary for a modern economy. The CTCC argued that only the state could combat inflation, unemployment, and the perpetual and unfavourable contrast of Quebec salaries with those in Ontario. One of the first tasks of the province would be to ensure the transformation of more of Quebec's natural resources in Quebec itself; foreigners were receiving not only the resources but the jobs that went with them. The CTCC also insisted that a modern economy required a modern school system. Only the state had the resources to untangle the chaos of the present system and solve the problems of access and cost. While the unions designed a rosy future for the state, the public morality enthusiasts attempted a broader alliance with all those people upset by the revelations of *abbés* Dion and O'Neill. Once the *Union nationale* flexed its own municipal muscle in 1957 to defeat Jean Drapeau, the moralists turned resolutely against Duplessis and began campaigning on a provincial level for political reform and a restoration of democracy. Some of them joined with intellectuals, journalists, and members of the new professions in a loose alliance known as the *Rassemblement*. Suspicious of all politicians, they pondered just how a social democratic society in Quebec might ensure equality, security, and justice. They did not believe either political party had the necessary purity. Nor were they sure they should sully their own hands by taking on an active political role themselves.

More than those of his opponents, Duplessis' own actions may

have precipitated political change. In 1958 he tempted fate by offering his organizers and a number of selected ridings to the federal Conservatives. Voters in the fifty chosen constituencies obeyed
and thus joined the massive Canadian sweep for Conservative John
Diefenbaker. But the victory released thirty-seven former federal
Liberals from Quebec for duty elsewhere. Even one who managed
to retain his seat found the prospect of opposition in Ottawa dis-
couraging. Jean Lesage and numerous former Ottawa colleagues
turned their eyes home. Perhaps there was something brewing on
the Quebec front. Certainly they could hardly be tarred with the
federalist brush now that the Conservatives were in office in Ottawa
thanks, in Quebec at least, to the *Union nationale*. Duplessis had
also worn out Georges Lapalme and Jean Lesage was more dynamic
and looked far better on television. Lesage took over the provincial
Liberal leadership in 1958 and Lapalme retired to pen a two-volume
political program combining every suggestion about modernizing
Quebec that he had heard or thought of over the last decade.
Duplessis may even have assisted the eventual Liberal victory by
dying in the autumn of 1959. He was known to be generous.

Duplessis' death gave a number of his opponents the chance to
play with political power. They had spent the decade arguing for
changes in the social and political pattern represented by the *Union
nationale* and its various flag wavers. Their own design was much
more similar to that of the rest of North America. Quebec, they
insisted, was backward, conservative, reactionary, and authoritarian. It had to be modernized, democratized, even purified. It had
to slough off the shackles of the past, notably those of religion
and nationalism. In fact the process had long been underway; in
the 1950s television both recorded and fostered much of it as its
rays shattered the ties of priest and politician to the people. Its
light reflected and beckoned an increasing similarity between
Quebec and the rest of North America. But at the same time
television magnified some of the cultural traits of French Canada, particularly the use of the French language. For all their
similarities, Quebecois were still different. There in fact was the
dilemma for the critics of the 1950s. To what extent could French
Canadians embrace the individualistic norms of North America
without becoming similar in all things? Perhaps for that reason
they turned to politics: the mastery of power might make the old
question of assimilation irrelevant.

SELECT BIBLIOGRAPHY

Behiels, Michael, and Ramsay Cook, eds. *The Essential Laurendeau.* Toronto: Copp Clark, 1976.

Brunet, Michel. "La Conquête anglaise et la déchéance de la bourgeoisie canadienne 1760–1793." In *La présence anglaise et les Canadiens.* Montreal: Beauchemin, 1964.

Caldwell, Gary, and B. Dan Czornocki. "Un rattrapage raté. Le changement social dans le Quebec d'aprés-guerre, 1950–1974: une comparaison Québec/Ontario." *Recherches sociographiques* 18(1977):9–58.

Confédération des syndicats nationaux. *En Grève! L'histoire de la C.S.N. et des luttes menées par ses militants de 1937 à 1963.* Montreal: Editions du Jour, 1963.

Cousineau, Jacques. "Charbonneau et le chef: légendes et réalits." *Le Devoir* (Montreal), 6 April 1974.

Cousineau, Jacques. "La gréve de l'amiante, les évêques et le départ de Mgr Charbonneau." *Le Devoir* (Montreal), 7 May 1974.

Daigneault, Richard. *Lesage.* Montmagny: Libre Expression, 1981.

Desbarats, Peter. *René: a Canadian in Search of a Country.* Toronto: McClelland and Stewart, 1976.

Dion, Gérard, and Louis O'Neill. *L'immoralité politique dans la province de Québec.* Montreal: Comité de moralité publique, 1956.

Falardeau, Jean-Charles. *L'essor des sciences sociales au Canada français.* Quebec: Ministère des affaires culturelles, 1964.

Falardeau, Jean-Charles, ed. *Essais sur le Québec contemporain.* Quebec: Les presses de l'Université Laval, 1953.

Groulx, Lionel. *Mes mémoires.* vol. 4. Montreal: Fides, 1974.

Lapalme, Georges-Emile. *Le vent de l'oubli.* Montreal: Leméac, 1970.

Lapalme, Georges-Emile. *La paradis du pouvoir.* Montreal: Leméac, 1973.

Lapointe, Renaude. *L'histoire bouleversante de Mgr Charbonneau.* Montreal: Editions du Jour, 1962.

Lévesque, Georges-Henri. "Prélude à la révolution tranquille au Québec: notes nouvelles sur d'anciens instruments." *Histoire Sociale/Social History* 10(1977):134–46.

McKenna, Brian, and Susan Purcell. *Drapeau.* Toronto: Clarke Irwin, 1980.

Ouellet, Fernand. "M. Michel Brunet et le problème de la Conquête." *Bulletin des Recherches historiques* 62(1956):92–101.

"Quebec Today." Special issue of *University of Toronto Quarterly* 27(1958).

Quinn, Herbert F. *Union Nationale: A Study in Quebec Nationalism.* Toronto: University of Toronto Press, 1963.

Ryan, Claude. "Un jugement sommaire du chanoine Groulx sur Mgr Charbonneau." *Le Devoir* (Montreal), 10 December 1974.

Tremblay, Louis-Marie. *Le syndicalisme québécois; idéologies de la C.S.N. et de la F.T.Q. 1940–1970.* Montreal: Les presses de l'Université de Montreal, 1972.

The province of Quebec.

19 Noisy Evolution

The Quiet Revolution fooled a lot of people. For six years the Liberal party of Quebec convinced itself and most onlookers that it had created something new and done so peacefully. By using the provincial government in a daring and innovative way, the Liberals had succeeded in slaying the ghost of Duplessis. Out of the ashes of his *grande noirceur* (great gloom) had arisen a thoroughly modern Quebec, glowing with enthusiasm and purpose and, except for language, looking and behaving very much like any other political entity in North America. In the hands of bureaucrats in pin-stripe suits, planning had succeeded in wiping out the past. For awhile almost everyone applauded. And then they began to wonder. For those within Quebec, the pace of change was either too fast or too slow. To those outside Quebec, the changes at first appeared welcoming but then became menacing. Just as Quebec was becoming so similar, it began reiterating its difference. Given all the modern trappings of that difference, it might well threaten the stability of Canada itself. Quebecois wondered uneasily, what next? And English Canadians demanded fretfully, what does Quebec want?

What in fact was Quebec doing between 1960 and 1966? The dates correspond to an electoral victory and an electoral loss for the provincial Liberals. They also are the habitual beginning and ending points for the Quiet Revolution. Logic alone would therefore associate the Liberals with a revolution. But the Liberals themselves made the association. From the catchy slogan of 1960, *c'est le temps que ça change* (it's time things changed), to the stunned incomprehension of their defeat in 1966, the Liberals appropriated all that was new and dynamic on the Quebec scene. In the name of a liberal society, modern, efficient, planned, and organized, they denounced their predecessors and despised their successors. They behaved indeed much like other rebels of the 1960s, whether across Canada or across the world, brandishing the wheel they had just invented and using it to roll over the past. In Quebec, however, the past could never be so easily dismissed. *Abbé* Groulx had long since referred to it as *notre maître le passé* (the past is our guide) and he was still alive in the 1960s. So was the past and the Liberals, for all their bravado, in fact incorporated much of it into their so-called revolution. Religion, language, and the family, the traditional institutions of nationalism, became the property of the state. So too did parts of the traditional domination of Quebec by foreign economic interests as the Liberals, with great fanfare, pursued state capitalism as the wave of the future. They even appropriated the nation itself and did so quite noisily too. Quebec was not a province like the others and henceforth the state would speak for the nation. The mathematical implication that state and nation were one, and both equal to Quebec, may have beguiled the efficiency experts of the 1960s but it was nothing new to long-time nationalists in Quebec. Perhaps the most fitting ending for the noisy evolution of the 1960s was the death of *abbé* Groulx in 1967, his priestly heart fearful over the assimilation of religion and the family by the state but his nationalist soul tickled by the economic and political daring.

The Liberals carefully prepared their coming in 1960. Thanks to Georges-Emile Lapalme and Jean-Marie Nadeau the party had restructured its membership, finances, and organization. In every county enthusiastic members responded to a desire to reform the party from the local level up. And all of them called upon the increasingly numerous critics of the *Union nationale*. So great indeed was their activity that during the election campaign in the late spring of 1960, many former *Union nationale* supporters publicly switched to the Liberals. Liberal candidates were locally known, a mayor here, a school board chairman there, or provincially recognizable: Jean Lesage, one time minister in the St. Laurent federal cabinet; Georges Lapalme, former leader of the provincial Liberals; René Hamel, the one Liberal member of the assembly who had been able to counter Duplessis' constant barbs; Paul Gérin-Lajoie, an Oxford-trained constitutional expert; and the superstar from television's *"Point de mire,"* René Lévesque, politicized by the strike at *Radio-Canada* in 1959. As a group, the candidates shone in contrast to those of the *Union nationale*: they had more education and a higher socio-economic status. In many ways they resembled the new urban professionals, intellectuals, and union leaders of the 1950s; certainly they had their support. But the Liberals sought a wider appeal than that and their campaign brochure deliberately mentioned a clerical relative for each of their candidates. For all the careful control of the campaign, however, chance had played a part in the election itself. Death had removed the one strong successor to Duplessis in the *Union nationale*. Paul Sauvé had had only one hundred days as premier to institute a number of political and administrative reforms which the Liberals subsequently enlarged upon and took the credit for. After his death early in 1960, the divided *Union nationale* could only come up with the unimaginative Antonio Barette, too gentlemanly to stoop to Duplessis' tricks but too conservative to change many of the *Union nationale*'s ways.

In comparison, the Liberals promised bright new minds with the express purpose of altering those ways. The new middle class would purify the public practices of the old *Union nationale* and, in the process, although they seldom said so, clear the way for their own social dominance. In some ways indeed, they resembled their forbears of the 1840s who had advocated responsible government as a political reform all the while counting the prestigious positions the reform would create. Lesage promised an enquiry into the alleged scandals of the *Union nationale*; he urged an end to political corruption and to patronage in the civil service. The Liberal program showered the province with pledges of hospital insurance, free schooling, a ministry of cultural affairs, an economic planning council, and a labour code. There was no advance notice of what would be the two major undertakings of the Lesage ministry: the secularization of education and the nationalization of electricity. Both came later, partly as a result of the very momentum the new government created—it announced a new project almost every day during the first month of its mandate—and partly as a means of keeping the headstrong and very individualistic members of the cabinet together. Except for Lesage, none of them had any ministerial experience; each one was anxious to try out the tools of power on his favourite idea, be it cultural, economic, political, or merely one of status. That the results were as coherent as the name Quiet Revolution implies is a tribute more to the public relations experts of the government and their journalistic supporters than to reality.

The takeover of the traditional institutions of nationalism was not therefore deliberate policy. Indeed many reformers, participants in, or supporters of the activities of the Lesage ministry thought they were ringing the death knell of nationalism. How could something as emotional and group-oriented as nationalism survive the rational individualism of true liberalism, whether in its nineteenth century variety of mutual tolerance or its more contemporary form of bureaucratic expertise? In Quebec at least, it may well have survived because the state gave it a new lease on life. Without quite meaning to, the Quebec government in the 1960s both undermined and appropriated the strength of three key institutions that had gone into the making of French Canada: religion, language, and the family.

The Catholic church may even have given the state a helping hand. Certain groups within the church had argued through the 1950s for a divorce of Catholic from national action. But the tie had always been so close that when the break did occur, some wondered whether there was much Catholic substance left. The same concern but for different reasons troubled Catholics all over the world and the Quebec church participated in a world-wide reformation of Catholic practice. Both the domestic and the international trends took their toll in Quebec as the number of new vocations declined and even the confirmed ones wavered. Men began leaving religious communities and the women followed suit. The departures may have reflected the basically social, rather than spiritual nature of the Catholic church's place in Quebec society. For by the 1960s, and increasingly so during the decade, socially prestigious and useful jobs could be found elsewhere; the church was no longer a major employer. But more than the professional religious were disappearing; the faithful were dwindling as well. Montreal's churches attracted only fifty percent of declared Catholics through the 1960s; in the suburbs, churchgoers offered social, not spiritual reasons for their continuing attendance. Certainly much had changed within the churches. The magic of procession, ritual, and the Latin language all vanished as the church sought modernity and relevance. Bingo replaced devotions and for sale signs appeared on church buildings.

It was perhaps easy enough then, and maybe even necessary, for the state to move in on certain areas traditionally administered by the church. The precedent of course had long been there: the state had given financial support to the church's social and educational endeavours for generations. But it had always done so discreetly, allowing the church the public display of charity and social service. Now it put its own mark on the terrain: a ministry of youth and social welfare already created by the Duplessis government in 1958; a joint federal-provincial plan of hospital insurance in 1961; a ministry of cultural affairs the same year; and a ministry of education in 1964. Each one not only confirmed a state presence but enlarged it; the state no longer assisted but directed. Clerics at the top and even the bottom of their many enterprises were replaced by provincial civil servants and state employees. On the whole the transfer was relatively quiet, secular bureaucrats being perhaps not much different from clerical ones.

The exception was education. There one could hear the creaking of the old department of public instruction, independent of all political authority since the 1870s, and defending its clerical masters in the Committee of Public Instruction against all attackers. By the 1960s the defence was untenable although many people in the public and the church still insisted upon it. Jean Lesage for example stamped "NEVER" on the suggestion that a genuine ministry of education control all the administrative, financial, and pedagogical aspects of schooling. Lesage's nevers rarely persisted. But his political skill did and he named a highly placed cleric, Monseigneur Alphonse-Marie Parent, vice-rector of Laval University, to head a provincial commission of enquiry into education in Quebec. The Parent Report recorded and upheld every criticism that had ever been voiced about the educational system and even added some of its own. In the name of modernity, science, and technology, of urbanization and the mass media, of the enlarged role of women and the emergence of new elites, Parent argued for the streamlining of education in Quebec. It ought to match the North American pattern in length of studies and accessibility to all, if not in precise institutions. And it ought to be administered by a single, secular authority. Only the state had the resources to undertake the task.

Parent was still penning the final volumes of his report in June 1963 when the Lesage government introduced Bill 60 to establish a ministry of education. The outcry from groups opposed to secularization, fearful of political influence, and anxious about the costs to the taxpayer was so loud that Lesage withdrew the bill momentarily. Opponents and supporters could have their say and they did so strenuously through the summer and autumn of 1963, but Lesage and the prospective first minister of education, Paul Gérin-Lajoie, intended to have their way. They had already made sufficient concessions, they thought, by incorporating another recommendation of the Parent Report into the original bill. A Superior Council of Education, again divided by religious denomination with the Catholic committee heavily weighted with bishops, was to oversee the continuing confessional character of the schools. The schools were thus not to be secular, but they were to be run by the state. Accompanying the change was the sound of construction, the roar of regional school buses, the tramp of student feet as the school leaving age was raised to sixteen and access made free to all secondary schools and the new junior colleges or CEGEP, and the rustle of diplomas granted to thousands of new lay teachers. The evolution of education in Quebec in the 1960s was decidedly noisy.

Much less provocative but just as definitive was the state's extending its protective umbrella to the French language. Lapalme had insisted on the addition of a French language bureau to his new cultural affairs ministry in 1961. The novelty of the ministry itself startled people: politicians from other provinces and countries wrote to him for information and advice; a farmer requested seed grain from the new minister of culture. In part the ministry merely co-ordinated under one authority the varying types of support the provincial government had been giving for years to museums, artists, and scholarship students. But it also intended to innovate and direct. The new ministry had four separate departments: the French language bureau, an office concerned with "French Canada beyond the borders," a provincial arts council, and a historic monuments commission. Except for the second, each of the others became important, indeed powerful instruments in the hands of subsequent governments who never questioned their duty to protect French Canadian culture. In fact by the mid-1960s, thanks both to the cultural effervescence of the time and to the cultural presumptions of the state, poets and politicians had taken on the role of definers of the people, leaving the church and the nationalists far behind.

In the process, by implication or design, the French language became the primary characteristic of French Canadians. For some people, notably the cultural affairs minister, that meant purifying the language and strengthening it. Lapalme remembered his own schooldays and the linguistic poverty of his teachers, trained in Rome for religion rather than in France for language. But for others, notably the younger writers of the mid- to late 1960s, the really distinguishing trait of French Canada was its popular idiom. *Joual* was a genuine Canadian creation and should be glorified as such. In a debate opened by *Les Insolences du frère Untel* in 1960 and raging through the decade, classically trained purists like Lapalme shuddered at the vulgarity of common language, while aspiring young writers like Michel Tremblay revelled in the down-to-earth reality of joual. Both nation and class were mixed up in the intense reaction to *joual*. The opponents had been raised on the tandem of faith and language, the inseparable support for a minority culture in North America. *Joual* seemed to become popular at the very time that external manifestations of the faith were diminishing. The decline of both religion and language thus appeared to be symptomatic: for all the worriers knew, barbarity lurked just the other side of an ill-constructed or badly pronounced sentence. As the language went, so perhaps went the nation. The exquisite use of French was, however, largely the preserve of the well educated middle class. They prided themselves that *Radio-*

Canada was extending that usage, but as soon as there was a
second French language television outlet in Montreal, a private
station in 1961, most viewers switched channels to more familiar
tones. Perhaps not surprisingly then, the new middle class fashioned
the instruments of the state in its own image and Lapalme's new
language bureau hovered over French like a mother hen.

Gradually being tucked under the wing of the state as well was
the family, the third of the trilogy of one-time defenders of the
nation. As the state took over the educational functions of the church,
it could not pretend, as the latter had done for so many generations, that the family was ultimately responsible for education.
Now the state claimed its own accountability for what the Parent
Report termed the autonomy of the person. Education entailed a
contract between the individual and the state; the family faded
into the background. And as the state enlarged secular hospital
care, the family increasingly became a shadowy entity. Hospital
insurance gave the sick greatly increased access to professional
care, but it also reduced the role of the family in the health care of
its members. The Quebec pension plan, carefully constructed in
1964 to be administratively different from that of Ottawa, had the
same effect: individuals who had been members of the public labour
force would contribute from their present earnings to their future
financial security; old age was no longer a family affair. And by
1965 the Lesage government was using what remained of the family unit in its increasing battles with Ottawa: Quebec needed a
family allowance scheme of its own designed in Quebec to suit
distinctive Quebec needs.

In fact those needs were increasingly less distinctive. Through
the 1960s Quebec families acquired the shape and the functions of
most other North American families. The birth rate plummeted to
the lowest in Canada from twenty eight per thousand in 1959 to
fourteen per thousand in 1971. The real quiet revolution may well
be there: while politicians were making loud noises in public, families were deciding in the privacy of kitchen, parlour, or bedroom
that enough was enough. Or the decision may have been the woman's alone as the availability and the personal, if not religious,
acceptability of the Pill permitted a certain autonomy. That autonomy in turn increased with more women and particularly more
married women joining the paid labour force. While the unions
fretted and advocated protective legislation, particularly the prohibition of night work, the government sanctioned much of the
autonomy in 1964 by changing its one hundred year old civil code
to eliminate the legal subjection of married women to their husbands. And once the federal government changed its divorce laws
in 1968 and the province established its own divorce courts the
following year, French Canadian women flocked to them as willingly
as other North Americans. Even by then, one family in twelve had
a woman as its sole support, poorer than the similar but far fewer
single-parent families headed by men. Throughout the 1960s then,

Quebec's families began to look increasingly like those elsewhere.

The coincidence of change within the family, the language, and the church and the intervention of the state in the three areas is remarkable. Each no doubt fed upon the other: social institutions like schools, hospitals, and welfare agencies were no longer able to cull the personnel or resources they needed from the church; at the same time the state was anxious to exercise the planning of a modern government. The state may even have assisted in sapping the internal cohesion of the church and the family. In the name of modernization it participated in and even instigated many of the changes and then in the name of nationalism it appropriated much of the strength of those institutions to its own account. By its intervention in three traditional areas of social and national integration, the state acquired a new force. Modernization and nationalism were quite compatible it seems.

The same compatibility appeared in another area of government intervention during the 1960s. The economic activity of the Lesage government made heads spin: no sooner did a minister have a bright idea than the civil service had the mechanism and the staff to carry it out. Much of the activity stemmed from the realization that the state could be used as a tool of economic development. It no longer need be just a supplier of roads and licences and a collector of minimal taxes; instead it could play a leading role itself. Some of the activity was a necessary response to the economically troubled times of 1957 to 1961. By the late 1950s, the postwar prosperity had petered out and with unemployment reaching as high as fourteen percent of the labour force during the winter of 1960 the government was expected to provide some cures. But the government's activities also had a nationalist overtone. New jobs in the public sector could be filled by French Canadians. The state might be able to solve the old problem of foreign economic domination of Quebec. By taking over and controlling much of the past, the government could prepare the future in its own way.

And so the major economic undertaking of the Lesage ministry was the nationalization of hydro-electricity. The process was neither quiet nor revolutionary. Twenty years earlier the wartime Liberal government had initiated the process by taking over the Montreal Light, Heat and Power Company to create Hydro-Quebec. In the 1960s Lesage's Liberal government simply took the next logical step of nationalizing the major remaining hydro-electric companies and while doing so brought Quebec into line with most other Canadian provinces. But what a commotion the proposal created. René Lévesque, the minister of natural resources, took to his favourite medium and announced on television his personal plan to integrate all the private, co-operative, and municipal hydro companies into Hydro-Quebec. Premier Lesage vetoed the plan with his usual "NEVER" and Lévesque's cabinet colleagues roared their resentment at not being consulted. So did the huge and largely foreign-owned Shawinigan Power Company, recognizing that it was at the top of Lévesque's list. The press and the public took turns shrieking the pros and cons of nationalization. The cabinet tore itself to shreds and then suddenly pulled together to support the policy and call a snap election on it. The only quiet aspect of the entire question was Lesage's assuring himself in the money markets that the government could borrow the vast sums necessary to buy out the private companies.

The election was exciting, if one-sided. The Liberals claimed they had found the key to Quebec's future. In one bold stroke they would put an end to economic colonialism in Quebec and make Quebecois *"maîtres chez nous"* (masters in our own house). *Abbé* Groulx recognized his slogan even if Lesage's speech writer Claude Morin, who later appeared in the *Parti québécois*, did not; Groulx even abandoned his usual electoral discretion to acclaim the policy and to vote for the second time in his life. René Lévesque stormed the province in person and on television and swayed almost all his listeners with his inimitable manner, total mastery of the details, and utter conviction. He quoted the government's own economic planning council to show that a unified hydro-electric system was the key to the industrialization of all the regions of Quebec and the necessary precondition not only of any policy of full employment but of Quebec's economic liberation in general. He added his own argument that the immense profits of the hydro companies would henceforth accrue to the state; they would even increase since the provincially owned Hydro-Quebec would not pay the federal tax imposed upon private companies. The funds would then permit the standardization and lowering of rates for electricity across the province. As an added bonus, Hydro-Quebec would open up managerial, engineering, and technical jobs for French Canadians. It was indeed a magic wand and the nonplussed *Union nationale* was either unwilling or unable to snap it. The Liberals increased both their popular vote to fifty-seven percent and their representation in the assembly to sixty-three.

The new Hydro-Quebec, dating from 1963, was only the most dramatic of the Liberal government's economic activities. Other activities revealed just the same fervour of organization and control. As early as 1961 the provincial economic planning council had been scrutinizing the province's economic potential and the role the government should play in it. In 1962 a provincially run finance corporation, the *Société générale de financement*, began as both holding company and lending institution for various Quebec enterprises. In 1963 the ambitious government undertook regional planning as well, turning economists and social scientists loose on the lower St. Lawrence and Gaspé regions. It structured ten administrative regions for the province in 1966 and parachuted more experts, civil servants all, into them. With their knowledge, techniques, and intricate plans they dazzled local groups who had been searching for answers to regional disparity since the 1950s. But the mutual appreciation did not last long as the bureaucrats from Quebec increasingly bruised regional sensitivity. Critics else-where even suggested that the government's interest in pensions, and particularly in a plan administered by Quebec rather than Ottawa, was determined more by the large sums of investment capital that a pension fund would contain than by the social benefits of pensions themselves. Indeed, no sooner was the Quebec pension plan inaugurated in 1964 than a government investment company, the *Caisse de dépôt et de placement*, appeared in 1965 to handle the deposits into the plan and the investment of them. Various other pension plans later put their monies into the *caisse* making it within fifteen years as big a financial institution as the *caisses populaires* or co-operative credit unions with assets of almost four-teen billion dollars. And at the same time, the Liberal government established a series of agencies to stamp a public seal on mining, oil exploration, forestry, and steelmaking. It littered the newspa-pers, the civil service, and the government account books with ac-ronyms: HQ, COEQ (later to become the OPDQ), SGF, FAEQ, SOQUEM, SOQUIP, REXFOR, SIDBEC. It was all very impressive, slightly mysterious, and ever so modern.

It was also expensive. In six years the Lesage ministry tripled the provincial budget. Some of the annual increases were larger than any since the late 1940s: twenty-four percent in 1959–60; twenty-seven percent in 1964–65. The government's proportion of gross expenditures in the province increased from seven and a half to twelve and a half percent. And the major recipients of govern-ment largesse were health, welfare, and education whose portion of the budget increased from thirty-five percent in 1960 to sixty-eight percent in 1965. That trend of spending, away from transportation and natural resources and into human resources and social serv-ices, was already visible in the Duplessis budgets of the 1950s, but the astronomical sums—budgets surpassing two billion dol-lars in 1966—were not. Gone were the days of balanced budgets as the provincial debt soared along with the other expenses. The cost of servicing it alone doubled between 1959 and 1966. The increasing indebtedness was government policy, partly to stimu-late the economy and partly to provide decent salaries for the vastly increasing number of public employees: civil servants, hospital workers, and teachers. Both succeeded but as unemployment de-clined, taxes rose: provincially, regionally, and municipally.

The enlarged government presence gave a boost to an economic trend visible since the 1920s. The service industries had gradually been amassing more and more of the workers of Quebec: forty percent had jobs in that sector—finance, transportation, commerce, teaching, construction, personal, professional, and governmental services—in 1941; sixty percent found work there in 1966. The new government employees were almost all in these categories: they organized, planned, charted, mapped, filed, and reported; they did not produce anything. The economists among them might speak happily of a post-industrial society, a sure sign of Quebec's mod-

ernity, but others wondered uneasily about the stagnation of manufacturing industries and the actual decline of primary production
in agriculture and forestry. Could an economy so top-heavy in non-
productive employment really be healthy? Montreal's mayor Jean
Drapeau, re-elected in 1960, professed no worries at all. His fancy
Place des arts, super highways, artistic subways, and extravagant
Expo 67 all attracted the attention and the tourists of the world.
And he had still more shimmering dreams of international league
baseball and even the Olympics. What more could one want, given
the construction jobs that accompanied the undertakings and the
commercial results of them? The magnet of Montreal's industries
and services was still strong enough to draw almost forty percent
of the population and more than fifty percent of the economic activity
of the province by the mid-1960s. And the province would always
come to the rescue of its star city should anything ever go wrong.
Actually one of the quieter concerns of the Quebec government during the 1960s was the need to distribute Montreal's wealth to other
areas of the province.

Much noisier was the Quebec government's dispute with Ottawa.
Here too the Lesage ministry hardly innovated; it merely trod more
firmly along a path well marked by previous Quebec governments.
But it dressed its demands in much more formal clothing. A ministry of federal-provincial affairs, headed by the premier himself,
began scrutinizing every aspect of relations with Ottawa in 1961.
And because few people on the outside grasped the assimilation of
the past that accompanied Quebec's noisy modernization, they did
not recognize the disguise. They thought they were now dealing
with a province like the others, an administration finally recognizing its social, cultural, and economic responsibilities. Instead
they confronted a province speaking for a nation and basing its
demands upon the needs of the nation. French Canada had become
Quebec and the provincial government was responsible for both.

What that responsibility entailed was more money, more power,
and more status. The new Quebec was expensive and insatiable.
By 1966 Lesage thought he had touched the bottom of the taxable
barrel in Quebec and still his expenses kept rising. What he needed
was a different distribution of revenue sources between Ottawa
and Quebec and he even asked the electorate in 1966 for a clear
mandate to negotiate such changes. In the meantime he squeezed
every possible source of increased federal funding and successfully
argued that much of that funding be reorganized to suit Quebec.
The province needed higher equalization grants, transfer payments
without strings attached from Ottawa's inexhaustible supply of
funds to Quebec's limited one. The province needed fewer shared-
cost programs, since their purpose as well as their financing was
often designed in Ottawa. And it wanted no grants-in-aid since
they tended to be entirely Ottawa's doing. But an end to such programs was not to mean an end to federal monies: Quebec should
have monetary compensation for its decision not to partake of joint

or one-sided ventures. It should be able both to opt out and to gain financially. And all along it should recuperate a larger share of the income, corporation, and estate taxes which continued to be collected by the federal government. By 1964 Lesage had so impressed his counterparts in the other provinces and in Ottawa that they agreed to virtually every demand.

But still it was not enough. In order to organize Quebec's social and economic life in conformity with its own spirit, the Quebec government established its own pension plan, apart from but compatible with that of Ottawa. Quebec civil servants worked faster and harder than those of Ottawa to design the scheme; their presentations at federal-provincial conferences were irrefutable and the Ottawa plan even incorporated some of the details of Quebec's. The politicians grumbled in public about the messiness of two separate plans, but the civil servants were able to co-ordinate their intricate calculations relatively simply. By the closing months of the Liberal ministry, Lesage was contemplating complete provincial jurisdiction over areas controlled by Ottawa: family allowances, old age pensions, manpower, and immigration. Why in fact should Quebec not recover full control of the many areas of provincial jurisdiction that Ottawa presumed to finance and direct? The prospect was irresistible and even though the electorate turned elsewhere in 1966, subsequent Quebec governments repeated the same demands. Lesage, remarked his economic adviser and subsequent *Parti québécois* finance minister Jacques Parizeau, taught them all how to work, to do great things with the state and do them well. The excitement was evident: French Canadians had learned the exercise of power.

The pride was infectious, and it demanded confirmation. Journalists, politicians, and the armchair makers of constitutions began debating special status for Quebec. The province had so transformed itself over the past few years, they claimed, that its relation to the other provinces and to Canada had necessarily to adjust accordingly. The new Quebec wanted substance for its autonomy, institutions to correspond to its inspiration, status for its new view of itself. Every possible formula was aired: particular status, special status, associate states, and co-operative federalism. Each had its advantage and disadvantage; none, insisted proponent and opponent alike, meant separatism. Each was merely an attempt to define what many Quebecois felt: that Canada was a country not of ten provinces but of two nations. When one of those nations corresponded to a province, it had to count for more than a province; when the other embraced nine provinces, it had to count for less. The political mathematics confused everyone and most English Canadians were thoroughly bewildered by the whole debate. In the field of external relations, the issues were more clear cut but hardly more reassuring. Quebec's new self-esteem required direct links with French-speaking countries abroad. The initial ones were with France: the *Maison du Québec* in Paris opened in 1961 and

French politicians deigned to recognize an extraordinary French presence on the other side of the Atlantic. By the later 1960s, Quebec and Ottawa were quarreling interminably over the protocol and principle of Quebec's interest in international affairs. Status was a touchy business.

Within Quebec the search for status could be presumptuous. From various quarters emerged a questioning of the Liberal government's appropriation of the national mantle. Although no government since the mid-1960s has denied any of the activities of the Lesage ministry and most have in fact enlarged upon them, each has had to take into account louder voices of protest from different sectors of Quebec society. One of the most organized of those voices has been that of federal Liberals from Quebec. If the Quebec government spoke for the nation, what were they doing in Ottawa? Along with their Liberal colleagues from the rest of Canada they had expected a Liberal presence in Quebec to ease their return to power in 1962. Instead, another protest group turned a potential victory into a Conservative minority. Twenty-six Social Credit members, invisible before the election, took their rural and working class unhappiness over the pace and nature of change in Quebec into the federal arena. Their presence may have annoyed the federal Liberals from Quebec but it probably also awakened other Liberals, indeed English Canada as a whole, to the turbulence in Quebec.

Once the Liberals returned to power at the federal level in 1963, the new prime minister, Lester Pearson, began exploring means of communicating that turbulence to the rest of the country. By appointing the Royal Commission on Bilingualism and Biculturalism in 1963 he clearly stated that Quebec's problems were Canada's problems. The entire country would solve them, not just Quebec alone. No sooner had commissioners André Laurendeau and Davidson Dunton issued a preliminary report in 1965 than some parts of the country began to respond. More support for French-speaking minorities in the other provinces suddenly materialized; more room appeared in the federal civil service for French speakers. But the later reports of the Commission confirmed what French Canadians had always known: the price of any real integration into the economy in terms of equal access to well-paying jobs was their own language. To find themselves on the lowest rungs of the socio-economic ladder in a province in which they constituted eighty percent of the population was injury enough; the added insult was to know that the English language was the only escape route. But even it was no guarantee since a unilingual anglophone consistently ranked higher than a bilingual francophone (two species given public exposure by the royal commission). In part, the Quebec government's economic and public service initiatives were designed to confront that long-standing problem by opening up new areas of work for French Canadians. That the work was exciting and at the same time comfortable is suggested by the number of federal civil servants who abandoned Ottawa to work in French for the Lesage government.

But there were others in Quebec uneasy over the tone of the provincial government's activities. Jobs were one thing, an interventionist government was perhaps even a very good thing, but did it have to be accompanied by such nationalist flourish? Pierre Elliott Trudeau, for one, thought not. Nationalism was an evil force, divisive and dangerous. It no more had its place in modern society than did Maurice Duplessis. Trudeau had spent much of his energy combatting Duplessis during the 1950s, although his attacks had always been distant and intellectual, never the close skirmishes of a Georges-Emile Lapalme in daily encounter in the legislature. And he tended to be almost as edgy about nationalists as Duplessis had been about communists. He saw them in every guise and always, under the surface, reactionary, irrational, and tribal. He had thought that Quebec's quiet revolution had shown them the door, but here they were popping back in by the windows so painfully opened after Duplessis's death. Easily enough then did the federal Liberals persuade Trudeau to take his anti-nationalism to Ottawa and to argue from there that the federal government had just as great a stake as Quebec in the future of French Canada. When flanked by the well-known journalist Gérard Pelletier and the even better known labour leader Jean Marchand, Trudeau was able to add eight more seats to the Liberal contingent from Quebec. But only when he became prime minister in 1968 could he summon the country-wide majority the Liberals had been seeking for years.

The presence of Jean Marchand among the federal trio of 1965 was linked to a much more complex tale of social protest. Marchand and the union central he presided, the CSN, were very close to the provincial Liberals and their reforming zeal in the early 1960s. He was on friendly terms with Jean Lesage and many a potential labour dispute was resolved amicably between the two of them. Much indeed of the evolution of the CSN had presaged and then paralleled that of Quebec society as a whole: deconfessionalization, radicalization, a concern for the development of the economy by means of an activist state, and for education and health care as the right of everyone rather than the privilege of the few. Through the early 1960s in fact, much to the chagrin of the rival union central, the FTQ, the CSN was a close ally of the Liberal government. The alliance was beneficial: new types of union members for the one and political support for the other. The relationship probably facilitated the extension of unions into the public service, something which Lesage initially opposed with his customary "NEVER". By 1964 he relented and a new labour code, besides streamlining the negotiation and conciliation process before the declaration of a strike, permitted the unionization of most workers in the public sector. The CSN took immediate advantage of the legislation and added thousands of members among teachers, hospital workers, and the professional employees of Hydro-Quebec. Together with the FTQ, the CSN protested the limits of the labour code and succeeded in having it enlarged in 1965 to permit the unionization of civil servants and their affiliation to the central of their choice. Again the numbers soared, particularly for the CSN. Over the six years of the Liberal ministry, membership in the CSN more than doubled, passing two hundred thousand by 1966.

But the proximity to government could prove awkward. With inter-union rivalry continuing, the FTQ could easily accuse the CSN of seeking government favour for certain types of workers at the expense of others. And in any serious confrontation between the government and its employees, as began to occur in the late 1960s, any semblance of ideological sympathy let alone social harmony quickly disintegrated. Moreover, as new union members, all those government employees created problems for the CSN since they were largely white collar workers and had to fit an organization designed for blue collar workers. And then the unions themselves began wondering about the middle class bias of the admittedly active provincial government. There were so many people left out of the reform rhetoric of the quiet revolution. What of the poor, now forced into the public limelight—in spite of Jean Drapeau's attempt to hide them behind colourful billboards—as private charity became public responsibility? What of the great majority of non-unionized workers? As both union centrals began fancying themselves as speakers for constituencies larger than their own membership, they became increasingly critical of the government. Some union leaders moved to the ideological left and began envisaging socialist solutions to Quebec's continuing economic problems. Others, such as Jean Marchand, were more worried by the nationalist tendencies of the provincial government. He departed for Ottawa to head off what he believed to be incipient separatism.

Much tinier groups in the early 1960s despaired of resolving either the national or the social question by peaceful means. A handful of youths took the movements for colonial independence in Asia and Africa seriously enough to apply their analysis and techniques to the Canadian situation. Quebec was a colony and the *Front de libération du Québec*, the FLQ, would set it free. The first homemade bombs struck military targets in 1963—a depot and a recruiting centre of the Canadian army—and then boxes of the royal mail in the upper class and largely English Montreal suburb of Westmount. Three years later the terrorists directed their force against symbols of working class exploitation by tossing bombs into a shoe factory and a textile mill. And in another four years they were able to capture the attention of the world by kidnapping a British diplomat, James Cross, and a provincial minister of labour, Pierre Laporte. If the FLQ was unperturbed by the theft and murder that accompanied their activities, most Quebecois were horrified. They were not prepared to sanction noisy revolution no matter what the bombs might be saying about the uneven distribution of power and wealth.

Sometimes flirting with the terrorists, sometimes shunning them, were a series of separatist associations in the 1960s. From left to right of the political spectrum and from working class youth to middle class intellectuals they had one thing in common: an independent state as the logical result of Quebec's past and present. They were never very numerous—together the conservative *Ralliement national* and the socialist *Rassemblement pour l'indépendance nationale* attracted only eight percent of the popular vote in the provincial elections in 1966—but they were noisy. Loudly some of them proclaimed that only an independent state could preserve French Canada's distinctiveness formed by history, Catholicism, and the French language. Just as vociferously others shouted that only an independent state could guarantee French Canada's future, notably the shaking off of a foreign economic presence. French Canadians could never hope to take their place in the economic sun of North America if they did not have complete control of the political and economic apparatus of the state. Lesage may have taken some giant steps in that direction, but his accommodations with Ottawa were a waste of time. The only real mark of autonomy was independence.

By 1966 both the noise and the evolution had left a number of people uneasy. Traditionalists distrusted the notion of an *état providence*, a providential state that did everything for everyone. They regretted the state's undermining of previous forces of social cohesion, such as the church. Radicals, on the other hand, suspected that the makers of the quiet revolution were too middle class and were fashioning the new Quebec too much in their own image. Rural dwellers eyed the urban pace and direction of change warily. Regional sensibilities chafed under the increasing economic dominance of Montreal and the new bureaucratic dominance of Quebec City. If workers, particularly those in public service employment, saw their wages rise, they also watched taxes increase and inflation eat away their gains. Federalists were surprised by the nationalist cloak that increasingly covered the activities of the provincial government and took their surprise to Ottawa. Nationalists on the other hand thought the cloak should envelop even more, perhaps as much as an independent Quebec. English Canadians both inside and outside Quebec wondered unhappily about the outcome of all this French fervour; for a while it had seemed so familiar, but gradually it became frightening. And in spite of the bomb throwers, women may have tossed the most explosive suggestion into the public forum in that their problems appeared to be related neither to class nor to nation. What that might mean for the future was anyone's guess. In the present, all of the protest combined to carve off ten percent of the Liberals' popular vote, offering two percent to the *Union nationale* and eight to the separatists. It still left the Liberals with the most votes, but fewer seats. The *Union nationale* victory of June 5, 1966, was, the Liberals liked to think, the end of the Quiet Revolution. But many of the groups that that noisy evolution had spawned went on to develop their own dreams of nation.

SELECT BIBLIOGRAPHY

The Canadian Annual Review. Toronto: University of Toronto Press, 1960–1966.

Clark, Samuel David. "Movements of Protest in Post-war Canadian Society." In *Transactions* of the Royal Society of Canada. 4th series, vol. 8. 1970. Pp. 223–37.

Daigneault, Richard. *Lesage*. Montmagny: Libre Expression, 1981.

Desbarats, Peter. *René: A Canadian in Search of a Country*. Toronto: McClelland and Stewart, 1976.

Dion, Léon. *Le Bill 60 et la société québécoise*. Montreal: HMH, 1967.

Dumont-Johnson, Micheline. "Les communautés religieuses et la condition féminine." *Recherches sociographiques* 19(1978):7–32.

Gérin-Lajoie, Paul. *Pourquoi le bill 60?* Montreal: Editions du Jour, 1963.

Guindon, Hubert. "Social Unrest, Social Class and Quebec's Bureaucratic Revolution." *Queen's Quarterly* 71(1964):150–62.

Jones, Richard. *Community in Crisis: French Canadian Nationalism in Perspective*. Toronto: McClelland and Stewart, 1967.

Lapalme, Georges-Émile. *Le paradis du pouvoir*. Montreal: Leméac, 1973.

Latouche, Daniel. "La vrai nature de la révolution tranquille." *Canadian Journal of Political Science* 7(1974):525–35.

Lemieux, Vincent, ed. *Quatre elections provinciales au Quebec 1956–1966*. Quebec: Les presses de l'Université Laval, 1969.

Moreux, Colette. *La Fin d'une religion?* Montreal: Les presses de l'Université de Montréal, 1969.

Sauriol, Paul. *La Nationalisation de l'électricité*. Montreal: Editions de l'Homme, 1962.

Simard, Jean-Jacques. *La longue marche des technocrates*. Montreal: Editions coopératives Albert Saint-Martin, 1979.

Smiley, Donald Victor. *The Canadian Political Nationality*. Toronto: Methuen, 1967.

Taylor, Charles. "Nationalism and the Political Intelligentsia: A Case Study." *Queen's Quarterly* 72(1965):150–68.

Tremblay, Louis-Marie. *Le syndicalisme québécois: Idéologies de la C.S.N. et de la F.T.Q. 1940–1970*. Montreal: Les presses de l'Université de Montréal, 1972.

Trudeau, Pierre Elliott. *Federalism and the French Canadians.* Toronto: Macmillan, 1968.

Voisine, Nive et al. *Histoire de l'église catholique au Québec 1608–1970.* Montreal: Fides, 1971.

" . . . women were to summon their courage and tenacity and reject separatist seduction."
Reprinted with permission—the Toronto Star Syndicate.

20 Feminism, Federalism, and the Independence of Quebec

Of all the turbulence that the Quiet Revolution generated, only three strains survived the fifteen year period 1966 to 1981 to become, perhaps, permanent features on the Quebec landscape. Feminism, federalism, and separatism, present as merely three elements of an immense questioning of every aspect of Quebec society, eventually distilled and diffused much of the turmoil of the late 1960s and early 1970s. Some of the questions were noisier than others, some were punctuated with bombs, some were dreams of an egalitarian society, and others were nightmares of kidnapping and murder. The differing views may have been at the origin of the Quiet Revolution itself and simply been deflected momentarily by the emphasis on government activity. Or they may have been the result of that activity. For as the state took over the traditional institutions of the nation, it turned language, the family, and at least the social aspects of religion into matters of public debate. Its involvement with economic institutions to demonstrate French Canadian skill and innovation raised the question of the equitable distribution of the wealth French Canadians now seemed so eminently capable of directing and producing. Thanks to television, every question posed in Quebec could be compared with international events: the clash of old and new nations in the Middle East; the imperialism of the superpowers in Vietnam; the demands of the civil rights movement and of women's liberation in the United States. Every query produced an increasingly dogmatic response until feminism, federalism, and separatism channelled them all into three concerns, narrower in number but broader in scope. Because they were three, a simple choice between YES or NO in a provincial referendum in 1980 was bound to be inconclusive.

The reappearance of feminism on the Quebec scene in the years after the Quiet Revolution was hardly surprising. Like its organized predecessor at the turn of the century it both emerged from and was illustrative of changing social and economic conditions. Like the individual exponents of feminism in the 1920s and 1930s demanding the provincial right to vote, it too had specific grievances. As more women, and especially more married women, entered the paid labour force, they encountered problems of discrimination, sexually segregated jobs, low wages, and no relief from domestic responsibilities. Having fewer children was one obvious response and that trend was evident long before the church gave up preaching the maternal mission of women. But so too was organizing in self-defence. Some women joined unions and by 1977 they made up one-third of all organized workers. Other women joined feminist groups, creating six new province-wide organizations between 1957 and 1973, five of them after 1966. Significantly, what none of them did—and this for the first time in the history of Quebec—was found new religious communities; many in fact left the existing ones. Partly there was more for women to do in the secular world. Partly there was less for religious women to do: the state's under-taking of education and health services added to the number of jobs for lay people. But many of those jobs were for men. As the secular replaced the cleric, men replaced women in positions of direction and leadership. Feminists thus had numerous reasons to look upon the Quiet Revolution as a mixed blessing.

In doing so they added a twist to the nationalist analysis of Quebec society, an analysis that had provided much of the vigour of the Quiet Revolution. Where nationalists found the economy dominated by anglophones—and enquiries by the federal govern-ment said it was so—feminists found the economy dominated by men. When a male economist updated the figures used by the Bi-lingualism and Biculturalism Commission to include those from the census of 1971, he found the domination even more pronounced: a unilingual anglophone earned sixty-four percent more than a unilingual francophone; a bilingual anglophone earned twenty per-cent more than a bilingual francophone. What he did not mention was that women earned less than any of them. The feminists had to take separate tallies to add the barrier of sex to that of lan-guage and ethnicity. Both nationalists and feminists wondered about the particular structure of Quebec's economy as an explanation for the lower wages and higher unemployment in the province. The nationalists picked out light industry—food processing, tex-tiles, shoemaking—as the villain and the feminists pointed out the heavy concentration of women workers in those occupations. Nationalists took a certain paternal pride in the increased role of the state in the economy since the 1960s; feminists demonstrated that the enlarged service sector was filled with low pay and low status jobs staffed by women. The segregation at least permitted women to defend their forty percent place in the paid work force when the increasing unemployment of the 1970s gave rise to the plea that women release their jobs to men. Even then it was the feminists who had to demonstrate that the unemployment rate for women was higher than that for men.

The social concerns of feminists were even more sharply deline-ated. Like most of their nationalist contemporaries, feminists wel-comed the diminution of religion in Quebec society. With the inauguration of civil marriage in 1968 and divorce courts in 1969, they gladly shook off another layer of the sacred from the family.

But the political role of the family remained intact, necessarily so for nationalists, distressingly so for feminists. Ever sensitive to the minority status of French Canadians, nationalists were disturbed by the dramatically declining birth rate. The revenge of the cradle might be a welcome addition to Quebec's historical scrap heap, but could French Canadians really afford zero population growth? Particularly when other groups in Canada continued to reproduce at a higher rate and to assimilate new immigrants. But feminists objected to the implications of such worries, that women were to be baby machines. Some feminists actually viewed the family as a patriarchal prison, its structure designed to favour men and to reproduce a sexual division of labour both at home and in the public work place. They pointed to women in the family bearing the brunt of inflation and unemployment, pulled into the paid labour force in response to the family's economic needs and out again to tend to its social and emotional demands. They demonstrated that such women did double duty since their household responsibilities rarely diminished when they took on paid work outside the home. Something was surely awry. As evidence the divorce rate skyrocketed after 1969 and most of the divorces were requested by women. Similarly, there was something strange about a social division of labour that had the state acquiring the church's prestigious role in education and hospitalization and leaving the more unpleasant tasks to women. Small groups of feminists, virtually without the assistance of church or state, coped with the fall-out of a sexist society: they were the ones, by the mid-1970s, to establish homes for battered wives and children, rape crisis centres, abortion referral services, and to organize birth control information and campaigns against pornography and sexual harassment.

Although the protests and the activities of the feminists implied that relations between the sexes were more crucial to the mechanisms of society than those between classes or ethnic groups, feminists had much in common with nationalists. Their origins, social class, and occupations were often the same. Sometimes they were even the same people, although it was more frequent to find feminists who were nationalists than the reverse. They all drew analogies from movements like their own elsewhere in the world. They all presumed to speak for a clientele larger than their own self-conscious groups: the feminists for all women, the nationalists for the entire nation. And their demands were strikingly similar. They both objected to the designation of roles on the basis of sex or of ethnicity. They both sought more status, as women in the family and in the public domain or as French Canadians in Canada. They both desired more autonomy, for women as individuals, for French Canadians as a collectivity. They wanted the same specific problems rectified: wage parity for Quebec and Ontario workers, and for women and men; access to professional training for French Canadians and for women; positions of economic and political power for French Canadians and for women. And then, in spite of their desire for autonomy, both insisted that they merited special consideration by public authorities because of their particular social burden: women bore children and French Canadians bore a culture. Finally, they both looked to the state as the instrument of their liberation.

Among themselves, feminists did not always speak with one voice. Their arguments ranged from a liberal desire that women make their own way in the world to a reformist recognition that laws and attitudes had to be changed if women were to become autonomous and then to the radical contention that short of a revolution little change was possible since society benefited from the oppression of women. Their remedies varied accordingly, from day-care centres to equal opportunity legislation and the removal of sexism from schoolbooks and the media, all the way to the abolition of the family and the rejection of men. Their organizations extended from minuscule consciousness-raising groups and self-defence classes to study sessions on women in politics, special committees within unions, and province-wide movements of education and social action. Even within the organizations, as much time could be spent discussing structure as substance because many feminists wanted to circumvent male patterns of leadership and command. After years of shouting with many voices they acquired both a means of coalescing their demands and a direct line to the government with the provincially created *Conseil du statut de la femme* (Council on the Status of Women) in 1973.

In terms of varied opinions their contemporaries among federalists were not much different. Indeed if feminists and nationalists had an ambiguous relationship with each other, so did federalists with the other two and among themselves. Both feminists and nationalists could be federalists and often were. But federalists could easily be neither and frequently were. They may have had the advantage of dominating the government of Quebec until 1976 but they were divided into four different political parties whose views on federalism served to distinguish Liberal, Conservative, *Union nationale*, and Social Credit from each other. Moreover they had to contend with federalist colleagues from Quebec in the House of Commons in Ottawa. Even when they shared the same political party, they were often diametrically opposed on the nature and the workings of federalism. Perhaps the only thing they had in common was an attachment to a federal form of government as the best for Canada and a belief that the relations between French- and English-speaking Canadians were basically political.

The shared belief in federalism was seldom strong enough to avoid wrangles between Quebec and Ottawa. Some of the disputes were just repeat performances of the old autonomy versus centralization play that the two had been staging for years. But some of them allowed for more contemporary issues. The demands of the Liberal government in Quebec in the early 1960s for more status, more power, and more money tested the resilience of the Canadian federation. Was there, the Royal Commission on Bilingualism and Biculturalism moodily asked but never answered, a means to recognize two nations in a country composed of ten provinces? Certainly Ottawa was not at all interested in having one of those provinces, much less a nation, accorded the least hint of international recognition. When the French president Charles de Gaulle did so by uttering the separatist slogan *"Vive le Québec libre"* (Long live free Quebec) in the midst of Expo 67 festivities, he was sent packing by Ottawa. And when the tiny African state of Gabon dared to issue a direct invitation to the Quebec government to participate in an international conference in 1968, it had to suffer the rebuke of severed diplomatic relations with Canada. Federalists in Ottawa stood upon the prerogatives of protocol; federalists in Quebec wondered why provincial matters that had international ramifications need necessarily pass via Ottawa.

Federalists in Ottawa and Quebec also had slogans to fling at each other. The meanings were never very precise even to those who uttered them, but they peppered the press and the various constitutional conferences that took place in the late 1960s and early 1970s. Prime minister Lester Pearson spoke of co-operative federalism before his retirement in 1968; his successor Pierre Trudeau philosophized about a just society, all the while badgering Quebec with his hostility to nationalism and English Canada with Quebec's threat of separatism. The provincial Liberals flirted momentarily with particular status but had difficulty distinguishing it from the *Union nationale*'s special status. Daniel Johnson, *Union nationale* premier between 1966 and 1968, tossed the much more threatening, if equally vague, *Egalité ou indépendance* (Equality or independence) into the ring. By the 1970s provincial Liberals were hedging their bets, faced as they then were with a separatist notion of sovereignty-association; to counter it they conjured up cultural sovereignty and profitable federalism. What the slogans disguised was a power struggle between Quebec and Ottawa over the nature and control of French Canada. When the debate concentrated on specific topics such as social policies, the French language, and the FLQ, it actually provided some substance to the slogans.

Social policies had traditionally been fertile ground for federal-provincial disputes and they became even more so in the years after the Quiet Revolution. Ever since the 1920s and increasingly since the Second World War, the Quebec government had been uneasy over federal desires to establish Canada-wide norms of social welfare. It protested the federal claim to jurisdiction in the field in the first place; it fretted over the suitability of Canadian norms for Quebec; it sighed over Ottawa's financial supremacy and unlimited spending power which allowed the federal government to do as it pleased in any case. But only when it undertook large scale social legislation itself in the early 1960s could it confront the issue squarely. Hospital insurance and contributory pensions provided funds, power, and popular policies, but they still were imitations of federal initiatives. To innovate, to be other than a mere executor of Ottawa's ideas, the provincial government, no matter what the party in power, had to have plans and designs of its own. The *Union nationale* was no sooner in office in 1966 than it named a provincial enquiry into health and social welfare. By the time the commission completed all of its reports, the chief investigator, Claude Castonguay, was the minister of health and welfare in the subsequent Liberal government of Robert Bourassa. There he implemented his own recommendation of 1967 for a province-wide compulsory scheme of medical insurance. The plan did indicate that co-operation with Ottawa was still possible since it was financed jointly by the federal and provincial governments. But almost all of his other ideas for coherently designed and specially tailored health care and social services to suit Quebec's particular needs conflicted with similar plans and powers in Ottawa.

However one defined those needs, the conflict led to arguments over the constitution. Some of Quebec's special needs were merely those of the provincial government whose appetite for power increased with the exercise of it. But some were also based on the notion that Quebec society was different from that of the rest of Canada. Castonguay had visions of family allowances, welfare benefits, and health services linked to plans for income security, manpower training, vocational education, housing, and leisure and all of it readily accessible in all the regions of Quebec. The plans required clarification of overlapping jurisdictions with Ottawa and expansion of Quebec's sole right to legislate in certain fields. Tinkering with the constitution became necessary to alter the British North America Act's distribution of legislative and financial powers between the federal and provincial governments. But in all the constitutional talks Quebec was never able to obtain a guarantee of provincial supremacy in all areas of social legislation. Because of that Quebec premier Robert Bourassa scuttled the painfully constructed Victoria Charter of 1971 for patriating and amending the BNA Act. For a few years thereafter the Quebec government limited its social policy ambitions to the single area of family allowances. Probably because the federal Liberal government was in a minority and therefore conciliatory position, Quebec was able to secure the right in 1974 to design a plan of its own without depriving Quebec residents of the federal money involved. Provincial federalists cheered, the technocrats filed away another dossier, and only a few feminists fretted over the implications of family allowances that increased substantially with each successive child.

While Quebec and Ottawa confronted each other on matters of social policy, they engaged in parallel activities to protect and promote the French language. Rarely crossing swords, they calmly staked out for themselves powers over the most specific and the most symbolic of the differences between French Canadians and other inhabitants of North America. For Quebec governments, again of whatever political stripe, the French language needed increasingly powerful legislative protection to offset the decline predicted by demographers and linguists. French also should adorn all the economic, social, cultural, and even political innovation since the early 1960s. Moreover, with a bit of help from the government, the language might even become an agent of assimilation of other groups in Quebec, a fitting response to what was happening to French Canadians beyond Quebec. To prevent the demise of French in Quebec, the provincial government had to muster its francophone majority and its legislative power. The *Union nationale* tried to do so gently in 1969 with a bill declaring French to be the prevailing language but not interfering with the traditional rights of parents to choose French or English as the language of schooling for their children. Massive French Canadian hostility to the legislation—ten thousand demonstrators in Montreal, twenty thousand in Quebec City—suggested that a gentle approach was no longer acceptable. The subsequent Liberal government was therefore more categorical. French became the official language of Quebec in 1974 and unless youngsters knew enough English to warrant entry into an English school, they would have to be educated in French. It seemed simple enough, but in fact the administration of the law was more chaotic than dogmatic. As a result, one of the earliest activities of the next government, that of the *Parti québécois*, was to cut through the administrative maze. As of 1977 only a child whose mother or father had been educated in English in Quebec could attend English schools. French was to prevail, not only in the schools, but in business, government, the professions, and even on signs in the street.

In the meantime the federal government was attempting to disprove Quebec's claim that beyond its borders the French language was doomed. Given the hostility of many English Canadians, the task was not always easy. But Liberal prime minister Pierre Trudeau, armed with the first reports of the Bilingualism and Biculturalism Commission, set out to accomplish it. His Official Languages Act in 1969 went beyond the minimal reference in the British North America Act to the use of French and English in the federal and Quebec parliament and courts to declare the two languages of equal and official status in Canada. His insistence on a greater French presence in the federal civil service and the armed forces doubled their representation over the decade 1966 to 1976. This was enough to send English Canadians scurrying to French language classes but not yet enough to balance the proportion of French to English in the overall population. But when Trudeau began flirting with multiculturalism, some French Canadians wondered if it were not a slap in the face of their supposed equality. Not surprisingly too, Ottawa and Quebec began squabbling over communications: Ottawa interested in the administrative control of interprovincial airwaves, Quebec concerned for the cultural policy that accompanied the language over those airwaves. And then in the early summer of 1976 the federal government appeared to support the claims of English-speaking pilots and air traffic controllers that the skies of Quebec were not safe if French crackled through the air. English Canadians had already begun to murmur that Trudeau was forcing French down their throats and now French Canadians, just months before a provincial election, began wondering about the seriousness of his claim to French equality.

Already they had seen the federal government's reaction to violence in Quebec. Burbling through the 1960s to reach a climax in the October Crisis in 1970, the violence was disturbing enough without the impression, whether deliberately fostered by Trudeau or not, that only he and the federal government could control the excesses of Quebec. On the eve of his first election as prime minister in 1968, and with all the media focussed upon him, Trudeau withstood an onslaught of bricks and bottles during a Saint Jean Baptiste parade in Montreal. Regiments of the Canadian army hovered in the wings of the city in the fall of 1969 as Montreal police and firefighters engaged in a wildcat strike and the city centre went wild. Throughout 1970 the federal RCMP appear to have worked at cross-purposes with the Quebec provincial and Montreal city police to track the FLQ and other bomb-flingers. And in the pre-dawn of October 16, 1970, the federal government, ostensibly at the request of the mayor of Montreal and the premier of Quebec, again sent federal troops to Montreal and imposed the War Measures Act to combat what the Act terms "insurrection real or apprehended."

If the insurrection was more in the wording of the law than in the streets of Montreal, the apprehension was real enough. No one knew if the kidnappings of British trade commissioner James Cross on October 5 and then of provincial labour minister Pierre Laporte on October 10 by two independent cells of the FLQ were isolated acts or the beginnings of a terrorist revolution. Was any public figure safe? Had all the arms and ammunition reported stolen over the past few years found their way into a secret cache of the FLQ? And was that organization, dedicated to social revolution and the forcible independence of Quebec, now about to bring down the government? No one knew, but many imaginations worked overtime as the FLQ measured out a few more hours of life to its captives with every demand for redress solemnly read over radio and television. Trudeau's invocation of emergency measures designed for war may even have heightened the apprehension. Certainly the sight of soldiers in the streets of their city was more frightening than reassuring to Montrealers. So too was the arrest without warrant of more than four hundred people, among them poets, singers, journalists, known public protesters, members of unions and of the legitimate separatist party; they were snatched from their beds on suspicion of FLQ sympathies and on the say so, it turns out, of federal cabinet ministers Gérard Pelletier and Jean Marchand. And then, the day after the imposition of the War Measures Act, the FLQ cell holding Pierre Laporte murdered him.

The double shock of wartime powers used during peace and cold blooded murder in a revolutionary cause numbed Canadians. Civil libertarians all across the country protested the unwarranted arrests. Some people accused Trudeau of using the power of the federal government to round up his provincial critics and silence legitimate opposition among nationalists and separatists. Quebec's three major union centrals, the FTQ, the CSN, and the teachers' union (the *Corporation des enseignants du Québec*), joined forces to denounce the War Measures Act. Other people worried more about the erosion of provincial power as a feeble premier Bourassa trembled in the federal shadow of Trudeau. But most Canadians, however queasy they might feel at the sight of the military, were even more unnerved by the thought of murder. Even the FLQ may have been taken aback. Cross and his captors were located early in December 1970 and after another few weeks of hide and seek the captors of Laporte were also found. In exchange for Cross, the first went to Cuba; the second went to jail. The sporadic reappearance of the FLQ for a year or so after the October Crisis seems to have been inspired more by police infiltrators than by any continuing terrorist enthusiasm. In 1971 the FLQ logician, Pierre Vallières, whose book *Nègres blancs d'Amérique (White Niggers of America)* had so captured revolutionary imaginations in 1969, publicly denounced terrorism as an effective means of bringing about social change or the independence of Quebec. He now advocated support for the separatist *Parti québécois*.

Somewhat surprisingly, neither Vallières' endorsation nor Trudeau's heavy-handed hint of guilt by association put the kiss of death on the fledgling separatist party in Quebec. The last thing, indeed, that René Lévesque, leader of the *Parti québécois*, needed for his infant party seeking the independence of Quebec by electoral means was the taint of radicalism, let alone revolution. The party was only two years old in 1970 when Lévesque had the dubious distinction of being quoted in one of the FLQ manifestoes. Beginning as a splinter group among Lesage's Liberals in 1967, the *Mouvement souveraineté-association* had carefully knit together previous separatist parties, finding it easier to come to an accord with the more conservative but politically pragmatic *Ralliement national* than the more socialist and dogmatic *Rassemblement pour l'indépendance nationale*. The new *Parti québécois* (PQ) accepted the historical analysis that led to the separatist slogan of 1967: "Cent ans d'injustice" (One hundred years of injustice) but tempered it with Lévesque's more charming but equally provocative "If you can't sleep together, you might as well have separate beds." The PQ denounced violence as an insane means of accomplishing social and political change. It soothed the Quebec and Canadian public with its highly popular, persuasive, and entertaining leader. René

Lévesque was able to convince many a listener that the leap from Quiet Revolutionary quarrels with Ottawa to separatist certitude was merely a matter of natural evolution. Even then, he smoothed out the blunt edges of separatism. What the PQ advocated was a new arrangement with Canada: a legally sovereign Quebec to confirm its existing cultural and territorial distinctiveness and at the same time an economic association, as an equal partner, with the rest of Canada. Lévesque's dream of nation was carefully fashioned to inspire, not to frighten.

Realizing the dream was not quite so easy. Within the PQ, Lévesque had to play upon his immense prestige and popularity just to keep the party together on touchy issues such as the language rights of minorities in an independent Quebec. He spent as much time containing radicals in his own ranks as he did explaining his Quebec option to English-speaking audiences across the country. Beyond the party, he had to convince people in Quebec that sovereignty, even if desirable, was at all feasible and he had to convince people outside Quebec that association, even if feasible, was at all desirable. Just as challenging was the task of persuading a conservative electorate that a home grown variety of social democracy was acceptable. That this could be done was evident from the first successes of the PQ in the provincial election of April 1970. Of the seven seats that the party won in the national assembly (so named in 1969), six were in working class areas of east-end Montreal. But there were also risks involved as evident two years later when the three major union centrals—the FTQ, CSN, and CEQ—staged a series of common front protests, strikes, and demonstrations against the slowness of contract negotiations in the public sector. In the spring of 1972 they succeeded in bringing the province virtually to a standstill. Even more unsettling was the ideological accompaniment of their activities. From a radically socialist standpoint they denounced the Liberal government of Robert Bourassa and many of the institutions of Quebec society. The electoral repercussions of such turbulence were unpredictable. For all the mildly left-of-centre *Parti québécois* knew, popular fear of social disorder could be as politically damaging to it as increased union hostility to the Liberals might be beneficial.

As the *Parti québécois* picked its way through the shoals of popular opinion, both luck and circumstance were on its side. It might easily have shared the fate of other third and fourth parties in Canada's electoral system and remained on the political fringe. Instead the *Union nationale* and the Social Credit party faded to that status in the early 1970s because of their inability to find a constitutional compromise between the federalist Liberals and the separatist-without-the-name *Parti québécois*. The PQ might also have succumbed to the combined strength of the provincial and federal Liberals, but on the provincial scene Robert Bourassa never was a match for René Lévesque. Bourassa promised one hundred thousand jobs during the election campaign of 1970 but subsequently created labour disputes with many times that number of workers. He launched the massive James Bay hydro-electric installations in Quebec's northland in 1971 but avoided the question of the temporary nature of the investment and the employment. He took only last minute measures to control the costs of the Olympics in 1976 and left to his successor the maze of their colossal escalation. Moreover, Bourassa was always in the shadow of Pierre Trudeau, a shadow Lévesque carefully avoided by having the *Parti québécois* play provincial politics only. Even with two personal defeats in the elections of 1970 and 1973 Lévesque was able to portray a stronger image than that of Bourassa.

The gradual pacification of social tensions in the province may have given the greatest electoral boost to the *Parti québécois*. If the party owed its birth to the turmoil of the late 1960s, it probably owed its eventual success to the dissipation of that turmoil in the mid-1970s. The PQ could on occasion misread popular temper as it did in 1973. Drawing on the socialist talk of the common front and emboldened by its own youthful presence, the party moved its social policies to the left and its political option to centre stage. It actually produced a budget for the first year of independence. At that the public balked. Popular opinion may well have been increasingly sympathetic to the *Parti québécois*, even though poll takers never could tell if the attraction was the leader, the constitutional stand, or the social policies, but the public was not yet ready for the clarity of the PQ budget. The Liberals ridiculed it, emphasized the economic woes of separatism, and kept their federalist option vague but visible: cultural sovereignty and profitable federalism. Until the PQ blurred its own policies, as it proceeded to do in 1974, it had to content itself with an increase from twenty-four to thirty percent of the popular vote and a new status as official opposition in the national assembly with six seats to the Liberals' one hundred and two.

By 1976, the *Parti québécois* had added political wisdom to its growing electoral support. It carefully avoided the words separatism or independence. It produced no budgets and held no mass rallies. Instead it quietly continued what were essentially feminist tactics of consciousness-raising by gathering small groups of congenial people in kitchens across the province to argue their way to the PQ position. It welcomed, but did not trumpet, the direct endorsation of the FTQ and may even have been glad that the CSN and the CEQ were more circumspect. It added economist Rodrigue Tremblay and television personality Lise Payette to its roster of impressive candidates. Assisted no doubt by the federal-provincial fracas in June over the use of French in air transport in Quebec, the PQ was able to convince forty-one percent of the electorate that it meant to govern better than Bourassa. As for sovereignty-association, well that would be the subject of a later consultation. By means of a referendum sometime in the future, the PQ would ask the people about future constitutional arrangements with Canada.

The strategy, the circumstances, and the luck held: on November 15, 1976, with seventy-one victorious candidates in an assembly of one hundred and ten, the *Parti québécois* became the government of Quebec.

Once in power, René Lévesque, as surprised as everyone else by the victory, had to enlarge his powers of persuasion. He tried reading history lessons to American businessmen to claim a doubtful analogy between the American Revolution and the eventual independence of Quebec. He spoke of adjustment rather than confrontation with the premiers from the other Canadian provinces. But he also tried direct bargaining with them over language rights: he would soften the provisions of the PQ language legislation if the other premiers were more supportive of French language teaching in their provinces. Momentarily the idea seemed interesting. But the French-speaking minorities outside Quebec made it clear they had no desire to be hostages in a separatist-federalist debate. And prime minister Trudeau reminded the provincial premiers that direct interprovincial negotiations were unseemly. Meanwhile in Quebec, Lévesque sent his ministers with economic portfolios to visit all the major companies in the province with assurances of stability. For those companies that had already packed up and departed after the PQ victory, Lévesque and his supporters could speak knowingly of the general trend westward of the North American economy. Perhaps the only discordant note the new government struck was its plan to nationalize the asbestos industry. American investors immediately saw socialist bogeymen and the PQ, perhaps deliberately, delayed its takeover of the Asbestos Corporation, an American firm, until late 1981.

Within the province, the promised good government largely meant social stability and economic realizations. Given the constraints on all governments at the time—huge deficits, high interest rates, inflation, unemployment, the energy crisis, and the declining value of the Canadian dollar—the new Quebec government performed remarkably well. It solidified its labour support by raising the minimum wage, dropping a number of charges against individual unions involved in labour unrest in the spring and summer of 1976, and reforming the labour code to specify the rights and obligations of unions. By 1979, it was having to legislate certain strikers back to work and was seriously weighing the value of the right to strike for public servants. It also had to cope with regional dissatisfaction. Geographically distant and economically underdeveloped areas of the province were not at all sure that their problems could be subsumed in a political struggle against Ottawa, an ethnic struggle against English Canadians, or a class struggle against exploiters. The agricultural policy of the *Parti québécois* was a partial response. Its purpose was to safeguard agricultural land from urban overflow and encourage diversification from dairying to livestock raising and feed grain production. The last two were designed to diminish Quebec's reliance on imports from western Canada. Another response was to assist the establishment of small and medium-sized industries in areas away from the major urban centres. In its economic policies the PQ clearly stated its preference for the private sector as the principal motor of the economy, without of course jettisoning the darling of Quebec development, Hydro-Quebec. It encouraged the modernization of Quebec's traditional textile, footwear, clothing, furniture, and pulp and paper industries. By late 1979 it could claim that eighty-thousand new jobs had been created during that year alone and that the per capita income in Quebec had reached ninety-five percent of the Canadian average. With that mark of success, the government turned its attention back to Montreal. There it marked the high technology industries as the next sector of economic growth and promised one major project to match the natural resources of each of the regions of Quebec. It fought the election of 1981 on the economy and won it.

But in the meantime it had taken a stunning blow to its pride. The idea of a referendum on Quebec's political future had been bandied about in the *Parti québécois* since 1973. If some members thought it politically wise to distinguish the election of a government from a constitutional choice, others thought the division would dissipate separatist zeal. They were not even sure there would be a referendum once the PQ settled comfortably into office. But Lévesque was categorical: he wanted one majority for a new government in Quebec and he wanted another majority to negotiate a new arrangement with Canada. He did not want the two confused. His government kept the idea of the referendum carefully before the public eye from the summer of 1977 on. It prepared a bill in June 1978 to regulate the consultation. In November 1979 it specified just how the campaign was to be organized. It revealed the question itself—a humble request for a mandate to negotiate sovereignty-association—in December and had the national assembly debate it in March 1980. Finally it settled the date for May 20, 1980. Each step was carefully measured around the vagaries of federal elections which produced a surprising Conservative victory in May 1979 and an equally unnerving resignation then reappearance of Pierre Trudeau as Liberal leader and prime minister again in February 1980.

What Lévesque did not foresee in his elaborate plans for the referendum was the potential confusion of feminism, federalism, and the independence of Quebec. In the period preceding the referendum, the three merged in a coincidental and curious manner. In the autumn of 1978 the *Conseil du statut de la femme* produced its first major report—*Pour les Québécoises: égalité et indépendance (For Quebec Women: Equality and Independence)*, the second half of the title gently mocking the constitutional debate in Quebec over the past dozen years. The report analysed the harm done to women by a sexual division of labour in the home and the public work place reinforced as it was by sexual stereotyping in the schools and the media. The implication was that a truly just society would permit an equal and autonomous place for women.

Just a year later, the Quebec government spelled out its argument for the forthcoming referendum campaign in *La nouvelle entente Québec-Canada* (*Quebec-Canada: A New Deal*). The booklet analysed the harm done to Quebec by more than two hundred years of English Canadian dominance reinforced as it was by a federal division of powers increasingly favouring Ottawa. The only just solution was equality by means of association and independence by means of sovereignty. A few weeks later, in January 1980, the provincial Liberals, now led by Claude Ryan, released *Une nouvelle fédération canadienne* (*A new Canadian federation*). Without denying some of the low blows French Canadians had received in the past, the Liberals argued that adjustments rather than radical change had always been the Canadian pattern and should continue to be in future. But then the Liberals proceeded to specify so many and such intricate changes that the federation was barely recognizable while the *Parti québécois* talked so sanguinely of association that its separatism could hardly be discerned. While the two smudged their options for political purposes, only the feminists implied that the debate might be irrelevant.

And yet the analogies among the three were both revealing and relevant. Feminism resembled federalism in the demand for more women or more French Canadians in positions of economic, legal, and political power. Feminism resembled separatism in suspecting that those very institutions, based as they were in the family or in federalism, were agents of sexual or ethnic discrimination. Sovereignty-association might well be as difficult to negotiate as an egalitarian marriage. Certainly the reaction of English Canada before the referendum was that of a spurned male: if a frivolous Quebec voted for separation, there would be no question of some new arrangement. For many federalists, indeed, separatism was unthinkable precisely because, without quite realizing it, they compared Quebec to a woman. Neither she, nor, by analogy, *la belle province*, had the right to independence. A separate Quebec, they feared, would deny its cultural mission in North America just as certain women were denying their prescribed role in the family to transmit values and refine behaviour. A separate Quebec would abandon French-speaking minorities in other parts of Canada, as horrendous a dereliction of duty as that of a mother abandoning her children. In the eyes of most of English Canada, Quebec had been behaving improperly since the 1960s, flirting with a long discarded French lover from across the sea, flaunting new found economic and administrative skills, and constantly wheedling more out of the federal government. The cracking of Confederation in the 1960s and 1970s was the cracking of the nineteenth century notion of separate spheres that had placed sexes and peoples, provinces and countries into mutually exclusive but supposedly complementary entities.

Images and reality of women coalesced in a most unexpected manner in the last few weeks of the referendum campaign. They may even have determined the outcome, for just as the polls were predicting a tiny majority in favour of Lévesque's option, the minister responsible for the status of women in his cabinet flung a sexist stereotype at her opponents. Lise Payette accused the wife of Liberal leader Claude Ryan of accepting her husband's political views without reflection and thus being no better than Yvette, the docile, submissive young girl of Quebec's school books. Feminists in the province had long been advocating the removal of such stereotypes from the schools and the media. But the Liberals took up the insult with a vengeance. Overnight, thousands of "Yvettes" emerged from their kitchens, held a public brunch in Quebec City, and then a monster rally of some fifteen thousand women in the Montreal Forum. There they listened to women quite unlike Yvette, speakers such as senator Thérèse Casgrain and federal health and welfare minister Monique Bégin and together they shouted their NO to Lévesque's request for a mandate to negotiate his new arrangement with Canada. They organized meetings all across the province and they captured the front page and editorial attention of a press delighted to record what it took to be an anti-feminist movement. The publicity for the Yvettes greatly disturbed Lévesque's YES supporters who were unable to obtain more than the tiniest of press references to the fortieth anniversary of women's right to vote in Quebec. Instead the media and the Yvettes called upon traditional female values to rescue the nation in distress. Loyal to the past and responsible for the future, women were to summon their courage and tenacity and reject the ruinous consequences of separatist seduction. It was the duty of women to say NO.

What the female-male distribution of the votes was on May 20 is unknown. But somewhere in the confusion over feminism, federalism, and the independence of Quebec, René Lévesque's dream of nation dissipated. Because of that very confusion, however, even the decisive results of the referendum—sixty percent NO and forty percent YES—could not provide a definitive answer to an almost four hundred year old question: how to be French in America. Lévesque may have known that as he fought back the tears and acknowledged the defeat of the referendum. "*A la prochaine*," he tossed to the crowd and the television cameras from across Canada. Literally, until the next time. Even on that gloomy night of May 20, 1980, Lévesque remained much too optimistic to suggest until the next dream.

A la prochaine. It's also the parting phrase of friends and lovers.

SELECT BIBLIOGRAPHY

Barry, Francine. *Le travail de la femme au Québec: l'évolution de 1940 à 1970.* Montreal: Les presses de l'Université du Québec, 1977.

Bernard, André. *What Does Quebec Want?* Toronto: J. Lorimer, 1978.

Brunelle, Dorval. *La désillusion tranquille.* Montreal: Hurtubise HMH, 1978.

Canadian Annual Review 1967–1970. Toronto: University of Toronto Press.

Canadian Annual Review of Politics and Public Affairs 1971–. Toronto: University of Toronto Press.

Desbarats, Peter. *René: A Canadian in Search of a Country.* Toronto: McClelland and Stewart, 1976.

Dumont-Johnson, Micheline. "Les communautés religieuses et la condition féminine." *Recherches sociographiques* 19(1978):7–32.

Fédération des femmes du Québec. *La participation politique des femmes du Québec.* Study no. 10 for the Royal Commission on the Status of Women. Ottawa, 1970.

Gagnon, Mona Josée. "Les femmes dans le mouvement syndical québécois." *Sociologie et Sociétés* 6(1974):17–36.

Harvey, Fernand. "La question régionale au Quebec." *Journal of Canadian Studies* 15(1980):74–87.

Jean, Michèle, and Marie Lavigne. "Le Phénomène des Yvettes: analyse externe." *Atlantis* 6(1981):17–23.

Lamothe, Jacqueline, and Jennifer Stoddart. "Les Yvettes ou: Comment un parti politique traditionnel se sert encore une fois des femmes." *Atlantis* 6(1981):10–16.

Lévesque, René. *Option Québec.* Montreal: Editions de l'Homme, 1968.

McKenna, Brian, and Susan Purcell. *Drapeau.* Toronto: Clarke Irwin, 1980.

Pelletier, Gérard. *The October Crisis.* Toronto: McClelland and Stewart, 1971.

Provencher, Jean. *René Lévesque: Portrait of a Québécois.* Toronto: Gage, 1975.

Royal Commission on the Status of Women in Canada. Ottawa, 1970.

Saywell, John Tupper. *Quebec 70. A Documentary Narrative.* Toronto: University of Toronto Press, 1971.

Saywell, John Tupper. *The Rise of the Parti Quebecois, 1967–1976.* Toronto: University of Toronto Press, 1977.

Stewart, James. *The F.L.Q. Seven Years of Terrorism.* Montreal: Simon and Shuster, 1970.

GENERAL BIBLIOGRAPHY

Blanchard, Raoul. *Le Canada français, province de Québec: étude géographique.* Paris: Fayard, 1960.

———. *Le centre du Canada français, province de Québec.* Montreal: Beauchemin, 1947.

———. *L'Est du Canada français.* 2 vols. Montreal: Beauchemin, 1935.

———. *L'Ouest du Canada français.* Montreal: Beauchemin, 1954.

Comeau, Robert, ed. *Economie québécoise.* Montreal: Les presses de l'Université du Québec, 1969.

Dictionary of Canadian Biography. vols. I–IV, IX–XI. Toronto: University of Toronto Press, 1966–1982.

Groulx, Lionel. *Histoire du Canada français depuis la découverte.* 2 vols. Montreal: Fides, 1960.

Hamelin, Jean, ed. *Histoire du Québec.* Paris: Privat, 1976.

Linteau, Paul-André, René Durocher, and Jean-Claude Robert. *Histoire du Québec contemporain.* Vol. 1: *De la Confédération à la crise (1867–1929).* Montreal: Boréal Express, 1979.

McRoberts, Kenneth, and Dale Posgate. *Quebec. Social Change and Political Crisis.* rev. ed. Toronto: McClelland and Stewart, 1980.

Robert, Jean-Claude. *Du Canada français au Québec libre.* Paris: Flammarion, 1975.

Rumilly, Robert, ed. *Histoire de la province de Québec.* 41 vols. Montreal: Fides, 1971.

Wade, Mason. *The French Canadians, 1760–1967.* rev. ed. 2 vols. Toronto: Macmillan, 1968.

INDEX